Hermeneutical Narratives in Art, Literature, and Communication

Also available from Bloomsbury

Language, Identity and Symbolic Culture, David Evans
Music as Multimodal Discourse, edited by Lyndon C. S. Way
and Simon McKerrell

Hermeneutical Narratives in Art, Literature, and Communication

Edited by Małgorzata Haładewicz-Grzelak
and Paula García-Ramírez

BLOOMSBURY ACADEMIC
LONDON • NEW YORK • OXFORD • NEW DELHI • SYDNEY

BLOOMSBURY ACADEMIC

Bloomsbury Publishing Plc, 50 Bedford Square, London, WC1B 3DP, UK
Bloomsbury Publishing Inc, 1385 Broadway, New York, NY 10018, USA
Bloomsbury Publishing Ireland, 29 Earlsfort Terrace, Dublin 2, D02 AY28, Ireland

BLOOMSBURY, BLOOMSBURY ACADEMIC and the Diana logo are trademarks
of Bloomsbury Publishing Plc

First published in Great Britain 2024
Paperback edition published 2025

Copyright © Małgorzata Haładewicz-Grzelak, Paula García-Ramírez and Contributors, 2024

Małgorzata Haładewicz-Grzelak, Paula García-Ramírez and Contributors has asserted
their right under the Copyright, Designs and Patents Act, 1988, to be identified as
Authors of this work.

For legal purposes the Acknowledgements on p. xxxix constitute an extension of this
copyright page.

Cover design: Elena Durey
Cover image © francescoch / Getty Images

All rights reserved. No part of this publication may be: i) reproduced or transmitted in
any form, electronic or mechanical, including photocopying, recording or by means of
any information storage or retrieval system without prior permission in writing from the
publishers; or ii) used or reproduced in any way for the training, development or operation
of artificial intelligence (AI) technologies, including generative AI technologies. The rights
holders expressly reserve this publication from the text and data mining exception as per
Article 4(3) of the Digital Single Market Directive (EU) 2019/790.

Bloomsbury Publishing Plc does not have any control over, or responsibility for,
any third-party websites referred to or in this book. All internet addresses given
in this book were correct at the time of going to press. The author and publisher
regret any inconvenience caused if addresses have changed or sites have
ceased to exist, but can accept no responsibility for any such changes.

A catalogue record for this book is available from the British Library.

A catalog record for this book is available from the Library of Congress.

ISBN: HB: 978-1-3504-0543-1
PB: 978-1-3504-0547-9
ePDF: 978-1-3504-0544-8
eBook: 978-1-3504-0545-5

Typeset by RefineCatch Limited, Bungay, Suffolk

For product safety related questions contact productsafety@bloomsbury.com.

To find out more about our authors and books visit www.bloomsbury.com
and sign up for our newsletters.

Contents

List of Figures	vii
List of Tables	ix
List of Contributors	x
Preface	xvii
Acknowledgements	xxxix

Part One Noematic *Lacunae* in Artistic Discourse

1 Hermeneutical Guidelines for Understanding the Self through Art *David Jaeger and Evan Underbrink* 3

2 Hieratic Communication in the Oeuvre of Kazimir Malevich, Vasily Kandinsky and Nikolai Roerich *Sally Stocksdale* 23

3 Painterly Motif of Kisses of Mary and Kisses of St Joseph in the Context of Iconography of *Unio Mystica* in the Baroque Period *Andrzej Kozieł* 55

4 Narrativity, Discourse Situation and the Opening of Elgar's Cello Concerto in E Minor, Op. 85 *Marta Falces Sierra* 71

Part Two Hermeneutic Diaphaneity in Literary Studies

5 Adinkra Symbols: From Visual Art Messages to a Literary Research Methodology *Violetta Jojo Verge* 87

6 Hermeneutical Narratives of the European Colonization in Africa in Graham Greene's *A Burnt-out Case* and Abdulrazak Gurnah's *Desertion* *Beatriz Valverde* 109

7 The Language of War in the Apocalypse Trope of Meg Elison's *The Book of the Unnamed Midwife* *Almudena Machado-Jiménez* 125

8 Prophesizing War in 'The Lament of the Deer' by Christopher Okigbo *Paula García-Ramírez* 149

Part Three Epistemic Spaces in the Geopsychic Universe of Visual and Verbal Communication

9   Local Amazigh Proverbs in Motion: Between Transmission and Interpretation *Fatima Ez-zahra Benkhallouq and Wahiba Moubchir* 163

10 Thirdspace Creation as a Geopsychic Dialogue with Tourists in the Karpacz Holiday Resort, Poland *Joanna Lubos-Kozieł and Małgorzata Haładewicz-Grzelak* 179

11 Creating Common Epistemic Spaces through Multimodal Stance-Taking Practices *Valentyna Ushchyna* 203

12 Elaborating a Heuristic Tool to Determine Fluency Spectrum for Deaf Pupils in Poland *Marta Wrześniewska-Pietrzak* 223

13 The Concept of *Wenming* (文明) ('Civility') as an Edusemiotic Strategy *Katarzyna Mazur-Włodarczyk, Małgorzata Haładewicz-Grzelak, Elżbieta Karaś, Joanna Kolańska-Płuska and Przemysław Misiurski* 241

Thematic Index 263

Figures

0.1.	Sculpture by Hana Purkrábková	xxiii
0.2.	A wayside shrine from the vicinity of Głuchołazy, Poland	xxvi
0.3.	A project of a monument authored by a Ukrainian agency and a socrealist monument extant in Ostrava, Czech Republic	xxvii
2.1.	*Sophia the Almighty Wisdom* by N. Roerich	24
2.2.	*Motley Life* by V. Kandinsky	25
2.3.	*Hinauf* by V. Kandinsky	27
3.1.	*The Kiss of the Virgin* by Michael Willmann	56
3.2.	*The Kiss of Mary* by Unknown painter	56
3.3.	*The Kiss of St Joseph* by Johaigunn Tscherning after Michael Willmann	58
3.4.	*The Bridegroom Leading the Bride* by Michael Willmann	58
3.5.	*The Assumption of the Blessed Virgin Mary* by Philipp Christian Bentum	63
3.6.	*The Vision of St Bernard of Clairvaux* by Michael Willmann	63
3.7.	*The Vision of St Lutgarde of Tongern* by Bernhard Krause	64
3.8.	*The Kiss of Mary* by Unknown painter	64
4.1.	Opening of Elgar's Cello Concerto, Op. 85	72
4.2.	Beethoven's Sonata No. 32, 2nd movement, bars 49–57	74
4.3.	Cello part, opening bars of Elgar's concerto, Op. 85	75
5.1.	A selection of Adinkra symbols	88
9.1.	Concise form of three levels of analysis	172
10.1	A futuristic vision of Riesengebirge tourism on a German postcard	180
10.2.	A venue for the first *flânerie*: transactional tradition in a design of a catering establishment	181
10.3.	Marking the boundaries of a phenomenological field in a townscape around Bistro Aurora	182
10.4.	Photos of the interior of the Bistro Aurora	194
11.1.	Modality on the axe of epistemic stance-taking	210
11.2.	Evidentiality on the axe of epistemic stance-taking	212
11.3.	Axe of epistemic stance-taking (modality+evidentiality)	218

12.1. Sample tasks from the application displayed to the respondent in the animated instruction prior to starting the test 230
13.1. The characters 文 and 明 written in the calligraphic style *jiaguwen* and *jinwen* 242
13.2. A canonical urban decoration showing 12 features of a socialist society, into which *wenming* is embedded 246
13.3. [遵守公共道德争当文明市民] This photo says: Observe public morality and strive to be a civilized citizen 247
13.4. Example of textuality relating *wenming* to propadeutic dimension ecological and natural aspects 253
13.5. A paper fan as a tourist brochure handed out at EXPO 2010 254

Tables

4.1. Discourse situation in narrative fiction and non-verbal music 78
4.2. Discourse situation in the opening of Elgar's Cello Concerto 80
9.1. Juxtaposition of differences between the Amazigh and French versions of proverbs 171

Contributors

Fatima Ez-zahra Benkhallouq, Professor, Department of Applied Languages to Culture
Cadi Ayyad University, Marrakesh, Morocco

Fatima Ez-zahra Benkhallouq holds a PhD in Linguistics and Culture, and has been Professor at Cadi Ayyad University (UCA) since 2005, where she is a specialist in sociolinguistics and Moroccan culture. She is interested in the social and cultural dimensions of languages, and works on the interaction between language, culture and the natural environment, particularly the Amazigh language in the Atlas Mountains. She has published several studies and individual and collective works on a national and international scale, for example, 'Figures of Cultural Transmission in Morocco' and 'Amazigh Idiomatic Expressions' (2022). She coordinated a project funded by the UCA, leading to the publication of several articles and a book entitled *Les Dispositifs d'Enseignement-Apprentissage à Distance en Période du Covid-19* (2021).

Marta Falces Sierra, Senior Lecturer, Department of English Philology
University of Granada, Spain

Marta Falces Sierra is Senior Lecturer in English Language and Literature. As a philologist, she has taught extensively on English stylistics, discourse analysis and pragmatics. Since 2011, she has also been involved in teaching the English for Musicology course at the Music Department of the same university. Her interest in language and music began in 1992 with the publication of *Pacto de Fausto: Aportaciones críticas a la etapa inglesa en la obra de I. Albéniz*. She has also published in the field of comparative poetry and music on Burdett-Coutts, Derek Walcott and T. S. Eliot. More recently, her research interests have focused on the textual analysis of Edward Elgar's Sea Pictures and music narrativity from a discourse perspective. She is a member of the research project 'A Microhistory of Spanish Contemporary Music: The International Peripheries in Dialogue' (MICINN, PGC2018-098986-B-C31 – Spanish Ministry of Science, Innovation and Universities).

Paula García-Ramírez, Associate Professor, Department of English Philology
University of Jaén, Spain

Paula García-Ramírez's main research interests are devoted to African literature, particularly Nigerian literature. In 1999, she published the book, *Introducción a la literatura africana en lengua inglesa*. Recently, she also published works on Chinua Achebe, Wole Soyinka, J. M. Coetzee and Ngugi wa Thiong'o.

David Jaeger, Independent Researcher
Cincinnati, Ohio, USA

David Jaeger's research interests include philosophy of law, phenomenology and the history of Western Philosophy. He is a member and secretary of the Society for the Phenomenology of Religious Experience (SoPheRe). David has two forthcoming articles for 2023, 'Mysticism and Variations on Scientific Metaphysics' and 'Phenomenological Approaches to Nature and Davidson's Anomalous Monism'.

Violetta Jojo Verge, Lecturer, Department of English and German Philology
University of La Laguna, Tenerife, Spain

Violetta Jojo Verge's research interests focus on African literature and postcolonial theory, as well as cultural, social and political studies related to Africa during the colonial, postcolonial and neocolonial periods. She has published on different social and cultural aspects regarding vital African issues and topics, including, 'Heirs of Wigs, Chalky Masks and Straight Hairs: The Bequest of Slavery and Colonialism', in Manuel Brito, Juan Sebastián and Amador Bedford (eds), *Insights and Bearings: Festschrift for Dr. Juan Sebastián Amador Bedford* (2007); and 'The Re-presentation of Africa and the African in the Anglophone West African Literature: Buchi Emecheta and Ama Ata Aidoo' (2015).

Małgorzata Haładewicz-Grzelak, Assistant Professor, Language Centre
Opole University of Technology, Opole, Poland

Małgorzata Haładewicz-Grzelak's main research interests are natural phonology and cultural semiotics, in particular the dyad of the sacred and profane in language. Her recent publications include a monograph, *Semiotactic Study of the Sacrosphere of Culture on the Material of Selected Examples of Visual Hierophanic Symbolics* (2019, in Polish) and '"Contiguity" as a Process of Semiotic Lenition in

Polish Socrealist Art (1949–1953)' with Joanna Filipczyk (2022). She has given sixty conference presentations.

Elżbieta Karaś, Assistant Professor, Faculty of Economics and Management
Opole University of Technology, Opole, Poland

Elżbieta Karaś's main area of scientific and research interest are issues in the field of business management, concerning modern concepts and strategies, quality, innovation and marketing. In recent years, her research projects have focused on aspects of the development of the economy and management of knowledge and information in the globalization. She is the author of numerous scientific publications presented at national and international conferences. Her recent publications, all in 2022, include, 'Organizational Culture – Asian Concepts of Kaizen, Gongfu and Xiushen,' co-authored with K. Mazur-Włodarczyk; 'Craft Development in Learning Organization (LO): Economic Approach,' co-authored with K. Łukaniszyn-Domaszewska; and 'Transformation of the Concept of Talent Management in the Era of the Fourth Industrial Revolution as the Basis for Sustainable Development,' co-authored with Artem Stopochkin, Inessa Sytnik and Janusz Wielki.

Joanna Kolańska-Płuska, Assistant Professor, Faculty of Electrical Engineering, Automatics and Computer Science
Opole University of Technology, Opole, Poland

Joanna Kolańska-Płuska's main research interests are the issues of renewable energy, numerical methods used in simulations, analytical algorhythms and the interface of machine/human communication. Her publications include, 'Implementation of ESDIRK (Kennedy-Carpenter) Method for the Purpose of Transient States in Long Line Investigation,' with Bernard Baron (2015); and 'Statistical Analysis of Data for Forecasting Electricity Production in a Selected Photovoltaic System,' with Piotr Gallus (2022).

Andrzej Kozieł, Professor, Institute of Art History
University of Wrocław, Wrocław, Poland
Chair of Art History and Cultural Heritage
University of Ostrava, Czech Republic

Andrzej Kozieł specializes in Baroque painting and drawing in Central Europe. He is also engaged in several projects promoting Baroque art in Silesia. His most recent books are *Michael Willmann and His Painting Workshop* (2013) and *Baroque Painting in Silesia* (2017).

Joanna Lubos-Kozieł, Assistant Professor, Art History Institute
University of Wrocław, Wrocław, Poland

Joanna Lubos-Kozieł's research interests include painting and sculpture of the nineteenth and early twentieth centuries, the religious art market and popular art of nineteenth and twentieth centuries. Two of her recent publications include: 'Ambiguous Heritage: "Plaster Saints", Cast-iron Christs and Other Mould-Made Catholic Sculptures from the Second Half of the 19th and the Early 20th Centuries' (2019); and 'Defaulting [+regional] in the Karpacz Holiday Resort (Poland)', co-authored with Małgorzata Haładewicz-Grzelak (2021).

Almudena Machado-Jiménez, Lecturer, Department of English Philology
University of Jaén, Jaén, Spain
President, Association of Young Researchers on Anglophone Studies

Almudena Machado-Jiménez has a PhD in Literatures in English from the University of Jaén, Jaén, Spain. Her research interests are utopian/dystopian fiction, gender studies and postcolonialism, particularly the notion of normative womanhood in contemporary patriarchal utopia written by women authors. Almudena's publications include, all in 2021, 'Bleak Bodies: Genetically Engineered Women in Louise O'Neill's (Anti-)Utopian Patriarchal Satire *Only Ever Yours*'; 'Patriarcavirus, Feminist Dystopias and COVID-19: Reflections on the Phenomenon of Gender Pandemics'; and 'On Utopus' Uterus: The Colonisation of the Body and the Birth of Patriarchal Utopia in Thomas More's *Utopia*'.

Katarzyna Mazur-Włodarczyk, Assistant Professor, Faculty of Economics and Management
Opole University of Technology, Opole, Poland

Katarzyna Mazur-Włodarczyk's main research interests are economic and management culture, perspectives related to the Belt and Route Initiative, the socioeconomic situation of the PRC, Sino-European business relations and sustainable development. Her most recent books are *Harmony in Chinese Economic Culture: The Perspective of Contemporary Socio-Economic Aspects* (2021); *Chinese Management Culture*, co-edited with Haifeng Huang and Maria Bernat (2021); and *Craft in China's Economic Culture*, co-authored with Iwona

Drosik (2022). In 2022, she received a scholarship from the Minister of Education and Science, Poland, for outstanding young scientists.

Przemysław Misiurski, Assistant Professor, Department of Enterprise Management, E-Business and Electronic Economy
Opole University of Technology, Opole, Poland

Przemysław Misiurski's main area of scientific and research interests is transport economics concerning modern concepts and strategies for the development of transport in Poland and in the world. In recent years, the main goal of Przemysław's research projects is to focus on the aspects of the effectiveness of rolling-stock investments in public transport companies. He is the author of numerous scientific publications presented at national and international conferences. Przemysław co-authored with Mazur-Włodarczyk Katarzyna, 'Industrial Harmony – A New Concept or a Newer Version of an Old Idea?' and 'Perception of the One Belt One Road Initiative by the Managers of Small Business Enterprises Located in Opole Silesia (Poland) – Results of Pilot Study', both in Eva Ardielli and Eva Molnárová (eds), *Development and Administration of Border Areas of the Czech Republic and Poland* (2021).

Wahiba Moubchir, Professor, Department of Languages and Humanities
École Normale Supérieure Marrakech, Marrakesh, Morocco
Permanent Member, Laboratory of Studies on Resources, Mobility and Attractiveness (LERMA), Faculty of Letters and Humanities
Cadi Ayyad University, Marrakesh, Morocco
Associate Member, Laboratory of Didactics and University Pedagogy
Cadi Ayyad University, Marrakesh, Morocco

Wahiba Moubchir received her PhD in the Geography of Tourism from Cadi Ayyad University in 2009. Her field of research is tourism and heritage. She has been involved in various research projects, the latest being the Erasmus Programme Concerning the Skills Development for Education and Applied Research in UNESCO's Mediterranean Biospheres Reserves (Edu Bio Med). Wahiba published several articles related to tourism and heritage, the latest being, 'Tourism in the Face of Covid-19: What Inclusive Reconstruction for an Accelerated Recovery of the Sector? The Case of the Tourist Operators of the Region of Marrakech-Safi' (2023).

Sally Stocksdale, Instructor of History
Towson University, Towson, MD, USA

Sally Stocksdale has a PhD in History from the University of Delaware, Newark, DE, USA. Her research interests include Russian and Soviet history generally; the cultural history of Russia, especially the Silver Age era; comparing Russian serfdom and American slavery, as well as the emancipation era in each country; Russian religious and philosophical history; and the history of Simbirsk Province in the Imperial period. She is also interested in the philosophical genre of phenomenology. Among her publications is her most recent book, *When Emancipation Came: The End of Enslavement on a Southern Plantation and a Russian Estate* (2022).

Evan Underbrink, Doctorante
Graduate Theological Union, Berkley, CA, USA

Evan Underbrink holds two MA degrees in Theology, one from Duke University Divinity School, Durham, NC (2018) and the other from Boston College, Chestnut Hill, MA, USA (2022). His research interests include hermeneutics, theology and the arts, especially the work of Dante. Among his most recent publications are, 'Milford: A Poet's Life in Spiritual Retreat' (2022); and a forthcoming collection of poems.

Valentyna Ushchyna, Professor, Department of English Philology
Lesya Ukrainka Volyn National University, Lutsk, Volyn Oblast, Ukraine

Valentyna Ushchyna's research interests concern relations between language, discourse, risk, power and society. She has published on political discourse, linguistics of risk communication and discursive stance-taking. Her most recent book is *Stance-Taking in the English Risk Discourse: A Sociocognitive Perspective* (2015, in Ukrainian).

Beatriz Valverde, Assistant Professor, Department of English Philology
Universidad de Jaén, Jaén, Spain

Beatriz Valverde has a PhD in English Philology from the Universidad de Jaén. She also has an MA in Spanish from Loyola University Chicago, Illinois, USA. Her main research interests are theology and literature, specifically in the work of Graham Greene; journalism and literature; and literature and cultural studies in English and Spanish. Beatriz has published extensively on these topics in international journals, such as *Anglia, English Studies, European Journal of English Studies* and *Revista Latina de Comunicación Social*, among others. In 2020, she co-edited with Mark Bosco, *Reading Flannery O'Connor in Spain: Andalusia in Andalucía*.

Marta Wrześniewska-Pietrzak, Professor, Department of Polish Philology
Adam Mickiewicz University, Poznań, Poland

Marta Wrześniewska-Pietrzak's main research interests are devoted to the language and identity of the d/Deaf. In 2017, she published a book, *Axiological Indicators of Identity in Texts Written by d/Deaf People and in 'Świat Ciszy' Community Newspaper* (in Polish). She also authored several papers referring to the (surdo)glottodidactics, including the problem of teaching Polish to the d/Deaf and students from migrant background in Polish primary schools. Marta is active in the area of religious language studies, being a co-organizer of a series of conferences in 2016, 2018 and 2022, *Język religijny dawniej i dziś* (Religious Language Formerly and Today). Among the articles she has published are, '"I Embrace with My Soul My Entire Beloved Homeland" – Homeland as a Value in John Paul II's Homilies' (in Polish, 2018), co-authored with Małgorzata Rybka; and 'Meetings in the Glow of Faith – A Few Remarks on the Persuasiveness and Attractiveness of the New Service of the Catholic Church' (in Polish, 2019), co-authored with Małgorzata Rybka.

Preface

Hermeneutics as a Pathway to Self-Knowledge

This monograph is a result of a pathfinding project dedicated to the approach to (meta-) communication as hermeneutic encounters through the agency of human activities, that is, communication seen as a tool for producing other tools.[1] The aim we set ourselves was thus to explore interpretative concretizations implicit in the modes of the givenness of phenomena. In particular, the purpose of this collection of essays is to explore the relationship between hermeneutics and the fine arts, including painting, music and literature as well as signage produced through engagement in communicative activities. Another analytical dimension assumed for the monograph was exploring connections between language and code, multiple avenues of human expression, between the hermeneutics of understanding, spiritual realities and imagined spaces (see here, e.g., Nielsen 2015).

Following one of the most well-known hermeneutic writers, Paul Ricoeur, narrativity is broadly introduced by asking:

> ce n'est pas la compétence apprise au cours d'une longue fréquentation des récits traditionnels qui nous permet, par anticipation, d'appeler narrativisation la simple reformulation de la taxonomie en termes d'opérations, et qui exige que nous procédions des relations stables aux opérations instables. (Ricoeur 1984: 78, as cited in Ablali 2008: 292) (One wonders if this is not the competence learned over a long frequentation of traditional stories which allows us, by anticipation, to call narrativization the simple reformulation of the taxonomy in terms of operations, and which demands that we proceed from stable relations to unstable operations.)

What follows, the 'hermeneutic keyword' for defining the perspective of this monograph, is the *encounter*, implying in general terms a meeting of the sender of a text with the receiver (addresser and addressee). These can subsume, for example, encounters of a reader with the author of a literary piece, artwork or any stretch of discourse, the encounter of the listener with the speaker on the plateau of spoken or orchestrated text, and even the incurrence of *the familiar* with *the alien*.[2] Religious experience can also be seen as an (asymmetrical) hermeneutic happenstance, effectuated through an engagement with particular symbols or texts.³

Hermeneutics, in general terms, can be seen as a science (or art) of dialectal interpretation, that is, an exegesis of the interaction of a reader with the text that is being read. James Risser broadly defines hermeneutics as a type of philosophy which, through its theoretical bent towards the praxis of interpretation, reveals that 'practical rationality is unique to our social life as a natural human capacity' (Risser 1997: 116). Particular versions of hermeneutics differed in the stance allotted both to the direction of that interaction and to the activities implied.⁴ For example, Ricoeur framed it as 'the study of the operations of understanding in their relation to the interpretation of texts' (1981: 43). Inna Semetzky, a semiotician, opts for a still wider understanding of the term, claiming that hermeneutics cannot be reduced to the interpretation of verbal texts only, but it also applies to any semiotic systems (e.g. images, symbols or cultural artefacts) with the objective of discovering their underlying and hidden meanings (Semetzky 2016: 240).⁵

At the earlier stages of its development, that is, in the period of antiquity, hermeneutical science was conceived of mainly as a set of rules for (rhetorical) interpretation of texts (Seebohm 2004: 6).⁶ Before Dilthey (as well as by Dilthey himself), the term 'hermeneutics' was predominantly applied in the epistemological dimension, that is, to facilitate interpretative reflections and on considerations of methods used by historical human sciences (Seebohm 2004: 1).⁷ Dieter Misgeld (1979) links hermeneutics, regarded as the theory of interpretative understanding, with the *Verstehen* approach to the study of society and culture: '[s]ince Schleiermacher and Dilthey, hermeneutics is a general theory of *Verstehen* as the access to all expressions of human individual, cultural and historical life. In the case of Dilthey in particular, such a general theory would be the basis of *Geisteswissenschafen*' (Misgeld 1979: 221). That move to position rhetoric as a paradigm for hermeneutics was aimed to enhance the rift between interpretative understanding and theoretical knowledge (ibid., 223).⁸ That Diltheyan opposition between understanding and explaining has been one of the pivotal hermeneutic tenets.⁹ As Driss Ablali (2008) points out, unlike 'understanding', 'explanation' is mainly connected with the natural sciences. The opposition between *Naturwissenschaft* (sciences of nature) and the *Geisteswissenschaften* (sciences of the mind), based on the famous Diltheyan phrase '[n]ature, we explain it, psychic life, we understand it', is tantamount to juxtaposing nature to man. Yet, as the scholar further emphasizes, 'the relationship between the two methods is not necessarily, as Ricoeur points out, exclusive' (Ablali 2008: 290).

Out of multifarious avenues through which the hermeneutics investigation developed, of importance is Hans-Georg Gadamer's case for going beyond the sphere of the control of science in appreciating the experiences of the truth as well as his strong stand on tradition, which is connected with processes initiating us into the way of life of a culture (Misgeld 1979: 225).[10] In particular,

> [b]y exploring an analogy between understanding a text representing a tradition of inquiry, or of literature and art, and a conversation, one can notice how understanding historically is not equal to assuming the role of a distantiated and distantiating observer just in noting the facts. Rather, one is assuming the role of partner in an interaction situation. One acts communicatively, to use Habermas' phrase. Gadamer speaks of participatory understanding. Participatory understanding cannot bring the object of its knowledge before itself in an objectivating fashion. Here one knows as one knows in speaking that what one says open up a variety of possibilities of reformulation. What is said stands in a definite, yet never quire predicable relationship to what is not said. There is not theory of definite descriptions here [...].The understanding of texts and of cultural traditions through them is the very paradigm case for a conception of philosophy that views itself as merely a more discursive form of daily communication.
>
> Misgeld 1979: 228–9

The importance of Gadamerian perspective is emphasized in particular chapters of this monograph. In fact, Gadamer links understanding with education, insisting that the success of understanding is educative as we learn from our interpretative experience. This is exactly what we want to bring into light with the different parts of our volume as we clearly connect the different areas of the Arts with Gadamer's philosophical humanism.

Notwithstanding, it is the hermeneutical thought as developed and evolving in Ricoeur's oeuvre which we deem the closest to the linguistic and semiotic thrust proposed in this monograph and which can serve as a meta-theoretical vignette for introducing and contextualizing the scope of this monograph. That said, the monograph by no means should be seen as an exposition of the application of Ricoeur's hermeneutics, yet it might be ventured to say that the emergent impact of this project is in a way conveyed by some of the Ricoeur's insights. Since in this monograph introduction there is no space to delve into intricate complexity nor retrospective details of the French thinker's theory,[11] we will accordingly focus on addressing just a few selected aspects, which are the most relevant to the trust of the project.

Hermeneutical Liaisons through Paul Ricoeur's Oeuvre

David Klem (1983: 26) points out that for Ricoeur, the weight of hermeneutic theory lies not so much in the justification of methods based on interpretation, but rather, on its ability to reveal the modus of human existence. Hence, the French philosopher, rather than focusing on what would be the rules for analysis of a particular discourse stretch or on elaborating analytical categories, saw his contribution into the theory of interrogation as fostering better understanding of a human being, as well as of the nexus between the man and the being in general (Klemm 1983: 60). The overarching question for Ricoeur thus was of an ontological nature: what it means to be a human being and what the specifics of human existence are (Rosner 1989: 6). In what follows, even though the concept of interpretation is key to Ricoeur's reflection, we will not find in his works a theory of interpretation understood as a collection of rules and procedures for text analysis (Rosner 1989: 5).

In any synopsis of Ricoeur's oeuvre, of paramount importance is the fact that the scholar was familiar with the (then) latest achievements of (structural) linguistics, of psychoanalysis as well as of semiotic theories, mainly in the structural version of Algirdas Greimas. Another crucial determinant of his thought was engagement and discussion with philosophers: both with his contemporaries and predecessors. Ricoeur's engagement with the critical chorus spurred a substantial number of scholarly perusals (e.g. Ablali 2008; Caussat 2008; Panier 2008; Ono 2008; Rosner 1989; Klemm 1983 *inter alia*). The most salient facet of that dialogue seems to be the 'combat amoureux' between Ricoeur's version of hermeneutics and (Greimassian) semiotics.[12] As Ablali (2008) upholds, this debate was implemented from *Semantique structurale* till *Du Sens II* and inscribes into a semiotic of the *discontinuous* (ibid., 291). Crucially, according to Ricoeur, 'the semiotics of Greimas, gives priority to explaining over understanding, in such a way that understanding becomes the path to explaining' (Ablali 2008: 292). What is more, understanding is shown operative at the level of narrative syntax:

> It is in the understanding of states and transformations, conjunctions and disjunctions, lack and satisfaction, that we can explain, for example, the

elementary structures of meaning. Because for the two positive deixes of the semiotic square to be considered as contrary, it is necessary that species of conjunction and disjunction correspond to them on the narrative plane. That lacking, the semiotic square would be irrelevant.

Ibid., 294

Another axis of his thought that might contextualize the project inscribed in the present monograph, and the final one to be addressed in this brief prolegomena, was his polemic engagement with 'incumbent' philosophical achievements (Kant and Husserl) as well as upgrading and refining the already developed hermeneutical thought (Dilthey, Heidegger). I will briefly synopsize this issue based on the elaboration by Rosner (1989).

Ricoeur's hermeneutics should be in broad terms understood as an attempt to overcome the rift between methodological hermeneutics by Dilthley and ontological hermeneutics by Heidegger (Rosner 1987: 8). Following Heidegger, contra Husserl, Ricoeur assumes that the situation of being-in-the-world (and by implication, in the history and culture) is prior to any specific perception, and pre-equips it with constraints which have influence on its course (Rosner (1989: 14). This tenet has a direct bearing on Ricoeur's hermeneutical programme: the most direct way of overcoming Husserl's idealism is for him transferring the cynosure of interpretative attention from the issue of subjectivity to the *mundane*. With this shift, the French philosopher establishes the act of consciousness as the final, and not the initial stage of understanding (Rosner 1989: 16).

Of importance is also the influence of Freud on Ricoeur's scholarly output. To wit, the French philosopher considered Freud's psychoanalysis to be an instance of a hermeneutic theory claiming that it is only through the interpretation of the meaning of all sorts of psychic figments (e.g. dreams) as well as of myths and artworks, the psychic content can be revealed (Rosner 1989: 27). The key points of the resulting programme of the new philosophy are captured by Rosner as follows: (1) the subject does not know himself; (2) self-consciousness is possible, however, the process of self-cognizance (awareness) is always mediated, both via the text understood as a target-meaningful product of the subject and via the Other (the interpreter). It is only through *altrui* that the dream is not self-expression but objectified text; (3) gaining consciousness is a diachronic process and its completion is not possible. Hence, in Ricoeurian hermeneutics, consciousnesses is a dynamic concept; (4) self-knowledge leads from meaning to existence, that is, to capture the fundamental means of existence, which is prior to all reflection. What follows, the process of interpretation is rooted in the structure of *Dasein* to overcome the claim of the idealistic *cogito*; (5) the only means to achieve self-consciousness by the subject is interpretation. What follows, the ultimate goal of interpretation is understanding oneself *vis-à-vis* a given symbol or a text, rather than understanding that symbol or that text *per se*; and (6) because hermeneutics – having questioned an abstract subject of philosophy – in its place introduced the *existing* subject, which is discovered through a hermeneutic process, thus, hermeneutics can be seen as an overcoming and a continuation of reflexive philosophy (Rosner 1989: 27 ff.).

The final aspect to be reported here is the contention with a hermeneutical vein as developed by Schleiermacher and Dilthey, which Ricoeur called 'Romantic hermeneutics'. The polemic developed in various avenues, but the main issue, which Rosner calls 'semantic controversy', regarded the fact that Dilthey considered psychology as the ultimate justification for hermeneutics (Rosner 1989: 39). The Diltheyan subordination of hermeneutics to psychology in practice meant that the teleology of hermeneutics was delving into the other's (the author's) life, rather than the delving into the meaning of the text.

On the other hand, Ricoeur, being familiar with the (then) contemporary achievements of structuralism, upheld the semantic autonomy of the text. Accordingly, for Ricoeur, the interpretation does not take place in the psychic plane but in the semantic one – the stand further developed in his theory of discourse (Rosner 1989: 44–5).[13]

Lacunae of Dialectic Engagements

To address pragmatically some of the theoretical postulations above and to link with the monograph content description below, we shall engage hermeneutically with sample tokens of visual discourse. The first interrogation relates to a sculpture, the digital documentation of which is given in Figure 0.1. The sculpture at the same time resonates with the hermeneutic thread of the *interpretation*, artistic discourse and creates *lacunae* in the seam between the *system* and the *speaker*, between *doxa* and *paradoxa*.

We might first of all recall the aforementioned 'bone of contention' between the Diltheyan hermeneutics and the Ricoeurian one, namely the objection to psychologism, that is, the main task of interpretation according to Dilthey being trying to recover the intention of the author. Contraire, Ricoeur upholds the semantic stance, which focuses on an inner response to the emotive horizon on which a given text evokes. In this line, the intentions of the author might indeed

Figure 0.1 Sculpture by Hana Purkrábková (object from the private collection of Jindřich Štreit, reproduction with the consent of the owner). Documented by Małgorzata Haładewicz-Grzelak at the exhibition '*Mimo město. Sovinec jako neoficiální centrum československé kultury 1974–1989'/Poza miastem. Sowiniec jako nieoficjalne centrum czechosłowackiej kultury 1974–1989* (Out of the City. Sowiniec as the Unofficial Center of Czechoslovak Culture 1974–1989). The exhibition was held at the Museum of Opole Silesia December 2019–August 2020.

be retrieved with the art historian's help: Hana Purkrábková was renowned for her criticism of the (Czechoslovak) state and the (Czechoslovak) society as such (Joanna Filipczyk, personal communication, February 2022), hence we have strong ground to assume that the artwork was aimed to express the artist's dissatisfaction with a (inertia) mentality of an average Czechoslovak citizen.

Yet, is it really necessary to know the political/personal views of the author and her biography to respond and relate to that visual text? Is not it feasible to extrapolate to the general (transcendental) dimension of humanity, rather than remaining on the specific take on the (supposed) inertia of Czechoslovak citizens? The transcendental in contrast to immanent, directly addresses the hermeneutical questions posed by Ricoeur. The first layer of engaging with the sculpture begs the ontological question. What/Who is this creature? Is it a human being or an animal? An animalized human or a humanized animal? What are the interpretative implications of adopting any of those assumptions?

This visual text might be for example addressed taking into account Roland Barthes' ([1973] 1975) caesura of 'textuality' regarding the impact on the receiving subject: (1) the text of pleasure, which 'contents, fills, grants euphoria, the text that comes from culture and does not break from it', versus (2) the text of bliss, which 'imposes a state the of loss, the text that discomforts, [...] unsettles the readers historical, cultural, psychological assumptions, the consistency of his tastes, values, memories, brings to crisis his relations with language' (Barthes [1973] 1975: 14). In accordance with the *jouissance* dimension, and 'the laceration the text of bliss inflicts upon the language' (ibid., 12), the sculpture is unsettling. What does it mean to be human, what are the characteristics of a human being, can we capture hypothetical exponential features of humanness?

Then ensues a question, 'lacerating' as Barthes would say, our concept of 'freedom'. The creature feels comfortable and cozy, lying in a relaxed position, as if on a coach watching a TV programme. As it looks calm and happy just lying there, thus might we say that it is enjoying its freedom? How deeply is freedom indexed by intentionality? Thus, the creature is free to do whatever it pleases, yet it happens that the only thing that the creature fancies is resting idly. A tangential issue, since the creature does not show any sign of uneasiness nor any coercion – what are thus the limits to our freedom and what does it mean to be free? Are there any values to uphold or to stand for? Could we thus say the creature is enjoying its freedom?

Pursuing that thread a step further, I asked a person from a 'millennial' generation, about the first impression that sculpture evoked, and the person immediately responded that this is a statement about acceptance, that is, accepting everyone that way they are, and accept oneself the way one looks, and accepting others in their peculiarities. Thus, we have a 'positive reading', related to the text of pleasure – focusing on acceptance and inclusivity of the creature, despite possible divergences with a canonical concept of a human figure. Nothing unsettling in that reading, simply the need to assume that everybody has a right to feel happy the way they are, the right to do what they please and to be what they are.

Thus, we are dealing with two separate or perhaps, complementary, hermeneutical horizons here. The first one, which focuses on general reflexivity, causes one to review one's own integrity and moral backbone. That is, admonishes to reach one's full potential as a human being, and is targeted as a purposefully painful critique. In Greimassian terms, prompts to review the actantial status of a reader of that visual text. The axiological focus would be on normativity and exclusion.

The other hermeneutical horizon departs from the opposite premise: inclusivity, acceptance and absolute freedom. This stand, however, is on a meta-level exclusive, since it bans any potential critique. Furthermore, an ontological query arises regarding the concept of 'freedom'. The creature assumes they are free to do whatever they want, free to be whatever they are. Yet, given that complacence with the status quo, will the creature ever make an effort to change their situation, that is, will there ever be a need to get up off the sofa? This is a standard hermeneutical question.

Thus, a hermeneutical horizon focusing on eliminating the boundaries and eliminating the rules, the need to 'strive' has a positive aspect of inclusion, in contradistinction to the former one, yet it begs the question: within the acceptance frame, should that creature be accepted as a *human being*? Then it ensues a Gadamerian hermeneutical circle: we are reverted back to the need to establish a new, or to abolish the incumbent definition of humanness. What is meant by to be 'human', as well as canonical values attached to it, become irrelevant.

Hermeneutics emerges at the seam of the two approaches as a dialogue. It is crucial to renegotiate between the two: only their mutual coexistence guarantees the full potential of a 'choice'. I am prepared to accept constructive criticism and set myself new, far-reaching goals, which all come with a cost and the need to make an effort and leave the comfort zone, yet, I am at the same time aware of the dyad exclusion/inclusion and necessity to respect the choice of *l'autrui*.

In that brief elenchus, it was thus hermeneutics that brought to light the divergences between the two horizons but perhaps it could also, by further interrogative delves, bring common ground on further interpretative circles. So, as Gadamer (1975: 103) remarks, the experience of an artwork reveals itself as an interpretation fact in which the viewer allows himself/herself to be determined by the limits appropriate to the work. That is, our experience completes and transforms the work of art.

The reciprocation is another dimension to take into account in hermeneutics. 'The text supersedes grammatical attitudes: it is the undifferentiated eye which an excessive author (Angelus Silesius) describes "the eye with which I see God is the same eye by which he sees me)"' (Barthes [1973] 1975: 16).[14] The seam where art joins the religious aspect is the transcendence, which in Ricoeurian tradition is one of the pillars of hermeneutics. To illustrate this facet, let us take a look at a documentation juxtaposed as Figure 0.2.

Figure 0.2 A wayside shrine from the vicinity of Głuchołazy, Poland, 16–17th century. Documentation respectively from 2017, 2019 and 2022. Author: Małgorzata Haładewicz-Grzelak.

All three photos show one wayside shrine (documented in the vicinity of the village of Głuchołazy, Poland), which according to the informative plaque near it, was erected in the seventeenth or even sixteenth century. The first photo (Figure 0.2, left) shows the documentation from 2017. We can see that on the one hand, the shrine was no longer active (there are no visible signs of devotion, such as, e.g., flowers, candles), yet, the shrine has been covered with fresh calcium and it remained in a *stasis* state as a cultural relic. Then, sometime in 2018, the shrine must have been dismantled and all that was left of its substantial materiality was the remains of the plinth (Figure 0.2, middle). The third photo in the panel, which is the documentation from 2022, shows that the shrine was put anew in a spot slightly to the left compared with the original position. Of course, research by an art historian, with insights into registers of official monuments of the region, would reveal the detailed procedures of renovation, yet, from a hermeneutic viewpoint, one basic question arises relating to the impact of 'human agency' here: is this *the same* shrine that (has) stood in almost that exact place since the sixteenth century?[15]

The informative plaque with the photo and the information about the shrine remained untouched after the renovation, with the same information as was provided for the version from Figure 0.2 (left). Officially then it is the same shrine. What then makes it *the same* shrine, assuming that much – if not all – of the original material substance has been removed and supplanted with new material, retaining a general shape of the original, but enlarging it, making it higher, enhancing the original's tectonic features and only approximating the spot on which the former one stood? All semiotic aspects point thus to the fact that the *sacrum* dimension related to that shrine remained after the renovation. The plaque still stands there informing that the shine was erected in the seventeenth or even sixteenth century. The transcendence of religious experience then can bridge the past and the present, spanning the obviousness of temporality, just as it happens in the reception and creation of a work of art, in compliance with the statement by Ricoeur that hermeneutics is an art of recognizing the discourse in an oeuvre (Ricoeur 1989: 236).

A final visual hermeneutic *elenchus* relates to the third thread of the thematic focus of this monograph, that is, the mundane aspect of experience. Figure 0.3 (right) shows an extent socrealist sculpture documented in Ostrava (Czech Republic). On the other hand, a rendition in Figure 0.3 (left) is a project (visualization) authored by the Ukrainian agency TS / D that has already gone viral. It is usually described in social media as 'a monument to shame and disgrace' and is supposed to turn the world's attention to the facet of the Russian invasion, that is usually disregarded: looting on a massive scale.

The monument is patterned after socrealist monuments which proliferated in the countries 'liberated' by the Red Army (e.g. Figure 0.3, right; see also Lubos-Kozieł and Haładewicz-Grzelak, this volume). We can see a Russian soldier standing on a stately pedestal, yet instead of a gun, flag, working tool, a child, an

Figure 0.3 Left: A project of a monument authored by a Ukrainian agency TS / D. Public domain. Right: A socrealist monument extant in Ostrava, Czech Republic. Photo by Małgorzata Haładewicz-Grzelak.

attribute which would canonically be expected in such a context, a soldier is holding a (stolen) toilet seat in his hands. On the rendition of that monument there is an inscription engraved, also in the English version: 'In tribute to the disgrace of Russian soldiers-looters.' The project relates to the fact of massive looting by the Russian Army in the occupied areas of Ukraine, the looting involving ordinary everyday objects after which, a residence, even if left intact from bombing, cannot be inhabited.

This visuality juxtaposed in Figure 0.3 involves in fact several hermeneutic loops. The first and the foremost relates to Schutz's concept of humour as an 'emancipating province' (Barber 2017). In particular, Barber argues for a wider understanding of humour, embracing space by far exceeding jokes, where 'interlocutors leap together into the humorous sphere and make jokes together' (ibid., x). In this case, it is important to be familiar with both the esthetic impact of social realism art and the philosophy behind it: art in Stalinism was conceived of as a tool for wielding in the battle for the well-being and happiness of the working class. The juxtaposition of assumed grandeur and importance of freeing the nations, the adopted ethos of *liberté, égalité, fraternité* with the mundane and pragmatic dimension (the toilet seat as an attribute) skillfully creates a tension, which 'transports both parties [that is, authors and recipients] into an encompassing humorous attitude in which everyday life statements and actions undergo a transvaluation' (ibid., 15). As a result, the final impact, a silent cry of ordinary Ukrainian citizens suffering during the war, is made the more acute.

The chapters comprising this monograph are a reflection of how hermeneutics can be envisaged through the prism of particular areas of study and modality (in a broad formulation, art, music or communication). Thus, we understand hermeneutics as a discipline that may link the researchers from different areas of interest and we focus our attention on how these academics 'interpret' the discipline on literary terms, because earlier hermeneutics did not put the emphasis on philology. So, the monograph is conceived to centre attention on how hermeneutics emerges in canonical contemporary research in humanities, bearing also in mind that it has become a common discipline in literary studies.

The Book: A Description of Subject-Provinces

In constructing the book, we invited an internationally diverse set of contributors who also hail from interdisciplinary studies to create an endeavour that would be global in scope. The result covers a range of themes, brought together by a binding focus on achieving methodological synergy in the form of a widely conceived hermeneutical prism. The volume thus strives to provide a platform for interconnecting different areas of thought and art rather than focusing on hermeneutics as such.

By looking through the hermeneutical prism at a selection of visual and verbal texts, this project groups them together to highlight the emerging internal linkages[16] between aspects such as the visual discourse of fine arts and communication. This covers, for example, musicological analyses, religious painting, as well as the *Umwelt* of African colonization, the meaningful richness of clothing in the African tradition, the hostile dystopian landscapes of Meg Elison, and the use of Christopher Okigbo's poetry for describing a world of violence and permanent conflict; as well as communication through sign language, or the urbanscapes of tourist dystopias.

In doing so, the book argues that everything is designed to create interplays 'between the idea of multiple realities: and particular works of art, artistic practices or literature, in which each clarifies the other' (Barber 2017: x). Furthermore, it can be recalled that earlier German hermeneutics grounds on humanism and the arts, so this collection of essays attempts to pinpoint the reading of the different interpretative experiences by means of linking art, music, literature and linguistics to validate rules and procedures of interpretation by means of incorporating visual and verbal literacy.

Accordingly, the volume attempts to elaborate on hermeneutics from a practical perspective, utilizing it as critical research and liaising with other areas of human creativity like art, literature or linguistics: hermeneutics, then, is here in an emergent nature. In general terms, it will be dedicated to the approach to (meta-)communication as a hermeneutic activity. We aim to explore interpretative concretizations implicit in the modes of the givenness of phenomena. We would like to look at communication as involving both the *tête-à-tête* interactions and the subsuming of an emerging influence of the contact with a work or art of any medium – (cf. Roman Ingarden and Roland Barthes). Hence, the notion of embodiment in looking at communication is crucial. Positioning hermeneutical narratives as the object of researching inquiry gives us freedom to distance from the established paths of interpretation and freedom to pursue novel perspectives.

The monograph comprises thirteen chapters almost uniformly divided into three domain parts, each devoted to a common field with the intention of providing coherence and cohesion to the volume. The monograph thus has a 'triptych' structure, with the literary part being the pivotal one, bridging the two 'flanking' ones: the artistic textuality and verbal and visual communication.

The chapters are mostly grounded on an 'insider's view' perspective, giving the reader access to idiosyncratic analytical data sets, such as, e.g., Amazigh proverbs, Chinese billboards, internet content of Ukrainian websites or to a selection of Adinkra symbols, a communication system developed among the Akan people from Ghana and the Ivory Coast. Thus, in one monograph, we offer the reader an exploration through specific cultural textscapes, mapped in the transcendence of the art dimension, in the space of literary expression as well as stretches of discourse, nonetheless without engaging in the pursuit of in-depth theory-specific issues.

In this general context, the part devoted to Fine Arts, 'Part One: Noematic *Lacunae* in Artistic Discourse', opens the volume. The thematic focus of the chapters gathered in the part evolves around what can be conceived as 'provinces of meaning', realized through different substantial modalities, e.g. painting and music. The other two parts focus on particular frameworks for the analysis of hermeneutics with a strong emphasis on interpreting particular texts and situations. In 'Part Two: Hermeneutic Diaphaneity in Literary Studies', there is a change in the scope thanks to the permeability of hermeneutics. This part has as cynosure of analytical attention literary works viewed from an array of analytical domains. The chapters gathered in 'Part Three: Epistemic Spaces in the Geopsychic Universe of Visual and Verbal Communication', are grounded in the analysis of both visual and verbal discourse and engage in explorations of the lifeworld of the subjects immersed in the spatiality of geopsychic transactions. The particular chapters put forward perspectives which are somewhat distinct in an overarching manner, ensuing from the epistemological specifics of particular fields of humanities.

We purposefully avoided putting emphasis on the ('badly burdened', as Husserl would say) term *discourse* in the title, although, admittedly, it was fostered by Ricoeur in the 1960s, since currently it is presumably the most exploited linguistic item, laden with a plethora of citational universes (e.g., critical discourse analysis, spatiality of discourse by Paul Chilton, etc.).[17] Positing *hermetical narratives* as the broad object of investigative inquiry gave us the freedom to stand aloof from the established paths of interpretation or citational spirals, and also opened avenues to pursue novel perspectives.

The objective was to envisage communication as involving both the *tête-à-tête* interactions and also subsuming an emerging impact of the contact with a work of art of any medium. That is, the assumption is to start from the artefacts as resources and follow their impact through the interpretations they generate. That impact is effectuated not on an analytical abstraction but on a perceiving subject, who is transformed through receiving that impact and also reacts to it.

Part One, 'Noematic *Lacunae* in Artistic Expression', addresses some of the multiple aspects of the givenness of the work of art, criss-crossed with the cultural opposition of 'sacred' and 'profane'. The part has four chapters: 'Hermeneutical Guidelines for Understanding the Self through Art' by David Jaeger and Evan Underbrink; 'Hieratic Communication in the Oeuvre of Kazimir Malevich, Vasily Kandinsky and Nikolai Roerich' by Sally Stocksdale; 'Painterly Motif of Kisses of Mary and Kisses of St Joseph in the Context of Iconography of *Unio Mystica* in the Baroque Period' by Andrzej Kozieł; and 'Non-verbal Music and Interaction: Narrativity, Discourse Situation and the opening of Elgar's Cello Concerto in E minor, Op. 85' by Marta Falces Sierra.

The chapter by David Jaeger and Evan Underbrink opening the volume, uses recent currents and arguments in Continental philosophy to provide an epistemological platform for the way in which the whole of Part One develops. Aiming at 'thematizing the invisible', the authors pursue the modes of the givenness of the artistic text in relation to one's own 'self-givenness' along with the 'givenness of the Other'. The resulting journey in the form that can be called an autoethnographic hermeneutics, proceeds along the coordinates of Richard Kerney's categories of *aesthesis*, *poesis* and *phronesis*, which correspond to the experiences of 'knowing', 'making' and 'practically living'. Assuming the state of self-alienation as a subjective default, the authors construct an interpretative web to enquire into the status of artistic experience in overcoming the inner hiddenness that leads into an open-ended, and hopefully, 'richer' sense of self-experiencing which also carries some important ethical consequences.

In her chapter, Sally Stocksdale offers a hermeneutical inspection of the roots and layers of interplay of the artistic output of landmark Russian painters of the so-called Silver Age: Kazimir Malevich, Vasily Kandinsky and Nikolai Roerich. She elaborates on the Slavophile beliefs of the luminaries of the period and shows how the province of art and belief of the godliness of a human being were reflected in the creative painterly oeuvre and how engaged it was in charting the Godly future of the civilization.

The premise of the chapter by Andrzej Kozieł is to search for a universal determinant of mystical experience as expressed through religious paintings of the Baroque period in Silesia (the region at the time belonging to Germany, now part of Poland). In particular, he traces the painterly motif of the Kisses of Mary and Kisses of Joseph through Silesian paintings of the nineteenth-century painting. Drawing on the output of the Catholic mystics of the period (St John of the Cross or Thomas of Aquinas), the scholar pinpoints some of the most important pictorial strategies that were adopted by artists who struggled to show the mystical union of the human soul with the divine essence.

The last chapter in Part One is by Marta Falces Sierra and it takes the opening of Elgar's Cello Concerto, Op. 85 as an illustration to trace aspects of narrativity in non-verbal music. The comparison of the rhetoric of discourse in both narrative fiction and music suggests that non-verbal music, if perceived as a story, does not take the form of a narration. Marta Falces claims that 'as the crafting of a story in a play is achieved through alternation of speech, advanced music moves are linked one to the other selecting, being selected by the former one or by self-selecting themselves to build their story'. This, together with the lack of narrative control and the performative dimension of the score, makes our perception of the 'music story' shift away from narrative fiction to drama.

Part Two, 'Hermeneutic Diaphaneity in Literary Studies', remaining within the realm of 'artistically marked texts' (the formulation by Elżbieta Chrzanowska-Kluczewska, 2017), shifts the analytical attention to the literary output. The part also comprises four chapters: 'Adinkra Symbols: From Visual Art Messages to a Literary Research Methodology' by Violetta Jojo Verge; 'Hermeneutical Narratives of the European Colonization in Africa in Graham Greene's *A Burnt-Out Case* and Abdulrazak Gurnah's *Desertion*' by Beatriz Valverde; 'The Language of War in the Apocalypse Trope of Meg Elison's *The Book of the Unnamed Midwife*' by Almudena Machado-Jiménez; and 'Prophesizing War in "The Lament of the Deer" by Christopher Okigbo' by Paula García-Ramírez.

Part Two opens with Violetta Jojo Verge's use of the Adinkra symbols, which acts as a link with the previous part. Particularly relevant is the bridge she creates between this artistic age-old communication system, developed by the Akan people from Ghana and the Ivory Coast, and literary works by West African women, particularly Buchi Emecheta and Ama Ata Aidoo. As happens in many animist cultures, both spiritual and physical dimensions cohabit in the collective imagination and so it helps to interpret the different spheres of human relationships – a symbology that attempts to create boundaries between the people as well as a common frame of reference in order to determine the limits of our interpretation (Gadamer).

Beatriz Valverde's chapter on Graham Greene and Abdulrazak Gurnah develop Yuri Lotman's semiotics in an attempt to show how both writers depict colonial landscapes from a common frame of reference even when they proceed from two different backgrounds. Such a richness of perspective will promote a new understanding of the colonial sphere in the African context.

An apocalyptic vision of gender's conflict in which men and women live completely apart is presented by Almudena Machado-Jiménez, who centres her attention on Meg Elison's *The Book of the Unnamed Midwife* (2014). While in the previous chapter, war is prophesized, human relationships are totally broken in the dystopian society presented in this chapter. The reader will find out a new exploitation of human relationships deeply rooted in the old structures.

Based on a similar landscape to that discussed in Beatriz Valverde's chapter, Paula García-Ramírez's quest for Christopher Okigbo's poetry focuses on the context and interpretation of the text by means of a poem inserted into a story for children. The function of this poem, if we bear in mind the contextualizing elements of it (oral tradition, aetiological meaning and so on), leads the reader to understand the consequences of an apocalyptic scenery of violence and abuse. How Christopher Okigbo's chapter deepens into the root of the conflict allows the reader to interpret the convulsive experience he is living in. The seer-poet elaborates on the explanation of African contemporary conflicts.

The final part of the monograph's structural triptych, 'Part Three: Epistemic Spaces in the Geopsychic Universe of Visual and Verbal Communication', has five chapters: 'Local Amazigh Proverbs in Motion: Between Transmission and Interpretation' by Fatima Ez-zahra Benkhallouq and Wahiba Moubchir; 'Thirdspace Creation as a Geopsychic Dialogue with Tourists in the Karpacz Holiday Resort, Poland' by Joanna Lubos-Kozieł and Małgorzata Haładewicz-Grzelak; 'Creating Common Epistemic Spaces through Multimodal Stance-Taking Practices' by Valentyna Ushchyna; 'Elaborating a Heuristic Tool to Determine Fluency Spectrum for Deaf Pupils in Poland' by Marta Wrześniewska-Pietrzak; and 'The Concept of *Wenming* (文明) ('Civility') as an Edusemiotic Strategy' by Katarzyna Mazur Włodarczyk, Małgorzata Haładewicz-Grzelak, Elżbieta Karaś, Joanna Kolańska-Płuska and Przemysław Misiurski. The main thrust of the contributions gathered together in this part relates to the systemic nature of the communication but also takes into account the role of the speaker, that is, the epistemic stance of the sender/author of the analysed textuality.

The topic of the contribution by Fatima Ez-zahra Benkhallouq and Wahiba Moubchir are the hermeneutic and immanent aspects of local Berber (Amazigh) proverbs as indexing values of a society of predominantly oral transmission of knowledge. The premise of the chapter is that the proverbs reflect specific thought patterns and are vital in transmitting intangible heritage across generations. The importance of a proverb in Amazigh (Berber) culture is reflected already in the name: (Amazigh) *awal idderr* literally means 'living word', which accentuates the power of the words bound together as a proverb as well as their pertinence to everyday life situations. The researchers also address the problems in intercultural translations, based on the same proverb uttered in French and Amazigh.

In their contribution Joanna Lubos-Kozieł and Małgorzata Haładewicz-Grzelak explore the hermeneutic and phenomenological potential of tourists' engagement with a non-place such as the Karpacz holiday resort, Poland. The analysis in particular makes use of the concept of 'third space' as elaborated by Edward Soja. The authors explore the interaction as a sort of transactional dialogue. In a way, both phenomenology and hermeneutics takes human experience as its object of enquiry. In compliance with canonical hermeneutical approach, authors were interested in what happens during the encounter of a tourist with the visual and verbal textuality prepared for their benefit by the Karpacz business entrepreneurs. This is done via two *flâneries* aimed at two of the multitude of Karpacz catering establishments operative in 2014.

The chapter by Valentyna Ushchyna deals with the hermeneutics of real-life online communication, utilizing the concept of stance-taking within the wider framework of 'objective hermeneutics'. The author shows some of the linguistic ways via which epistemic stance-taking becomes an integral part of the shared epistemic spaces creation, where the dynamics and ecology of meaning-making presupposes interaction and collaboration. To be more specific, the focus of this study is on the epistemic stance-taking in the Covid-19 discourse, based on the study of the content of two Ukrainian bloggers related to the Covid pandemic. Because knowledge concerning Covid-19 is insufficient, epistemic possibilities build upon uncertainty and unpredictability. The study uses an objective hermeneutic approach as the methodological framework that allows disclosing of the concealed structures of discourse and enables explanation of the complex processes of social semiosis in post-modern computerized society. Within the objective hermeneutic paradigm, analysis of stance-taking presupposes taking into account personal attitudes of individual speakers (stance-takers) along with the domineering social structures framing their discursive actions and interactions.

Marta Wrześniewska-Pietrzak investigates challenges and opportunities of using the PJM-PL vocabulary test with two distinct languages: the Polish Sign Language and Written Polish. In this way, the chapter inscribes into the discussion on the controversies besetting the so-called Deaf-culture in Poland that is, (a diasporic) community of hearing-impaired users of sign language in Poland. In particular, the author addresses the problems occurring in educational reality that a hearing-impaired child is faced with. These problem ensue, first of all, because of the predominant negative bias towards teaching the sign language in Poland, the lack of competences in sign language of educators at all levels and, most of all, the so-called oralist approach that demands that a child ultimately align with the phonic milieu, notwithstanding the fact that a phonic language is always (if at all) acquired by a hearing-impaired child as a foreign one. One of the burning issues to remedy this plight is thus developing diagnostic procedures to correctly diagnose the language competencies across modalities (phonic versus gestural language) of a child. The chapter relates the steps of creating such a diagnostic tool and explores its propaedeutic potential. Although the tool was developed for Polish, there is a potential to extrapolate specific steps into other languages.

Katarzyna Mazur-Włodarczyk, Małgorzata Haładewicz-Grzelak, Elżbieta Karaś, Joanna Kolańska-Płuska and Przemysław Misiurski address in their chapter the edusemiotic aspect of billboards promotive of the concept of *wenming* (文明) ('civility') as part of the urbanscape of the People's Republic of China (PRC), coupling it with the Gadamerian hermeneutics. In particular, the authors focus on the concept of *Bildung* as fostered by Gadamer, in the sense of formative propaedeutics. The analysis shows the compliance of the edusemiotic approach with the social hermeneutics, and isolates *wenming* as a landmark edusemiotic marker, of hermeneutical nature, pivotal in creating an ecosystem of cultural significance.

Synopsizing, by tracing the maze of communicative activities of a human being, the book interrogates the multiple identities created by assuming various stances towards the givenness of the texts. The synergy of diversities within the book offers the reader engagement in a hermeneutics of human creative output, bringing together particular simplex aspects. It also contributes to understanding hermeneutics in a very broad sense, that is, as the art of interpretation, proceeding through contradictions and complementarities of the *being-in-the-world*, that is, the experience of selfhood through communication and through the existence of *the Other* given to us phenomenologically. The universal experience of truth (as exposed by Gadamer) will allow us to revisit some of the outstanding elements of humanism, historicism and education. The threefold perspective we have used lead us to conclude that hermeneutics allow us to relate different areas of knowledge: art, literature and education with the purpose of illustrating many possibilities of interpretation in a deeply changing society.

Notes

1. We would like to thank Morwenna Scott and Laura Gallon for their help during all the stages of proceeding this monograph.
2. In line with Ricoeurian thought, 'Comment procéder à cette analyse conceptuelle de ce que signifie agir pour un homme ? ... c'est-à -dire de ce que l'on dit lorsqu'on énonce de manière compréhensive pour autrui ce qu'on fait, ce pourquoi on le fait, ce qui pousse à agir comment et avec quels moyens on le fait, en vue de quoi on le fait' (Ricoeur 1977 : 5).
3. We aimed thus at viewing communication through its products and tools as involving both the *tête-à-tête* interactions and also subsuming an emerging impact of the contact with a work or art of any medium.
4. We will not delve into particular vicissitudes of hermeneutics here.
5. The scholar also points out that: 'Etymologically, the Greek words *hermeneuein* and *hermeneia* for interpreting and interpretation are related to the mythical god Hermes, a messenger and mediator between gods and mortals, who crosses thresholds and traverses boundaries because he can understand both languages even if they appear totally alien to each other' (Semetsky 2016: 240).
6. In particular, 'According to the *Epinomis*, those who practice the hermeneutical art, the *hermeneutioke techne,* are called *exegetai. Exegesis,* interpretation, is the word that set us on the right track. In the Hellenistic period, the at of interpretation is called *grammatike* exegesis although occasionally we also find *hermeneia eis ti*' (Seebohm 2004: 13). As Misgeld observes, it was Hans-Georg Gadamer's oeuvre *Wahreit und Methode* which, being the most important work on hermeneutics, for the first time specifically traced the roots of hermeneutics to ancient rhetoric (Misgeld 1979: 222).
7. The same reference for a fundamental phenological critique of hermeneutics in the nineteenth century.
8. Gadamer's case for 'experiences of the truth that transcend the sphere of the control of science' (Misgeld 1979: 225) is connected with his strong stand on tradition, which 'are processes initiating us into the way of life of a culture' (ibid., 225).
9. With the caveat that according to Ablali, Dilthley's theory specifies three types of understanding (Ablali 2007: 288–9).
10. In this connection, Seebohm motivates the importance of hermeneutical consciousness, which as he claims, consists in 'the consciousness of attitudes in the understanding of one's own cultural tradition' (Seebohm 2004: 5).
11. Such an in-depth and exhaustive retrospective of Ricoeur's thought is provided, for example, in Rosner (1989) as an introduction to the collected works published as Ricoeur (1989).
12. For example, Ono traces the influence of Émile Benveniste on Ricoeur as the two figures who perspicuously marked the poststructuralist landscape, pointing out that,

'in his hermeneutical, historical and literary research, Ricoeur repeatedly borrowed from Benveniste the concepts of "instance of discourse", "historical event" or "linguistic time"' (Ono 2008: 326).
13 This issue is further developed by Ricoeur as the Appropriation of the text by the reader (Rosner 1989: 47).
14 Varela calls such elusive boundary states, where the decomposition of an entity triggers the processes in integrating that entity 'imbricating' (overlapping) (Varela 1976).
15 According to the information on a plaque, the tradition mentions it was erected as an expiation for sins, which was then a common procedure, see, for, example the custom of erecting the so-called expiation crosses.
16 Gregory Bateson put it this way: 'the contrast between a part and the whole, whenever this contract appears I the realm of communication, is simply a contrast in logical typing. The whole is always in meta-relationship with its parts' (Bateson 2000: 267).
17 The same goes with another catchy term, *multimodality*.

References

Ablali, Driss. 2008. 'Sémiotique et herméneutique: Le texte et l'action'. *Semiotica*, 168 (1/4): 287–304.
Barber, Michael. 2017. *Religion and Humour as Emancipating Provinces of Meaning*. Contributions to Phenomenology Series, vol. 91, x. Springer: Dordrecht.
Barthes, Roland. [1973] 1975. *The Pleasure of the Text* (Le Plaisir du Texte). Éditions du Seuil, trans. Richard Miller. New York: Hill and Wang.
Bateson, Gregory. 2000. *Steps to an Ecology of Mind*. Chicago, IL: University of Chicago Press.
Caussat, Pierre. 2008. 'La philosophie face à l'univers des signes: Positions et propositions de Paul Ricoeur surla sémiotique et la sémiologie'. *Semiotica*, 168 (1/4): 365–87.
Flemonds, Douglas. 1991. *Completing Distinctions*. Boston, MA: Shambala.
Freeman, Melissa. 2007. 'Performing the Event of Understanding in Hermeneutic Conversations with Narrative Texts'. *Qualitative Inquiry*, 13 (7): 925–44.
Gadamer, Hans Geoog. 1975. *Truth and Method*. New York: Seabury Press.
Klemm, David E. 1983. *The Hermeneutical Theory of Paul Ricoeur: A Constructive Analysis*. Lewisburg, PA: Bucknell University Press.
Misgeld, Dieter. 1979. 'On Gadamer's Hermeneutics'. *Philosophy of the Social Sciences*, 9: 221–39.
Nielsen, Cynthia. 2015. *Interstitial Soundings: Philosophical Reflections on Improvisation, Practice, and Self-Making*. Eugene, OR: Cascade Books.
Ono, Aya. 2008. 'Le parcours du *sens*: Ricoeur et Benveniste'. *Semiotica*, 168 (1/4): 325–39.

Panier, Louis. 2008. 'Ricoeur et la sé´miotique: Une rencontre "improbable"?' *Semiotica*, 168 (1/4): 305–24.

1950. *Philosophie de la volonté: Le Volontaire et l'involontaire*. Paris: Aubier.

Ricoeur, Paul. 1977. 'Le discours de l'action. In Dorian Tiffeneau (ed.), *La sémantique de l'action*, 3–144. Paris: Éditions du CNRS.

Ricoeur, P. 1981. *Hermeneutics and the Human Sciences*. Trans. J. B. Thompson. Cambridge: Cambridge University Press.

Ricoeur, Paul 1984. *Temps et récit, II. La configuration du temps dans le ré´cit*. Paris: Seuil.

Ricoeur, Paul. 1989. *Język tekst, interpretacja. Wybór pism*. Trans. Katarzyna Rosner and Piotr Graff. Warszawa: Państwowy Instytut Wydawniczy.

Risser, James. 1997. *Hermeneutics and the Voice of the Other: Re-reading Gadamer's Philosophical Hermeneutics*. Albany, NY: State University of New York Press.

Rosner, Katarzyna. 1989. 'Paul Ricoeur – filozoficzne źródła jego hermeneutyki'. In Paul Ricoeur, *Język tekst, interpretacja. Wybór pism*. Trans. Katarzyna Rosner and Piotr Graff, 5–60. Warszawa: Państwowy Instytut Wydawniczy.

Seebohm, Thomas M. 2004: *Hermeneutics. Method and Methodology*. Dordrecht: Kluwer Academic Publishers.

Semetsky, Inna 2016. 'Monstrous Hermeneutics: Learning from Diagrams'. *Semiotica*, 212: 239–58.

Varela, Francisco. 1976. 'Not One Not Two'. *Coevolution Quarterly*, 12: 32–67.

Acknowledgements

Every effort has been made to trace copyright holders and to obtain their permission for the use of copyright material. However, if any have been inadvertently overlooked, the publishers will be pleased, if notified of any omissions, to make the necessary arrangement at the first opportunity.

Part One

Noematic *Lacunae* in Artistic Discourse

1

Hermeneutical Guidelines for Understanding the Self through Art

David Jaeger and Evan Underbrink

Introduction: The Person is a Stranger to Itself

Any phenomenon which is universal is by that very predicative value difficult to decipher. The proverb, 'Fish do not know what water is,' is perhaps applicable here, as we argue that the experience of being a stranger to ourselves is an essential element within each human being. We might at the outset highlight a few common examples which seem to be particularly defined by a concentration of this predicative value of self-strangeness. For instance, when I wake up in the night and cannot remember where I am or even my own name, and must wake up more for these things to return to me, the uncanniness of spending time simply looking at myself in the eye in a mirror, or when I meditate upon my thumb or foot and consider the very strange fact that it is my appendage and, in some sense, myself. There is an uncanniness of myself in these experiences, where I wonder at myself as a being both in time, but also in space. I perceive myself as perceiving myself, and in this find a sort of alienation and horror.

Yet, I cannot perpetually be within this experience of total strangeness. We need to interpret in order to survive, to make sense of the phenomena, to function and flourish. Yet, hermeneutics is often 'more an art than a science', and among other things, to interpret is to deal with the longstanding question of the relation between the visible and invisible. The question of this relationship between what appears to us in the world and those subtle, invisible conditions of phenomenality, has challenged phenomenological thinking for decades. The inexhaustibility of interpretation is also guaranteed, as Jean-Luc Marion emphasizes in the concept of 'saturated phenomena' ([1989] 2002: ix). This relation between the visible and invisible is further complexified when it is turned upon the self[1] that is not fully transparent to itself. The self that experiences the strangeness of phenomena is also to itself a stranger.

This condition gives rise to incomprehensibility and self-alienation, which can manifest in a variety of ways. I may be disgusted with the mistakes I have made in my past, or realize that an intention to do good was centrally motivated by egoism, or some other experience of self-revelation (for example, someone pointing out to me an uncomfortable truth about which I had not perceived). These experiences and more speak to the confrontation between that which the self perceives of itself, and that which it does not. In other words, we encounter, or re-encounter ourselves as being strange, motivated by impulses too complex for us to fully understand, and bearing negative aspects and traits we like to ignore or avoid. To maintain this state of confrontation within the self leads to an experience of horror and paralysis. I may, for instance, be so concerned with the nature of egotism present within my acts that I fail to act at all, for good or ill. Or, I may push away the person who would otherwise allow me to understand myself better.

This horror and paralysis in encountering our own self-estrangement may also be inevitable; yet, these emotions need not be the defining traits of this experience. 'O heaven and earth, this is wondrous strange,' cries Horatio, the outsider who observes, and Hamlet, who is in the liminality of self and other, the day and the night, the dead king and living prince, responds: 'and therefore as a stranger give it welcome'.[2] The stranger we are to ourselves confronts us, yet we may elect to assume a posture of welcome or abhorrence to the strange. From this, the question of hospitality naturally follows: how do we welcome the stranger that is ourselves to ourselves?

Hospitality must be maintained by some intermediary element. As Ricoeur notes ([1990] 1992), we construct our self-identities through the world about us, and through relation to others. This opens the call to explore specifically how the arts operate hermeneutically within the context of self-understanding.

Art Addressing the Incomprehensibility of the Self

In order to understand how art helps us to address this perception of ourselves being comprised of an inner hiddenness which can lead to self-alienation, we begin with some basic observations on what we mean by 'art' and its interpretation. Particular works of art are in themselves an interpretive task, an '*Aufgabe*', and interpretation 'involves a community of interpreters, rules of interpretation and a history of interpretation' (Mohanty 1989: 52). We may consider the example of interpreting as it manifests in the act of reading.

In the act of attentive, 'active' reading, much will occur in consciousness, along with various kinesthetic responses; I may scan my eyes across a page, or listen to the voice of another (physically present or prerecorded), or read aloud in my own voice. In reading, I am also required to 'fill in' aesthetic sense through use of the imagination and/or rational meaning from the text, very similar to the sort of operation that one would perform in a phenomenological essence-analysis. Great works of writing, and indeed any work with deep artistic meaning or 'beauty', will likely leave us with a sense of excess on the first or even after multiple readings – there is more to be understood, but my understanding falls short of what I desire or have intended.

In line with one of Marion's ([1989] 2002) best known concepts, a text, whether it is the most cross-referenced literary work in the world, or the humble dime-store novel, is a saturated phenomenon.[3] This concept responds to what Kant ([1781-7] 1996, A70/B95: 124) calls 'ontological predicates', namely, *quantity*, *quality*, *modality* and *relation*. These fundamental categories or limits on cognition (along with perhaps a few others)[4] are pushed up against and breached in a saturated phenomenon. Key examples of this are events, paintings, the unique singularity of an individual person and our own bodies. We can thus see that such an experience of saturated phenomena is liable to emerge not only when reading, but within most encounters with art, provided that we recognize that the saturation can come not only from the excess of the 'object', but also from an interior inability to fully perceive.

I may read a poem, observe a scene or taste a French omelette dozens of times, each in a different context, and find that every instance leaves me with a sense of confusion or wonder, provided that I am attentive to it as a saturated phenomenon. The implication is that our means of knowing the universe is not exclusively, or perhaps even primarily, through the idea of rationality. We argue that we 'know' the universe, at least partially, as an aesthetic idea.[5] Saturation, too, is not limited to the times when I find myself humbled or awestruck, but can be found in more common and everyday phenomena.

Art need not be always breathtaking; indeed it may be argued that the pots and pans of the kitchen, a park bench or a baseball game all contain the prerequisite qualities for being 'art', and their often underwhelming-ness stems from my own inability to constitute them in all their depth as aesthetic, even poetic, objects. This inability varies in intensity, based upon my own experience and perception, as well as the context and presentation which amend objects to poetic reception. It is simply easier for me to see the art of an object when it is placed in a gallery rather than a gutter.

This saturated experience of art makes us more aware of the invisible, both within mundane objects such as paint, ink, coffee beans, stone, etc., and also within ourselves. Invisibility in phenomenology is not concerned with speculating about 'invisible' phenomena such as the oft-used thought experiment of an elephant in the room which one can neither confirm nor deny. Generally, there have been two dominant strands of thinking of the invisible. In line with Merleau-Ponty, one can think of invisibility as co-inhering within the appearing of phenomena. For example, in each act of perception, there are essentially hidden/invisible aspects of the correlated objects of perception; the classic Husserlian example of this is the awareness that objects as perceived are essentially given to be perceived one-side-at-a-time in adumbrations (Husserl 2005: 97*)*. The showing of one profile of the cube suggests the possibility of being viewed otherwise (where these invisible possibilities are given through imagination).

This view of invisibility accords with Merleau-Ponty's preference for the primacy of perception. In Michel Henry's approach to invisibility ([1988] 2009) the view is different and more radical. He speaks of a phenomenology of 'manifestation'; and requires four guiding maxims – Husserl's call to the things themselves, the validity of originary giving intuitions,[6] the correlation between reduction and givenness (the more one applies phenomenological reduction, the more excess of givenness) and lastly: '*so much appearing, so much Being*' (Henry 2019: 5, emphasis added).

These last two axioms allow one to investigate the self-manifestation of Being as hidden *by phenomenological necessity*, and this 'appears', perhaps paradoxically, as 'non-apparent'. Following the phenomenological method one finds that this invisibility is not so much something *inaccessible* but rather something that exists as a dynamic component of the relational nature of any experience (Nitsche 2020: 555). Henry is especially poignant here:

> Is it not possible that ... certain phenomena cannot appear, not by a defect, but because they cannot do so in principle? Does the method of phenomenology (unveiling, putting into light) always and necessarily coincide with its 'object' (the phenomenon to manifest)? Or, is it not possible in certain cases that the 'identity between the object and the method of phenomenology loses its evidence'? For example, when it is a matter of phenomenalizing life ... which escapes in principle from the domain of the visible ... then the identity between the object and the method of phenomenology is broken abruptly. It

would give way to a heterogeneity so radical that it is first presented to thought as an abyss.

Henry 2019: 11

If one adopts this phenomenology of Life as one's starting point, then in some sense it makes sense to speak of *noesis* as a form of *poesis*.⁷

Remaining a Stranger to Oneself

When we speak of the self as stranger, we are considering 'strangeness' as a predicative value which Bernhard Waldenfels and Peter Costello note can be found in someone or something else – a person, a monstrous act or phenomena of nature, non-human technology, possibly even some aspect of the unknown God (Waldenfels [2006] 2011: 126; Costello 2012: 11). The stranger can be the Other, yet it in some way confronts us. It can also occur within 'the sphere of ownness'. We have seen how my own ego or my lived body may appear with strangeness as I find a new desire awakened within me, if I realize a latent talent, lose an ability that I once cherished, or even if I just find myself in a radically new context. In speaking of the alien, the foreigner, the stranger, we are discussing that which permeates the boundary between the visible and invisible. In this vein, although I may be able to assimilate aspects of what at first appears strange or foreign into my horizon of understanding, the most intimate sense of the alien or the strange will always escape me.

It is vital to understand that this ever escaping horizon of understanding is also located within ourselves as the object of our perception. We remain strangers to ourselves. We have noted aspects of the invisible and offered a sketch which suggests that to interpret is to be receptive to the givenness of a text as saturated, and as offering itself to perception, essentially opening a horizon of the foreign within the text. The interrelationship of these two aspects may also be seen in Derrida's conception of the messianistic within phenomena ([1997] 2000: 77). On a 'messianistic' reading, just as with the saturated phenomenon, the essential quality of that phenomena ever lies outside the full reach of the comprehension, and I know that the infinite 'ideal' sense is always *to come*, never finally *arriving*. This interplay of waiting draws us into the otherness of the text or experience, an otherness that will resist a totalizing and final interpretation.

Following this, our hermeneutic experience recognizes Derrida's idea that interpretation is an impossible act, and an act of mourning, allowing one to appreciate that our goal ought not be a full reduction of the strangeness of ourselves. Such a reduction or removal of all strangeness is foremost impossible. Yet, even if it were possible through some aberrant form of 'therapy' or nearly fanatical self-observation, it would be an egregious act of inhospitality to this stranger that is us. Hence, the nature of our interpretations, according to Derrida (ibid.), has a Janus face: we locate ways to interpret ourselves in order to understand the stranger, but in understanding the stranger we are also ever letting ourselves up to the utter mystery we are to ourselves (ibid., 9).

Our ideal is not that the self should be reduced into utter comprehensibility, where I cease to be a stranger to myself. Instead, we can appreciate our experience of the phenomenon of the self as stranger analogously to how we experience all strangers. Thus, a hermeneutics which stems from the perception of art, and indeed other methods, will fall under the ethical consideration of hospitality. For instance, it would be inhospitable to think of any stranger who has confronted us as being inherently an enemy because of their strangeness. Nor would it be hospitable to claim or to operate under the misunderstanding that we fully comprehend this stranger.

Our ideal is thus instead to consider how art can be a particularly helpful hermeneutic tool to approach the stranger who is ourselves, as we remain hospitable in sharing the experience of art. The dialogue formed through art within the self who is perceiving, and the self who is partially perceived can be one that directly honors the messianistic essence of the phenomenon, by nature of the shared hermeneutical object of focus incorporating this saturation of meaning within its own essence. Art thus allows for a multiplicity of interpretations, including the interpretation which allows us to interpret, but also be hospitable, to ourselves.

This power of art to generate an interpretation of ourselves arises naturally from exposure to particular works of art. It is evidenced whenever a person identifies themselves within a character, or is affected by some aesthetic experience. When I read Dante and experience a passion for his literary works, this by its very nature provides some furtherance of my self-understanding; I discover that I am the sort of person who loves to read Dante, which is not something I knew before I picked up *La Divina Commedia*. This revelation leads me into a further exploration of the constant strangeness of myself, as I am led to consider *why* it is that I like Dante, what in his material inspires or resonates with me, and how I approach the text differently in different stages of my life and in each further reading.

However, this naturally arising awareness, when analysed, can yield guidelines which better facilitate these revelations, and even help us to maintain a hospitality to ourselves as the stranger.

Hermeneutics of the Self through Art: Three Guidelines

Having considered the relationship between self, art and self-strangeness, we now attempt to develop these concepts into more explicit hermeneutic guidelines. As Gadamer (2007: 131) points out, the work of art is, among other things, an injunction that one must change oneself. This holds true, whether it is a change in one's ethical comportment in the world (as an artistic photograph of shell-shocked children in a war-ground may call me to do something about war), a change in worldview (as the film about a group outside of my social milieu may lead me to understand how others perceive and grasp values) or a change in self-understanding (as a cubist painting may point to latent perceptual possibilities in me).

All forms of artistic media provide access to horizons that affect one's view of oneself and the environing world. We must navigate through these horizons, that they might change us. Or, more precisely, the artistic media to which we expose ourselves, and how we elect to interpret that media within our lives, plays an essential role in determining how we understand the self. We look at media as being more than the simple choice of taste or preference, or as the more complex means of interpersonal communication of identity within differing social groups, but as being an essential component of how the self understands and structures its reality. We are the art with which we are surrounded, as well as the response to that art, and the choice of art with which we decide to surround ourselves.

Insofar as this is true, it is possible to form some discernment between different approaches for the consideration of art, without a recourse to purely subjective 'taste', and highlight the best possible elements for interpretation. We may disagree about the optimal moral life and the deontological injunctions which follow such ethical principles, but we nevertheless can evaluate how various forms of art more or less effectively function as part of the process of a human to conform to those values.

Our primary concern is guidelines for the reception, appreciation and criticism of art which lead one to self-understanding. We may therefore, for instance, critique propagandistic pieces of art as being inherently based in the reduction of self-understanding, in order that the perceiver may more perfectly fit within the self as desired within the propaganda's ideology. Art which intentionally answers the question of the self for the self, e.g. 'I am first a party member' or 'I am defined by hating x group,' can therefore be seen as lesser than art which provokes the receiver into a greater exploration of who they are, and secondarily assists the self in becoming more virtuous.

We can be even more specific, to say that a hermeneutics of art should hold a heuristic based upon its capacity to engage ourselves in self-realization and self-improvement. Being able to see that a painting is beautiful is a good thing. Better, we argue, is being able to perceive the painting's beauty along with perceiving one's affective response to that beauty as a means for greater self-knowledge. At least equally or even better is the ability to encounter art that one finds ugly and aesthetically abrasive, and yet nevertheless have a developed method of growing through the negative experience of art. I learn just as much if not more about myself from the art I do *not* like as I do considering the art I do.

This capacity for the comparison of different methodologies allows for the proposal of a phenomenological hermeneutics of art that seeks to best promote better practices of art interpretation. This general comparison of methodologies in art criticism is also beyond our current scope; however, what particularly interests us here is that the interpretation of art has been proven as a means for greater self-understanding, and the method of this interpretation can be shown to affect the outcome: a well-constructed hermeneutic will lend to better self-understanding gleaned from the experience of the art. Furthermore, at this stage of our inquiry an ethical mandate emerges that indeed we *ought* to construct for ourselves the best possible framework for understanding art that we can. This is exactly because, as we have shown, art defines us and what we know about ourselves. If, for instance, I have an ethical mandate not to allow myself to become a radicalized pawn for an unethical government, then it is required that part of that process of avoiding radicalization is to develop a hermeneutic that can differentiate between and reject self-definition through the propaganda of the said unethical government.

Before turning from this ethical mandate to the proposal of three guidelines, we briefly pause to explain the usage of the term, 'guideline', in relation to our hermeneutics of self-understanding through art. We have for natural reasons avoided the word 'law' because the relation between experiencers and art is so complex as to reject any such stiff definition. A similar reasoning though to a lesser extent, can be found by the limited use of the term 'rule'. Guidelines amend themselves to a certain degree of exploration upon the fringes; a guideline can welcome its bending. Rules and laws do not, and should not. The terms 'model' and 'framework' may be applied to this hermeneutic, with the understanding that the framework contains the three guidelines, and perhaps more as inquiry develops on this topic.

Guidelines, models and frameworks generally tend to work best insofar as they are created in dialogue with, and in application of, some greater theory. It is for this reason that our guidelines can be understood as the particular application of Richard Kearney and Kascha Semonovitch's 'poetic phenomenology' (2011a) into a poetic hermeneutic of self and art. Thus, we will appropriate the Aristotelian terms of *aesthesis*, *poeisis* and *phronesis* into our guidelines.

Aesthesis as Performativity in Self-Interpretation

Our first guideline concerns a hermeneutics of *aesthesis*. By this, we are taking into consideration how the 'active' consumption of art reveals and influences one's self-interpretation. We may now consider the *aesthesis*, this 'taking-in' of our hermeneutic model, as having three operative aspects: contextualization, foreignness-familiarity and identification-reflection. Contextualization is the taking in of information based on what we already know or can reasonably expect to learn. This is art most familiar to us, or communicated in its most prosaic qualities: names, dates, historical events and periods, subject matter, colour, dimension, scale, medium, material, function; the sunny land of facticity and broadly understood or understandable information about the phenomenon. Polonius tells us of his acting days, saying, 'I did enact Julius Cesar. I was killed i'th' Capitol. Brutus killed me.'[8] This taking-in is a necessary precondition for the other forms of *aesthesis* to develop into their full expression in the abundant giving of the art. It is through studying Shakespeare that we come to better appreciate the character of Polonius, the world of Shakespeare's Globe, and the various acting in-jokes which make Hamlet's response, 'It was a brute part of him to kill so capital a calf there,' to achieve its full humour.

However, for our hermeneutic directed at self-understanding, contextual *aesthesis* is only useful insofar as it benefits the other operant forms. The process of making facts familiar to oneself is not, in itself, revelatory. The context must be brought in as the further developing material for the other two aspects of *aesthesis*: the *aesthesis* of foreignness-familiarity and of affectation-identification.

The operative principle of foreignness-familiarity within the guideline of *aesthesis* is to maintain as much as possible a perpetual awareness of the foreignness of the art, which in itself is only possible because there is an implicit familiarity. Our language is intentionally resonant with Derrida's reading of Plato's *Sophist*, of the 'parricide foreigner' or the 'foreign son' (Derrida [1997] 2000: 9). For Derrida the deconstructionist, there is an utter risk involved with welcoming the foreigner, who may turn out to be either saint or assassin. For our purposes and understanding of a hermeneutics of *aesthesis*, we might consider empathy as playing a central role in expanding our horizons in connection to the other. In this sense, an act of what Husserl called 'associative pairing' plays a central role. (Moran and Cohen 2012: 57).[9] While I may not have a direct embodied contact with the creator of a work, nor even in a sense comprehensively with the work itself, a work allows itself to be approached in a way that resembles an experience of interpersonal empathy. Of course, the work may not present other humans as subjects; in the case of abstract painting, for example, there may not be any obvious subject at all, and this may lead one to ask how such a work may affect one's interpersonal understanding.

Nevertheless, this consideration allows us to consider the *aesthesis* directed at art as a kind of wager (Kearney 2015: 112–45). We may take in propaganda, which forms us into precisely the sorts of people we do not wish to be. Yet, we must understand that in this wager, we are not permitted the choice between wagering or abstaining. Art, propaganda, message, video, algorithm; the fruit for *aesthesis* ever surrounds us and even more defines us in an era of constant technological visitations. Our wager is therefore either to intentionally choose the art which influences us, or to passively allow technological companies to select our wager, with their hermeneutics which privilege volume, reinforcement of any habit or activity, and the continuous 'feed' of information and outrage into our understanding of self and world.

In order to prudently employ this guideline of *aesthesis*, to make this wager wisely, we must intentionally call to mind the strangeness of the art-other so that we avoid collapsing it reflexively into our own limited self-knowledge; yet at the same time, we must recognize that there are points of familiarity, of communication, between myself and the art-familiar. What arises from this marriage, sometimes quarrelsome, sometimes amicable, is the birth of a new interpretation both of ourselves and the art. We know we have successfully accomplished the aim of this hermeneutic when we gain a better understanding of ourselves, and a better understanding of the text. The central assumption of this aim is that the art-phenomena to which we draw our attention contains within itself an abundance that facilitates this relationship.

The third aspect of affectation-identification is similarly developed upon the lines of a dichotomy, with a few significant distinctions. While our second aspect proceeded upon the wager of taking in art as the external other, in the wager of the foreign and familiar, our third aspect turns to the intaking which has an internal origin. Further, while foreignness and familiarity operate simultaneously within the experience of the phenomenon of art, we may speak of affectation and identification as being of a first and second order of operations, respectively. While these two orders obviously interpenetrate within a continuous cycle as the art gives itself to the perceiver, we may consider that the affectation generally precedes the identification, with the identification leading naturally into further affectations and so forth.

Affectation concerns that which evokes something within us, as it were, without our direct conscious desire. This may, in one sense, be considered a kind of *anagnorisis*.[10] However, we must qualify this term. There is, naturally, the sort of self-revelation through art where we are, as it were, serendipitously made aware of some 'deeper' aspect of self which manifests in an altered perception of self, world and other. King Laugh arrives, as Van Helsing tells us, and we can do nothing but open the gates and let him in.[11] These sorts of *aesthesis* ought to be recognized and valued; but the very randomness and radical subjectivity of their nature precludes them from hermeneutical consideration of this first order.

Instead, we might speak of the order of affectation as having a hermeneutical sensitivity toward how the art we receive provokes a response within us. This may be an emotional response: pleasure in the reading of Dickens, or contextualized delight within the technical mastery in a long-take from Hitchcock. The important thing is to develop one's own methodology of art reception in such a way that one is aware of these sentiments. Yet, affection goes beyond sentiment as well. I ought to be aware of the way in which art, when meditated upon, affects my train of thought, perception of myself in time-space, and the various sensual aspects of self which can be brought into the experience of the phenomenon: all reception of art is experienced from an embodied reality. Hence, our reception of art ought to take into account touch, taste and smell, along with the more common sight and hearing. This line of inquiry, while at the fringe of our current scope, brings interesting questions such as the following for later meditation: what is the fitting smell to accompany Van Gogh's *Starry Night*? How are we structuring the spaces of our art museums to harmonize well with the presented art? How can touch be incorporated into the reception of sculpture?

Aisthesis as Identity in Self-Interpretation

Turning to the second order of our third aspect for the hermeneutical guideline of *aisthesis* within our framework of a phenomenological hermeneutics of art, we recognize that identification plays a vital role within our development of the self through art. Generally, where art becomes hermeneutically significant for the understanding of the self is when we approach it with the intention of identification.

Our first-order feelings, emotions, perceptions, impressions and assumptions upon the encounter with art lead us to further self-understanding precisely when we say, 'I am such a figure as this,' in response to a narrative; or 'this sings in me rightly' with music; or 'those eyes, that expression, is as my own' in terms of visual art. This identification is most often not uniform or even entirely rational. I identify myself within Ebeneezer Scrooge's humbugging about Christmas, and at the same time his nephew's impassioned defense of the holiday, reflecting perhaps the interior dialectic of any great holiday – a mixture of cynicism and joy. It is by placing myself within this dialectic, these differing roles, that I find some comprehension of myself.

Our second hermeneutical guideline fits broadly into Kearney and Semonovitch's understanding of *poesis* within his poetic phenomenology (2011a: 3–29). Kearney and writes that '*poiesis* connotes a making, a putting in order, a creation of the beautiful, of the novel' (ibid.: 11). This *poiesis* is often seen in opposition to *aesthesis*, and within our current venture one might question how precisely we can simultaneously aesthetically receive and poetically make as a mode of understanding ourselves from an encounter with art. However, it is precisely through a poetic imagination that art transcends a passive reflection of ourselves through aesthetic information, reception and affectation, and becomes our active interaction and participation within the art.

An example of this point may prove helpful, drawn from a great work of literature. When Dante the pilgrim arrives at the garden of terrestrial paradise near the end of his *Purgatorio*, he arrives upon a bucolic scene:

> Already my slow steps had carried me
> Into the ancient wood so far, that I
> Could not perceive where I had entered it.
> And lo! my further course a stream cut off,
> Which tow'rd the left hand with its little waves
> Bent down the grass that on its margin sprang
>
> Dante [1555] [1966–8] 2008: 262

We may, of course, take in the contextual information that there is an obvious parallel of Dante being lost and confused within another wood. I would argue, in resonance with Dietrich von Hildebrand (1977: 38), that we may derive affectation from the well-presented sense of action, the sound of the words, even identify with the pilgrim the sweet sense of rest by a river after a long mountain climb. However, we enter a new level of understanding ourselves through the phenomena by performing an act of imagination in terms of the art. This we may say is performed in two different modes of making: in remembering, participating, and responsively generating.

In the first mode, we called to mind the image at the heart of the English word 'remember', that of putting limbs back upon some past thing. This requires a work of imagination. We may elect to feed our imagination by visiting today the sights of Italian woods and rivers which may have inspired the poet, and seek to conform our imagination as closely as possible to what Dante may have held in his mind. We may, on the other hand, remember the scene through our own rivers, woods and mountains, which hold particular significance for ourselves.

In this realm of *poiesis*, either method is appreciable, although the latter engages us with questions of hospitality and translation of the author. We come to understand ourselves better either way, as by exercising the imagination, we create a space which is truly an aspect of ourselves. The text is of Dante's Eden; but through our imagination we generate our own Eden with Dante. Childbearing is perhaps the best metaphor for this kind of poetic work, as what is created ends up sharing the features of both myself and the inspiring art. I am within my imagination before art better aware of myself, as being present with and within the imagination spurred to life by the art. It is in the end as much my Eden as it is the Eden of Dante's *Purgatorio*.

It is from this observation that the second mode of imagination stems: I can move about, speak, sing, set things on fire within my Eden shared with Dante. I, in a sense, write myself into the poem of Dante paired with the aspect of affectation-identification within our *aesthesis* guideline, we see an operation of imaginative action[12] which leads to received affectation of our own activity, that then leads on to us identifying ourselves within something of our imaginative action. Do I choose to cool my feet in the river? Climb one of the trees, pluck the hem of the pilgrim's robe and ask him what he thinks of being lost once again within a woods? Each activity creates its own affective phenomenon within me, which I am then free to consider for what it might reveal about the sort of person I am.

The final mode itself develops out of this sort of imagination. I am able not only to perform an internal *poiesis*, but actually make something which stands in conversation to what I have experienced. *Poiesis* as conversation with art is a particular mode of revelation in which I encounter my own voice, and can permit myself to be surprised by its qualities: beauty, ugliness, pain, an uncomfortable awareness of our unpolished nature. A poem that one considers to be poorly written can be just as revelatory in this hermeneutic guideline as a good one, perhaps even more so. We are often adroit in ways that unify us with others; our failures are often wholly personalized. Furthermore, the particular medium of art in which we choose to respond helps us to refine our ways of perceiving the world. Painters might better and better perceive texture by considering what sort of trees grow in this Eden. Poets have for centuries found their voice by trailing in Dante's wake.

Phronesis as Othering in Self-Interpretation

Our third and final guideline is founded within the concept of *phronesis,* which can take the form of a 'diacritical hermeneutics' (Kearney and Semonovitch 2011a: 3). Here, art performs the function of the Other by which we come to perceive ourselves. Art, in some sense, is an incarnation and distillation of communication from the other which, to varying degrees based upon the perceiver and the art, opens itself to a response. However, the art which we select, and precisely what forms this response we give to it, is to some measure determined by our own personal judgment. This judgment enters into a hermeneutic circle, where we determine the art by which we understand ourselves, and are in turn determined by that art. By reading Rainer Maria Rilke, I am simultaneously learning myself in light of Rilke, and becoming someone who has read him.

A second heuristic to the diacritical hermeneutics around our phronesis is to select that art which brings us into a community. As the self is not only a person or object, but also the network of relationships[13] in which it is embedded, we learn of ourselves by using art as the basis for communication with the other. Relationships formed through a common engagement with horror movies, or artisanal coffee roasting, or any form of artistry, proceed to make the self-understandable to itself.

A third heuristic would entail that we should not allow our presuppositions about what constitutes good art to prevent us from recognizing that art we do not initially find appealing or meaningful can still affect our subjectivity in a way that reveals self-strangeness and consequently brings an expansion of self-awareness. As we have noted, artistic experience allows us to become other to ourselves, and ideally, to appreciate the otherness of the Other. Here, three particular experiences where overcoming an initial presupposition enabled me to experience greater richness within a work of art and in my self and communal experience come to mind.

As a first example of this: there was a time when I could not appreciate Mark Rothko paintings. Standing in front of one at the Cincinnati Art Museum, I remarked, 'Well this is stupid painting; it's just some patches on a canvas. I don't understand what it means.' And in response, the person next to me remarked, 'No! Look at how the painting breathes! Think about the painting as a series of varying perceptions! Look at how the blue's texture varies in parts, pay attention to the gaps in the spaces, the outlines of the canvas; try to see the middle blues as popping out to greet you.'

I tried to understand the person's suggestions, and surely enough, after a few moments of paying attention to these details, it did seem to me as if the painting was more 'alive' and even conveying a sense of motion that I had previously not been able to perceive. In this interaction, I took away a few hermeneutic lessons. Not least of which was that it was not the painting's stupidity at issue, but rather my own; I was not properly attuned to my own possibilities of aesthetic reception.

As a second example: I have a friend who works in video production. He once sent me a clip from his film project in which he acts as an African American police officer who takes visible pleasure (for example, eating from a bucket of popcorn and grinning widely) in watching white people being robbed, abused and even killed. As a person with a 'white epidermal schema' (to borrow a term from Franz Fanon (2008), I was initially without a satisfying interpretation of the film clip. What message was my friend trying to convey with his script? In this case, he was willing to answer the question, and explained that he was trying to show the contingency of white privileges in the twenty-first-century United States. 'Things,' he went on,

> could easily have been otherwise. I wanted to give the white viewer a sense of what it is like to be a black person in this country who can't rely on police resources or many of the other things that white people might take for granted. For a lot of black people, it feels like white people just look on in amusement as black Americans are killed.

While it might seem trivial (obviously, things could always have been otherwise, and always could be otherwise), it made for an opportunity for hermeneutic self-reflection. This experience drew me into the recognition that there were times when I was unconscious of some of the ways that my skin colour created a feeling of a social 'safety' (for example, feeling safe to call the police to come to my house at 1am, or not typically fearing that I will be shot when I am pulled over at a traffic stop in the United States).

A third example comes from aesthetic insensitivity; this happened with the co-author of this paper. I was attempting to read from my computer screen while we were in a room full of our friends watching a film together. He motioned to me, 'Pay attention to the film. Now is a chance to learn to develop your aesthetic sense. Think – why did the director choose *that* angle, *that* setting, etc.' My initial response to the experience I had been having (paying attention to something that didn't pertain to the community experience of the moment), had been one of indifference. In calling me to a greater awareness, my friend draws me out of myself, and in doing so, invites me to participate in the meaning-making that is film.

Here, we would argue that calling the members in one's human community to new interpretations of the work of art is a way of drawing both ourselves and the others out of familiarity with oneself and into a metaphorical space of sorts, that invites us to a 'deeper' constitution of meaning. This is one of the great 'utilities' at play in the arts, that it allows for this hermeneutic openness in a space that is perhaps not as explicitly politically charged as, for example, a political rally, or a protest. When aesthetic reception occurs in an atmosphere of leisure, there can be a relaxation of attitude which facilitates hermeneutic openness. On the intersubjective level, the gracious stranger who invites me to view the painting differently, the media-creator who explains her work to me, or the friend who invites me to appreciate new details, creates a space for 'community', even if this is sometimes in a limited and transient modality.

Phenomenologically, we wager that in allowing a hospitality to self that allows for one to appear as 'strange' to oneself in one's own radical singularity combined with an openness to the manifestation of the other person that helps one to appreciate their radical singularity, we 'make space' for the condition of being 'neither the same, nor different' from the other. Far from being merely entertaining or a form of escapism, these sorts of aesthetic experiences work on self-hood and community by enabling us to experience non-quantitative value in a way that we could not attain on our own. In these experiences, art is an 'Other' that bears the potential to draw us all out of ourselves and into a surplus of meaning.

Conclusion

In this chapter, we have briefly considered the hermeneutics behind the relationship between ourselves and the phenomenon of aesthetic experience that is in part created by human endeavour, which we may briefly call art. We considered art in terms of its appearance as a type of 'knowing' distinct from propositional knowledge, as 'saturated phenomenon' and 'messianic' phenomenon, both of which imply a sense of inexhaustibility and impossibility of a final interpretation; even attempting a totalizing view can be seen as 'inhospitable' and foreclosing the possibility of intellectual and perhaps (inter) personal growth. In light of this, we adopted Kearney's threefold schema of aesthesis – something akin to a discerning selection of the art that we take in, in light of the ideal of self-improvement and increased self-awareness (especially with increasing awareness to what can be considered 'strange' within us). The second aspect of this, poisis, then entails 'remembering', calling to mind this strangeness, and using imaginative inquiry to draw us into new intellectual and affective horizons. Lastly, phronesis is a sort of ethos that comes with aesthetic reception and production; we are 'called' (perhaps in a Heideggarian sense) to use all of our experiences with art to foster new and 'deeper' horizons within our lifeworld experience.

Every civilization, culture, home and person has in them and about them some element which, satisfying no physical or material need, yet still is a necessity, the exclusion of which negates the whole. Humanity, and humans, cannot be bracketed from this particular phenomenon. In spite of this, the very universality of this phenomenon poses a difficulty in its being deciphered. There is a kind of bait and switch with how art is treated within our contemporary society: on the one hand, the 'starving artist' is treated as a dreamer, producing nothing of 'real' value; on the other, marketing and image consultation remains a lucrative field of expression, provided it is in service to a sellable product. What we find at the root of this disjuncture is that art, whether from Frieda or Fritos, performs an essential role in the individual constructing their identity. From such an assertion is inferred that the individual begins, and we argue remains, with a fundamental incomprehensibility of understanding themselves.

Notes

1 There is a question of the capitalizing the concept of 'self'. As we have seen throughout phenomenology literature, there is a considerable amount of variegation on this. For example, Anthony Steinbock, along with several other phenomenologists, seems to capitalize when they want to emphasize what seems to be a more metaphysical position on S/selfhood. For our analysis, though, we agreed

to the lower-case usage, since our paper does trend more to the functionalist/ practical than the strictly metaphysical (David Jaeger and Evan Underbrink).

2 William Shakespeare, *Hamlet*, Act 1, Scene 5. A thorough treatment of *Hamlet* as a preeminent example of the self-encountering and coming to terms with itself and its own history through art is beyond the scope of this essay. However, the consideration of this play might be revelatory as to the psychology of Hamlet and Gertude, without recourse back to directly psychoanalytic interpretive frameworks.

3 Marion's concept of 'saturated phenomena', as we understand it, is a concept that is formulated in order to be able to talk about phenomena in a way that works around what some have seen as 'necessary' categories of cognition. Even if we cognize any given phenomena through these categories, so the argument goes, it is not *exhaustive*. If one accepts this argument, then not just profound or mysterious things, but even everyday 'humble phenomena' are considered to be 'saturated'.

4 For a list of 'incorrigible ontological relations', see Galvez (2015).

5 For employment of this argument see Nesteruk (2014: 236). The gist of the argument is that in its refusal to be exhausted cognitively (rational knowledge both moves slowly towards infinity, and we can see fundamental limitations in our cognitive rational knowing), the universe gives itself to be *known* aesthetically prior to being known cognitively. Interestingly, Graham Harman (e.g. 2017), one of today's most influential thinkers in the 'speculative realism' movement, also makes a case for aesthetics as first philosophy.

6 See Louchakova-Schwartz (2022: 705) for an explanation of the concept of 'originary self-giving' in Husserl.

7 See Hart (1992) for an analysis of these relations.

8 Shakespeare, *Hamlet*, Act 3, Scene 2.

9 Entry titled 'Assoziation' (Moran and Cohen 2012: 45).

10 By means of clarification, Merriam-Webster dictionary defines the entry for 'anagoresis' as: 'The point in the plot ... at which the protagonist recognizes his or her or some other character's true identity or discovers the true nature of his or her own situation.'

11 Stoker, *Dracula* ([1897] 1997).

12 This may seem like a hermeneutic circle and perhaps thus in the eyes of some, a worthless imaginative exercise. It need not be a vicious circle though, if one attempts to hold firm to the phenomenological epoche's methodological attempt to suspend presuppositions. In the course of doing this, one can recognize that although one is working within one's imagination (arguably a condition of possibility for phenomenology, see Aldea 2012), one is 'spiralling' and not necessarily lost in a solipsistic reverie. In Anthony Steinbock's (2021) words, one can remain 'ontologically naive' about the imagination.

13 Human and non-human.

References

Aldea, Andrea Smarnada. 2012. 'Phantasie and Phenomenological Inquiry – Thinking with Edmund Husserl'. Unpublished PhD diss., Emory University, Atlanta, GA.

Alighieri, Dante. [1555] [1966–8] 2008. *The Divine Comedy*. Illustrated ed. Trans. Charles H. Sisson, ed. Giorgio Petrocchi and Charles S. Singleton. Oxford: Oxford University Press.

'Anagnorisis'. *Merriam-Webster.com Dictionary*, Merriam-Webster. Available online: https://www.merriam-webster.com/dictionary/anagnorisis (accessed 2 August 2022).

Costello, Peter. 2012. *Layers in Huserl's Phenomenology*. Toronto: University of Toronto Press.

Derrida, Jaques. [1997] 2000. *Of Hospitality* (De l'hospitalité). Trans. Rachel Bowlby. Stanford, CA: Stanford University Press.

Fanon, Franz. 2008. *Black Skin, White Masks*. Trans. C. L. Markmann. London: Pluto Press.

Gadamer, Hans-George. [1960] 1998. *Truth and Method* (Wahrheit und Methode: Grundzüge einer philosophischen Hermeneutik). Trans. Joel Weinsheimer and Donald Marshall. London: Bloomsbury.

Gadamer, Hans-George. 2007. *The Gadamer Reader*. Ed. Richard Palmer. Evanston, IL: Northwestern University Press.

Galvez, Julian. 2015. *Our Incorrigible Ontological Relations and Categories of Being: Causal and Limiting Factors of Objective Knowledge*. Buenos Aires: published independently. ISBN 978-15-21402405.

Galvez, Julian Manuel. 2015. *Our Incorrigible Ontological Relations and Categories of Being*, philarchive.org. Available online: https://philarchive.org/archive/GALOIO (accessed 29 July 2023).

Harman, Graham. 2017. *Object Oriented Ontology: A New Theory of Everything*. London: Pelican Books.

Hart, James. 1992. 'Being's Mindfulness: The Noema of Transcendental Idealism'. In John Drummond and Lester Embree (eds), *Phenomenology of the Noema*, 111–35. Boston, MA: Springer.

Henry, Michel. [1988] 2009. *Seeing the Invisible: On Kandinsky* (Voir l'invisible. Sur Kandinsky). Trans. Scott Davidson. London: Continuum.

Henry, Michel. 2019. 'Four Principles of Phenomenology'. In Scott Davidson (ed.), *The Michel Henry Reader*, 5–29. Evanston, IL: Northwestern University Press.

Hildebrand, von Dietrich. 1977. *The Heart: An Analysis of Human and Divine Affectivity*. Chicago, IL: Franciscan Herald Press.

Husserl, Edmund. [1931] 1960. *Cartesian Meditations* (Méditations cartésiennes: Introduction à la phénoménologie). Trans. Dorian Cairns. Boston, MA: Kluwer Academic.

Husserl, Edmund. 2005. *Phantasy, Image Consciousness, and Memory (1898–1925)*. Ed. Rudolf Bernet, trans. John Brough. Dordrecht: Springer.

Inverso, Hernan. 2021. 'Phenomenology of the Inapparent: A Methodological Approach to the New Realism'. In Guillermo Ferrer, Syvaine Gourdain, Tolbert Garrera and Nicolás Alexander Schnell (eds), *Phänomenologie und spekulativer Realismus. Phenomenology and Speculative Realism. Phénoménologie et réalisme spéculatif*, 1–13. Würzburg: Königshausen & Neumann.

Kant, Immanuel. [1781–7] 1996. *Critique of Pure Reason: Unified Edition* (Kritik der reinen Vernunft). Ed. James Ellington, trans. Werner Pluhar. Indianapolis, IN: Hackett.

Kearney, Richard. 2015. *Carnal Hermeneutics*. New York: Fordham University Press.

Kearney, Richard and Kascha Semonovitch. 2011a. 'At the Threshold: Foreigeners, Strangers, Others'. In Kearney, Richard and Kascha Semonovitch (edss), *Phenomenologies of the Stranger*, 3–29. New York: Fordham University Press.

Kearney, Richard and Kascha Semonovitch (eds). 2011b. *Phenomenologies of the Stranger*. New York: Fordham University Press.

Kristeva, Julia. [1988] 1994. *Strangers to Ourselves* (Étrangers à nous-mêmes). Trans. Leon Loudiez. New York: Columbia University Press.

Louchakova-Schwartz, Olga. 2022. 'Religious Experience in the First-Person Perspective: The Lived Body and Perception of Reality'. *Religions*, 13: 704–18. Doi.org/ 10.3390/rel13080704.

Marion, Jean-Luc. [1989] 2002. *Being Given: Towards a Phenomenology of Givenness* (Étant donné: Essai d'une phénoménologie de la donation). Trans. Jeffrey Kossky. Stanford, CA: Stanford University Press.

Mohanty, Jitendra Nath. 1989. *Transcendental Phenomenology: An Analytic Account*. Cambridge: Blackwell.

Moran, Dermot and Joseph Cohen (eds). 2012. *The Husserl Dictionary*. London: Bloomsbury Academic. Academia.edu. Available online: https://www.academia.edu/10194179/The_Husserl_Dictionary (accessed 29 July 2023).

Nesteruk, Alexi. 2014. 'The Universe as a Saturated Phenomenon: The Christian Concept of Creation in View of Modern Philosophical and Scientific Developments'. *Theology and Science*, 12 (3): 236–59.

Nitsche, Martin. 2020. 'The Invisible and the Hidden within the Phenomenological Situation of Appearing'. *Open Theology*, 6 (1): 547–56.

Ricoeur, Paul. [1990] 1992. *Oneself as Another* (Soi-même comme un autre). Trans. Kathleen Blamey. Chicago, IL: University of Chicago Press.

Ricoeur, Paul. [2004] 2006. *On Translation* (Sur la traduction). Trans. Eileen Brennan. London: Routledge.

Shakespeare, William. [1603] 1997. *Hamlet*. Introduced and annotated by Cedric Watts. Hertfordshire: Wordsworth Editions.

Steinbock, Anthony. 2021. *Love as Critique and Participation*. Evanston, IL: Northwestern University Press.

Stoker, Bram. [1897] 1997. *Dracula*. Hertfordshire: Wordsworth Editions.

Waldenfels, Bernhard [2006] 2011. *Phenomenology of the Alien: Basic Concepts* (Grundmotive einer Phänomenologie des Fremden). Trans. Alex Kozin and Tanja Stähler. Evanston, IL: Northwestern University Press.

2

Hieratic Communication in the Oeuvre of Kazimir Malevich, Vasily Kandinsky and Nikolai Roerich

Sally Stocksdale

The Context: The Cultural and Belief System of the Silver Age in Russia

Hermeneutics has to do with the process of interpretation.[1] In hermeneutic methodology, interpretation involves a dialogic, or dialectical, or interactive relationship, with reciprocal reinforcement between the reader and a text, or an observer and the subject being observed – the phenomenon. In that phenomenological process, of the hermeneutical coming together of the (bracketed or suspended) subject and the object (the thing itself, the content, the noema – what is thought about), communication is taking place, and understanding of both the self and the other (the content or context) comes forth. Therein lies the meaning.

Noted for his work in Hermeneutic Phenomenology, Paul Ricoeur was interested in the process of communication between the observer/interpreter and the object. He considered that because man expresses and manifests himself through language, man is 'no more than language' (Deodato and Sitoy 2010: 1–4). Because he considered language polysemic, the 'hermeneutics of language' has to do with specific words – symbols. Ricoeur held that a symbol had the capacity to accommodate polysemic communication, defining it as 'any structure of signification because every symbol is a sign or a particular linguistic expression that communicates meaning' (ibid., 1–4). Because words (symbols) become the vehicle for and the mediator of communication, they have transformative power. Meaning happens as a result of the self-reflection that occurs after any hermeneutical interaction (Ricoeur 1978: 100–6). Thinkers of the Russian Silver Age[2] believed that the word, the symbol, the icon had theurgic properties, and that art not only telegraphed divine messages, but the *act* of art was divine work

(Rosenthal 1997: 20; Billington 1966: 329ff., 478ff.).³ Indeed, one luminary, Father Pavel Florensky, the great Russian Orthodox priest, theologian, philosopher, linguist and mathematician, nicknamed the 'Russian Leonardo' for his versatility in talents, held that one's sheer existence was nothing other than a symbol, or, in his words, an icon. By symbol, Florensky meant both visual and verbal communication.⁴ In hermeneutic fashion, the artists of the Silver Age were both products and progenitors of the zeitgeist of that era. Though not a comprehensive list, what follows are some of their prevailing ideas and beliefs.⁵

In varying degrees and expressed in different ways at different times, the luminaries of the day all seemed to subscribe to the idea that the world had reached a pivotal moment in history (see Figure 2.1). No doubt in part exacerbated by the closure of the nineteenth century as well as a reaction against the mainstream theories of Comtean positivism and materialism, the sentiment prevailed that all the old ways were coming to an end, and the world stood on the threshold of a new beginning. A new world, and new myths were on the horizon.⁶ Silver Age artists combined human agency with artistic creativity for the purpose of charting a better future. This was predicated on the idea that art had theurgic power⁷ (Rosenthal 2010: 241).

Sometimes this search for and construction of new myths entailed reaching back, deep into traditional, folk or even ancient history, in order to discover, or

Figure 2.1 *Sophia the Almighty Wisdom* by N. Roerich, 1932. Courtesy of the Nicholas Roerich Museum, New York.⁸

Figure 2.2 *Motley Life* by V. Kandinsky, 1907. The Städtische Galerie im Lenbachhaus, Germany. Courtesy of the Kandinsky Museum.[10]

rediscover, restore and reconnect with the past. Why? It was deemed pure, authentic, whole, contained, naturally spiritual, harmonious, ritualistic (as in repetitive, cyclic) and uncontaminated by modernity, positivism, materialism and foreign, inorganic characteristics. There was a mystical component too, in that ancient culture was viewed as closer or even closest to *the* source: God. We can also interpret this irresistible retrospective pull towards and longing for the past, the pastoral, the archaic, arcadia, as a structural, albeit subconscious phenomenon of the human condition, which has to do with a circular, cyclic, eternal return interpretation of life. Indeed, ancient or primitive or traditional culture, and often, literally, actual geographic places were considered the harbingers of both humanity's origins and original, sacred wisdom (see Figure 2.2).[9]

Closely related to this urge to go back to the source, was a kind of ethno-spiritual atavistic memory, recalling a pristine, uncontaminated, original, authentic culture. One of the discoveries was Primitivism. Like many terms cited in this chapter, Primitivism (or Neo-primitivism as it was known in Russia at the time) had many variants across Western Europe, the differences being found in geographical-ethno-cultural and historical aspects of local regions. For the Silver

Age luminaries, the Russian, or Slavic peasant and rural, village ways of life were lauded. Often, Slavic and ethnic tribes, such as the Scythians or Zyrians, or Polovetsians, were looked to.[11]

Another example of this 'looking backward in order to chart a future' theme was Eurasianism. It was (and is) a kind of proto-postcolonialism meets a little bit of Slavophilism;[12] a geo-cultural-religious interpretation of Russian history and identity that decentred European hegemony, the 'West' and modernity, and privileged Russia's Asian source, especially in the Mongols. For Eurasianists, the Mongols 'unified' Russia, jettisoning the localities of and competition between the numerous Slavic principalities from the thirteenth to the fifteenth centuries. Eurasianists also considered that the Mongols effectively 'saved' Russia from the Catholic West, with the latter's perceived trappings of hierarchy, scholasticism and power resting in the figure of the Pope. Above all, Eurasianists saw both the historical salience and the democratic nature of the Eastern Orthodox Church as central to Russia's future.[13]

Closely related to these was traditionalism, which eschews modernity and seeks to restore a pristine, pre-modern community where culture, language, religion and truth are transmitted from generation to generation. Traditionalism considers the essence of society as spiritual, and that there is a cosmic, divine order, originating with God. An important transmitter of traditionalism is language, for it is deemed to have theurgic, or divine power in its action. That is, words, functioning as symbols or icons, have the power to create, imbue and materialize the invisible, to make the imagined into the concrete (Sedgwick 2004: 16 and 21–5; Arnold 2019: 41–4). Therefore, traditional society is perceived as hierophanic – embodying and manifesting the sacred.

It is here that we can discern a traditionalist route to another model community which gained a following among the Silver Age thinkers, especially after the Revolution when Russia was saturated with utopian projects intended to transform the world and when, seemingly, both art and science had been liberated from the trappings of the autocracy's authoritarian controls. This search for, and anticipation of a utopian community of the future was Cosmism, a blend of cosmogony, eschatology and messianism; a kind of anthropocentrism meets scientific alchemy, with a splash of Hermeticism.[14] Cosmism's founder, the ascetic intellectual Nikolai Fedorov, envisioned a perfected, utopian community in the entire living organism of the cosmos, the ultimate goal being the will, indeed obligation to overcome death. That is, a unity of universal salvation; literally, the ascension of all, including the resurrection of the dead. If God became man in Christ, then man can emulate Christ, and overcome death.

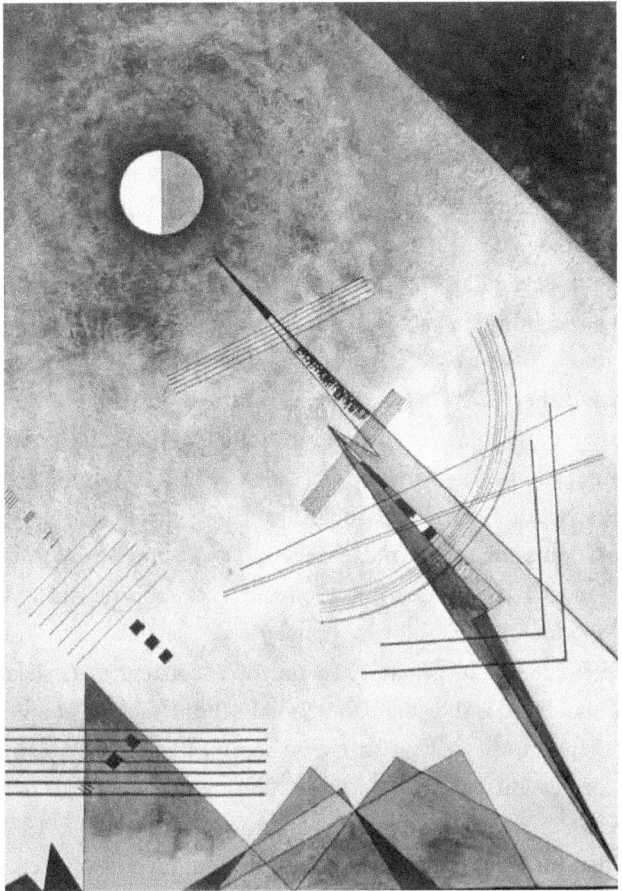

Figure 2.3 *Hinauf* (Upward) by V. Kandinsky, 1925. Courtesy of the Kandinsky Museum.[17]

Evincing a characteristic typical of the Russian world view, namely, bearing 'within oneself a responsibility for all', Fedorov anticipated that this model could be implemented by using technology and science to unite with God, i.e. henosis/theosis. Because Fedorov considered Russian culture pristine, and where ancestor wisdom and communality naturally resided, he anticipated that it could fuse with the future advancement of technological knowledge. Thus, Fedorov, and others such as Kazimir Malevich,[15] envisioned 'rocket science', 'space travel' and 'space colonization', as the only means to reconcile, merge with God, and restore unity. Unlike here on earth, where chaos reigned, the cosmos and celestial heavens was the place where the resurrected could reside (see Figure 2.3).[16]

Who could be agents for change? 'Spiritual godfather of the Silver Age' and 'God-seeker', Vladimir Soloviev, drew on the Slavophile belief in Russia's historical and cultural distinctiveness, and discerned that Russia itself was in an ideal position to mediate and bring about world unity – a reintegration of the East and West; the spiritual and material; the religious with the secular; the divine with the human. That Russia was situated both geographically and culturally, between the East and the West, Soloviev and others considered it a mediator, an intermediary of sorts, with the self-assigned messianic task of saving the world from apocalypse, effecting a kingdom of heaven on earth and totalizing unity. Because Russia was considered far less contaminated by modernity, and therefore purer than the West further convinced luminaries of Russia's special mission. Further, because Russia had not experienced the Enlightenment or the Reformation, its culture was far less watered down by Humanism, scholasticism and reason. All this boded well for the perception of Russia's special mission of spearheading world unity and henosis.[18]

Another agent was found in the Godman. Although he did not invent the concept of Godmanhood, Soloviev popularized it at this time (Young 2013a; Cassedy 1991: 538–9). In general, and indeed according to Eastern Orthodox dogma, Godmanhood is shorthand for theosis – the act/action, of uniting with the divine, and therefore self-deification. If God became human, then man can become God – the deification of man. Indeed, in the mystical theology of the Eastern Orthodox Church, deification connotes union with God (Lossky 1976: 9). This is not an egotistical, hubristic auto-divinization. Reminiscent of theurgic tenants, Union with God is possible only because of God. Salvation as deification, that is, the craving for *physical* renewal through contact with the divine, is at the very centre of the Christian East (Gustafson 1996: 38). The fact of Christ's transfiguration makes possible ours. Like Christ, man embodies, carries a kernel of the divine in himself. Therefore, Godmanhood is the foundation of the deification of humankind. For when one pursues this salvation, others will be influenced, initiated and inspired. In a millenarian fashion, when all human beings devote themselves to this salvation, God's Kingdom will be '"*in all,*" and God will be "*all in all and all will be one in Him*"' (Gustafson 1996: 41, original emphasis).

In the Silver Age cultural milieu, it was incumbent for the artist, a creator, to become a Godman. Notice the action component. Acting as a kind of midwife, mediator, this would help accelerate humanity's salvation/deification.[19] Also consider what is suggested, implied, given in this phenomenological, hermeneutic communication: the subject (the artist) interacts with, has communication with the object (the art that the artist produces; art which comprises symbols that communicate meaning). Yet more hermeneutic conversation occurs: the subject (the artist) is in communication, in relationship with the viewer (the initiate); *and* the viewer (the intiate) is in a (subjective) communicative relationship with the art object.

Meanwhile, Friedrich Nietzsche's work became all the rage within Russian elite society during the late nineteenth and early twentieth centuries. Essentially, his clarion call to act – to set yourself free from and transgress and replace established norms and myths – was irresistible to Silver Age luminaries. Even if many of them were not direct devotees, Nietzschean thought was in the water. Fellow traveler of many Russian God-seekers, including Vasily Kandinsky, Annie Besant stated: 'Nietzsche belongs distinctly to us!' Indeed, Nietzsche's Superman could easily have overlap with the idea of Godmanhood in that it personified the idea of acting on and authoring one's self-determination, self-actualization and represented an elite, prophet-like, (artistic?) spiritual aristocrat who could lead the masses to spiritual self-perfection. As one Silver Age religious intellectual proclaimed 'the "Superman" is the path from man to God'.[20]

Yet another current which made a huge and lasting impact was Theosophy. 'Divine wisdom,' Theosophy was founded in 1875 by the Russian spiritual guru, Helen Blavatsky. Setting 'in motion the Big Occult Bang' (Lachman 2015: 360–81), Blavatsky cobbled together a set of Theosophic tenets drawn from one or more aspects of Buddhism, Neoplatonism,[21] Brahminism, Kabbalism, Gnosticism, Rosicrucianism, Hermeticism, esotericism,[22] pantheism and more! Its tenets included the promise of unity; the idea that all religions share a set of fundamental beliefs; that all that has happened in the past is recorded on a kind of cosmic film reel; that creation is a geometrical progression beginning with a single point; and that we have all been here before, in reincarnations, but do not remember. Therefore, in a kind of Nietzschean clarion call, Blavatsky encouraged followers to use their will to stop the cycle and self-actualize. In doing so, and reminiscent of the Pythagorean theory of 'learning as remembering', followers would fast-track the learning curve of life. Therefore, Theosophy held that we are all Godmen in the making. Obviously, there was overlap with some tenets of other religious/spiritual/intellectual currents at the time. For example, the ascension paradigm of Theosophy resembles a kind of Christian Jacob's Ladder, or Buddhist layers of consciousness, an ascension across the seven Hermetic planetary zones, the Eastern Orthodox Hesychast union with God, or an upwardly progressing pyramid twisting and turning, hurling upwards to the God-head. All this said, perhaps this is why Gary Lachman has stated that 'abstract art grew in theosophic soil' (2015: 376).[23]

The above is just a summary of some of the main currents of the Silver Age cultural ethos. What follows is a discussion of how some aspects of these manifested in the artistic creativity of Kazimir Malevich, Vasily Kandinsky and Nikolai Roerich.

Artistic Trailblazers of Spiritual Expression

Kazimir Malevich: 'Painting against the Grain'[24]

Born in a rural village in the Kiev Governorate of the Russian Empire, Kazimir Malevich (1879–1935) was a pioneer of geometric abstract art,[25] the founder of avant-garde Suprematism, an art theorist, and a devout Christian mystic, indeed, a 'radical Protestant' (Sidorkin 2011), who held that, 'Art in its highest manifestations is a path to cosmic consciousness' (Gill 2014: 57). Radical Malevich was. He declared to one critic that, 'Art does not need us and it never did.'[26] Yet, he considered that, utilizing 'creative intuition', the artist's purpose was to initiate 'cultural renovation' and achieve 'divine perfection'; while the purpose of art was to 'transform'. Indeed, the role of the artist, according to Malevich, was to be shaman-like, a clairvoyant, a prophet, a 'social and cultural hero', a Moses-like leader, who will lead initiates to God. Malevich considered that he could 'elevate himself into a Deity' (Gill 2014: 53–4, 56–8). In occult fashion, he believed the new world would be revealed. Similar to his conception of the cosmos, Malevich considered art, in and of itself, as alive, unfolding, evolving, always becoming and of spiritual essence.[27]

Although his Suprematism manifesto, *From Cubism and Futurism to Suprematism: The New Realism in Painting* (1915), reads as a contemptuous, Nietzschean, nihilistic attack on the bourgeois, recognizable, realistic, reproductive, mimetic, perspectival, subject oriented, objective art of the past, in fact, Malevich used Christian motifs and theological history in his vision for the future of art, the role of the artist, and his artistic theories. As Gleb Sidorkin (2011) has pointed out, Malevich asserted that artists needed to emulate Jesus Christ by opening up the path to the heavens for others. Moreover, he argued that just as Christianity abolished the representational mundane aspect of the Mediterranean civilization and replaced it with an objectless world, Suprematism aimed to put forth nothingness as its new light. It was a new vision for art, one of pure sensation. When Malevich called on the courageous to 'spit' on the 'altar' of conventional art theory, he was rejecting what he considered the artistic idolatry of the past (Malevich 1915). It was the artist's job to liberate art from its past, thus purging it of all biographical details associated with its authors, and emancipating it from objects, objectivity and the 'tyranny of easel painting', as well as setting the artist free in the process (Billington 1966: 485).

Malevich defined Suprematism from the Latin *supremus*, meaning 'ultimate' or 'absolute', as non-objective art in which feelings, sensation, emotion and intuition were paramount. In this regard, it was the articulation of one of the signature characteristics of the Silver Age era: eschewing 'realistic' depictions, logic and objective art, and privileging, revealing the occulted, the hidden, the unseen realities via signs and symbols. But Suprematism did not reject reality. It was presenting a new aspect of it, where geometric, essentialized, often overlapping forms floated freely in space evoking a vast cosmos; and where colour and texture were liberated from subject matter.

Malevich drew spiritual inspiration from the 'essentialized shapes from the ubiquity of black-and-red cross-stich embroidery and the striking rectilinear facades of pristinely white-washed village houses and stuccoed hearths' (Mudrak 2004). For during his formative years, his family moved from one Ukrainian village to the next, living on or near sugar beet farms. He had a deep affinity for the cottage industries and folk art of the region, including arts and crafts, embroidery, motifs, *kilimi*, woven carpets comprising geometricized designs (associated with the right bank of the Dnieper) and floral/nature compositions (associated with the left bank of the Dnieper), and *lubki* (a kind of wooden lithograph from which peasants created prints of folktales, carnivalesque humor and satire and homespun wisdom). The Slavic, peasant, village culture was an enduring influence on the artist (ibid.).

Malevich was equally influenced by the Russian 'esoteric VIP', P. D. Ouspensky (Lachman 2015: 386). Regarding art, Ouspensky declared that an 'artist must be a clairvoyant' and make 'others see what they do not see by themselves'; art penetrates the phenomenal and reveals the noumenal (Gill 2014: 55, 57); and it was '"divine" essence' (Billington 1966: 329). Ouspensky was obsessed with time, specifically, as in the Nietzschean sense (or more correctly, Pythagorean), the 'eternal return'. That is, the belief that we repeat our lives. But unlike Nietzsche, who asserted that only the Superman was strong enough to overcome repetition and achieve his/her potential, Ouspensky was concerned with how one could stop the cycle all together. To do this, Ouspensky rationalized, one had to *remember* one's past (lives); remember the *real* you, the spirit that inhabits your body (Lachman 2015: 390).

Equally important to Ouspensky was the concept of space, in terms of a conception of reality. Obviously, the thinker understood that our spatial perception was three dimensional. But contemporaneously recent inventions and discourse such as the X-ray, electromagnetic waves, the wireless telegraph, the particle emitting electron, the wave theory of light and more, seemed to confirm what spiritualists and philosophers had suspected for centuries – that there is more to reality than meets the eye. Some of these included ideas like matter/forms exist, but in a transparent state; there are vibrating wavelengths in the ether, which penetrate matter; and all matter emits particles into the ether – indeed, that ether itself is *the* source of all matter (Henderson 2014: 233–4).

Reminiscent of Plato's cave analogy, Ouspensky believed in an occulted reality, the *real* reality, the fourth dimension. For Ouspensky, this meant that we see the world in slits, or slices, or as Malevich called them, cuts, thus confusing spatial phenomena with temporal ones (Henderson 2014: 241–2). In layman's terms, understanding the fourth dimension might proceed as follows: if a line might represent a one dimensional reality; and a plane might represent a two dimensional one; and then a cube illustrates the third dimension (which is our reality); then in the fourth dimension, we would see everything, all of time, all of 3D space, from all sides, simultaneously. There would be no up and no down, and no past and no future, but an infinity of timeless space, with simultaneous bursts of pulsating, vibrational colour. Ouspensky believed that because we can only 'see' the realities of the fourth dimension in 3D, that is, in splices, this explains why we have the concept of time. That is, on a trajectory of, say, cubes, each splice, or cube, represents a point in time (Henderson 2014: 241).[28]

Influenced by the wildly intriguing at the time Charles Hinton 'tesseract', which was meant to illustrate four-dimensional reality, Ouspensky believed *this* was the make-up of 'the other side', the *real* home of our consciousness, the occulted reality. And the mediator, connecting matter and consciousness, indeed, the make-up of the fourth dimension was ether – an invisible, gaseous, mist-, or smoke- or steam-like substance (Henderson 2014: 233–6, 241–2).

We can see a substantial realization of these assumptions in Malevich's oeuvre. Often Malevich's paintings would present white canvases conveying the vast cosmos with coloured 'planes' suspended in the dimension, representing a kind of 'cut' or splice. Malevich called these 'semaphores' of colour, which burst forth like '"fireworks" … before our eyes' (Henderson 2014: 242). As a result, in Malevich's Suprematism paintings, colour is both independent of (liberated), and yet in relationship with the composition.

Malevich was 'a kind of artistic prophet of the space age' (Billington 1966: 485). Indeed, he called himself the 'president of space' (Kovtun and Douglas 1981: 236), and exclaimed that 'man's path lies through space' and '"man" is preparing on the earth to throw his body into infinity ... towards the absolute' (Billington 1966: 485–6). For Malevich, space represented a kind of symbol of 'purification', 'deliverance', an 'annihilation of the self', where one would dissolve into and merge with God (Billington 1966: 485; Gill 2014: 258). In addition, space in Malevich's Suprematism paintings was analogic with cosmic space, where gravity was overcome. 'In fact,' as Malevich wrote (Kovtun and Douglas 1981: 236), 'in man, in his consciousness, there is a striving towards space, a yearning to "take off from the earth"'.

Charlotte Gill (2014: 53) has explained that this 'urge to take off from the earth', so prominent in Malevich's oeuvre, was rooted in one of the prevailing fads among the avant-garde at the time: shamanism. It was 'an anthropological and ethnic spiritualism, centred on the fundamental mystical and healing powers of the shaman', the latter of which serves as an intermediary, a mediator, a prophet of sorts, who possesses clairvoyant talents and who assists in cultural renovation, cosmic consciousness and salvation. And the vehicle or means by which this might take place was art (Gill 2014: 53–4). Here we see a classic example of language and beliefs associated with the theurgic properties of art, the role of the artist, man's search for ancient, timeless wisdom and cosmic consciousness and the urge to unite with God.

Vasily Kandinsky: Substantiating the Invisible[29]

Born in Moscow, Vasily Kandinsky (1866–1944) is considered the originator of abstract art.[30] He was an artist, a lawyer, a devout Eastern Orthodox Christian, an ethnographer, a cultural anthropologist, an art theorist, a connoisseur of colour and geometric forms on canvas, and was interested in capturing invisible essences and ether – the biochemical, auric, ethereal, vibrational, mists and dematerialized realities that he believed existed beyond the naked eye. Whereas Malevich conceived of ether in spatial terms, Kandinsky considered it as the 'all-pervading substance' of space (Henderson 2014: 234). Indeed, Kandinsky interpreted it as an 'elastic jelly or whirling fluid', or 'smoke steam', which not only permeated everything, but was the substance of all material.[31]

In his abstract art manifesto of 1911, *Concerning the Spiritual in Art* (1977), Kandinsky laid out his vision for art, the role of the artist and his artistic theories. Perhaps not as polemical as Malevich, Kandinsky was just as radical. He called for a spiritual revolution in painting; a movement to liberate art from the shackles of the 'mechanized, industrial world' (Kandinsky [1911] 1977: vi). He invoked that art should 'counter the whole nightmare of the materialistic attitude, which has turned life of the universe into an evil, purposeless game' (ibid., 1–2). The abstract element in art, Kandinsky hypothesized, should emerge from its prior concealment, just as tomorrow that which was concealed will be revealed (Warren 2013: 91–2).

Like Malevich, Kandinsky argued that art must depart from the objective world and natural representation. But distinct from Malevich, who wanted to liberate art for *its* sake, Kandinsky believed that art should express the artist's inner feelings; inner reality. Still, Malevich considered that creating non-representational art was the way for an artist to release artistic creativity (Stupples 2001: 11, 25). This is not different from Kandinsky, who believed an artist had an 'internal necessity', a kind of mystical irrepressible urge to express and create (Ringbom 1966: 391–2; Kandinsky [1911] 1977: 33ff.). Even so, Kandinsky put forward the idea of a 'third element' of art, where artistic periodization and authorship would be rendered moot by the new, spiritual art. When Kandinsky wrote of this 'eternal artistry', he was explaining that artistic fads were just that, and that true art would not conform to the standards, the pre-established theory or conventions of any given epoch, which straitjacketed or repressed expression. Rather, the artist must express a sacred inner spiritual *feeling*. As a result, while the painting will become a repository of that artist's feeling, it is its own, in and of itself, forever. In doing so, it will contribute to the 'improvement and refinement of the human soul' (ibid., 34–5, 54). This is not so different from Malevich's view that the artist must go beyond reason (*will* it) and reject simply portraying the exterior. No. Each painting represented an 'event' in the artist's spiritual state at the moment of creation. And that *process*, of documenting spiritual evolution, which Malevich called 'the forming element' represented a kind of 'soul journey' with the goal of reaching cosmic consciousness (Gill 2014: 56).

For Kandinsky, spirit (God) manifests itself via sound (vibrations). Because Kandinsky considered the artistic equivalent of music was colour, he wanted to project sound from the colours in his paintings (Ashmore 1977: 329ff.). Just as musicians do not rely on the material world to express feelings, nor should art. Indeed, and certainly intrigued by Goethe's *Theory of Colors* (1810), in which the philosopher documented the allegorical, symbolic and mystical characteristics of colour; and influenced by Theosophists Annie Besant and Charles Leadbetter's *Thought Forms* (1905), in which they identified correspondences between colours and emotions, Kandinsky conceived of colours in an almost animistic way – ascribing human qualities, emotions, even personalities to them. Kandinsky likened the human soul to the piano, and the latter's keys being the equivalent to colours, which produced rhythm and musical notes, thus setting in motion a cacophony of spiritual, vibrational waves expressing and influencing emotion in the viewer, a kind of initiate.[32]

Thus, in Kandinsky's paintings, colours and shapes symbolically both depicted *and* telegraphed the occulted reality, unleashed, free floating in the cosmos, transmitting messages via feelings, interiority which they corresponded to. Here, he believed that his paintings could both transmit to, and instill in the initiate a higher vibrational level of cosmic consciousness and awaken spirituality (Ringbom 1966: 405–6, 408). Obviously, for Kandinsky, the connection between colours and music suggested that he was a synesthete – or more correctly, a chromesthete – a sensory condition where more than one of the senses is linked to another, in this case, colours and feelings. As phenomenologist Michel Henry stressed ([2005] 2009: 88), Kandinsky was unique because of his conception and use of colour: on the one hand colour was a universal in that everyone recognizes, say, red. On the other hand, each individual *experiences*, senses red differently, subjectively. This was a radical conception of the role of colour in art.

Later, in his, albeit abstruse, *Point and Line to Plane*, originally published in 1926, Kandinsky examined the geometric elements of painting. The surface of the canvas is the 'plane'. A point is the 'proto-element', the reference point. That is, the first in a series of steps which make up the composition. Lines, whether straight, angular, or curved, serve as 'forces' that reveal space, and serve as compasses directing movement. Combined, the point and line create both balance and contrast, as well as feelings, whether joy, anger, harmony or tension and so on. In short, they have a compositional relationship. It is interesting to note that, like Malevich, Kandinsky's paintings were based on lines and colour, the two distinguishing characteristics of the Christian icon.[33]

Geometric shapes were significant to Kandinsky because, in a kind of Pythagorean sense, he believed objects in motion in the cosmos vibrate and produce sound, albeit inaudible to the human ear. The entire universe was a cosmic composition. And, like Malevich, he subscribed to the concept of sacred geometry as the foundational blueprint of life in the cosmos.[34] The pyramid was significant because: (1) he used it as a metaphor for the artist, who, like the tip of the pyramid, proceeds like an arrow or a vanguard, pointing the way to the future; and (2) as a metaphor, symbol, icon, it is a vessel which holds humanity and, spiraling upward, the pyramid uplifts humanity into space/heaven/higher consciousness. Still, Kandinsky considered the circle the most important primary form because he believed it was a window into the fourth dimension (see Figure 2.3).[35]

Kandinsky drew spiritual inspiration from various pagan, ethnic tribes in Russia, which was both rooted in his Buriat (Mongolian) heritage and a result of an ethnographical/anthropological expedition undertaken as a young man to the remote Vologda region, roughly 400 miles north of Moscow, where he studied primitive, peasant law and remnants of pagan religion which evidenced elements of animism, atavism and ancestor worship. Describing this experience as if he had travelled to 'another planet', or had 'entered into a painting', Kandinsky intuited a spiritual connection to the land, with its 'unending forests' and 'brightly hued hills', punctuated with the inhabitants' wonderfully painted, 'like a folksong', and carved wooden houses. The vibrant, animated activities of the trade fairs, with their musical cacophony of voices and sounds, and the various ethnic tribes of the region, especially the Zyrians, with their 'white faces, red-painted cheeks and black hair', who seemed to be 'brightly colored living pictures on two legs', made such an impression on him that Peg Weiss (1986) has argued that it 'reverberated' in his artwork 'to the very end'.[36]

Especially, Weiss (1986: 9) insists, Kandinsky was taken by the 'salvation' beliefs and motifs of the 'shamanistic' aspects of various tribes' culture, incorporating them in his art and, therefore, demonstrating his belief in 'art as a metaphor for cultural healing and salvation'. In the cosmologies of these various tribes, the shaman had a special kind of 'knowing' (gnosis), which included ecstatic, 'trance' experiences that 'transported him to other realms', and which were transmitted from the One. He was typically depicted as an 'old man' with a staff, the latter of which was a symbolic representation of a horse which carried (uplifted, ascended) him with 'power and speed', across time and space in order for him to fulfill his purpose.[37] This is remarkably reminiscent of Merkavah mysticism, which features apocalyptic stories of ancient heroes who ascend to heaven on horses or chariots; or the Hermetic ascension through the cosmos.

Kandinsky was also taken with the warrior, or musketeer, or *streltsy* figures and archers who rode on horses. Weiss suggests that in the patron Saint George, whom the Orthodox Church honors twice a year, Kandinsky saw overlap with the peasant folk hero *Egori* the Brave, both personifying the ideal, heavenly warrior defending the community from invaders, and the latter representing a kind of shamanistic intercessor. Weiss persuasively explains that Kandinsky would identify with the shaman's purpose and conceive of art as 'the means by which "man speaks to mankind about the supernatural"'.[38]

Both Charlotte Gill (2014) and Peg Weiss (1986) identify the shamanistic elements of Malevich's and Kandinsky's cosmology of beliefs and how these are depicted in their art. However, Gleb Sidorkin (2011) and Sixten Ringbom (1966: 415) make it clear that both artists were devout Christians, with the former pointing out that the New Testament was the 'primary reference and metatext' for Malevich, keeping a copy of it on his desk for his entire life. And Ringbom notes that Kandinsky himself conceded that his conception of art was 'Christian'. For it harbored 'in itself the necessary elements' for salvation. The positions of Gill and Weiss and those of Sidorkin and Ringbom are not necessarily mutually exclusive. For history has shown that examples of religious syncretism abound. In addition, that the Eastern Orthodox Church dogmatized mysticism in the form of Hesychasm in the fourteenth century meant that a transition to and acceptance of other manifestations of mysticism could well be seamless.

Nikolai Roerich:[39] Art as Embodied Vignettes

Artist extraordinaire, Nikolai Roerich (1874–1947) was another dazzling luminary of the Silver Age. Arguably best known for his set designs and costumes for the 1913 Paris season of Sergei Diaghilev's Ballets Russes, which featured Igor Stravinsky's *The Rite of Spring*, Roerich's versatility went well beyond art. He was an archaeologist, an explorer, a historian, a cultural anthropologist, an ethnographer, a philosopher, a poet, a lawyer, a peace activist, a Nobel Peace Prize nominee, and, like Malevich and Kandinsky, a follower of Theosophism.[40] Indeed, Roerich believed he was the reincarnation of Leonardo da Vinci (Shenkman 2013).

Although he would be influenced by Asia's shamanistic traditions, the starting point of understanding Roerich's world view is Russian Christian Orthodoxy. Among the many defining characteristics of the Eastern Church, it was its dogmatized component of mysticism that would be a central feature of Roerich's life. And then there were the icons,[41] which, in their formulaic contents and compositions, as well as in their stylistic qualities in terms of both line and colour, transmitted spiritualism both symbolically and mystically (Drayer 2005: 29; McCannon 2000: 273, 280–1, 287). Equally significant was his upbringing at his family's manor estate, Izvara. Here, he was steeped in the intelligentsia's culture of the country estate as well as greatly influenced by the nature all around him. He was especially taken with the Slavic folk and ethno-archaic and ancient histories and myths. Reminiscent of the ideal of traditionalism discussed above, in time, Roerich believed that the original, cultural essence of a people was of the spirit (Drayer 2005: 2–6, 11, 29, 34–6, 99, 120–2; McCannon 2000: 275–8; Roerich 2017c: 13).

Over the course of his life, Roerich produced over 7,000 paintings and a number of writings, manifestos of sorts, which documented his archaeological, ethnographic and spiritual expeditionary travels as well as his beliefs. One of his greatest missions in life was to work to protect cultural artifacts from the ravages of war and conflict. For he considered them beautiful relics in their own right, embodied, material evidence of our connections to our ancient past. For Roerich, this was also related to a kind of proto-structuralist belief, indeed, in line with the tenets of Hermeticism, that all of humanity shares commonalities in terms of myths, totems, attributes, organization – and origins.

Roerich was drawn to the 'Heart of Asia', a.k.a. 'High Asia', the 'Abode of Light', the 'sacred Symbol of Ascent', the 'roof of the world', the Tibetan Plateau, where the Himalayas cupped its south-western border and the Altai Mountains crowned its northern reaches. For he believed that this was the cradle of Russian civilization, where, he discerned, its folklore, symbols, archetypes, myths and poems originated (Roerich, 2017b: 11; ibid., 2017c: 11, 94; McCannon 2000: 274, 280, 292; Drayer 2005: 15).

In addition, Roerich was drawn to this land because he believed it was, literally, geographically, physically, *the* place on earth which was closest to heaven; and where the sacred Hindu, Jain, Buddhist Mount Meru was located – these cosmologies considering it the centre of the world and the nexus which connected heaven and earth (Roerich 2017b: v; ibid., 2017c: 18). For Roerich, the Heart of Asia was also the harbinger of all cosmic knowledge, a 'repository of the wisdom of the ages, the heart of the planet, the place to which one returns after death, and from which one emerges reborn' (ibid., 2017b: v). While many of his paintings depict retrospective scenes – a recollection of former pristine civilizations and communities, such as the Viking, pagan Slav and Mongol heritages,[42] Roerich also depicted one of the future – a unified, spiritually conscious world. Therefore, he believed that somewhere, in the most remote impenetrable ice capped mountains of the Altai region, the legendary mystical kingdom of Shambhala was tucked beneath the clouds and mist – one of its connotations being the abode where the spiritual and the material worlds unite, as well as the nexus between the eternal and the here and now. (Roerich 2017b: 83ff.; ibid., 2017c: 71, 116; Drayer 2005: 101, 132, 139–40).

The mystique of Shambhala also included the idea that it was only visible to the initiated; only accessible to the truly spiritually enlightened. Thus, Shambhala was both a visible, spatial, fragrant place, as well as an invisible one, the latter being metaphysical, accessible to anyone searching for heightened consciousness, divine wisdom, purification and liberation; the word itself meaning sacred. Roerich fully subscribed to the local legend that the sacred wisdom of all ages and religions was deposited deep in a remote cave somewhere in the region (Roerich 2017b: 123ff., 131ff.; ibid., 2017c: 71 81, 92, 112; Drayer 2005: 83ff., 175–7).

In his writings, Roerich discusses the many myths and stories in the spiritual cosmologies of the region. Many of his paintings feature motifs such as the fabled wind horse, which rides through the air as the bearer of good fortune and spiritual enlightenment, symbolized by a flaming jewel which it carries on its back; or the extra-terrestrial Chintamani, an emerald green, thought (or intention) gem, that can give one soothsaying powers and heighten an individual's vibrational frequency, and was purportedly brought to earth by the Sirians (Roerich 2017c: 86, 100; Drayer 2005: 1, 86, 118, 129). (Obviously, the Chintamani was similar to the philosopher's stone in Western alchemy, the symbol of which is the squared circle.) A pagan symbol that Roerich noticed ubiquitously in the region also made an impression. Carved on stone and woven into fabrics, its iconic design presented alternate versions, one consisting of three circles stacked in the shape of a pyramid sitting above wavy lines and the other of three dots enclosed in a circle. Seeing in it the triune theme in all of nature and human constructs, Roerich appropriated the sacred sign, incorporating it in his Banner of Peace, the universal symbol of The Roerich Pact, created in 1935, which was devoted to protecting cultural artifacts. It was also featured in many of his paintings, telegraphing the sacred, circularity of life, the eternal return and what he (like Steiner, see n. 38) considered as the three most important aspects of life – art, science and religion (Roerich, 2017b: 13; Nicholas Roerich Museum New York).

One of many intriguing components of the Shambhala myth has to do with the spiritual heroes, or warriors, who, in an atavistic fighter tradition, defend the 'fiery doctrine'. The latter is shorthand for telegraphing the essence of spiritual maturity and elevated consciousness, consisting of wisdom, beauty, purity, ineffable love and radiance.[43] But the Shambhala legend also had a military component as part of an eschatological prophecy which involved the last king who, in a trance-like state, would intuit when an invasion by barbarians would commence, and thus gather an army comprising virtuous soldiers and archers, thousands of elephants and horse-drawn chariots and weapons. Of course, the epic battle would result in victory, thus ending history. Perfect peace would radiate across the world, uniting East and West, and the material with the metaphysical.[44]

In his many treatises, Roerich laid out his vision for the future of art, the role of the artist and his artistic theories. He was so inextricably connected to creativity that he once stated that, 'I would perish unless I devoted my life to art' (Drayer 2005: 5). As a devotee of Agni Yoga, he fully subscribed to its ideas, such as there is a 'creative relationship of human thought to the energy or fire of which the universe is made'; and 'Happiness lies in serving the salvation of Humanity' (ibid., 18).

Similar to both Malevich and Kandinsky, Roerich believed that art could communicate much better than words, noting that art was 'the best international language'. It 'will unify all humanity'. He held that his paintings would 'lead humanity to a future more magnificent than its past'. He perceived aesthetic culture as of the spirit, stating 'art is the universal medium of expression, and an evidence of the dominant spirit in life'. His aim was to 'better the lives of the masses' and bring all of humanity together in mutual harmony and cooperation. 'Perhaps physically separated souls can begin to understand one another through Art, the language of the highest blessings.' And, 'Creation is the purer prayer of the spirit.... Only through ... wisdom can mankind arrive at union and mutual understanding. To understand is to forgive' (Drayer 2005: 13, 27, 34, 39, 40–1).

Many of Roerich's paintings depict 'High Asia' as well as the legends, myths, epics, tales and songs associated with the region. For, in a kind of pseudo-Jungian way, he believed, they 'introduce[d] an understanding of higher concepts into the consciousness' (Roerich 2017c: 13). But these were not realistic paintings, the likes of which both Malevich and Kandinsky eschewed. In fact, they are more like dreams, 'filtered through his memory, imagination, and emotions' (Drayer 2005: 31). If we understand abstract art to be about revealing that which cannot be seen, or the spiritual, or interiority, or visionary, Roerich's art *was* abstract. His artistic style is unique, characterized by an iconic, two dimensionality, reproducing what Roerich saw *in* the landscape: 'broad flat lines, for everything is stripped clear of all ornaments and arabesques' (Drayer 2005: 141). His paintings exude vivid, seemingly pulsating, vibrational, luminous, mystical, other worldly colours – indeed, 'color-harmonics' as one reviewer has described them (ibid., 17). Refracted light images shine across the skies and are reflected in crystal beds in cave settings. And they are imbibed with an ethereal, anticipatory, spiritual quality. The mountains, the sky, the light, the snow, the rocks – here were two different worlds at once. Yes, Roerich's compositions are 'landscapes', but only of sorts. They are neither realistic nor objective. Like the Christian Orthodox icon, they are seemingly windows into a heavenly realm, sensual and sensory, 'mood landscapes',[45] external depictions of an inward journey, documenting a place in the here and now, our three-dimensional world, yet communicating to the viewer, the initiate, about the place of the future.

Therefore, a recurring feature, symbol, icon of his paintings is mountains, the 'metaphors of life', whose correspondences include the long, lonely, and arduous trek one must climb in order to attain elevated consciousness, and proximity to heaven. (Drayer 2005: 15, 92, 129; Roerich 2017c: 18, 28). When he painted the 'eternally moving ocean of clouds, with untold varieties of mist' (Roerich 2017b: 19) he was speaking to the fact that these represented the ethereal, gaseous veil, perhaps in the tradition of *The Cloud of Unknowing*, the demarcation line between earth and heaven, and between our earthly orientation and enlightened consciousness. (Similar to Malevich and Kandinsky, Roerich believed ether was an invisible, pervasive substance which surrounded all matter.) Often his scenic panoramas had animistic qualities and depictions, the landscape being the memory keeper. (Drayer 2005: 14–15, 96–7; Roerich 2017e: 35–40).

Conclusion

Although Malevich, Kandinsky and Roerich were unique in their own respective ways, as the above demonstrates, they shared many characteristics and beliefs. This is because they were embedded in both the Silver Age epoch and the longer trajectory of Russian history.

Regarding the widespread belief that the world was hurtling towards apocalypse, each artist possessed an element of urgency, a call to action, and participated in charting a better future – one which would be distinguished for its unity, self-deification and heightened consciousness. There was a component here of autochthony in their retrospective search for a pure and spiritual template to utilize. Each was attached to and inspired by his ethno-Slavic-Eurasian heritage. Although they looked back and saw value in the rich archaisms of the past, they also looked to a cosmic future where love, peace and unity would prevail. Each had an expansive, spiritual, cosmological interpretation of life. Each was drawn to a kaleidoscopic, syncretic amalgam of mystical and spiritual traditions in terms of both recent fads and ancient beliefs. This included their base, Eastern Orthodox Christianity.

As artists, they were motivated to liberate art from the past. Fully subscribing to an occultized reality and an expansive cosmic trajectory, they applied their beliefs to art. They wanted to liberate both the artist and art itself from former formulaic, theoretical constraints. They shed the heretofore established artistic theory and philosophical norms, such as perspective, logic and reason, and privileged colour, form, line and space. Above all, they had a theurgic interpretation of art. The content of their paintings contained iconic symbols and signs which corresponded to and telegraphed didactic, polysemic messages about both an occulted reality and spiritual apotheosis. Seeing themselves as theurgic practitioners, prophet like leaders, Godmen, they conceived of art as roadmaps for heightened consciousness and, especially, union with God. Their creations were hieratic conversations about henosis. They believed art had alchemic, transubstantiative power. Their colour and form motifs and stylistic methods were repetitive in nature.

However, this new abstract art of the Silver Age was a modern manifestation of an old one; indeed a timeless aesthetic. As it has long been known,[46] this new spiritual art was just the most recent installment of an old one. As Mircea Eliade schooled, 'Originally all art was sacred[,] ... it translated religious experience and a metaphysical conception of the world and of human existence into a concrete, representation form' (qtd by McCannon 2000: 271). This was theurgy: divine-, or God-working, or godlike action.

As it was noted at the beginning of this chapter, Paul Ricoeur held that all communication consists of symbols, and is hermeneutic in nature. Especially, he held that meaning results from the self-reflection that occurs after any hermeneutical interaction takes place. That interest in the art of Malevich, Kandinsky and Roerich persists to this day leaves no doubt about the accomplishment of their aims: to use art to draw attention to and generate interest in the nature of reality and spiritual maturity.

Notes

1 The author would like to thank the Landeshauptstadt München Staedtische Galerie im Lenbachhaus und Kunstbau Münchenand (available online: https://www.lenbachhaus.de/en/discover/collection-online/detail/das-bunte-leben-30036433) and the Nikolai Roerich Museum in New York for letting her publish photos of paintings from their collections.
2 The Silver Age was a literary, artistic, cultural and spiritual peak in Russia from roughly the 1890s to the 1920s. Although many sources cited herein define and discuss its many aspects, for an interesting analysis see Ariev (2012).
3 *Theurgy* is a mode of communication, the act of being in relationship with God. The fifth-century Neoplatonic philosopher Proclus believed that God communicates with us via repeated symbols, signs, imprints on material, embodied objects and those symbols' correspondences, or synthemata as he called them, assist with

deification and ascension – union with God. Synthemata can appear in different (material, embodied) formats, such as dance or art or texts, be they myths, narratives or representations. Repetition of communication is a ritual, and functions as liturgy. Indeed, repetition – that is, ritualized embodied symbols – has the capacity to reach more initiates. Here is the crucial connection between theurgy and art. Theurgy is a blended, mixing, hermeneutic, dialogically communicative, experiential, ritualistic process between God and 'fields of human activity', such as 'hieratic art' (Tanaseanu-Döbler 2013: 88, 108, 126, 145, 189, 230, 248, 282). The icons of the Eastern Christian Church operated as theurgy well before the connection between theurgy and art was defined during the Renaissance (ibid., 195). The artist has long been considered a theurgist. A theurgist is an 'esoteric ritual specialist' (ibid., 189). However, the theurgist, or conjurer, or soothsayer, or shaman, or prophet, or Godman, cannot perform theurgy without God. This is the divine component of theurgy. It happens because of grace, because of God's energies. Theurgy stresses that the soul in an individual has a kind of irrepressible urge to connect with God, and that it is only possible through certain repetitive, pseudo-liturgical practices, acts, such as prayer and/or offerings or art. In this regard, art substitutes for, or is a form of prayer. Thus, the theurgist, the artist is a mediator of sorts, as well as a transliterator, telegraphing God's word to the initiate. See Tanaseanu-Dobler (ibid., 188–96); Bychkov (1993: 18); and Chiaradonna and Lecerf (2019). In this chapter, I refer to two specific terms connected with references to the sacred: 'hieratic' and 'henosis'. 'Hieratic' has several meanings. I utilize its meaning as a form of communication involving the invocation of the divine and divine knowledge, and transmitting that knowledge (from above to below, from the invisible to the visible) via symbolic correspondences and signs in order to inspire deification (Tanaseanu-Dobler 2013: 191–4). 'Henosis' is understood as the act of uniting with the divine, the One, God, and therefore perfecting oneself; the deification of the self.

4 See Cassedy (1996: 98); and Bychkov (1993: 7–10).
5 Stupples (2001) emphasizes the roles of Neoplatonism, the European avant-garde, and the concept of evolution. The oeuvre of Carlson stresses Theosophy (discussed below), while that of Rosenthal highlights the occult. Billington stresses promethianism (1966: 478–92).
6 I borrow this expression from Bernice Glatzer Rosenthal's studies (1997, and 2002). However, Kazimir Malevich wrote this phrase in 1919 (Stupples 2013: 257). See also Rosenthal (2002: 39–40); Carlson (1993); and Kornblatt and Gustafson (1996). Drawing on Billington (1966: 514–15), Raleigh (2017: 10–11) has reminded us that apocalypticism during this time period was a peculiarly Russian phenomenon.
7 Consider Malevich's *Black Square* (1915) which was introduced as part of the *Last Futurist Exhibition of Paintings 0,10* (1915–16). The numerical ending of the

exhibition's title represented a levelling; a reduction of all things to zero; a new beginning, and from there progressing into the future, into a new world liberated from all of the old forms and norms. There, in the tradition of the Eastern Orthodox icon's location in homes, *Black Square* was displayed in the upper corner of the exhibit. In the tradition of the icon, *Black Square* was formulaic, its message not being verbal, but sensual, the spiritual content being delivered by the image itself. Malevich believed the square was the totality of all creation. The viewer (the initiate) perceives an infinity of the cosmos, as well as, possibly, God's eye mirroring back to you the sublime nature of life. However, Malevich introduced *Black Square* two years earlier, as the backdrop to the set of the avant-garde Cubo-Futurist opera *Victory Over the Sun*, 1913. Written in *Zaum* language (transrational, sound symbolism) and performed in a nonlinear libretto with unorthodox rhythms, the story is about a collection of futurists who want to overthrow reason, rational thought, logic and time, epitomized by the Sun, a powerful symbol of timelessness, and significant to folk culture. The play ends with an airplane crashing onto the stage, thus the 'new' symbolically overcoming the past. The set itself replicates Charles Howard Hinton's tesseract, discussed in his books, *A New Era of Thought* (1888) and *The Fourth Dimension* (1904), and which was meant to replicate the concept of four-dimensional space – that is, a 4D analogue of a cube. The Tesseract is considered a precursor to the concept of 'spacetime'. For a full analysis of the opera, see Douglas (1981); and Valentine (2016). See *Black Square* by Malevich, available online: https://www.wikiart.org/en/kazimir-malevich/black-square-1915 accessed 23 April 2023).

8 In the public domain, available online: https://www.wikiart.org/en/nicholas-roerich/saint-sophia-the-almighty-wisdom-1932 (accessed 23 April 2023).

9 See K. Malevich, *Peasant Women in a Church* (Stedelijk Museum, Amsterdam, Netherlands, 1912). Camilla Gray describes the composition as a 'static fused mass of repeated gesture and expression. Three-dimensional space has been almost ... crowded out'. The huddled figures are 'reminiscent of the "crowd-scenes" in Byzantine icons – [and] have lost any separate identity of form, face or gesture. Only a cylindrical pattern of shapes emerges.(...) [with] brilliantly contrasted colour highlighting' (Gray 1990: 148), available on line: https://www.wikiart.org/en/kazimir-malevich/peasant-women-in-a-church (accessed 23 April 2023).

10 Peg Weiss describes the 'bright medley of figures and action' in 'old Russian costume converging on a town bordering a river'. 'The whole composition is [composed of] ... contrasts: life and death, old and young, love and hate, peace and war,... Central ... is the figure of a [green] long-bearded old man.' Could this be the 'old sorcerer' of the Zyrian cosmology, whose staff symbolically represents his horse, which he rides to 'other worlds'? See Weiss (1986: 8–9). For an analysis, see also: https://www.kandinskypaintings.org/colourful-life (accessed 29 August 2022).

11 See McCannon (2000: 294), who explains the difference between primitivism and archaism, the former meaning using the past as a means or a device to advance a future oriented agenda, and the latter being an attraction to an ancient era, 'for its own sake'.
12 Slavophilism was a Russian manifestation of a nineteenth-century pan-European counter-Enlightenment which eschewed rationalism, reason, and universalism, and embraced and promoted the Romanitc Era's ideals of feeling, empathy, and individual experience. Slavophiles believed that the simple, humble Russian peasant was both the personification and harbinger of an authentic, pristine Russian culture. They also believed in a spiritualized essence of culture and religious cosmogany.
13 See Bassin, Glebov and Laruelle (2015: 1–12); Laruelle (2008); and Arnold (2019).
14 Hermeticism was a Hellenistic system of occultism that flourished in the first and second centuries AD. It refers to the body of spiritual philosophical work attributed to one Hermes Trismegistus. That is Hermes, the 'Thrice-Greatest', the legendary sage who was the embodiment of the Greek God Hermes (the God of writing and messages, and mediator between mortals and the divine – the Greek equivalent of the Roman God Mercury) and the Egyptian God Thoth (the God of knowledge, magic, wisdom, thought and meditation) in Ptolemaic Egypt. (Both Hermes and Thoth were considered psychopomps, i.e. soul guides.) Often viewed as the source of the *prisca theologia* (sacred ancient theology), Hermes imparted cosmic wisdom, utilizing 'negative theology'. That is, instead of knowing (gnosis) through reason and argument (episteme), the initiate 'awakens' in mystical silence, via experiencing God. (This is similar to the Hesychast meditation methodology and dogma of the Eastern Orthodox Church. See Stocksdale (2021: 209–24).) Thus, knowledge and experience of God is not reserved for the learned but available to all, via meditation. Some tenets of Hermeticism include alchemy; theurgy; the phrases 'the One, the All' (all things flow from the One), and 'As above, so Below' (everything in the cosmos is inextricably related, and the cosmos is a living organism of which we are all parts); consciousness can exist outside of the body; and via meditation one merges with God, thus self-deifies. The latter can be a literal out of body experience, or sometimes described as an ecstatic, inner-soul journey – a.k.a. cosmic consciousness. See Lachman (2011: 11–34, 63–64, 98; and 2015: 79–85, 97–9, 130–6, 350).
15 See *Suprematism*, K. Malevich 1915 (space dwellings) (Geometricization/architecture for the future).
16 See Hagemeister (1997: 185–9); Young (2013b); and Masing-Delic (1992: 76–104). Gallaher (2019: 203) puts Fedorov's cosmism in the category of proto-transhumanism. Hagemeister explains that Cosmism was part of a much larger trend that emerged after the 1905 Revolution, known as God-building. For the revolution proved to many in this period that it was not enough just to seek God (as the withdrawn, first set of luminaries in Russia's Silver Age are labelled), but to actively implement change; create a better world. Thus, in this context, 'action' was a

loaded term, a sign, a symbol, with specific meaning. See Rosenthal (1977, 2002: 27–50); and Lippman (2020: 223–39). In Eastern Orthodox dogma, theosis refers to being made God-like; deified.

17 The Spiritual Triangle; the upward and forward movement of heightened consciousness, the propelling spirituality. In the public domain at: https://commons.wikimedia.org/wiki/Category:Wassily_Kandinsky#:~ (accessed 23 April 2023).

18 For further discussion of these topics, see Lincoln (1998: 267); Gottlieb (2012: 492–503); Kornblatt and Gustafson (1996: 3–28); Gustafson (1996: 31–48); Lachman (2003: 213–14); Holland and Nesterov (2014); and Dowler (2010: 234–6). Iswolsky (1947: 16) described Soloviev as the 'bearer of Russia's highest spiritual ideal', while Young (2013a) and Lincoln (1998: 266), explained that Soloviev applied philosophical analysis to religious dogma. Quoting Semen Frank, Poole (2008: 201) described Soloviev as 'the greatest of Russian philosophers'. The statement that Russia did not experience the Enlightenment or the Reformation can be problematic. Each injected reason, the concepts of progress and free will, modernity, secularism and Humanism (with an emphasis on the individual) into the culture of Western Europe. Soloviev considered that, because of modernity (the Enlightenment), Western civilization had rejected God, and was reduced to 'striving to substitute something for the rejected gods'. See Poole (2008: 208); and Zhuk (2004). In the mid-nineteenth century, Slavophile Ivan Kireevskii pointed out that, because Christianity came late to Russia, this also inoculated it from Catholicism's hegemony in Western Europe. See Davidson (2009: 4).

19 See Gustafson (1996: 36–40); Young (2013b); Rosenthal (1997: 85; and 2002: 61); and Gallaher (2019: 201–2ff.). For an account of the mechanics of this self-deification, see Bychkov (1993: 27–9); and Gustafson (1996: 42–7).

20 See Rosenthal (2002: 38 and 51–3ff.). For quotes see Rosenthal (1997: 13) and (2002: 52, 53). See also Grillaert (2008: *passim*, especially chs 2 and 4). Grillaert points out that Nietzsche's books were not allowed in Russia until 1898 (19–20). Here, the apophatic nature of the Eastern Orthodox Church could find superficial overlap with Nietzscheanism. As theologian Vladimir Lossky has explained, apophaticism enables one to 'transcend all concepts' and therefore, allows one to be transformed so that union with God is possible (Lossky 1976: 238; and Bienstock 1940).

21 A mystical religious, metaphysical philosophical system, Neoplatonism emerged in the third century AD. Developed by Plotinus and his successors, its primary tenet is a belief that all things emanate from the One, including nous (the intellect), which in turn, produces forms/matter. It considers that, because both spirit and matter are combined in humans, they have the capacity, the urge to reunite with God. See 'Neoplatonism', *Stanford Encyclopedia of Philosophy*, available online: https://plato.stanford.edu/entries/neoplatonism/ (accessed 11 January 2023).

22 Esotericism connotes inner secrets, understood by a select few; its essence being the attainment of knowledge (gnosis) of the unseen, not via faith or belief, but

experience. There is a split in Western Esotericism regarding the route to gnosis, between those that advocated passive contemplation (i.e. *via negativa* – which, again, is in line with the Eastern Orthodox Church's Hesychast methodology) and active participation in the way of ritual, symbolism, and practices (i.e. *via positiva*). See Stocksdale (2021: 209–24); and Lachman (2015: 30, 152–3, 217–18). Its core beliefs include: correspondences; self-divination; the cosmos is a living organism; imagination is the source of spiritual knowledge; and master to initiate transmission. See Versluis (2000: 21, and the previous note).

23 For a solid discussion of the dimensions of both Theosophy and the occult in Russia, see Rosenthal (1997); Carlson (1993, 1997, 2012); and Lachman (2015: 360–81).
24 See Malevich's works that I refer to above.
25 By 'abstract art' we mean non-objective, non-representational, non-perspectival, non-figurative, non-rational, dematerialized art, including the elimination of pictorial content. If abstract art was about portraying that which cannot be seen, then, by definition, it was occult.
26 This apocryphal quote attributed to Malevich is linked by scholars to a letter written by the artist to one of his critics, Alexandre Benois. See in Kovtun and Douglas (1981: 235, 238, 241, see note above).
27 See also Billington (1966: 483); Stupples (2001: 12–14, 27, 29); and Malevich ([1915] 1976).
28 Of note, Father Florensky considered that the two dimensionality of the Eastern Orthodox icon, with its flat plane surface and linear outlines, was the closest artistic representation that we have of the spiritual dimension of reality, or the fourth dimension. (Florensky [1922] 1996: 64–6).
29 See Figures 2.2 and 2.3.
30 Both Malevich and Kandinsky have been considered, separately, as the founders of abstract art (Galenson 2008: 236).
31 Father of Anthroposophy (a kind of scientific, humanist approach to spiritual wisdom seeking), Rudolf Steiner, who greatly influenced Kandinsky, considered that ether was the invisible current along which thoughts travelled from one person to another. See Henderson (2014: 234, 236–8); and Lachman (2015: 392–4). He also held that, 'Art, religion and science' were 'inseparable ...', asserting that the artist connected humanity with the 'Divine' by raising the former up to the latter (Ringbom 1966: 391).
32 See Kandinsky ([1911] 1977: viii, 25); Ringbom (1966: 389–91, 396–402). Following Versluis (2000: 27), I use the word 'initiate' deliberately. That is, in theurgy, art is conceived of, and functions as, a device to awaken consciousness in initiates.
33 Kandinsky ([1926] 1979: 9–11, 17, 25, 32–3, 36, 38, 4–8, 53–4, 57, 67, 77, 79, 123); Billington (1966: 517); and Stupples (2001: 28).
34 Malevich's and Kandinsky's paintings evidence their affinity for the relationship between points, lines, curves, forms and colour in space, as well as their interest in

the symbolic correspondences which those characteristics communicate. Practically every study on each artist mentions their beliefs regarding geometry. For Malevich, see the fascinating study by John Milner (1996). For Kandinsky, see Campos (2018).

35 Henderson (2014: 238); Ringbom (1966: 391, 395); and Kandinsky ([1911] 1977: 6–12, 54).
36 Weiss (1986: 1–3, 5, 7, 11).
37 Weiss (1986: 4–5, 9–12). Kandinsky's painting *Motley Life* (1907) is most often cited to communicate such examples of timeless, and possibly atavistic, cultural symbols and beliefs.
38 Weiss (1986: 1–5, 10–13).
39 Roerich remains a controversial figure. For example, see Garafola (1990–1: 401–12); or Kalyan (2021); or Znamenski (2011: esp. 155–217); or Osterreider (2012). See Figure 2.1.
40 One of Blavatsky's staunchest devotees was Roerich's wife, Helena, who translated the sage's work, *Secret Doctrine*, into Russian and, via purported transmissions from her spiritual guru, one Master Morya, developed a formula for ethical living according to Theosophic philosophy, which she and Roerich called Agni Yoga, with one of its goals being to unite all the world's religions into one.
41 An analysis of iconography is beyond the scope of this chapter. However, well before the emergence of artistic theurgy (see Footnote 3), the Orthodox icon was a sacred, material, embodied bearer of the divine. In it lives divine energy. The source of this sacred nature is found in the rationale behind 'the word made flesh'; the 'spiritual' can only express itself in 'matter'; and if the flesh is deified, then so is the object (art). That Silver Age artists were embedded in their geo-cultural-historical lifeworld, means that they could well have implicitly (if not explicitly) subscribed to these characteristics. For more information see Lossky (1976: 10, 189); Osipova (2016); Stocksdale (2021: 209–24); Bychkov (1993: 42, 67, 77–95); and Ware (2015: 32).
42 Roerich regretted that the violence of Mongol invasion overshadowed what he considered to be the genius of artistic talent that Asia produced (Drayer 2005: 11).
43 In Roerichism (and many spiritual traditions) fiery is a term loaded with symbolism corresponding to many things. Some of these include spiritual (or even material, bodily) transformation/transubstantiation; cleansed, purified by a spiritual fire (but not burnt); an ecstatic, possibly out of body experience; heightened consciousness; and, in eschatological terms, the fire through which the world will pass at the end of time. The metaphor appears ubiquitously in all of Roerich's writings and is featured in many of his paintings. For example, see Roerich (2017a; and 2017c: 18).
44 See Znamenski (2011: 3ff.); and Roerich (2017c: 17, 62, 77–8, 94ff.; and 2017e: 35–40).
45 I borrow this expression from Gusarova (2013), who uses it in the context of analysing the Symbolist art movement in Russia.
46 See Ringbom (1966) and Massimo Introvigne (2016).

References

Primary Sources

Kandinsky, Wassily. [1911] 1977. *Concerning the Spiritual in Art*. Trans. with an introduction by M. T. H. Sadler. New York: Dover Publications.

Kandinsky, Wassily. [1926] 1979. *Point and Line to Plane*. New York: Dover Publications.

Malevich, Kazimir. [1915] 1976. 'From Cubism and Futurism to Suprematism: The New Painterly Realism'. In John E. Bowlt (ed. and trans.), *Russian Art and the Avant-Garde theory and Criticism 1902–1934*, 116–36. New Yorrk: Viking Press.

Nicholas Roerich Museum New York. [1935]. 'Roerich Pack and Banner of Peace'. Available online; https://www.roerich.org/roerich-pact.php (accessed 5 January 2023).

Roerich, Nicholas. 2017a. *Fiery Stronghold*. New York: Nicholas Roerich Museum.

Roerich, Nicholas. 2017b. *Heart of Asia*. New York: Nicholas Roerich Museum.

Roerich, Nicholas. 2017c. *Himalayas: Abode of Light*. Bombay: Nalanda Publications.

Roerich, Nicholas. 2017d. *Realm of Light*. New York: Nicholas Roerich Museum.

Roerich, Nicholas. 2017e. *Shambhala*. New York: Nicholas Roerich Museum.

Secondary Sources

Ariev, Andrei. 2012. 'The Intelligentsia without Revolution: The Culture of the Silver Age'. *Russian Culture Center for Democratic Culture*, 1–28. Available online: https://digitalscholarship.unlv.edu/cgi/viewcontent.cgi?article=1013&context=russian_culture (accessed 28 February 2022).

Arnold, Jafe. 2019. 'Alexander Dugin and Western Esotericism: The Challenge of the Language of Tradition'. *MONDI: Movimenti simbolici e sociali dell'uomo*, 2: 3–70.

Ashmore, Jerome. 1977. 'Sound in Kandinsky's Painting'. *Journal of Aesthetics and Art Criticism*, 35 (3): 329–36.

Bassin, Mark, Sergey Glebov and Marlene Laruelle (eds). 2015. *Between Europe and Asia: The Origins, Theories, and Legacies of Russian Eurasianism*. Pittsburgh, PA: University of Pittsburgh Press.

Bienstock, Gregory. 1940. 'Church and God-Manhood in Russian Religious Philosophy'. *Marxist Internet Archive* by Paul Flewers. Available online: https://www.marxists.org/archive/bienstock/1940/russian-church.htm (accessed 1 January 2022).

Billington, James H. 1966. *The Icon and the Axe: An Interpretive History of Russian Culture*. New York: Vintage Books.

Bychkov, Victor. 1993. *The Aesthetic Face of Being: Art in the Theology of Pavel Florensky*. Trans. Richard Pevear and Larissa Volokhonsky. Crestwood, NY: St. Vladimir's Seminary Press.

Campos, Isabel Sobral. 2018. 'The Ecology of Kandinsky's Abstraction: A Trembling World of Beings and Things'. *symplokē*, 26 (1–2): 237–50; *Oceania in Theory*, 237–313.

Carlson, Maria. 1993. *No Religion Higher than Truth: A History of the Theosophical Movement in Russia, 1875–1922*. Princeton, NJ: Princeton University Press.

Carlson, Maria. 1997. '*Chapter Five*: Spiritualism, Theosophy, Freemasonry, and Hermeticism in Fin-de-Siecle Russia'. In Bernice Glatzer Rosenthal (ed.), *The Occult in Russian and Soviet Culture*, 135–52. Ithaca, NY: Cornell University Press.

Carlson, Maria. 2012. 'Fashionable Occultism', in *The Theosophical Society in America*. Available online: http://www.theosophical.org/publications/quest-magazine/2301 (accessed 9 July 2012).

Cassedy, Steven. 1991. 'Pavel Florenskij's Philosophy of Language: Its Contextuality and its Context'. *Slavic and East European Journal*, 35 (4): 537–52.

Cassedy, Steven. 1996. 'P.A. Florensky and the Celebration of Matter'. In Judith Deutsch Kornblatt and Richard F. Gustafson (eds), *Russian Religious Thought*, 95–111. Madison, WI: University of Wisconsin Press.

Chiaradonna, Ricardo and Adrien Lecerf. 2019. 'The Soul, Theurgy and Religion'. In Edward N. Zalta (ed.), 'Iamblichus', *The Stanford Encyclopedia of Philosophy* (Fall). Available online: https://plato.stanford.edu/archives/fall2019/entries/iamblichus/ (accessed 21 May 2022).

Davidson, Pamela. 2009. 'Cultural Memory and Survival: The Russian Renaissance of Classical Antiquity in the Twentieth Century'. Inaugural Lecture, School of Slavonic and East European Studies, University College London, 21 May, 1–41. Available online: https://discovery.ucl.ac.uk/id/eprint/69111/1/Cultural%20Memory%20FINAL%20REVISED%20VERSION.pdf (accessed 31 May 2022).

Deodato, Alexis and Itao Sitoy. 2010. 'Paul Ricoeur's Hermeneutics of Symbols: A Critical Dialectic of Suspicion and Faith'. *Kritike: An Online Journal of Philosophy*, 4 (2): 1–17.

Douglas, Charlotte. 1981. 'Victory Over the Sun', *Russian History*, Twentieth-Century Russian and Ukrainian Stage Design, 8 (1–2): 69–89.

Dowler, Wayne. 2010. *Russia in 1913*. DeKalb, IL: Northern Illinois University Press.

Drayer, Ruth. A. 2005. *Nicholas & Helena Roerich: The Spiritual Journey of Two Great Artists and Peacemakers*. Wheaton, IL: Quest Books.

Florensky, Pavel. [1922] 1996. *Iconostasi*. Trans. Olga Andrejev. Crestwood, NY: St. Vladimir's Press. Part of this book in English translation is available online: file:///C:/Users/sally/Documents/Florensky%20Iconostasis.pdf (accessed 6 June 2022).

Galenson, David W. 2008. 'Two Paths to Abstract Art: Kandinsky and Malevich'. *Russian History/Histoire Russe*, '"Festschrift" for Richard Hellie: Part 2' (Spring–Summer/Printemps–Été), 35 (1–2): 235–50.

Gallaher, Brandon. 2019. 'Godmanhood vs. Mangodhood: An Eastern Orthodox Response to Transhumanism'. *Studies in Christian Ethics*, 32 (2): 200–15.

Garafola, Lynn. 1990–1. '"The Enigma of Nicholas Roerich": *Nicholas Roerich: The Life and Art of a Russian Master* by Jacqueline Decter, The Nicholas Roerich Museum (Rochester, VT: Park Street Press, 1989)'. *Dance Chronicle*, 13 (3): 401–12.

Gill, Charlotte. 2014. '"An Urge to Take Off from the Earth": How Malevich Embodies the Role of "Shamanic Artist"'. *North Street Review: Arts and Visual Culture*, 17: 53–62.

Gottlieb, Christian. 2012. 'Russian Philosophy and Orthodoxy'. In Augustine Casiday (ed.), *The Orthodox Christian World*, 492–503. New York: Routledge.

Gray, Camilla. 1990. *The Russian Experiment in Art, 1863–1922*. New York: Thames and Hudson.

Grillaert, Nell. 2008. *What the God-Seekers Found in Nietzsche: The Reception of Nietzsche's Ubermensch by the Philosophers of the Russian Religious Renaissance*. Amsterdam: Rodopi.

Gustafson, Richard F. 1996. 'Soloviev's Doctrine of Salvation'. In Judith Deutsch Kornblatt and Richard F. Gustafson (eds), *Russian Religious Thought*, 31–48. Madison, WI: University of Wisconsin Press.

Gusarova, Alla. 2013. 'Symbolism and Russian Art'. *Heritage*, 2: 39. Available online: https://www.tretyakovgallerymagazine.com/articles/N2-2013-39/symbolism-and-russian-art (accessed 1 March 2022).

Hagemeister, Michael. 1997. 'Chapter Eight: Russian Cosmism in the 1920s and Today'. In Bernice Glatzer Rosenthal (ed.), *The Occult in Russian and Soviet Culture*, 185–202. Ithaca, NY: Cornell University Press.

Henderson, Linda Dalrymple. 2014. 'Abstraction, the Ether, and the Fourth Dimension: Kandinsky, Mondrian, and Malevich in Context'. *Interalia Magazine: An Online Magazine Dedicated to the Interactions between the Arts, Siences and Consciousness*. Available online: https://www.interaliamag.org/articles/linda-dalrymple-henderson-abstraction-the-ether-and-the-fourth-dimension-kandinsky-mondrian-and-malevich-in-context/ (accessed 7 April 2022). Reproduced from Kunst Sammlung Nordrhein Westfalen (ed.), *Kandinsky Malewitsch Mondrian – Der weiße Abgrund Unendlichkeit: Kat. K20 Kunstsammlung Nordrhein-Westfalen*, 233–45. Ghent: Snoeck Publishing Company.

Henry, Michel. [2005] 2009. *Seeing the Invisible: On Kandinsky*. Trans. Scott Davidson. New York: Continuum.

Holland, Rupert and Andrei Nesterov. 2014. 'The Theories of the Slavophiles: On the Relationship between State and Society in Russia'. *GeoHistory: Practical Perspectives on a Complex Region*, 22 August. Available online: https://geohistory.today/state-society-russia-slavophiles/ (accessed 8 March 2022).

Introvigne, Massimo. 2016. 'New Religious Movements and the Visual Arts'. *Nova Religio: The Journal of Alternative and Emergent Religions*, 19 (4): 3–13.

Iswolsky, Helene. 1947. 'Vladimir Soloviev and the Western World'. *Russian Review*, 7 (1): 16–23.

Kalyan, Arundhati. 2021. 'Cultural Misrepresentation of the East in Nicholas Roerich's Art'. *Inquiries*, 13 (02). Available online: http://www.inquiriesjournal.com/articles/1876/cultural-misrepresentation-of-the-east-in-nicholas-roerichs-art (accessed 15 May 2022).

Kornblatt, Judith Deutsch and Richard F. Gustafson (eds). 1996. *Russian Religious Thought*. Madison, WI: University of Wisconsin Press.

Kovtun, E. F. and Charlotte Douglas. 1981. 'Kazimir Malevich'. *Art Journal*, 41 (3): 234–41.

Lachman, Gary. 2003. *A Dark Muse: A History of the Occult*. New York: Thunder's Mouth Press.

Lachman, Gary. 2011. 'The Quest for Hermes Trismegistus: From Ancient Egypt to the Modern World. Edinburg: Floris Books.

Lachman, Gary. 2015. *The Secret Teachers of the Western World*. New York: Jeremy P. Tarcher/Penguin.

Laruelle, Marlene. 2008. '"The White Tsar": Romantic Imperialism in Russia's Legitimizing of Conquering the Far East'. *Acta Slavica Iaponica*, 25: 113–34.

Lincoln, Bruce W. 1998. *Between Heaven and Hell: The Story of a Thousand Years of Artistic Life in Russia*. New York: Penguin Books.

Lippman, Erich. 2020. 'God-Seeking, God-Building, and the New Religious Consciousness'. In Caryl Emerson, George Pattison and Randall A. Poole (eds), *The Oxford Handbook of Russian Religious Thought*, 223–39. Oxfor: Oxford University Press.

Lossky, Vladimir. 1976. *The Mystical Theology of the Eastern Church*. Crestwood, NY: St. Vladimir's Seminary Press.

Masing-Delic, Irene. 1992. *Abolishing Death: A Salvation Myth of Russian Twentieth-Century Literature*. Stanford, CA: Stanford University Press.

McCannon, John. 2000. 'In Search of Primeval Russia: Stylistic Evolution in the Landscapes of Nicholas Roerich, 1897–1914'. *Ecumene*, 7 (3): 271–97.

Milner, John. 1996. *Kazimir Malevich and the Art of Geometry*. New Haven, CT: Yale University Press.

Mudrak, Myroslava M. 2004. 'The Art World: Kazimir Malevich and Ukraine'. *Zorya Fine Art: Twentieth Century Masters Contemporary Art*. Availale online: https://zoryafineart.com/publications/view/10 (accessed 8 April 2022). This is reproduced from *The Ukrainian Weekly*, 11 April 2004, no. 15, vol. 72.

Osipova, Irina. 2016. 'How to Read and Comprehend a Russian Icon'. *Russia Beyond*. Availale online: https://www.rbth.com/longreads/Russian_icons/ (accessed 8 May 2022).

Osterreider, Markus. 2012. 'From Synarchy to Shambhala: The Role of Political Occultism and Social Messianism in the Activities of Nicholas Roerich'. In Birgit Menzel, Michael Hagemeister and Bernice Glatzer Rosenthal (eds), *The New Age of Russia: Occult and Esoteric Dimensions*, 101–34. München: Kubon & Sagner GmbH.

Poole, Randall A., The College of St Scholastica. 2008. 'The Greatness of Vladimir Solov'ëv: A Review Essay'. *Canadian Slavonic Papers*, 50 (1/2): Canadian Contributions to the XIV International Congress of Slavists, OHRID, Macedonia, 2008 (March–June), 201–23.

Raleigh, Donald J. 2017. 'Introductory Essay: Stravinsky's Russia and the Politics of Cultural Ferment'. In Severine Neff, Maureen Carr and Gretchen Horlacher (eds), with John Reef, *The Rite of Spring at 100*, 1–16. Bloomington, IN: Indiana University Press.

Ricoeur, Paul. 1978. *The Philosophy of Paul Ricoeur: An Anthology of His Work*. Ed. Charles E. Reagan and David Stewart. Boston, MA: Beacon.

Ringbom, Sixten. 1966. 'Art in "The Epoch of the Great Spiritual": Occult Elements in the Early Theory of Abstract Painting'. *Journal of the Warburg and Courtauld Institutes*, 29 (1): 386–418.

Rosenthal, Bernice Glatzer. 1977. 'The Transmutation of the Symbolist Ethos: Mystical Anarchism and the Revolution of 1905'. *Slavic Review*, 36 (4): 608–27.

Rosenthal, Bernice Glatzer (ed.). 1997. *The Occult in Russian and Soviet Culture*. Ithaca, NY: Cornell University Press.

Rosenthal, Bernice Glatzer. 2002. *New Myth, New World: From Nietzsche to Stalinism*. University Park, PA: Penn State University Press.

Rosenthal, Bernice Glatzer. 2010. 'Religious Humanism in the Russian Silver Age'. In G. M. Hamburg and Randall L. Poole (eds), *A History of Russian Religious Philosophy, 1830-1930: Faith, Reason, and the Defense of Human Dignity*, 227–47. New York: Cambridge University Press.

Sedgwick, Mark. 2004. *Against the Modern World: Traditionalism and the Secret Intellectual History of the Twentieth Century*. New York: Oxford University Press.

Shenkman, Yan. 2013. 'Nicholas Roerich: An Extraordinary Life'. *Russia Beyond*. Available online: https://www.rbth.com/arts/2013/12/05/nicholas_roerich_an_extraordinary_life_31389 (accessed 24 April 2022).

Sidorkin, Gleb. 2011. 'Kazimir Malevich: A New Gospel in Art'. HAA 176m, (Spring): 1–23, https://www.scribd.com/document/91617708/Kazimir-Malevich-A-New-Gospel-in-Art (accessed 24 April 2022).

Stocksdale, Sally. 2021. 'Communication with God: Utilizing Michel Henry's Radical Phenomenology to Analyze Hesychastic Meditation'. In Malgorzata Haladewicz-Grzelak and Marta Boguslawska-Tafelska (eds), *Intersubjective Plateaus in Language and Communication*, 209–24. Bern: Peter Lang Publishers.

Stupples, Peter. 2001. 'Malevich and the Liberation of Art'. *New Zealand Slavonic Journal*, 86: 11–36.

Stupples, Peter. 2013. 'Florensky and Malevich: The Image and Materiality'. *South African Journal of Art History*, 28 (2): 250–61.

Tanaseanu-Döbler, Ilinca. 2013. *Theurgy in Late Antiquity: The Invention of a Ritual Tradition*. Gottingen: Vandenhoeck & Ruprecht.

Valentine, Olivia A. 2016. 'Rejecting Reason and Embracing Modernized Art: How *Victory Over the Sun* Revolutionized the Russian Avant-Garde'. *Vanderbilt Historical Review*, 39–48. Available online: https://ir.vanderbilt.edu/bitstream/handle/1803/8359/Rejecting-Reason.pdf?sequence=1&isAllowed=y (accessed 24 March 2022).

Versluis, Arthur. 2000. 'Western Esotericism and Consciousness'. *Journal of Consciousness Studies* 7 (6): 20–33.

Ware, Timothy. 2015. *The Orthodox Church: An Introduction to Eastern Christianity*. London: Penguin Books.

Warren, Sarah. 2013. *Mikhail Larionov and the Culture of Politics in Late Imperial Russia*. Burlington, VT: Ashgate.

Weiss, Peg. 1986. 'Kandinsky and "Old Russia": An Ethnographic Exploration'. *Syracuse Scholar*, 7 (1): 1–20.

Young, Sarah J. 2013a. 'Russian Thought Lecture 8: Vladimir Solov'ev: Godmanhood, Sophia, and Erotic Utopianism'. *Dr. Sarah J. Young: Russian Literature; History and Culture*, 18 February. Available online: https://sarahjyoung.com/site/2013/02/18/russian-thought-lecture-8-vladimir-solovev-godmanhood-sophia-and-erotic-utopianism/ (accessed 28 February 2022).

Young, Sarah J. 2013. 'Russian Thought Lecture 9: Nikolai Fedorov and the Utopia of the Resurrected'. *Dr. Sarah J. Young: Russian Literature; History and Culture*, 5 March. Available online: https://sarahjyoung.com/site/2013/03/05/russian-thought-lecture-9-nikolai-fedorov-and-the-utopia-of-the-resurrected/ (accessed 25 May 2022).

Zhuk, Sergei I. 2004. *Russia's Lost Reformation: Peasants, Millennialism, and Radical Sects in Southern Russia and Ukraine, 1830–1917*. Washington, DC: Woodrow Wilson Center Press.

Znamenski, Andrei. 2011. *Red Shambhala: Magic, Prophecy, and Geopolitics in the Heart of Asia*. Wheaton, IL: Quest B.

3

Painterly Motif of Kisses of Mary and Kisses of St Joseph in the Context of Iconography of *Unio Mystica* in the Baroque Period

Andrzej Kozieł

Introduction

One of the most characteristic features of the religious iconosphere of the Silesia region (currently Poland and the Czech Republic) in the Baroque period is the presence of various types of representations of the Holy Family, i.e. Jesus, Mary and St Joseph in the intimate scenes of the Kiss of Mary or the Kiss of St Joseph (Kozieł 2006: 117–66).[1] As many as sixty representations of this type in the form of paintings, graphic and drawing artworks are extant till today. They come from almost all of historical Silesia territory in the pre-1740 borders: from Żagań (Sagan), Zielona Góra (Grünberg) in the West, to Cieszyn (Teschen) and Opava (Troppau) in the East. In most cases, these are small-size devotional representations that used to serve for individual devotional practices, such as, for example, the painting on a copper plate of the Kiss of Mary with a scene of Joseph's wedding with God the Father by Michael Willmann (1630–1706) from the collection of Gemanisches Nationalmuseum in Nuremberg.

Nonetheless, large-scale representations of Kisses which served as altar paintings also exist, such as, e.g. the canvas painting the Kiss of Mary made in 1695 in the workshop of Willmann for the side altar in the parish church of St Martin in Jawor (Jauer) (Figure 3.1). The extant representations of Kisses include works of good artistic quality executed by professional artists, such as *The Kiss of Mary* by Ignaz Günther (1727–1807) at the filial church in Janov (Johannestal), as well as the craft of folk artists, the best example of which is the charming canvas of an anonymous painter in the collections of the Museum of Cieszyn Silesia in Cieszyn (Figure 3.2). Importantly, in no other region of Europe do we find so many preserved works from the Baroque period, and so diverse in terms of the iconography and form, the main theme of which would be the representations of the Kisses of Mary and the Kisses of St Joseph.

Figure 3.1 *The Kiss of the Virgin* by Michael Willmann, 1687, oil on canvas, parish church of St Marcin, Jawor. Photo by Franciszek Grzywacz.

Figure 3.2 *The Kiss of Mary* by Unknown painter, with the scene of Joseph's wedding with God the Father, 3rd quarter of the 18th century, oil on canvas, Museum of Cieszyn Silesia, Cieszyn.

In this contribution, I will attempt to analyse such representations in a broader context of aspects of the mysticism of the Baroque period. In the first part, I will discuss the influence and role of the Confraternity of Saint Joseph in Krzeszów (Grüssau) in the interpretation of the mystical marriage of the 'Soul' with the Created Trinity, that is, Jesus, Mary and St Joseph. The next section is devoted to the modus of interweaving mystical underpinnings (e.g. by St Bernard of Clairvaux, St John of the Cross or Thomas of Aquinas) behind the scene of Mary kissing Jesus or St Joseph kissing his Son as a visual sign of virgin love. Finally, I will focus on general implications of the analysed material as an exponent a supra-denominational visual language that served to graphically communicate content related to the spousal mysticism.

The Mystical Exponents of the Assumptions of the Confraternity of St Joseph

The appearance of *Kisses* in Silesia and their dynamic spread in that area was related to the activities of the religious confraternity of Saint Joseph, which was established in 1669 in Krzeszów on the initiative of the abbot of the local Cistercian monastery, Bernhard Rosa (1624–1696) (Kozieł 2006: 117–66). The Krzeszów confraternity was developing rapidly. In 1694, it had already 43,000 members, and in the first half of the eighteenth century that number reached 100,000 (Rose 1960: 75–6; Lutterotti 1962: 104). To cater for their piousness needs, fraternal prayer books were published and the obligatory representations of the Holy Family as the Created Trinity were produced in large quantities, referred to as 'Jesus, Maria, Joseph' or abbreviated as 'J. M. J.' (Mikuda 1985: 48–66; Kozieł 2006: 128–30).

The text of the second edition of a fraternal prayer book *Ehren=Kränzlein*..., (Honor=Wreath), which in 1678 left Ignatz Schubart's printing house in Kłodzko (Rosa 1678), apart from fraternal statutes, rules and prayers, included also foundations of the mysticism of the Created Trinity – namely, an exposition of the original mystical concepts of the marriage of the 'Soul' with the Created Trinity, that is, with Jesus, Mary and St Joseph. As ensues from the content of the prayer book, Jesus, Mary and Joseph constituted 'one soul and one body', because they were all 'merged' in Jesus thanks to their mutual virginal love. Saint Joseph was the one who went through all three stages of love towards the full union in the Trinity, hence he was a model for the soul of every Christian, aiming at the union with God. The process of developing God's likeness in the soul of a Christian, captured by Abbot Rosa in the form of a mystical marriage of the soul with the Created Trinity, was composed of three stages known as: (1) the ring of thoughts (*Denk=Ring*); (2) the ring of fidelity (*Treu=Ring*); and (3) the ring of love (*Liebes=Ring*), the culminating stage in which there was an ecstatic union of the soul-bride with God and the spiritual 'habitation' of the Bridegroom with the Holy Trinity and the Created Trinity in the soul of a Christian (Fitych 1984: 119–165; Fitych 1990: 95–157).

It was the duty of each member of the Confraternity of St Joseph to have his own representation of the Created Trinity and to say daily prayers in front of it. As a result, the incorporation of the mystery of the mystical marriage of the soul with the Created Trinity into the devotional practices of the members of the brotherhood of St Joseph resulted in the appearance of fraternal devotional representations of the Created Trinity in the new 'mystical' type of *Kisses*. Also, the mystery of the mystical marriage of the Soul-Bride with the Created Trinity was associated with the use of fraternal images, and the culmination of the mystery– the act of the 'love contract' of the Bride with the 'Holy Human Trinity J. M. J.' – was to happen 'in front of the painting with J. M. J.' (Kozieł 2006: 137–40).

Figure 3.3 *The Kiss of St Joseph* by Johann Tscherning after Michael Willmann, 1678, engraving, National Museum, Warsaw.

Figure 3.4 *The Bridegroom Leading the Bride* by Michael Willmann, after 1697, distemper on panel, former Cistercian Abbey, Lubiąż.

These new fraternal representations were designed by Michael Willmann, the most eminent painter of the Baroque period in Silesia, in collaboration with the abbot Rosa. It was at his request that Willmann designed three model types of 'mystical' images of the Created Trinity: *The Kiss of Mary*, *The Kiss of St Joseph* (Figure 3.3) and *The Kiss of Mary with a Scene of the Wedding of St Joseph with God the Father*. The latter directly related to the fraternal mystery of the three wedding rings (Kozieł 2000: 139–41; ibid., 2006: 137–40). However, regardless of the specific variant of the representation, its main theme is a sensual kiss, which was usually shown in the foreground and in the central part of the painting. This clear emotional-sensual expression of the *Kiss of Mary* and *The Kiss of St Joseph* definitely prevails over the theological and symbolic meaning of the representations, relegating their eschatological or counter-reformation meanings to the background.

Mystical Roots of *Unio Mystica* Representations

From the vantage point of the mysticism of the Created Trinity, the scene of Mary kissing Jesus or St Joseph kissing his Son were a visual sign of Jesus, Mary and St Joseph's mutual, virginal love. The members of the Holy Family who were 'merged' by a kiss, are Mary and St Joseph. They 'melted' with agape in Jesus, constituting together a mystical 'seed of Church' open to the love of every Christian. Thanks to this love, the married soul (as the seed of the church) could be united with God. The nexus of this relationship was the person of Jesus, while Saint Joseph assumed the role of a kind of intermediary between the Holy Trinity and the members of the Christian community.

There is no doubt that this original avail of a kiss as an image of mystical love was taken from the famous unfinished *Sermons* of St Bernard of Clairvaux on *the Song of Songs*, where the three-step path of spiritual improvement of the soul was described as three kisses: respectively on the foot, on the hand and on the mouth. The kiss on the lips itself signified the mystical union of the Bride and Bridegroom, i.e. a human being with the divine entity. St Bernard of Clairvaux even compared the kiss on the lips and its role to the person of the Christ, claiming that, 'the kiss itself is nothing other than an intermediary between God and men, Jesus Christ, a man who, as God, lives and reigns with the Father and the Holy Spirit for all ages and ages' (S. Bernardi 1879: 794).

It is not known who first came up with the idea to show the *unio mystica* of a Christian's soul with the Created Trinity by means of the representation of a kiss placed on the lips of Jesus by Mary or St Joseph. It could have been a famous poet and mystic Johannes Scheffler (1624–1677), known as Angelus Silesius, who from at least 1671 until his death in 1677 collaborated with the abbot Rosa. Angelus Silesius was the inspirer of Krzeszów's 'mystical' devotional initiatives and in his songs published in 1668 as *Heilige Seelen=Lust...* (Angelus Silesius 1668: 259–62) and seven years later as *Cherubinischer Wandersmann...* (Angelus Silesius 1675: 210–13), he devoted two pieces to a mystical interpretation of a kiss on the mouth.

It could well have been the Abbot Rosa himself, who was familiar with the writings of St Bernard of Clairvaux, because in 1678 he prepared a selection of the most important prayers as well as Marian and Passion sermons written by the Mellifluous Doctor, which were included in the scheme of prayer service spread over nine days (novenas) (Rosa 1772). Regardless of who was the author of this concept, the Krzeszów paintings of the Kisses of Mary and the Kisses of St Joseph undoubtedly became one of the most original representations of *unio mystica* in all of the European religious art of the Baroque era.

The depiction of the highest, culminating stage of the mystical path, in which the human soul reaches the spiritual union with the divine essence in love, was one of the most difficult tasks for modern mystics, theologians and artists cooperating with them. It was due to the essential qualities of this spiritual experience. First, *unio mystica* took place in the mind or soul of a person and hence was idiosyncratic and personal in nature. As St Thomas Aquinas wrote in *Summa Theologica*, God being known on the 'affective and experiential' path, penetrates the mind of the subject who knows Him, that is, the human soul, enriching it with His presence. However, it is an internal process that is the spiritual experience of a particular human being and takes place completely beyond the human senses, including the artist's sense of sight (St Thomas of Aquinas [1911] 1971: 220).

Second, the mystical union of the human soul with the divine essence is completely imageless, which was emphasized by almost all Christian mystics. In the words of St John of the Cross – the greatest early modern analyst of mystical experience, achieving the spiritual union of the human soul with God is possible only when the soul 'empties itself and detaches from all forms and knowledge' that are stored in its memory and are created by its imagination and fantasy. This is because

> God's Wisdom, with which the mind is to unite, has no form and is not subject to any limitation and to any differentiated and detailed understanding. It is completely clean and simple. [...] The soul, then, must become equally pure and simple, and not encapsulated in certain specific concepts, or shaped into an outline of a form, concept or image.
>
> St John of the Cross [1975]: 176

Third, the result of *unio mystica* was the spiritual union of the human soul with the divine being in love, which meant the abandonment by the human being of his personality within the hitherto existing boundaries and identity. For Master Eckhart, the birth of God in the 'depths of the soul' (*Seelengrund*) of man meant the mystical identification of man – the image of God with his pattern. As the German mystic vividly explained,

> If we press the seal against green or red wax, or against a canvas, a painting will appear in this place. However, if we press it down so tightly that it passes through the wax and nothing is left that it does not penetrate, the wax then forms one with the seal, without any differentiation. Something similar happens to the soul when, by true knowledge, it touches God; then it is completely fused with Him in the image and likeness.
>
> Master Eckhart 1986: 235–6

Fourth, the mystical union of the human soul with the divine essence concerned the extremely delicate, direct relations between man and God, which from the point of view of the Church as an institution mediating in these relations, could raise doubts. By presenting a human being as spiritually fused with the divine essence, it was easy to cross the imprecise boundaries between what was an acceptable religious image and what at that time was already treated as sacrilege and for what – as shows the famous case of the papal condemnation of Miguel Molinos and his mystical doctrines of Quietism – there ensued severe consequences (Kołakowski 1997: 344). So, how did Baroque artists portray something that was not visible, that had neither form nor its own identity, and was problematic from an ecclesiastical point of view?

Pictorial Strategies as Visual Hermeneutics of Mystical Experience

Although the issue of *unio mystica* iconography in the art of the Baroque period is still waiting for its monographer, we can try to pinpoint some of the most important pictorial strategies that were adopted by artists who wanted to show the mystical union of the human soul with the divine essence. For rarely do we come across any representations that would directly refer to the texts of modern mystics describing the path of mystical experience. Works such as e.g. the famous copperplate cycle by Anton and Hieronimus Wierix composed of nine representations of the stages of mystical ascension according to St John of the Cross, including the culminatory scene of the Flow of God's Love, which is shown through the use of the heart symbol (Mauquoy-Hendrickx 1980: 1425–34; Clifton 2012: 639–66), are exceptions in this regard. Most often, the artists presented *unio mystica* in a kind of roundabout way, referring to other texts or representations treated as a kind of a surrogate symbolic figure. This type of strategy was, e.g., using various types of illustrations of the text of the Song of Songs. The love affairs of the Bride and the Bridegroom described in this biblical work were interpreted by many church authors, including St Bernard of Clairvaux, as an allegorical description of the human soul's pursuit of the mystical union with Christ.

This in turn provided the basis for creating illustrations not only of the text of the Song of Songs, but also of various types of literary works inspired by the words of this biblical work. An example is the work of the Antwerp Jesuit Friar

Herman Hugo, extremely popular in Europe, *Pia desideria*. It was published for the first time in 1624 in Antwerp by the publishing house of Hendrik Aertsen and later repeatedly reprinted and translated into particular national languages (Praz 1964: 83–6; Reimbold 1978: 93–162).

The forty-six graphic illustrations by Boëtius and Bolswert included in this work, showing the love adventures of the human soul – the Bride striving for mystical union with her Bridegroom – Christ, became the basis of a supra-denominational visual language, which was used to illustrate the content related to the spousal mysticism. Both Catholics and Protestants availed of graphic illustrations from *Pia desideria*, using them as prototypes not only for graphic illustrations in devotional prayer books and songbooks, but also for monumental paintings. This latter practice is best evidenced by the painted decoration of the ceiling of the Great Hall in the palace of Lubiąż (Leubus) abbots in Moczydlnica Klasztorna (Mönchmotschelnitz) (Figure 3.4), made after 1697 by the workshop of Willmann (Kozieł 2008b: 294–310), or a series of fourteen paintings on the lowest floor of the gallery in the former Lutheran church in Kościelec (Hochkirch) near Legnica (Liegnitz), created by an unknown painter at the end of the seventeenth century (Szupieńko 2002: 192–9).

The text of the Song of Songs was also used to interpret the scene of the Assumption and the Coronation of the Blessed Virgin Mary by the Holy Trinity in terms of the spousal mysticism. St Bernard of Clairvaux presented this scene in his Marian sermons as an allegorical-mystical *unio mystica* image and a model for all people who seek union with God: 'Our Queen is ahead of us, ahead of us. And She was so gloriously received that the young slaves boldly follow the Lady, crying: "Draw us after you, we are running after the scent of your oils"' (PnP 1, 3). (Song 1: 3) (S. Bernardi 1879: 415). Hence, baroque artists often portrayed the scene of the Assumption and Coronation of the Blessed Virgin Mary by the Holy Trinity as an image of the pursuit of Mary – the Bride – for a spiritual reunion with her divine Bridegroom – Christ (Figure 3.5). The procedure consisted in giving the traditional depiction of this scene some 'spousal' attributes, such as wreaths of lilies and roses placed on Mary's head, which were a symbolic visualization of the biblical words spoken by the Bride to the Bridegroom: 'Cover me with flowers, sprinkle apples, because I am sick with love' (Song 2: 5).

Another way of showing *unio mystica* was to use scenes of mystical visions of saints. Although in essence mystical visions were not the result of the spiritual union of the human soul with the divine being, but generally they arose only on the occasion of mystical devotional practices, nonetheless the visualizations of mystical visions were treated as symbolic representations of *unio mystica*

Figure 3.5 *The Assumption of the Blessed Virgin Mary* by Philipp Christian Bentum, 1748, oil on canvas, Parish Church of St Bartholomew and St Hedwig, Trzebnica. Photo by Jerzy Buława.

Figure 3.6 *The Vision of St Bernard of Clairvaux* by Michael Willmann (Lactatio Bernardi), around 1682, oil on canvas, Parish Church of St of the Holy Savior, Warsaw. Photo by Jerzy Buława.

(Stoichita 1997; Kramiszewska 2003). It concerned mainly those scenes in which there was an interaction between a human person and a divine, being the interaction that was impossible in the real world. As examples, let us mention the representations of the *Lactatio Bernardi* scene, extremely popular in European art, in which Maria sprinkled the dry lips of St Bernard of Clairvaux with drops of milk (Dewez and Iterson 1956: 165–187) (Figure 3.6), or the Ecstasy of St Teresa of Avila, stabbed to the heart by a seraphim with a red-hot blade of a golden spear (Cortuguera 2010: 255–63).

Sometimes the radicalism of these representations is surprising, in which there was even a physical communion of saints with Christ, as in the case of the representations of the Vision of St Mathilda of Hackeborn, in which she received from Christ his heart as a pledge of an eternal covenant (Kozieł 2006: 344), or the Vision of St Lutgarde of Tongern, in which the saint was embraced by the Crucified Christ and allowed to drain the mortal wound in his side (Dębińska

Figure 3.7 *The Vision of St Lutgarde of Tongern* by Bernhard Krause, 1772, oil on canvas, pilgrimage Church of St Visitation of Our Lady, Bardo. Photo by Mirosław Łanowiecki.

Figure 3.8 *The Kiss of Mary* by Unknown painter, with the scene of Joseph's marriage to God the Father, around 1700, oil on canvas, Chapel of St Holy Family, Doudleby Castle. Photo by Martin Mádl.

2009: 96–8; see Figure 3.7). We should remember, however, that all the scenes of mystical visions presented by the artists were grounded in literary prototypes taken from officially published religious works, which were approved by the church censorship before being sent for printing.

Conclusion

Against this background, the Krzeszów representations of the Kisses of Mary and the Kisses of St Joseph appear not only as original, but also as an exceptionally accurate and mature solution to the problem of imaging *unio mystica* in religious art of the Baroque period. Of course, as in most other representations of the mystical union of the human soul with the divine being, the symbolic figure of a kiss on the mouth was used in the images of Krzeszów. However, compared to other representations, it is distinguished by its universality and the laconic expression.

Contrary to the illustrations of texts inspired by the Song of Songs or representations of mystical visions of saints, requiring the viewer to know their literary prototypes, the Krzeszów's *Kisses* were generally understandable even for uneducated viewers, because they referred to the members of the Holy Family and the loving affection they shared. Showing just this popular religious topic could not raise any doubts from the point of view of theological correctness. And most importantly, thanks to the artistic skill of Willmann, the *unio mystica* works as shown in Krzeszów were visually attractive. Kisses of Mary and Kisses of St Joseph are characterized by a static, central and uniplanar composition aimed at providing the viewer with spiritual participation in the presented scenes through an emotional reaction to the viewed depiction of a kiss and identification with the person of St Joseph.

Although the original concept of the mystical marriage of the soul with the Created Trinity had over time gradually became forgotten, the representations of the Kisses of Mary and the Kisses of St Joseph stemming from it kept moving the feelings of viewers, and their popularity exceeded the borders of Silesia, as evidenced by numerous examples of the reception of these images in the territory of Bohemia, Moravia and the Polish-Lithuanian Commonwealth (Kozieł 2008a: 892–3; Figure 3.8). Even after the activities of the Josephine Confraternities in Silesia terminated at the beginning of the nineteenth century, these representations continued to enjoy unwavering success. Amongst the numerous paintings of the Kisses of Mary that were created at the time we can mention for example the painting from the collection of Joseph Langer (1865–1918), preserved to this day (Organisty 2002: 29). The visual power of the impact of 'kissing' images was also appreciated by their first researchers (Kloss 1934: 98–9), who often fell under the spell of these 'sensually sweet' representations. Today, no one needs to be convinced of the pan-European significance of the mystical achievements of the artists such as Jakob Boehme (1575–1624), Daniel Czepko von Reigersfeld (1605–1660), or Johannes Scheffler, known as Angelus Silesius (Kosian 2001).

The concept of the Silesian mysticism has become a permanent element of the description of spiritual life in Europe of the modern era, and the most outstanding representatives of the Silesian school of spirituality now occupy a prominent place in the Pantheon of the most important mystics of all time. The analysis of the phenomenon of the mysticism of the Created Trinity in Krzeszów and the accompanying mystical representations shows, however, that the supra-regional significance of Silesian mysticism is not limited only to textual works, but also extends to the original representations of the Kisses of Mary and the Kisses of St Joseph, which we can boldly consider a Silesian against the background of the then European *unio mystica* iconography.

In terms of overarching interpretative conclusions, we can recall that for Ricoeur ([1972] 1989), hermeneutics is an art of recognizing the discourse in an oeuvre. Nonetheless, the discourse is given to us solely within and through the structure of that oeuvre. What follows, as the scholar subsequently concludes, interpretation constitutes an answer to that perennial alienation, which is 'established by man in the works of discourse, comparable to the objectification that constitutes the works of his work and his art' (Ricoeur [1972] 1989: 236).

In this respect, the analysis traced the struggle to grasp and convey visually the human soul's pursuit of the mystical union with Christ thought visual discourse of Baroque painters in Silesia. We have seen how artists elaborated symbolic inventory, which on the one hand, was to mediate, coincide with and also to portray eternal experience of agape, revelation and bridge the alienation of human condition.

Notes

1 All the illustrative material in the chapter are my authorship, with the publication permission. The text features toponyms in their current version in Polish, but also gives the German version, as they functioned before 1945, in parentheses.

References

Primary Sources

Angelus Silesius = [Johannes Scheffler]. 1668. *Heilige Seelen=Lust Oder Geistliche Hirten=Lieder Der in ihren JESUM verliebten Psyche gesungen von Johann Angelo Silesio, und von Herren Georgio Josepho mit außbündig schönen Melodieyen geziert. Anjetzo auffs neue übersehn und mit dem Fünfften Theil vermehrt*. Breßlaw: in der Baumannischen Erben Druckerei.

Angelus Silesius = [Johannes Scheffler]. 1675. *Cherubinischer Wandersmann oder Geist=Reiche Sinn= und Schluß=Reime zur Göttlichen Beschauligkeit anleitende / Von dem Urheber aufs neue übersehn und mit dem Sechsten Buche vermehrt den Liebhabern der geheimen Theologie und beschaulichen Lebens zur Geistlichen Ergötzligkeit zum andernmahl her=auß gegeben*. Glatz: Ignaz Schubart.

S. Bernardi [Abbati primi Claraevallensis]. 1879. *Sermones*, In: *PATROLOGIAE CURSUS COMPLETUS...*, vol. 183. PARISSIS.

John of the Cross = św. Jan od Krzyża. [1975]. *Droga na Górę Karmel* [Ascent of Mount Carmel]. In *Św. Jan od Krzyża. Dzieła* [John of the Cross, collected works]. (Trans. by O. Bernard of God's Mother). Vol. 1. Kraków: Wydawnictwo Karmelitów Bosych.

Meister Eckhart = Mistrz Eckhart. [1986]. *Kazania* [Sermons]. (Trans. W. Szymon OP). Poznań: AA.

Rosa, Bernhard. 1678. *Ehren=Kränzlein / Dem / Hochheiligen Patriarchen / JOSEPHO, / Pflege Vater / CHRISTI JESU, / Bräutigam der Jungfräuli= / chen GOttes Gebährerin / MARIAE. / Auß den schönsten Tugend-Blumen / seines heiligen Lebens, und unterschiedlichen / Bet= und Lob=Büchern, abgepflocket und / zusammen gebunden / Durch BERNARDUM ROSAM, / deß heiligen Cistert. Ord: im Klo= / ster Grüssau / Abbten und Herrn / Zu absonderlichen Geruch und =brauch der auffgerichten Bruderschafft deß Heiligen / Josephi in besagtem Kloster. / neV aVs gefertIget In gröbereM DrVCk / zV hILff breshaffter aVgen*. Glatz: Maria Barbara Schubarthin.

Rosa, Bernhard. 1772. *Neufach / abtrieffender Hönigseim / aus dem Leben und Tugenden des Hönigfliessenden / Kirchen=Lehrers / Bernardi, / Abbtens zu Claravall, / Cisterciensis Ordinis; / davon sich / der grosse Brenen=Schwarm / Vieler begierigen Seelen / durch Neun diensttätige Andacht / zu loben wünschet, / schon Anno 1678 / von dem Hochw. Hochedelgeb. in Gott geistl. / und andächtigen Herrn / Herrn Bernardo Rosa, / Des Fürtlichen Stifts Ordinis Cisterciensis zu / Grüssau Abbten / schriftlich abgefasset / anjetzo aber / durch die Hochwürdige, Hochedelgeb. / in Gott geistliche und andächtige Frau / Frau Anastasia Röslerin, / zu S. Marienthal Ordinis Cisterciensis, in der Oberlausitz, / regierender Abbatißin, und Domina / zu Druck gebracht.*

Thomas of Aquinus. [1911] 1971. *Suma teologiczna* (The Summa Theologiae). Vol. 19: *Religijność*. Trans. F. W. Bednarski OP. Londyn: Veritas.

Secondary Sources

Clifton, James. 2012. 'Secret Wisdom: Antoon Wierix's Engravings of a Carmelite Mystic'. In Celeste Brusati, Karl Enenkle and Walter Melion (eds), *The Authority of the World. Reflecting on Image and Text in Northern Europe, 1400–1700*, 639–66. Leiden: Brill.

Corteguera, Louis R. 2010. 'Visions and the Soul's Ascent to God in Spanish Mysticism'. In Coulum Hourihane (ed.), *Looking beyond: Visions, Dreams, and Insights in Medieval Art and History*, 255–63. Princeton, NJ: Penn State University Press.

Dębińska, Anna. 2009. 'Ikonografia św. Lutgardy na Śląsku, w Czechach i na Morawach w czasach baroku'. MA thesis, vols 1–2, University of Wrocław, Wrocław.

Dewez, Leon and Albert van Iterson. 1956. 'La Lactation de saint Bernard. Légende et iconographie'. *Cîteaux in de Nederlanden*, 7: 165–87.

Fitych, Tadeusz. 1984. 'Bernarda Rosy nauka o św. Józefie w świetle koncepcji mistycznych zaślubin duszy z "Trójcą Stworzoną"'. *Colloquium Salutis. Wrocławskie Studia Teologiczne*, 16: 119–65.

Fitych, Tadeusz. 1990. *Trójca Stworzona. Nauka o św. Józefie na Śląsku*. Lublin: Towarzystwo Naukowe Katolickiego Uniwersytetu Lubelskiego.

Florisoone, Michel. 1980. *Jean de la Croix. Iconographie Générale*. Brügge: Desclée, De Brouwer.

Kloss, Ernst. 1934. *Michael Willmann. Leben und Werke eines deutschen Barockmalers*. Breslau: Ostdeutsche Verlagsanstalt.

Kołakowski, Leszek. 1997. *Świadomość religijna i więź kościelna. Studia nad chrześcijaństwem bezwyznaniowym XVII wieku*, 2nd ed. Warszawa: Wydawnictwo Naukowe PWN.

Kosian, Józef. 2001. *Mistyka śląska. Mistrzowie duchowości śląskiej. Jakub Boehme, Anioł Ślązak i Daniel Czepko*. Wrocław: Wydawnictwo Uniwersytetu Wrocławskiego.

Kozieł, Andrzej. 2000. *Rysunki Michaela Willmanna (1630–1706)*. Wrocław: Wydawnictwo Uniwersytetu Wrocławskiego.

Kozieł, Andrzej. 2006. *Angelus Silesius, Bernhard Rosa i Michael Willmann, czyli sztuka i mistyka na Śląsku w czasach baroku*. Wrocław: Wydawnictwo Uniwersytetu Wrocławskiego.

Kozieł, Andrzej. 2008a. 'Silesia Mystica. Śląska ikonografia mistyczna i jej recepcja w Czechach i na Morawach w czasach baroku'. In Helena Dáňová, Jan Klípa and Lenka Stolárová (eds), *Slezsko, země Koruny České. Historia a kultura 1300–1740*, Vol. B, 889–905. Praha: Národní galerie v Praze.

Kozieł, Andrzej. 2008b. 'Willmann i barbarzyńcy, czyli słów kilka o dekoracji malarskiej stropów z dawnego pałacu opatów lubiąskich w Moczydlnicy Klasztornej'. In Andrzej Kozieł (ed.), *Opactwo Cystersów w Lubiążu i artyści*, 294–310. Wrocław: Wydawnictwo Uniwersytetu Wrocławskiego.

Kozieł, Andrzej. 2013. *Michael Willmann i jego malarska pracownia*. Wrocław: Wydawnictwo Uniwersytetu Wrocławskiego.

Kramiszewska, Agnieszka. 2003. *Visio religiosa w polskiej sztuce barokowej. Ze studiów nad ikonografią hagiograficzną*. Lublin: Towarzystwo Naukowe Katolickiego Uniwersytetu Lubelskiego.

Lutterotti, Nikolaus von. 1962. *Vom unbekannten Grüssau. Altgrüssauer Klostergeschichten*. Ed. Ambrosius Rose. Wolfenbüttel: Grenzland-Verlag.

Mauquoy-Hendrickx, Marie. 1980. *Les estampes des Wierix. Conservees an Cabinet des Estampes de la Biblioteque Royal Albert Ier*. Vol. 2. Bruxelles: Alan Wofsy Fine Arts.

Mikuda, Barbara. 1985. '"Pietas Austriaca" – Zum Freskenzyklus Michael Willmanns und zur Josephsverehrung in Grüssau'. *Zeitschrift für Ostforschung*, 34: 48–66.

Organisty, Adam. 2002. *Joseph Langer (1865–1918). Ein schlesischer Maler, Konservator und Sammler*. Trans. D. Petruk. exh. cat., Bielefeld-Brackwede, Rathaus, 25.05–23.06.2002. Kraków Modulus Verlag.

Praz, Mario. 1964. *Studies in Seventeenth-Century Imagery*. Rome: Edizioni di storia e letteratura.

Reimbold, Ernst Thomas. 1978. '"Geistliche Seelenlust". Ein Beitrag zur barocken Bildmeditation: Hugo Hermann (!), Pia desideria, Antwerpen 1624'. *Symbolon. Jahrbuch für Symbolenforschung*, 4: 93–162.

Ricoeur, Paul. [1972] 1989. 'Hermeutyczna funkcja dystansu [Hermeneutic distance function]'. In Katarzyna Rosner (ed.) and trans. Katarzyna Rosner and Piotr Graff, *Język, tekst, interpretacja. Wybór pism*, 224–45. Warszawa: PIW.

Rose, Ambrosius. 1960. *Abt Bernardus Rosa von Grüssau. Nach Notizen des P. Nikolaus von Lutterotti*, Stuttgart: Brentano Verlag.

Staedel, Else. 1935. *Ikonographie der Himmelfahrt Mariens*. Strassburg: Heitz.

Stoichita, Victor Ieronim. 1997. *Das mystische Auge. Vision und Malerei im Spanien des Goldenen Zeitalters*. Trans. A. Knop. München: W. Fink.

Schnell, Hugo. 1951. 'Die Darstellung von "Mariä Himmelfahrt" in Süddeutschen Barock'. *Das Münster*, 4: 19–44.

Szupieńko, Stanisław. 2002. 'Mistyka oblubieńcza w programie dekoracji malarskiej kościoła poewangelickiego w Kościelcu koło Legnicy'. In Andrzej Kozieł and Beata Lejman (eds), *Willmann i inni. Malarstwo, rysunek i grafika na Śląsku i w krajach ościennych w XVII i XVIII wieku*, 192–9. Wrocław: Via Nova.

Weddigen, Erasmus. 1988. 'Zur Ikonographie der Bamberger "Assunta" von Jacopo Tintoretto'. In M. Petzet (ed.), *Die Bamberger 'Himmelfahrt Mariae' von Jacopo Tintoretto, Internationales Koloqium in München 27. und 28. Januar 1986 und Restaurierungsbericht*, 61–112. München: Karl M. Lipp Verlag – Bayerisches Landesamt für Denkmalpflege.

4

Narrativity, Discourse Situation and the Opening of Elgar's Cello Concerto in E Minor, Op. 85

Marta Falces Sierra

Introduction: The Score

Over the last decades, the question of music as semiotic material has been widely discussed from various stances, both by modern musicologists and philologists. As a matter of fact, for linguists, written music on the score resembles the closest material to their object of study. The score becomes their best opportunity to approach the untranslatable musical experience. No matter how abstract music code may be, it looks like a text on the written paper (see Figure 4.1).

Accordingly, the score becomes the graphological representation of how sound and rhythm are crafted to 'say', to 'utter' something expressive in a unique way, in so far the music sign is ultimately abstract. Nonetheless, one may easily infer that the score is, at the least, just the beginning of what may be understood as a musical aesthetic experience. In the course of an inspiring description of how she 'listens', Evelyn Glennie, the Scottish percussionist, declared: 'I read the music. [...] I will follow the instructions, the tempo markings, the dynamics. I will do exactly as I'm told. [...] So therefore, if I translate this piece of music, [...] my career would probably last about five years' (Glennie 2003).[1]

The perception of a *music piece* as a coherent, quasi-narrative text in which a series of connected events are woven together as it does for a *language piece*, implies the presence of complex relationships of cohesive elements at work. Many of us, after a concert, will reflect on the fact that musicians play by heart, not to mention how composers store in their minds the music piece during the process of composition. As such, sound in music discourse should be understood as all other signs 'in the context of what has gone before, what is cotemporal and what follows' (Toolan 2016: 135).

Figure 4.1 Opening of Elgar's Cello Concerto, Op. 85. Reprint of the original Novello edition. Available as open access: https://www.free-scores.com/download-sheet-music.php?pdf=24338 (accessed 29 July 2023).

Textual coherence in language depends equally on the same type of crafting. Grammatical and lexical cohesive links at work tie *events* together and let the reader recognize the text as a coherent independent unit. Grammatical procedures including elements that point out backwards or forward in the text (anaphoric and cataphoric references), processes of substitution, ellipsis and explicit links between sentences are some of them. In my view, all these processes have their music counterpart, although 'sav[ing] language from representation' (Dayan 2006: 131). Consider Beethoven's Sonata No. 32, 2nd movement Arietta (*adagio molto semplice e cantabile*), which may be regarded as a core example of the cohesive power of cataphoric reference in a music text (see Figure 4.2). The referred event bursts in bar 49 (12/32 time signature) after a slow and apparently endless transition (number of bars are actually 100 for all sections are repeated). The harmonic progression clearly indicates that the *referent* is to come in order to give complete sense of the preceding structure.

All in all, music as a code encapsulates a much more complex, comparably richer number of textual 'grammatical' elements than language can provide. Textual cohesive tools in music act simultaneously at the vertical axis (key) and horizontal axis (rhythm or melody). Can one say, though, that these choices a music text may exhibit contribute to its perception as a story?

The Story

This article approaches the idea of music narrativity within the scope of comparative discourse stylistics. It aims to go beyond the boundaries of the *music text* to enter the idea of *music as a story*. Indeed, any *story* encompasses material of textual nature. Recently, Toolan (2016) has addressed the question of musical narrativity by developing an initial idea of how listening to music may be perceived as imagining a story both in and through music, 'though admittedly', he says, 'one that is vague in all particulars' (Toolan 2016: 130). At the opening of his essay, he acknowledges what may seem a familiar perception, namely, the idea that 'at a concert performance of a purely instrumental composition, many in the audience will experience the work as a kind of *story*' (ibid., 130, emphasis added).

Setting aside the obvious cases of vocal music, even of music explicitly written after a literary idea or scenic description, it seems worth exploring how this *story telling* may work for absolute music. The question is whether this vague musical

Figure 4.2 Beethoven's Sonata No. 32, 2nd movement, bars 49–57. Reproduced by kind permission of Universal Edition AG, Wien.

story can also be perceived as a piece of musical narrative fiction. The assumption that the understanding of any work of art, not just music, can be experienced as a story – however vague its nature may be – necessarily implies its perception as the aforementioned telling of a series of connected events in time. Both, the connection between music textual patterning and the way it may signify, say, as an emotional abstract story, is also put forward in a different way in Sampson:

> Despite all the resources of language, [...] [music]does not create linguistic meaning. [...]. For if its meaning were something external to itself, that music had to indicate or mimic, all 'abstract' music – including everything that's purely instrumental, apart from film scores and programme music –would be 'meaningless'. Yet, that's not our experience. We experience it as *meaningful*, even when it's *not* evoking a particular emotion: as something that it is non-arbitrary, that coheres in a recognisable form, creating patterns and pleasurable sensation.
> [2016] 2018: 115

Can it then be stated that the perception of a story presumes the perception of a piece of narrative? Music narrativity entails the acceptance that events in time are transmitted by a specific voice (a teller/a narrator) who manages to create a perspective on the story; there must be also characters whose actions, words and thoughts are presented. Moreover, these characters interact among one another during the plot, which must be internally contextualized in a concrete setting and organized in time. In general terms, this metaphor goes beyond the consideration of a music piece as a *story* to the perception of a music piece as *narrative*. And, should it not also be necessary to regard *fiction* as part of this category? For a music piece is not, say, like a journalistic report is, but clearly a piece of figment narrative. Lastly, the incorporation of *fiction* as a category also implies the acceptance of a new rhetoric of discourse.

Let us consider the following example. Figure 4.3 corresponds to the six opening bars of Elgar's Cello Concerto in E minor, Op. 85. E minor means

Figure 4.3 Cello part, opening bars of Elgar's concerto, Op. 85. Reprint of the original Novello edition. Available as open access: https://www.free-scores.com/download-sheet-music.php?pdf=24338 (accessed 29 July 2023).

one sharp (F) on the key signature and, more importantly, that this key is the relative minor of G major,[2] which indeed influences the narrative tone of the story due to the degree distribution in the scale, as the tone colour of the cello does.[3] Time signature (4/4) shapes time spam, four beats (semibreve) until next strong one. The parallel tie on A notes between 2nd-3rd and 3rd-4th measure, and octave apart in each case blurs the boundaries between measures. The outcome is that the expected strong beat one every four disappears. Thus, the sense of time duration in the event is expanded: there is nowhere during the move to lean on, nowhere to take breath until the strong beat at the end of the event. No rest. At this point, the first beat in bar 5, accompanied by a fortissimo (*ff*), precedes a long rest (two beats and, two beats, and one and a half with a fermata). This means the rest will be held as long as the conductor decides.

Its consideration as the opening of that *abstract* story suggests two different types of questions regarding its narrativity: one dealing with the textual crafting of the score and another one focusing on its discourse nature. The first group would include queries such us: can this 'event' be identified as the opening of something? How many 'music utterances' can be found? Are they repeated in any sort of way? Is there a way of knowing if there is something coming next? What can be anticipated about its story by looking at the score? From the description above, it is possible to state that the story opens with one long expanded statement, ending loudly, with a long breath as if expecting something else to come. Repetition as a connector highlighting, imitating or questioning former events is also worth mentioning, although not found (yet). However, there is a second set of questions, In this case, queries like the ones listed below lead to the scenario of discourse stylistics: Who is speaking? Who is the narrator? How many participants/characters are there? Who is controlling the story? Who is being addressed? Next section will try to provide some answers taking the notion of *transmutation* (Steiner 1995) as the point of departure.

Discourse Situation: Music Narrative?

As part of his inaugural lecture at Oxford University (1994–5), George Steiner defended the position that knowing about something implies the recognition of something which has been previously experienced:

> Every act of reception of significant form, in language, in art, in music, is comparative. Cognition is re-cognition, either in the high Platonic sense of a remembrance of prior truth, or in that of psychology.
>
> Steiner 1995: 1

His claim let him incorporate the idea of *transmutation* as intersemiotic translation in the same fashion Roman Jakobson (1959) did some decades ago. This is to say, a poem may be transmuted into a music score, a score into a poem, or why not, a score into a story:

> A poem, a play, a novel can never be separated altogether from the illustrations or other pieces of art which it inspires, from its settings to music, from the films, radio versions, television treatments which are based on it. Roman Jakobson called this motion of a text 'transmutations'. They seem to me vital to the disciplines of understanding and valuation in comparative literature.
>
> Steiner 1995: 16

Being aware of the risk involved in a task of comparative nature like this one, it is precisely the scenario I have chosen for this chapter, namely, how a discursive perspective may contribute to a better understanding of the possible narrativity in a musical experience. In this search, it is examined if the rhetoric of discourse in verbal narrative fiction can be discursively transmuted into the rhetoric of discourse in a music piece. In order to check how transmutation may work in this context, the opening of Edward Elgar's cello concerto in E minor, Op. 85. has been taken as an example.

Table 4.1 contrasts the rhetoric of discourse in both narrative fiction and music. The table is divided in two columns. The left column contains the classical representation of how different communicative layers operate in narrative fiction (Leech and Short [1981] 2007: 259), while the right column includes my initial attempt to transmute Leech and Short's (ibid.) diagram into its music counterpart.

In the left-hand column of Table 4.1, the communicative discourse is hierarchically organized into four different levels: (1) author – reader; (2) implied author – implied reader; (3) narrator – narrate; and (4) character – character. *Implied reader* and *implied author* are abstractions which stand for the author we readers infer from the reading of the text and the 'hypothetical personage who shares with the author, not just background knowledge but also a set of presuppositions, sympathies and standards of what is pleasant and unpleasant, good and bad, right and wrong', respectively (Leech [1981] 2007: 259). The third and fourth discourse levels below the dotted line (*narrator-narratee*, *character-character*) let us enter the realm of fiction. In it, the teller controls the narration, reporting actions and letting us know about characters thoughts and words, overall creating a perspective by focalizing the narrative in a particular manner.

In the process of transmuting the discourse situation from narrative fiction to non-verbal music, as shown in the right column of Table 4.1, all communicative levels have a counterpart. *Author-reader* are replaced by *composer-listener*. In the same fashion, the abstractions *implied author* and *implied reader* are replaced by their homologous *implied composer* and *implied audience*. However, from the third level of description downwards (that is, below the dotted line which separates non-fictional categories from fictional ones), some difficulties are overtly noted relating the second set of questions posed in the previous section of this chapter: Who controls the fictional music story? Who is the teller of this set of 'connected vague events' (Toolan 2016: 130)? How does focalization operate in a music composition?

These queries have answers in narrative fiction. For instance, it is common knowledge that a piece of narrative fiction may neutralize some of the above mentioned communicative levels, affecting its focal point as a result. The fusion between narrator and character layer of description in 1st person narratives, can be taken as a good case of this situation. No story, however, can give up its teller as a narrative device through one or another voice. Conversely, for non-verbal music, even if different musical genres are also expected to exhibit different discourse situation schemes, the unanswered question about the lacking narrator remains. What else do all these results suggest?

Table 4.1 Discourse situation in narrative fiction and non-verbal music

Narrative fiction		
Context of situation (?)		
Adresser	**Message**	**Addressee**
AUTHOR		READER
IMPLIED AUTHOR		IMPLIED READER
NARRATOR		NARRATEE
CHARACTER		CHARACTER

The fantastic are diluted and subject to the rules generated by the development of this narrative strategy.

Discourse Situation: Music Interaction

At the If there were no telling voice controlling discursively a music narration, why is it that the story can still be perceived? How is it crafted? Along with Toolan's contribution to this discussion (2016: 142–3), I would like to bring forward further reflections on the matter which have been particularly useful in my search for a focalizing narrative voice. There are three aspects of Klorman's claims on the theory of *multiple agency* in chamber music that I are particularly relevant here. The first one has to do with *interaction*. Within the context of his analysis of Mozart's string quartet in G Major (K.387), we read: 'The above analysis is unusually concerned with *which instrument utters a particular musical statement and how the others respond*' (Klorman 2016: 121, emphasis added). My belief is that this stance, which may be seen to work smoothly for chamber music, also expands to other musical forms or genres, as it will be illustrated through the example below.

His second proposition serves particularly to the distinction between *fiction/non-fiction* narratives and the way they exhibit different discursive representations. Here, Klorman contrasts interaction in chamber music with the sonata form. The presence of what he calls a 'strong sense of mission and trajectory' in the later is signalled as the key concept in order to differentiate the development of the story for each of these aforementioned musical forms:

Non-verbal music		
Context of situation (?)		
addresser	Message	addressee
COMPOSER		
		LISTENER
IMPLIED COMPOSER	IMPLIED AUDIENCE	
NARRATOR ?		NARRATEE ?
INSTRUMENTAL event	INSTRUMENTAL event	

> The open-ended nature of conversation allows it to freely follow a meandering path, with new twists and turns introduced with phrases like 'by the way'. [...] Not so in musical *discourse*, where certain tonal evens are essential for the completion of the form and require the participation of all parties.
>
> Klorman 2016: 127, emphasis added

The third and last aspect turns toward *performance*. With explicit avoidance of the term *conversation*, multiple agency is defined as follows 'the notion that a chamber music score is, above all, *something to be played*, an encoded musical exchange in which each player assumes an individual character, similar in many respects to a theatrical script' (emphasis added). All in all, Klorman's (ibid.) ideas tackle three key concepts in our search of music narrativity as discourse: interaction, fiction and performance.

Table 4.2 represents the discourse situation of the opening events in Elgar's cello Concerto in E minor, Op. 85, particularly the first 19 opening bars (see Figure 4.1). In this diagram, musical discourse categories have been assigned the specific information coming from the piece. Thus, at the first communicative level, Edward Elgar addresses the *score/story* to the concrete listener, say Mr X in this case. The second level respectively corresponds to their abstractions: an early twentieth-century British composer addressing a twenty-first century Classical music lover. The concerto as a narration, then, occupies the third communicative level, but once more, it seems there is no teller. Only by reaching the character-character level of interaction, the development of the story can be again described. In this

Table 4.2 Discourse situation in the opening of Elgar's Cello Concerto

	Context of situation	
Addresser	**Message**	**Adressee**
COMPOSER		LISTENER
Edward Elgar		Mr. X
IMPLIED COMPOSER		IMPLIED AUDIENCE
20thC British composer		Classical music lover
NARRATOR		NARRATEE
(?)		(?)
CHARACTER		CHARACTER
Cello's event	(bars 1-5)	Woodwind's event
Woodwind's event		
		String's event

regard, *Elgar's Cello concerto* opening move has a sense of lengthy time duration in which there is no chance to get a breath, not a strong beat to rest until the end of the event in bar 5. In this fortissimo on an E note, the tonic clearly marks the end of the move, and it precedes a long rest, a lapse. Also in bar 5, the woodwind section (flute, fagot, oboe and clarinet) self-selects itself, not reopening the topic, not developing it with a bound opening move, but just repeating the end of the former cello event. They do it imitating the original event as they were giving time to next event. The woodwinds turn also selects harmonically on the dominant of Em the string section, which initiates the main theme, a new move in bar 8.

Conclusion

Results in this analysis suggest that it is in plays where the *story* is crafted through dramatic tension as it is in music. The story shares the same 'strong sense of mission and trajectory' (Klorman 2016: 127) that both fictional narratives or music sonata form entail. Alternatively, attributing an open-ended nature to conversation exchanges would be suitable for non-fictional instances of natural everyday verbal exchanges, not for dramatic interaction.

The analysis above also suggests that the discourse of non-verbal music, if perceived as a story, does not take the form of narrative. Tension and the flow of the aforementioned connected events is also achieved by interaction. If they are experienced as a fluent series of connected moves and compared to verbal narration, they could only be regarded as instances of free direct speech events, namely, utterances without a reporting clause.

In a way, this was subsidiarily tackled in Toolan (2016: 140). As part of his discussion of narrativity and the idea of themes in music and literature, *Macbeth* was chosen as the literary work to illustrate his ideas. Can anybody doubt Macbeth is a *story*? However, can be the story of Macbeth be regarded as a narration? Undoubtly not. As any other play, the story of *Macbeth* is crafted dramatically by interaction, and therefore, as it seems to be for the music story, it lacks narrative control.

In the same way the crafting of a story in a play is achieved through alternation of speech, adjacency music moves are linked one to the other selecting, being selected by the former one or by self-selecting themselves to build their story. Similarly, alternation in dramatic interaction also occurs by the allocation of turns into next speaker or by self-selection. Lapses, overlapping or repetitions are devices which contribute to craft the story. In Boykan's own words, 'it is useless to know that a motive is repeated, without taking into account when is repeated, without recognizing that motivic transformation is a response to a new situation, not just harmonic conceit, or decoration for the sake of "variety"' (2004: 3). Putting all these ideas together, and despite all literature about *music narrativity*, I would dare state that narrativity could be regarded as a deceptive term. Otherwise, the classical discursive dichotomy between *story* and *narration* become central for the perception of a music piece as a story.

Finally, there is one more element which relates the story in a play and in a music piece: *performance*. As dramatic discourse in literature needs performance to be completed, music discourse equally does. No matter linguists, literary critics and philologists look at the score as the ultimate object of study. Only when the magical moment the music text goes beyond the score and becomes performed, the music piece becomes real; just as the dramatic text does when it takes off from the page and gets on stage to tell its story directly to the audience.

Discursively, this scenario incorporates an extra communicative layer: the presence of the stage director, or the conductor/soloist in the case of music performance. Beyond the fictional crafting, the audience has the opportunity of attending a concrete *reading* of the score, as the audience attends a concrete reading of a play. Only when the music comes to life on stage, then, the conductor may be understood as a narrator, just as the director of a play does. In both cases, though, the interpreter and the theatre director are external participants to the fictionality implied in a dramatic play or music piece. However, it is my belief that this is the only case in which either a play or a music piece can be said to be externally *focalized* at a meta-textual discursive level. In the light of these final remarks, let me conclude returning to Elgar's concerto, specifically to the 1967 Jackeline Dupré performance at the Wood Lane studios, that vague dramatic story externally focalized by the conductor Daniel Barenboim and addressed to an invited audience; a dramatic story crafted through the interaction between the cello moves as performed by Jackeline Dupré at conversation with those moves allocated to the rest of the instruments as performed by the New Philharmonia Orchestra.[4] But this is a different story.

Acknowledgements

Special thanks to Prof Michael Toolan (U. of Birmingham, UK) for all the stimulating talks on music narrativiy during my visit to Birmingham in 2016; specially those about this cello concerto. I would also like to thank Prof. John Rea

(Schulic School of Music, McGill University, Montreal, Canada) for introducing me to Dr Klorman's recent research.

Notes

1. Evelyn Glennie was diagnosed profoundly deaf at the age of 12. The quoted excerpt comes from a 2013 talk. Here, she tells the audience how she feels music in her body. For a full account of her words, see: https://www.ted.com/talks/evelyn_glennie_how_to_truly_listen.
2. Major and their relative minor keys share the same key signature but they have a different tonic; relative minor scale start one and a half semitones below their major one. Also, major and their relative minor keys have a different degree distribution in the scale.
3. NOTE TEXT MISSING.
4. This performance is part of documentary film directed by Christopher Nupen, *Jacqueline Du Pré and the Elgar Cello Concerto* (1967).

References

Primary Sources

Beethoven, Ludwig. [1822] 1978. *Sonatas para piano (Vol. 4)*. Madrid: Real Musical. Spanish edition by Ramón Barce. Reprint of the original Wiener URTEXT edition.

Elgar, Edward. 1921. *Concerto in E minor Opus 85 for Violoncello and Orchestra*. Published by Masters Music Publications Inc. Reprint of the original Novello & company limited edition. Availale online: https://www.free-scores.com/free-sheet-music.php?partition_centrale=12480&compositeur=edward-elgar (accessed 25 February 2022).

Secondary Sources

Boykan, Martin. 2004. *Silence and Slow Time: Studies in Musical Narrative*. Lanham, MD: Scarecrow Press.

Dayan, Peter. 2006. *Music Writing Literature, from Sand via Debussy to Derrida*. Aldershot: Ashgate.

Glennie, Evelyn. 2003. 'How_to_truly_listen'. *TED*, February. Availabble online: https://www.ted.com/talks/evelyn_glennie_how_to_truly_listen (accessed 25 February 2022).

Jakobson, Roman. 1959. 'On Linguistic Aspects of Translation'. In Fang Achiles and Reuben Arthur Brower (eds), *On Translation*, 232–9. Cambridge, MA: Harvard University Press.

Klorman, Edward. 2016. *Mozart's Music of Friends: Social Interplay in the Chamber Works*. Cambridge: Cambridge University Press.

Leech, Geoffrey and Mick Short. [1981] 2007. *Style in Fiction*. London: Longman.

Nupen, Christopher. 1967. *Jacqueline du Pré and the Elgar Cello Concerto*. Omnibus, BBC1.

Sampson, Fiona. [2016] 2018. *Lyric Cousins: Poetry and Musical Form*. Edinburgh: Edinburgh University Press.

Steiner, George. 1995. 'What is Comparative Literature? An Inaugural Lecture Delivered before the University of Oxford on 11 October, 1994'. Oxford: Clarendon Press.

Toolan, Michael. 2016. 'Musical Narrativity'. In Raphaël Baro and Françoise Revaz (eds), *Narrative Sequence in Contemporary Narratology*, 130–50. Columbus, OH: Ohio State University Press.

Sampson, Fiona. [2016] 2018. *Lyric Cousins: Poetry and Musical Form*. Edinburgh: Edinburgh University Press.

Part Two

Hermeneutic Diaphaneity in Literary Studies

5

Adinkra Symbols

From Visual Art Messages to a Literary Research Methodology

Violetta Jojo Verge

Introduction

The Akan people from Ghana and Ivory Coast have developed a communication system during centuries based on the Adinkra symbols – explanation here for an ordinary reader – e.g. a set of symbolic drawings, having both evocative, decorative and ritual use.[1] These have allowed them to arrange both the physical and spiritual universe, facilitating to classify, encode and transmit, to the dead in funerals, messages about their experience in their religious, social, moral and political daily life. Hence, Adinkra, here, can be envisaged as a visual and substantive hermeneutical commentary emanating from these women writers to the living society, having in mind that aso ebi used to be practiced in the past only by women. Being attracted to the Adinkra symbols ever since I was a child in Ghana, when I grew up; I read and inquired about their meanings and utility because I always saw them everywhere. When, years later, I started my research and after recollecting feasible information I wanted to bring forward the knowledge and philosophy behind the symbols and use them in a new approach to African Literature. In order to achieve this, I elaborated a research perspective, stemming from Hall's theory of representation, where I interweave advances in literary studies, with the hermeneutic dimension of particular symbols, emphasizing parallels in the achievements of African women writers as a narrative web of Adinkra relations. The selection of Adinkra symbols to be analysed below is given in Figure 5.1.

a) NKYIMU   b) AKOBEN   c) NEA ONNIM NO SUA A, OHU   d) SANKOFA   e) ODENKYEM   f) ASASE YE DURU   g) EPA   h) AKOKO NAN

Figure 5.1 A selection of Adinkra symbols that are the object of the present analysis (own elaboration).

From Representation to Re-presentation: The Struggle of African Women Writers

The concept of 'representation' has been approached from a variety of perspectives, the most prominent of which stem from phenomenology (Husserl), hermeneutics (Ricoueur) or semiotics (cf. Fenk (1997) for an overview. For example, Sokolowski points out that the phenomenological theory of truth, rather than

> moving between mental or semantic entities and real entities, operates entirely in the domain of presentation. It distinguishes varieties in the kinds of presentation (the simple, the categorical, the propositional, the confirmatory) and speaks about the identities that are achieved within the new manifolds that these varieties introduce.
>
> Sokolowski 2000: 102

In my work, I rely on Stuart Hall's theory (1997), which regards 'representation' as an intermediary between concepts and language, through which we may refer both to the 'mundane', that is, the experienced world of objects or events, and to the imaginary, implying possible worlds of fictitious objects and events (Hall 1997: 17). Furthermore, the scholar emphasizes the importance of 'participants of culture' as factors giving meaning to objects, people or events (ibid., 3). This implied meaning, in turn, is contingent on the way they are represented as well as on the ensuing narratives about those objects, that is, words, stories told about them, images produced, or emotions evoked and associated with them, and finally, the way we classify them and construct ensuing axiology (ibid., 3). Hall adds that meaning is directly related to the construction of identity, related to 'questions of how culture is used to mark out and maintain identity within and difference between groups' (ibid., 3). This means that all kinds of elements are essential in the composition of texts, and so my interest in the concept of representation emanates not only from the literary but also from any other source.

Furthermore, Hall refers to Michel Foucault's crucial contribution to the advancement of the concept of representation, highlighting how the French philosopher diverged his attention to the importance of the production of knowledge and not only meaning in language. Hence, Foucault (1994) changed his object of study – a corpus of language – and substituted it by what he calls 'discourse', in which historical particulars and contexts, as well as the relations of power, play an important factor in representing and thus producing social knowledge. For him (1994), representation at this point is the production of knowledge, about something or someone, under the constraints of the historical moment and political power. Additionally, Foucault, who was interested in the observation of how the production of knowledge regulates the working of power in social practice, challenges the position of the subject. Hall uses Foucault's discussion of Velazquez's *Las Meninas* to expound the idea that we adopt the vantage point indicated by the discourse, and having identified with them, succumb to its meanings, and thus become its 'subjects' (Hall 1997: 60). For him, Foucault's powerful argument is that the meaning of this painting is always involved in a process of emerging and thus, never fixed. That being so implies that 'For the painting to work, the spectator, whoever he or she may be, must first 'subject' himself/ herself to the painting's discourse and, in this way, become the painting's ideal viewer, the producer of its meanings-its subject' (Hall 1997: 60).

In the case of this research, I used the term 'representation' with a hyphen 're-presentation' to highlight that there is a second chance, afresh, anew with respect to any previous idea or situation, which is particularly applicable to the creative output of African women writers. In trying to bring forward female characters and their realms, African female writers write back to their male peers, who mostly present female women characters either as silenced women or completely absent from any social and political scenario in their work. It was an ordeal for African women to write and when they did, it was difficult to publish. If they did, it was even harder to be read. Though what turned out to be the worst of all was that critics took no heed of their texts. Consequently, the term 're-presentation' also refers to the courageous act of many women writers, who had to try more than once. They did not give up writing; rather they kept on doing it until they got to be acknowledged as writers.

Kadiatu Kanneh (1998) agrees with Hall's explanation on the evolution of the concept of representation mentioned above. She explores texts that have installed biased discourses around race, depending on the historical time, the political ideology and economic aims. She observes how these discourses, associated to different fields and disciplines, have constructed with words, metaphors and images a corpus of knowledge about African peoples and their continent in diverse historical moments. Furthermore, she studies the cross-references that appear in different and sometimes contradicting narratives, which shed light on her suspicion of how many texts have been the launching pads for all sorts of ideas and images. Sometimes, these have interpreted and inevitably invented an idea of Africa and her peoples to suit the colonial machinery. Finally, Kanneh adds the element of race to Foucault's theoretical approach. Therefore, the addition of this aspect makes her theory suitable to explore the specific African experience. In this sense, I followed her strategy of bringing together the factors that constitute the cornerstones for the construction of an authorized image of Africa by outsiders. For example, in my analysis of Adinkra symbols, I focus on the issue of race and its effects on the representations of Africa and Africans, which have triggered the need of Africans to restore their identity, especially visible in the oeuvre of two landmark female writers; Ama Ata Aidoo's *Our Sister Killjoy* (1977) and Buchi Emecheta's *The Joys of Motherhood* (1979).

Kadiatu Kanneh not only relies on scientific or commercial texts but also on ethnographical works and historical narratives. Before her, this approach was pioneered by Edward Said (1994), who, focusing on the nineteenth- and twentieth-century modern Western empire, especially investigated novels as cultural forms, assuming their key importance in the creation of imperial experiences and attitudes. Moreover, Said insists on the need to not only focus on narrative fiction, but also pay attention to those cultural forms 'position in the history and world of empire' (ibid., xii). He highlights the importance of the effect of narratives of these stories:

> my basic point being that stories are at the heart of what explorers and novelists say about strange regions of the world; they also become the method colonized people use to assert their own identity and the existence of their own histories. The main battle in imperialism is over land, of course; but when it came to who owned the land, who had the right to settle and work on it, who kept it going, who won it back, and who now plans its future—these issues were reflected, contested, and even for a time decided in narrative.
>
> Ibid., xii–xiii

Kadiatu Kanneh (1998) has also inferred that those texts underscored the idea of the existence of different races and turned into a body of discourse on racism. First, she believes in the process of connecting time and comparing the narratives produced in the nineteenth century with those in early twentieth century. Second, she also thinks that it is important to examine the places in which those texts were produced. And, finally, she takes into account the diverse disciplines that framed writing into particular ideologies of the historical period with the corresponding authors' political engagement. This approach unveiled how the meaning of Africa was defined through the establishment of a corpus of narrative, which produced descriptions and definitions about Africa engrossing an imaginative concept and a body of knowledge about the continent and its peoples for diverse purposes. We should not forget that mostly non-Africans wrote those texts in the past:

> The movement between African and European contexts reveals how Africa and its identities have been crucially informed by the impact of knowledges and interests from *outside* the continent. The reading of literary texts alongside and against theoretical, political and ethnographic writings is intended to emphasise, [...] the necessity of approaching literary texts as a nexus for the re-articulation of—culturally and socially mediated—ideological material.
>
> Kanneh 1998:1

Homi K. Bhabba (1994: 34) influences Kanneh in the explanation of the 'in-between space' that will be used to stress the problems of confusing cultural diversity with cultural difference. Thus, this encounter makes reference to the cultural representation in 'this clash of signification on the borders and limits of cultures, which acknowledge and mediate cultural meaning always as the articulation of difference and otherness' (Kanneh 1998: 17). This last reference can be taken into account as a twofold opportunity to approach, on the one hand, diverse texts from more than one discipline in order to study and compare the representations of Africa and Africans, scrutinizing the question of race. On the other hand, to pin down the idea behind this research: a hyphenated 're-presentation' as explained above. Hence, in elaborating the analytical perspective, I relied on the authority of Kanneh's research as I shared her idea of including any literary narrative diverse sources. I also used texts that belong to other disciplines such as travel writing, ethno-philosophy, anthropology, ethnography and colonial literary works to accomplish my analysis.

Chikwenye Okonjo Ogunyemi's Vernacular Theory

In developing my approach, to Adinkra symbols, I have always preferred to search for an adequate framework that can suit the African experience and its particularity. Theories dealing with Africa and African texts are mostly emerging from the postcolonial theory. As indicated in the introduction, my goal is to imbricate achievements in African female literary studies with the hermeneutics trust of *aso ebi* cloth. In compliance with that, in this section I would like to present Chikwenye Okonjo Ogunyemi vernacular literary theory, which has allowed critics and scholars to read African women's texts under a new light. This discussion will serve as a background onto which I will present selected aspects of Adinkra symbols in the analytical section.

In contrast to *Toward the Decolonization of African Literature* (1985), in which the authors Chinweizu, Onwuchekwa Jemie and Ihechukwu Madubuike – the 'Bolekaja' group – prescribe, guide and criticize some African authors, Ogunyemi's monograph *Africa Wo/Man Palava* (1996) recompiles facts from the Nigerian ethnic groups' original oral myths, and compares them with her studies on some African women writers' early literary works. She elaborates a vernacular literary theory based on a multicultural and multilingual literary tradition. This theory springs from the oral Yoruba and the Igbo ethnic groups' myths, unavoidably intertwined with the pidgin and the English realities of the colonial and the postcolonial experience (cf. Ogunyemi 1996).

Ogunyemi's main trope for the creation of this approach is motherhood or mothering. She highlights the similarities among some African myths and Egyptian, Greek, Roman and Christian ones. To explore the African vernacular myths she starts with Osun, worshiped in the precolonial Yoruba-land as the water goddess. She is the variation 'on the theme of the great, ancestral mother in a hostile universe. Her greatness lies in her policy of containment of her anguish for the good of all' (ibid., 23). For Ogunyemi, Osun's myth is a blueprint for Nigerian women writers, and this can be expanded to many African women authors, who started to write in the second half of the twentieth century:

> Osun's story encapsulates several principles: motherhood, gender problems, woman's independence, fe/male interdependency, woman´s carrer, economics, aesthetics, domesticity, sustenance, fertility to ensure the future, interest in the environment, quarrel and mediation, *siddon look* tactics, that is, 'sit down and cogitate,' a belligerent form of pacifism.
>
> Ibid., 26

The truth and role of umpire or peacemaker that *Osetura/Esu* was expected to perform in this myth could be the same founding ground for African womanism, since Ogunyemi displays the idea behind this ideology in a very clear statement:

'In the womanist venture, four principles, call them the four C's – conciliation, collaboration, consensus and complementarity between women and men – predominate' (ibid., 126). The Nigerian academic further introduces the Yoruba divination text composed of 256 verses, known as *Odu*, who, as she explains, is the wife of the divination *orisa*, *Orunmila/Ifa*. In another version, she is *Obatal*'s wife, the creating *orisa*. Hence, Ogunyemi infers that *Odu*, that 'is a female essence', is at once connected with 'divination and creativity through wifehood' (ibid., 27).

Undoubtedly, Ogunyemi grounds her theory through placing this myth in the women's realm, and retrieves the authority of storytelling and writing from the men's exclusive hands. What is of paramount importance for the present discussion is that in order to develop her theory on the repetitive sequences, she brings in a significant analogy between cloth and the African women writers' texts. She deduces that the repetition of patterns in both African typical cloths and literature can inform of a particular tradition. In fact, she admits that she borrowed this idea from Anne Adams' talk at the University of Bayreuth in 1986, in which she compared some African women's texts and the *lappa*. According to Buchi Emecheta's glossary included in her novel *Kehinde*, the *lappa* is a 'traditional woman's costume, a length of cloth wrapped around the waist' (Emecheta 1994: 144). Ogunyemi (1996: 4) provides further details:

> The simple two or three yards of fabric is versatile: it can be used as a dress, a blanket, a pillow, a curtain or screen, a mattress or mat, a sheet, a bed cover, a tablecloth, an umbrella, headgear, a baby carrier, a sling, a wall decoration, or an *aju* to cushion and protect the head from the load it carries. Its common placeness ensures its position as a symbol of African womanhood.

Ogunyemi adds that the *lappa* is not only used by women as a wild card, but also by men to cover themselves at any time. The scholar stresses the use of the *lappa* as the soother for the heavy weight held by women on their heads, or the babies on their backs or on their way to and from markets or farms. Definitely, this Nigerian critic likens the *lappa* to African women's writing: 'Women's novels, like the *lappa*, are intended primarily for women who mostly bear burdens, yet they are indispensable for communal use' (Ogunyemi 1996: 4). Ogunyemi chooses to launch her vernacular theory based on the frame of reference of motherhood, though not from a feminist point of view in this case. Motherhood alludes to the condition of a woman as being a creator or engenderer, 'resulting in an intricately woven lappa with patterns replicated with slight variations, as with the Yoruba aso ebi'. For her, this concept rather belongs to the Yoruba people in Nigeria, meaning 'cloth for kin', and referring to the practice of wearing identical cloths 'at crowded affairs like weddings, funerals, chieftaincy, inaugurations, or political gatherings' (ibid., 10). Friends and families wear the same to satisfy their Yoruba traditions. The parallelism this critic finds between the *aso ebi* in Nigerian life and the Nigerian women's fiction urges her to use the *aso ebi* as a metaphor for the reassessment of African women's writing. She affirms that womanism[2] is the repetitive pattern that pervades their narrative. I lean on this statement of her theoretical discourse and the expanded idea of womanism with the four 'C's to include the social and political commitment and participation in many African women writers, especially Ama Ata Aidoo and Buchi Emecheta.

Okechukwu Nwafor has enriched this discussion explaining that aso ebi is a combined word where 'aso means cloth while ebì means family' (2013: 1). In addition to what Ogunyemi calls the practice of wearing, Nwafor asserts, based on his research on the Nigerian middle and lower classes in Lagos, that recently the 'aso ebì practice is predominantly an urban phenomenon' (2). His historical account traces this practice back to the times of colonial modernity, although also looks into contemporary African society as observed in his quotation from 'The Fabric of Friendship':

> In recent times it has become a city phenomenon and has diffused into other groups in Nigeria. *Also peoples from other West African sub-regions* engage in *aso ebì* activities and the practice has risen above family affiliation such that a stranger and an uninvited guest may seek recognition through *aso ebì*.
>
> Nwafor 2013: 3, emphasis added

These stressed words reaffirm that the essence or concept of the *aso ebi* is not limited to the Nigerian community. Therefore, I decided to approach both Ama Ata Aidoo and Buchi Emecheta as participating in the *aso ebi* celebration of writing, in which their repetitive patterns are not only limited to a gender role but also open out to other social and political aspects, which I will discuss later.

The Adinkra *Aso Ebi* Cloth as a Hermeneutic Scripture

W. Bruce Willis (1998: 1) asserts that the translation for the term Adinkra is 'a message one gives to another when departing'. The burial ceremony is celebrated as a final rite of passage from this world to the most important world, the abode of the dead ancestors, who intercede for the living in all their affairs. Rooted in the oral tradition of the Akan people, as Willis clearly pinpoints (Willis 1998: 43), they are a cultural element which links the past and the present as well as today and the future. To this, G. F. Kojo Arthur (2001: 10) adds:

> Communication can be accomplished through the use of discrete graphical representation of commonly held ideas and views. In this way, ostensibly, 'non-literate' societies may produce, through the use of their symbols and signs, a literature which pervades their environment by being emblazoned on their clothes, tools, and other common material artifacts.

For him, the Adinkra symbols are icons and metaphors that stand for a whole system of thought, religious belief, social behaviour and political organization based on a common experience that hold together the Akan people (cf. 12). His analysis reveals the richness of the kaleidoscopic interpretations that his re-reading of the Adinkra cloth has conveyed. He concludes that if we take into account variables such as the colours of the cloth background and the infinite combinations of the symbols, then we can read each Adinkra cloth as an illustrated book, in which knowledge is stored through its own narrative (cf. 123).

The Adinkra symbols do not conform to a static system of illustrations and thoughts. Every experience has yielded a new form for artistic expression. Nowadays, the symbols can be found everywhere as decorative designs not only on the funeral cloths and others, but also carved into furniture such as the sacred stool, moulded into facades of government buildings, welded to jewellery and other adornments for daily use. It is significant to remark that this is not a dead system. It continuously renews itself, maintaining its abiding quality of communicating knowledge, and adapting to fit the needs of the Akan community's changes with the requirements of the present everyday life.

Kofi Anyidoho intertwines both artistic works and Adinkra symbols with Ogunyemi's theory (2000: 3, emphasis added) regarding the repetitive patterns of the *aso ebi*:

> The cultural landscape of Ghana as seen in her literary and performing arts is dominated by an amazing range of defining metaphors and symbols,[3] of which a certain core group constitute various *patterns of recurrence*. While some of these metaphors emphasize achievement and celebration, others underscore the need for critical evaluation of self.

The evolution of the Adinkra symbols is due to the capacity for adaptation of the African community. It is no wonder that, in addition to the traditional old symbols, the Akan Christians have incorporated new colours and symbols that represent Good Friday or Easter. Although the Akan people constitute a large community from diverse regions in Africa, Kojo Arthur tends to unify their cultural and religious idiosyncrasy and unique and unified institutions. However, this author acknowledges that the commercial contacts with the Islamic African community has caused a cultural exchange where both groups have lent and borrowed from each other words and symbols (Arthur 2001: 21–3). His research compares the diverse theories regarding the origin and history of the ideograms or ideographs, and wonders if these symbols can be understood as a writing system. Then he delves into the essence of his analysis: the Akan cloth. His intention is to focus on the function of the Akan cloth as a communication mechanism. Kojo Arthur quotes Susan Domowitz's *Wearing Proverb: Anyi Names for Printed Factory Cloth*: 'proverb cloths offer an accessible public voice to those who are constrained to silence' (Arthur 2001: 19). In talking so, she particularly refers to the Adinkra cloth. Arthur also quotes Kwesi Yankah's *The Proverb in the Context of Akan Rhetoric: A Theory of Proverb Praxis*, related to the 'textile rhetoric':

> Yankah on the other hand, notes that the cloth design, along with the mode of wearing it may be used 'not just to praise political heroes, to commemorate historical events, and to assert social identities, but also as a form of rhetoric—*a channel for the silent projection of argument*'.
>
> Arthur 2001: 19, emphasis added

In selecting both quotations, Arthur insists on the aspect of the communicative power of the Adinkra cloth, in which symbols speak out the silence of the people dressed in that way. I have stressed the last sentence in the quotation above, since it is crucially related to Ogunyemi's literary trope: her analogy between cloth and women's texts and the reception of those texts. Kojo Arthur also adds that the Adinkra cloth is not only used for the funeral and other sacred ceremonies, but also for the swearing ceremony of the king and the queen mother. Hence, it is a cloth worn by both male and female members of the Akan society and also offered as a 'parting cloth' when someone is sent to exile (Arthur 2001: 20–5). He highlights the significance of the colours used for the printing of the Adinkra symbols and the background of the cloth. Furthermore, Kojo Arthur (ibid., 20) defends that the Adinkra symbols become a 'multilayered ideogrammatic language', in which the culturally specific becomes at once universal in dealing with concepts common to everyman. In any case, Kojo Arthur's most relevant affirmation for my argument is that 'the adinkra cloth is pregnant with text', and that 'the symbols and the patterns of stamping them in the cloth constitute text that needs to be examined for what it encodes' (ibid., 26). This feature of communication, which transforms the Adinkra cloth from a mere piece of material into a cloth embellished with woven voices emerging from the printed symbols, will turn into an essential issue in my approach to both Aidoo and Emecheta.

The Analysis: Adinkra Symbols as a Pre-text Voicing Re-presentation

I embrace the analogy between some African women writers' texts and the practice of the *aso ebi* cloth – as this latter is practiced among African women – as Ogunyemi suggests in her theory. Even though there are particularities that diverge, Ogunyemi's analogy is based on the similarities that converge. She equates the repetitive designs in the *aso ebi* cloth of all the African women, who belong to a group in an event, to the recurrent patterns of thought or themes that create similarities in African women writers' texts. This recurrence unveils a fascinating tradition in African women writer.

By bringing together various theoretical approaches such as Ogunyeni's position, Kojo Arthur's affirmation that the Adinkra cloth could become a text, and Bruce Willis's affirmation that the Adinkra symbols are clearly linked to proverbs and the oral tradition of the Akan people. Thus, I conceived my research as an *aso ebi* activity, in which I have chosen Ama Ata Aidoo and Buchi Emecheta out from the growing group of West African women writers. Both are wearing the same cloth printed with Adinkra symbols that speak out their stories and their worries. These re-presentations are loaded with narratives about political, social and spiritual predicaments. Their divergences in the *aso ebi* cloth constitute the characteristics of the individuality in each writer. Meanwhile, the similarities lie on the recurrent patterns that form the aso ebi, which highlight the existence of a tradition that Ogunyemi analyses when theorizing on the West African women writers' narrative. These recurrent motifs contain the encoded traditional, social and political messages related to the Adinkra symbols I analyse in this research.

My approach focuses on analysing the Adinkra symbols as a pre-text in which I studied the contents related to the tenets of these symbols. Therefore, each part fits to the message that each symbol conveys and its relationship with Aidoo's and Emecheta's narratives. Now let me probe into the divisions of the imaginary

Adinkra *aso ebi* cloth and extract the symbols that create similarities and individualities. Each symbol with its proverb and meaning will become the mouthpiece of the narrative that decodes the messages of the voices emerging from previously silenced people (Figure 5.1).

Each symbol guides the readers to take heed of the main worries, ideas and themes, which some African women writers re-present. Sometimes they converge into common grounds and on other occasions diverge into their own particularities. Each symbol is framed in the ideas I presented above, regarding the issue of re-presentation in diverse texts from other disciplines in addition to the literary narrative. At the same time, I consider some social, political and scientific theories, which have built up a girdle of racism around many texts from previous decades that are now subjected to observation here.

Nkyimu

I have selected this Adinkra symbol (Figure 5.1a) as a point of departure for my inquiry since it represents the idea of proficiency and intelligence required to divide the cloth before printing the symbols on it with the natural dyes. I assimilated the sectioning of an Adinkra cloth with both the methodology I developed and the general organization of the sections in this research, my own work mimicking the Ghanaian craftsmen.

The starting point is the concept of re-presentation, which is essential in my approach. In this sense, the methodology I have followed relies on the cross-sectional sources developed above, especially Stuart Hall's elucidation on the evolution of the concept of representation, Kadiatu Kanneh's race factor departing from Foucault's idea of representation, Edward Said's assertions regarding the importance of the colonial narratives about the strange peoples and the places in the world, and Franz Fanon's analysis on the psychological effects of colonialism. All these cross-sectional approaches will serve to reveal the doubly marginalized condition of African women as both women and writers. Therefore, the meaning encoded in my hyphenated term 're-presentation' conveys the anew chance to discuss and freshly present again, having also in mind the issue of race.

Additionally, I inquired into Chikwenye Okonjo Ogunyemi's concept of motherhood, which creates or engenders common threads that weave metaphorically a cloth called *lappa* in Nigeria. And I also embraced Ogunyemi's analogy between the text and the *aso ebi*, accomplishing the function of creating a kin group through the use of repetitive patterns. All this has helped to turn my corpus into an Adinkra *aso ebi* so as to study both the thoughts and lessons embedded in the new re-presentation of Africa and Africans and the forms of art used to achieve this goal.

Akoben

This symbol (Figure 5.1b) stands for a horn that is blown to call the people to come together and do something or help the rest of the community. Thus, I introduce the external elements that, in addition to the inherent desire of becoming writers, have prodded West African writers to balance stories about Africa and Africans, as if they were blowing the *Akoben* horn for the community of writers.

Chinua Achebe's insistence on putting right the image of his people has made him call for a new self-representation by Africans themselves. Indeed, this aspiration encouraged both Ama Ata Aidoo and Buchi Emecheta. Aidoo wanted to become a writer ever since she was a girl at school; exactly as Buchi Emecheta who had also fancied to become a writer. Both have written to improve and go further the African male self-representation by adding the African women's voice in their new re-presentation.

In order to organize the effect of those external factors that moved African intellectuals to re-present themselves, I have relied on Sarah Robinson and Alastair Niven's (2016) view on how the image of Africa and Africans was downtrodden in the writings of David Livingstone, Mary Kingsley and Joseph Conrad, calling attention to the power of literary discourse when it comes to distorting people and their land. I have also depended on Dorothy Hammond and Alta Jablow's (1992) reading of more than 500 works of fiction and non-fiction by British authors about sub-Saharan Africa from the sixteenth through to the twentieth centuries. Gaurav Desai's expanded definition of the concept 'colonial library' (2001) has served me to show the epistemological colonization of the 'native African minds', and has derived in what I call a body of discourse and counter-discourse about Africa and Africans generated by the colonizers, colonialists and colonized. Likewise, both Frantz Fanon and Edward Said have yielded enough argumentation to justify the idea of the *Akoben* (war horn) calling African writers to the action of self-representation, which is extended to women writers in this research.

Finally, Chinua Achebe's critical essays centred my attention on the issue of race. Most of the 'colonial library' books demean Africans and this, as if it were an *Akoben*, motivated Achebe to start writing about his people and country.

Furthermore, his writing turned into the *Akoben* that called other writers to recover Africa's lost dignity. Definitely, this stimulated Ama Ata Aidoo and Buchi Emecheta to write from their own point of view their self re-presentation as African women.

Nea Onnim No Sua A, Ohu

This significant symbol (Figure 5.1c) conveys a very popular message for West African peoples. It translates into, 'If you no know you go know,' as any Ghanaian would repeat in diverse social situations. It suggests that only through the acquisition of knowledge can one live and grow. It urges people to keep on learning in order to keep flowing with life.

Achebe defends the writer's function as a teacher who regenerates society. Franz Fanon's overcoming of the racial inferiority complex in Africans or Nadine Gordimer's insistence that only a committed writer can take the responsibility of writing for the sake of education and change, are among the clear examples I have followed to demonstrate the necessity for improvement in African society in two decades. Along with it, special emphasis is also given to how African women writers were committed in three ways: 'as a writer, as a woman and as a Third World person' (Ogundipe-Leslie 1987: 10). Within this late consideration, I deal with the issue of labelling these African women's writings as feminist literature. Both Ama Ata Aidoo's and Buchi Emecheta's rejection to this label is delineated through Emecheta's process of teaching the Igbo cultural particulars and their traditions, and Aidoo's moral, social and political lessons. Thus, I appreciate that these authors re-present the problems with the only aim of teaching for change. Or, as the symbol *Nea Onnim No Sua A, Ohu* suggests, one can live and grow only through the acquisition of knowledge.

Sankofa

This is one of the most deeply rooted Adinkra symbols (Figure 5.1d) since it calls for looking back to ancestral art forms and culture so as to recover African identity. Precisely, this was banished during the colonization period and further. For W. Bruce Willis (1998), *Sankofa* is the icon that stands for African cultural awakening, inviting to bring from the past what is precious to construct a new prosperous future. Moreover, Anyidoho (2000) puts forward what he calls 'The *Sankofa* principle' to explain the recurrent attitude of contemporary Ghanaian writers and art performers of intertwining both the present and past to endow their artworks with proposals for the future.

After the independence of Ghana, UNESCO encouraged African intellectuals and politicians to establish an agenda for the revival of African culture. Kwame Nkrumah, the first Ghanaian president, was one of the pioneers in this endeavour. Moreover, intellectuals, writers, poets and playwrights have participated in this re-emergence of the African identity. For example, Kayper-Mensah wrote his poems on some Adinkra symbols as a way of ensuring the regeneration of old traditions, so as to keep on transmitting the ancient vernacular knowledge of Africans.

At that point, I bring into discussion intellectuals such as Chinua Achebe – inviting artists to bring back through memories and imagination the history and stories of their people; Ngügï Wa Thiong'o – dealing with the idea of setting Africa as the central point of departure to learn other cultures and his desire to decolonize the educational system in his country re-evaluating oral tradition. Chinweizu, Onwuchekwa Jemie and Ihechukwu Madubuike's recommendation to render into English all the African resources from the traditional proverbs, jokes, legends, metaphors and other stylistic features, in such a way that they conserve the African flavour; and Abiola Irele's legitimacy of embracing the oral realm into the written texts.

Consequently, I intertpret how both Aidoo and Emecheta accomplish the *Sankofa* maxim of looking back to get the gems, and divide their behaviour intro three main modes: correspondence, duplication and substitution. Just like any *aso ebi*, this Adinkra *aso ebi* will reveal to have similarities and particularities in its re-presentation.

Odenkyem

This symbol (Figure 5.1e) looking more like a turtle represents, in fact, a crocodile, which is considered an animal able to live in and out of water. It conveys a message of the importance of flexibility and prudent adaptability, since in these lies the wisdom of overcoming difficulties for the sake of survival.

Under this Adinkra symbol, I will focus on the issue of language. Chinua Achebe debunks Roscoe's idea that the African literature written in European languages can only be considered as an appendage, irritating many African writers and intellectuals (Arndt 1998 63). Ngügï Wa Thiong'o's critical essays and conferences have always proposed the idea of writing in African languages and then, if necessary, translating the works into European languages. F. Abiola Irele (2001) acknowledges that the emerging African literature is challenging the Western classical canon and trying to become different. On the other hand,

Chinua Achebe defends the idea of embracing the English language, although with the condition of adapting it to represent the African particularities in the literary works, promising to 'do unheard of things with it' (Achebe 1976: 9).

This debate on the issue of language conveys an analysis on Buchi Emecheta's strategies to accomplish her re-presentations, intertwining English and pidgin, Igbo and Yoruba languages. I relied heavily on Susan Arndt's nomenclature and specific terms so as to organize my explanation of this phenomenon in Emecheta's use of language to re-present the cultural particularities of her people. In the case of Aidoo's strategies, it is especially seen in her combination of both Mfantse and English. In looking for the origins of the African narratives both Aidoo and Emecheta draw from diverse sources to produce their African works in the first two decades after independence. Ngügï Wa Thiong'o (1993, 1997) serves as the launching pad for this discussion, since during the 1980s his intention was to ground the African novel roots in the African oral literature. Moreover, Ali Mazrui et al. (1999) were aware about the issue of genre related to the African literary written productions ever since they appeared in the 1930s. Chinua Achebe's process of re-storying, which was necessary to overcome the trauma of dispossession that Africans experienced, implies the use of the traditional cultural resources for the new written narratives.

Encouraged by Odamtten's work (1994) I have embraced a term linked to science to provide African writing a new rightful label: 'African polyphyletic literary category,' which best fits to this new written literature that sprouts from so many origins. This produces a kind of eclecticism, which is mainly based on the diverse sources both Aidoo and Emecheta include in their narrative. In this sense, they participate of the Adinkra symbol, *Odenkyem*, in which the importance of flexibility and prudent adaptability are necessary to overcome difficulties and for the sake of survival. In the case of these two writers, their narrative, interviews and miscellaneous pieces have demonstrated the successful combination of vernacular elements and a new literary re-presentation.

Asase Ye Duru

This symbol (Figure 5.1f) suggests that the Earth, which is heavier than the sea, sustains life. It is like a mother that gives life, sustains her children, and cuddles them when they die to bury them in her womb again. In the Adinkra *aso ebi* that stands for texts in both Aidoo and Emecheta, this symbol acquires a holistic dimension. The messages emanating from the previous discourses on African Mother Earth have created a distorted image that has blown the *Akoben* – war horn – for the Africans to set right this undesirable situation. Among these repairers are both Aidoo and Emecheta with their re-presentations. Through the combination of both Kadiatu Kanneh's considerations on some writers' political and economic commitments to suit their engagements with the powers in command, and Ngugi Wa Thiong'o's idea about the spiritual connection between land and people, we come close to understand both Ama Ata Aidoo's and Buchi Emecheta's Adinkra *aso ebi*.

I included diverse approaches such as Kanneh's categories: the experiential, the visual and the historical, to analyse the evolution of the meaning of Africa. Mudimbe's argumentation is based on the deformity and discontinuity of the discourse on African history, which is based on the ideological and sociological discourse about Africa. Taking into account Sister Joseph Thérèse Agbasiere's analysis on the history and identity of the *Ibi* people, and Cheik Anta Diop's defence of the historical connectedness in order to create a historical consciousness of a people, Emecheta's works present a new historical narrative that I consider to be a re-presentation of her people's history. In the case of Aidoo's texts, Cheik Anta Diop's thought is promising for Aidoo's pan-Africanist vision on the discourse of the African peoples' historical connections (1983: 59–68).

The last two categories – experiential and visual – proposed by Kanneh are seen in how both Aidoo and Emecheta perceive and re-present the geographical notions about Africa. For example, in examining how African economy greatly depends on women's efforts, especially those from the rural world, the markets appear as a space for economic, social and political interaction. If Emmanuel Obiechina (1975) considers the literature associated to popular Onitsha market as the cradle of the African novel, both Aidoo and Emecheta confirm that some African markets and the peoples involved in them present the African society's complexities, including the differences between rural and urban spaces, which are re-presented in these writers' fiction. Finally, African Mother Earth has been continually sustaining life at the historical, experiential and visual levels as the symbol *Asase Ye Duru* suggests, as well as protecting all its sons and daughters.

Epa

The Adinkra symbol *Epa* (Figure 5.1g) represents two cuffs, and they refer to enslavement. Although this ideogram is related to the concepts of law, order, justice and control, I analysed it as a representation of the slave trade and other kinds of enslavement and subjugation.

J. D. Fage and William Tordoff's *A History of Africa* (2002) have been enlightening to discern how both Emecheta and Aidoo re-present all kinds of enslavement. Regarding Aidoo's treatment of slavery, I have followed Anyidoho's analysis on the slave forts spread throughout the slave coast of Ghana, which demonstrates how these have become a significant metaphor in Ghanaian culture (2000: 13). Moreover, Kwadwo Opoku-Agyemang's approach on the stone buildings as the source of an infinite number of thoughts and thousands of images runs parallel to his affirmation that, 'Slavery is the living wound under the patchwork of scars' (2000: 23).

The two cuffs in the Adinkra symbol *Epa* fit the postcolonial enslavement that Aidoo re-presents in her work, such as silence, skin colour, religion, language, inferiority complex, easy money and the yoke of neo-colonialism. In the case of Buchi Emecheta's fiction, her narratives of enslavement, in which the enslaved characters do not complain about the 'cuffs', but she does. I pinpoint profitability and survival as justifications her characters offer to explain the slave trade that takes place in the markets. At that point, Emecheta is re-presenting the new kinds of bondage through which the enslaved people only change masters.

Akoko Nan

This Adinkra symbol (Figure 5.1h) graphically stands for the hen's feet as Bruce Willis and Kojo Arthur affirm. It represents protective parenting and parental admonition. Its aim is to correct the behaviour of younger people for their own benefit. Commitment and responsibility are crucial to accomplish this hard task in writing. Aidoo's self-infliction is one of the causes her writing has been neglected by the African male critics, although there already was the tradition of self-assessment practice in the Ghanaian theatrical performances (Aidoo 1971: 14). She has washed her people's dirty linens in public. Furthermore, Kofi Anyidoho defends that the idea of self-appraisal already existed in the traditional Ghanaian drama and oral narrative.

To examine oneself and one's people demands to travel or be away from one's hometown, as Ogunyemi has articulated in her theory around the term 'Been-toism' (1996: 264). This is related to the common terms 'been-to' or 'bintu', used mostly in English-speaking West African countries to identify those who have been to other places away from their original birthplace. The important issue here is the displacement that endows the displaced person with a double vision that causes change in the perception of reality as Homi Bhabha also afirms in *The Location of Culture*.

The tradition of self-examination serves to approach the works of both Emecheta and Aidoo and analyse the two possibilities for reprimanding: what do you do that causes hurt to others? And what do you do to yourself? Aidoo exposes the African maladies in the 1960s and 1970s and the heritage of the colonial and postcolonial eras. Meanwhile, Emecheta warns about the influence of the obsolete traditions coming from a remote past, which were still imposed in the first half of the twentieth century and still present in some African countries. This attitude has served to awake Africans and revise 'where the rain is beating them'. Achebe uses this expression – a Nigerian saying – on numerous occasions, referring to the search for the reasons behind any problem. Definitely both Aidoo's and Emecheta's intentions correlate to the *Akoko Nan* symbol, suggesting commitment and responsibility through protection and parental admonition.

Conclusion

Finally, to sum up, the route I have chosen as a methodology for my research can be related to hermeneutics on a twofold dimension. Starting with Michel Foucault's and Stuart Hall's concepts of re-presentation to finish with the Adinkra symbols whose philosophical basis preserve tradition and explain how the African world establishes its relationship with culture. I demonstrate how the Adinkra symbols I analyse are extremely useful to understand the physical and spiritual universe of some African writers. To achieve this, I have added Kojo Arthur's theoretical approach to those symbols he understands as a written system. His research also delves into the essence of the Akan cloth, which reaffirms the functions of this symbolic cloth as a communication mechanism. As regards to representation, Kadiatu Kanneh agrees with Hall's explanation of the evolution of the concept of representation mentioned above. She explores texts that have installed biased discourses around race, depending on the historical time, the political ideology and economic aims. My conclusive contribution to this field rests on the use of the hyphenated term re-presentation, to highlight that there is a second chance, afresh, anew with respect to any previous idea or situation. In this sense, African women writers bring forward women characters and their realms by writing back to their male peers, who mostly present women characters either as silence or completely absent entities from any social and political scenario in their work. For this reason, I have included references to Ama Ata Aidoo and Buchi Emecheta as her novels may be considered reflections on the Adinkra symbology and how to read it into their novels.

Notes

1 The Adinkra symbols are initially stamped on traditional cloths used during a funeral ceremony. See, e.g.: http://www.adinkra.org/htmls/adinkra_index.htm (accessed 6 May 2023).
2 Womanism is the theory that embraces both 'Alice Walker's theory of black woman's identit' and 'an affirmation of motherhood' as the central issue (Newell 2006: 152). This theory focuses on the African women's oppression, although seeking communal solidarity through conciliation with men since both genders become supplementary. Recall that for Ogunyemi, African womanism is also based on the four 'C's, 'conciliation, collaboration, consensus and complementarity between women and men' (1996: 126), as I mentioned above.
3 Kofi Anyidoho particularly refers to the Adinkra symbols here.

References

Achebe, Chinua. 1976. 'Colonialist Criticism'. *Morning Yet on Creation Day*, 3–24. New York: Anchor.
Agbasiere, Joseph Thérèse. 2000. *Women in Igbo Life and Thought*. London: Routledge.
Aidoo, Ama Ata. 1971. 'Commitment'. *Burning Issues in African Literature. Cape Coast English Department Workpapers*, Special Issue, 1: 10–14.
Aidoo, Ama Ata. 1977. *Our Sister Killjoy*. London: Longman.
Anyidoho, Kofi. 2000. 'National Identity and the Language of Metaphor'. In Kofi Anyidoho and James Gibbs (eds), *FonTomFrom: Contemporary Ghanaian Literature, Theatre and Film*, 1–22. Amsterdam: Rodopi.
Arndt, Susan. 1998. *African Women's Literature: Orature and Intertexuality*. Trans. Isabel Cole. Bayreuth: Bayreuth University.
Arthur, G. F. Kojo. 2001. *Cloth as Metaphor: (Re)Reading the Adinkra Cloth Symbols of the Akan of Ghana*. Legon: Centre for Indigenous Knowledge System.
Bhabha, Homi. 1994. *The Location of Culture*. London: Routledge.
Chinweizu, Onwuchekwa Jemie and Ihechukwu Madubuike. 1985. *Toward the Decolonization of African Literature: African Fiction and Poetry and Their Critics*. London: KPI.
Davidson, Basil. [1966] 1992. *Africa in History: Themes and Outlines*. London: Phoenix.
Desai, Gaurav. 2001. *Subject to Colonialism: African Self-Fashioning and the Colonial Library*. Durham, NC: Duke University Press.

Diop, Cheik Anta. 1983. 'De la identidad cultural'. *La afirmación de la identidad cultural y la formación de la conciencia nacional en el África contemporánea*. Trans. Pedro L. Gómez. UNESCO, 59–68. Barcelona: Serbal.

Donowitz, Susan. 1992. 'Wearing Proverb: Anyi Names for Printed Factory Cloth'. *African Arts*, 25 (3): 82–7.

Emecheta, Buchi. 1979. *The Joys of Motherhood*. Oxford: Heinemann Educational, 1994.

Emecheta, Buchi. 1994. *Kehinde*. Oxford and Ibadan: Heinemann Educational Publishers.

Fage, J. D. and William Tordoff. 2002. *A History of Africa*. London: Routledge.

Fanon, Frantz. 1986. *Black Skin, White Mask*. Trans. Charles Lam Markmann. London: Pluto.

Fanon, Frantz. 2001. *The Wretched of the Earth*. Trans. Constance Farrington. London: Penguin.

Fenk, August. 1997. 'Representation and Iconicity'. *Semiotica*, 115 (3/4): 215–34.

Foucault, Michel. 1994. 'Las Meninas'. *The Order of Things: An Archaeology of the Human Science*, 3–16. New York: Vintage.

Hall, Stuart (ed.). 1997. *Representation: Cultural Representations and Signifying Practices*. Milton Keynes: Open University.

Hammond, Dorothy and Alta Jablow. 1992. *The Africa that Never Was: Four Centuries of British Writing about Africa*. Prospect Heights, IL: Waveland.

Irele, F. Abiola. 2001. *The African Imagination: Literature in Africa and the Black Diaspora*. Oxford: Oxford University Press.

Kanneh, Kadiatu. 1998. *African Identities: Race, Nation and Culture in Ethnography, Pan-Africanism and Black Literature*. London: Routledge.

Mazrui, Ali A., Mario de Andrade, M'hamed Alaoui Abdalaoui, Daniel P. Kunene and Jan Vansina. 1999. 'The Development of Modern Literature since 1935'. Ali A. Mazrui (ed.), *General History of Africa, Volume 8: Africa since 1935*, 553–81. Oxford: James Currey, UNESCO.

Mudimbe, V. Y. 1988. *The Invention of Africa: Gnosis, Philosophy and the Order of Knowledge*. London: James Currey.

Mudimbe, V. Y. 1994. *The Idea of Africa*. Bloomington and Indianapolis, IN: Indiana University Press.

Newell, Stephanie. 2006. *West African Literatures: Ways of Reading*, Oxford Studies in Postcolonial Literatures in English. Oxford and New York: Oxford University Press.

Newell, Stephanie (ed.). 1997. *Writing African Women: Gender, Popular Culture and Literature in West Africa*. London and Atlantic Highlands, NJ: Zed Books.

Nwafor, Okechukwu. 2013. 'The Fabric of Friendship: *Aso Ebi* and the Moral Economy of Amity in Nigeria'. *African Studies*, 72 (1): 1–18.

Obiechina, Emmanuel. 1975. *Culture, Tradition and Society in the West African Novel*, African Studies Series, 14. Cambridge: Cambridge University Press.

Odamtten, Vincent O. 1994. *The Art of Ama Ata Aidoo: Polylectics and Reading against Neocolonialism*. Gainesville, FL: University Press of Florida.

Ogundipe-Leslie, Molara. 1987. 'The Female Writer and Her Commitment'. In Eldred Durosimi Jones (ed.), *Women in African Literature Today*, vol. 15, 5–13. Oxford: James Currey.

Ogunyemi, Chikwenye Okonjo. 1983. 'Buchi Emecheta: The Shaping of a Self'. *Komparatistische Hefte*, 8: 65–77.

Ogunyemi, Chikwenye Okonjo. 1996. *Africa Wo/Man Palava: The Nigerian Novel by Women*. Chicago, IL: University of Chicago Press.

Ojo-Ade, Femi. 1983. 'Female Writers, Male Critics'. *African Literature Today: Recent Trends in the Novel*. Vol. 13, 158–79. London: Heinemann.

Opoku-Agyemang, Kwadwo. 2000. 'Cape Castle: The Edifice and the Metaphor'. In Kofi Anyidoho and James Gibbs (eds), *FonTomFrom: Contemporary Ghanaian Literature, Theatre and Film*, , 23–8. Amsterdam: Rodopi.

Robinson, Sarah and Alistair Niven. 2016. *Discourses of Empire and Commonwealth: 192*, Cross/Cultures. Leiden: Brill.

Said, Edward W. 1994. *Culture and Imperialism*. New York: Vintage.

Sokolowski, Robert. 2000. *Introduction to Phenomenology*. Cambridge: Cambridge University Press.

Wa Thiong'o, Ngũgĩ. 1993. *Moving the Centre: The Struggle for Cultural Freedoms*. London: James Currey.

Wa Thiong'o, Ngũgĩ. 1997. *Decolonising the Mind: The Politics of Language in African Literature*. London: James Currey.

Willis, W. Bruce. 1998. *The Adinkra Dictionary: A Visual Primer on the Language of Adinkra*. Washington, DC: The Pyramid Complex.

Yankah, Kwesi. 1989. *The Proverb in the Context of Akan Rhetoric: A Theory of Proverb Praxis*. Frankfurt au Main: Peter Lang.

6

Hermeneutical Narratives of the European Colonization in Africa in Graham Greene's *A Burnt-Out Case* and Abdulrazak Gurnah's *Desertion*

Beatriz Valverde

Introduction

In his essays and lectures, Chinua Achebe often railed against the European critics' depiction of African authors – and by extension all Africans – as 'unfinished Europeans who with patient guidance would grow up' (Achebe 1988: 46) and develop a European identity.[1] Following this train of thought, Achebe ultimately stated that white writers should stop writing fiction about Africa altogether, since even when they were trying to be helpful showing the devastating effect of European colonization of the continent, white authors did fail to understand Africa and ended up essentially perpetuating existing stereotypes (Allen 2012: 118).

Graham Greene set various literary works in different territories in Africa: a travel book, *Journey without Maps* (1936), a novelist journal, *In Search of a Character* (1961) and two novels – *The Heart of the Matter* (1948) and *A Burnt-Out Case* (1960). In reference to Greene, Achebe stated that his representation of Africa in the aforementioned works did not reinforce existing stereotypes, mainly since '[h]e didn't want to explain Africans to the world. He made limited claims and wasn't attempting to be too profound' (Phillips 2003). Greene scholarship, however, has argued that Greene used Africa as the scene for his spiritual explorations (Roos 2009: 59). In addition, scholars have affirmed that in his portrayal of Africa and the Africans, the British writer displayed an underlying Eurocentric view which 'reinforced and spread the idea of physical and social differences between the Europeans and the non-European races, rendering the latter an inferior position to the former' (Aladaylah 2012: 122).[2] What is more, Mazumder claims that Greene's portrayal of non-white characters as 'either naïve, illiterate, or quarrelsome and greedy' (2021: 114)[3] indicates an obvious othering and marginalization of the non-Europeans in the novel, in contrast with the sympathetic presentation of the whites as the good characters (ibid., 113).[4]

Asked in an interview about Achebe's statement on the convenience of white authors not writing fiction about Africa, the recent Nobel Prize winner Abdulrazak Gurnah observed: 'I don't think Achebe is right in that advice, or whatever you might call it—prescription? I always feel: let anybody write about whatever they want, then we'll read it and make up our minds' (Allen 2012: 118). In this vein, what Gurnah advocates is a critical dialectical interpretation on the part of the reader of any fictional representation of Africa.[5] In his view, this hermeneutical activity will help to better understand the world we live in, what we are about and what we have done and are doing; out of it, argues the Zanzibari born writer, will come 'a bit of understanding about how we might do things differently' (Iqbal 2019: 39).

Following Gurnah's argument, in this chapter I will examine the fictionalized depiction of the European community in two colonized territories in Africa, the Belgian Congo in Greene's *A Burnt-Out Case* (1960) and the British protectorate in Zanzibar in Gurnah's *Desertion* (2005). More concretely, taking its cue from Yuri Lotman's theory of cultural semiotics, and specifically his concepts of semiosphere and frontier, this essay analyzes the presence of different coexisting semiospheres in these works, focusing mainly on the presentation of the European semiotic space and their attitude towards the other. I will conclude that Greene and Gurnah, aiming to question both, the European ambivalence towards the colonizing mission and her own 'system of civilization', offer a depiction of a heterogenous European semiosphere that show uncanny similarities: on the one hand, Europeans who either impose their concept of civilization on the native population, to whom they do not give the status of an existent semiosphere, or show a(n) (un)conscious patronizing attitude towards Africans. On the other hand, in both novels we find a sympathetic portrayal of other Europeans who, being in the frontier of their own semiosphere, favor a hermeneutical activity that allows them to question their own modes and conceptions and who, as a result, reach a certain level of understanding of the African semiotic space.

Embodiments of Colonization in the Narrative on European Imperialism in *A Burnt-Out Case* and *Desertion*

In her insightful study of whiteness and masculinities in M. G. Vassanji's *The Book of Secrets* (1994) and Abdulrazak Gurnah's *Desertion* (2005), Pujolràs-Noguer establishes three different embodiments of whiteness in relation with what she terms the experience of the empire, specifically in the British protectorate of Zanzibar: the soldier/estate manager, Richard Burton in *Desertion*; the administrator, Frederick Turner; and the orientalist, Martin Pearce (2019: 134). As Pujolràs-Noguer explains, whereas the first two characters embody the view of masculinity and whiteness as a superior condition in relation with the non-Europeans, Pearce clearly challenges that representation (136). According to Pujolràs-Noguer, the questioning present in Gurnah's novel 'emanates from a significant shift: in contraposition to the European perspective that shaped colonial literature, in Vassanji and Gurnah's texts [...] what allows us to visualize colonial masculinities as bodies-not-at-home is *precisely the non-white perspective* of their narrators' (135, emphasis added). Later on she insists on this idea: 'it is no longer about how the European sees the non-European but how the non-European inspects the European' (147). From this perspective, the only possible defamiliarizing depiction of male, white characters in the colonial phenomenon would be through non-European eyes. With the analysis of the colonial performance through the eyes of European characters in *A Burnt-Out Case*, I will question this assertion.

The embodiment of colonization depicted in the narrative of the empire in Greene's *A Burnt-Out Case* – in this case of the Belgian Congo right before its independence – does not differ significantly from Gurnah's. The Europeans don't constitute a homogeneous group regarding their perspective on imperialism. While the administrators and the colons (represented by the Governor, the owner of the *Otraco* company, and more significantly by Rycker) embody the well-anchored identities of the imposing empire, despising and/or ignoring the native population, Father Superior and the priests in the leprosery – with the exception of Father Thomas – through their hermeneutics of intercultural communication, question the necessity of whitening the conquered territories. In this line of thought, I will argue that, as Pujolràs-Noguer claimed in her analysis of the colonizers in *Desertion*, the hermeneutical standpoint of Europeans concerning the non-whites in *A Burnt-Out Case* is directly related to their (lack of) recognition of themselves as masculine, white bodies. To further strengthen this argument, I will examine how this (lack of) recognition aligns with the semiotic experience between the Westerners and the Africans in Greene's and Gurnah's novels. Henceforth, drawing upon Lotman's theory of cultural semiotics, I will demonstrate how through the introduction of Western characters that challenge the hermeneutics of the European colonization, based on a superior role of whiteness, both Greene and Gurnah aim to point to the ambivalences and paradoxes of the colonial experience in Africa.

In Yuri Lotman's exploration of the semiotic experience and, more specifically, the construction of meaning in both physical and symbolic spaces, the concept of semiosphere – a notion inspired by Vladimir Vernadski' biosphere – has a prominent role. Lotman defines the semiosphere as 'the semiotic space necessary for the existence and functioning of languages' (Lotman 1990: 123); or, to put it in other words, the 'semiotic space, out of which semiosis itself cannot exist' (ibid., 2005: 208). For Lotman, all semiotic space is based on two main foundations: first, every semiosphere constitutes a unified mechanism; therefore, it needs another semiosphere to identify its structure and borders. At the same time, however, all semiotic space is characterized by its heterogeneity (ibid., 1990: 125; and 2009: 114), defined by the diversity of elements it contains and by their different functions in the semiotic experience: '[t]he languages which fill up the semiotic space are various, and they relate to each other along the spectrum which runs from complete mutual translatability to just as complete mutual untranslatability' (ibid., 1990: 125).

In the process of construction of meaning, in order to maintain a certain level of coherence, the semiosphere requires the existence of a frontier. In this train of thought, Lotman argues that '[c]ompletely stable invariant semiotic structures do not exist at all, generally speaking. [...] Semiotic systems, encountered in the semiosphere, display an ability to survive and to be transformed and, like Proteus, become "others"' (2009: 114). Focusing on the structure of the semiosphere, its centre presents the most developed and structurally organized languages (ibid., 134). On the contrary, its periphery – where the normativity is not so effectively imposed on the semiotic space – is extremely dynamic due to the constant exchange of information with other semiotic spaces (ibid., 134). Consequently, if the semiosphere is to be transformed, its margins become a space of utmost significance:

> The border of semiotic space is the most important functional and structural position, giving substance to its semiotic mechanism. The border is a bilingual mechanism, translating external communications into the internal language of

the semiosphere and vice versa. Thus, only with the help of the boundary is the semiosphere able to establish contact with non-semiotic and extra-semiotic spaces.

Ibid., 2005: 210

What characterizes the border of any semiosphere is its permeability, which allows the admission of information coming from other semiotic spaces. In Lotman's words, this border is 'constantly transgressed via intrusions from the extra-semiotic sphere which, when bursting in, introduce a new dynamic, transforming the bounded space and simultaneously transforming themselves according to its laws' (2009: 115). The frontier represents thus a catalyst through which external information become part of the internal structure of the semiosphere, producing new texts that can transform the normativity that rules a given semiotic space. Building on this theoretical framework, in the following sections I will turn to a cultural semiotic artifact, the hegemonic European empire in the African continent in order to conceptualize its central language as well as its frontiers in its hermeneutical experience with the semiosphere of the native population in *A Burnt-Out Case* and *Desertion*.

Normative Embodiments within the Colonizing Experience

As both a symbolic and material construct, the government agency of the empire would act as the centre of the European semiosphere, and its duly constituted representatives would formulate and regulate the semiosis with other spaces. Within this centre, in *Desertion* we find the ruthless but efficient estate manager, Richard Burton, who is in charge of keeping order and who represents 'to perfection the organizing and civilizing streak [...] he runs the estate with exacting accuracy, organizing land and labour in such a way as to procure the success of the imperial enterprise' (Pujolràs-Noguer 2019: 140). Regarding his connection with the diverse semiospheres present in the East African coast, Burton's hermeneutical process is rather limited: there is not a real engagement on his side that may elicit feedback that would challenge his understanding of the other semiospheres with whom he coexists. He expresses contempt for the African population in the area with his racist undertones:

> Look at this region. The niggers here have been corrupted by the Arabs, by their religion and their ... their perfumed courtesies. The Arabs themselves do not

amount to much. They are mostly bluster, not capable of a day's work unless their lives depended on it or there is a bit of loot and pillage in it.

Gurnah 2005: 83

In his view, Africa can be another America for white colonization as long as Arabs are impoverished and expelled and Africans 'starve and die off in the encounter with civilization. No need to bleat to me about morality or responsibility. It's inevitable, it's scientific. There is no cruelty in this outcome, and it has happened everywhere, again and again, in exactly the same way' (ibid., 83–4). His inability to speak neither of their languages informs his lack of interest in engaging with the other semiospheres.[6] Tellingly, the only language function he can communicate in Swahili is ordering: 'Burton can push a bit of Swahili, but I don't think he could describe the destiny of British possessions in Africa in that language. It's more carry that, bring this, and don't ever do that again. It does not sound right when you hear him in spate' (Gurnah 2005: 92).

The language of the centre of the European semiosphere in *A Burnt-Out Case* is also formulated by the administrators of the empire, the members of the government in the capital and the *Otraco* company, the monopolist of trade on the river. The main representative of the administration in the area of the leprosery where the story takes place is Rycker, the owner of a palm oil factory. In line with Burton, Rycker embodies the hermeneutics of whiteness and maleness of the empire: on the one hand, he is proud of teaching Marie, his wife, the ways of being the perfect female spouse of a colonist: 'I've trained her to know what a man needs' (Greene 2001: 36). His engagement with the native semiosphere in the region is limited to imposing the Western morals and modes on them and his communication with the Africans evokes Burton's: 'You know you have to shout to them a little. They understand nothing else' (ibid., 34). Rycker represents the centre of the European semiosphere in the Belgian colony: from his position the Western hermeneutics is without any shadow of doubt the only appropriate way of understanding the world. Due to his lack of engagement with the African semiosphere, he has become inflexible and incapable of further development. As a consequence, when he is the reflector in the narrator's discourse, the native semiosphere is considered a non-structure and Africans are seen as non-humans:

> Rycker and his wife drove into town for cocktails with the Governor. [...] in the bush thirty kilometres before they had passed *something* sitting in a chair constructed out of a palm-nut and woven fibres into the rouge and monstrous apperance of a human being. Inexplicable *objects* were the fingerprints of Africa.
>
> Greene 2001: 61, emphasis added

At the centre of the (white, male) European semiosphere in *A Burnt-Out Case* we find two more relevant characters: Father Thomas and Parkinson. The priest, rooted in the Western way of life has failed to engage with the semiosphere of the Africans with whom he has coexisted for two years. Proof of it is his longing for Europe (Greene 2001: 88) and his inability to sleep due to his fear of darkness (ibid., 86–7). His lack of engagement affects as well his (mis)communication with the natives who live in the leper colony, as the Father Superior tries to show him when Father Thomas assures that Deo Gratias and Querry prayed all night when they were lost in the forest:

> 'I asked Deo Gratias. He said yes. I asked him what prayers – the Ave Maria, I asked him? He said yes.' 'Father Thomas, when you have been in Africa a little longer, you will learn not to ask an African a question which may be answered by yes. It is their form of courtesy to agree. It means nothing at all.' 'I think after two years I can tell when an African is lying.'
>
> Greene 2001: 87

What is more, Father Thomas, in contrast with the ecumenical standpoint of the rest of the priests in the seminary, embodies the pre-Vatican II moral hermeneutics of the Catholic Church. In his view, the role of a priest in Africa must be evangelizing the native population (Greene 2001: 83). Revealing in this sense is his argument with Father Superior about moral appropriateness of having Marie Akimbu teaching children when she gives birth to a baby every year from diverse fathers. Whereas Father Thomas asks 'What kind of example is that?', the Superior simply answers '*autres pays autres moeurs*' (Greene 2001: 85, original emphasis).

The last character who embodies the languages of the centre of the European semiosphere is Parkinson. He is a journalist who has totally lost his vocation and whose professional performance is driven by his ambition, showing no regard whatsoever for truth (Valverde 2020: 113). Even though he experiences first-hand the situation of the Belgian colony, not only does he refuse to engage with the African semiosphere, but he uses it (Dobozy 2002: 437) to continue conveying in his chronicles the romantic clichés of the continent that the Victorian writers and explorers spread out: 'The eternal forest broods along the banks unchanged since Stanley and his little band' (Greene 2001: 97). Being aware of the powerful role of media in society – often the only way for citizens to have access to what happens in the world – Parkinson's chronicles could have become a peripheral text, extremely significant in further questioning the romanticized vision of the European public of Africa. Much on the contrary, he does not only disdain information accuracy – despite being corrected about the geographical mistakes he makes and being accused of lying – but also his own audience: 'They won't know the bloody difference' (ibid., 98). In this sense, Parkinson pushes the inflexible hermeneutics of the centre of the European semiosphere to its limits, since he chooses to lie and re-invent Africa for his readers.

Colonial Idealists: A Well-Intentioned Paternalistic View of Colonization

All semiotic spaces, as Yuri Lotman states, show a certain level of internal heterogeneity. The languages of the centre of the semiosphere can be altered by contacts with other semiotic spaces with the inclusion of new information through the translating mechanism of the frontier (Lotman 2005: 210). Still in the centre of the European semiosphere, we find an embodiment of whiteness different than Burton, Rycker, Father Thomas and Parkinson. Frederick Turner in *Desertion* and Doctor Colin in *A Burnt-Out Case* are the formers' counterparts in the sense that their vision of the colonizing experience is felt as a responsibility to guide (Gurnah 2005: 84) the natives – in line with Achebe's denouncement of the view of Africans as unfinished Europeans that could be patiently taught the 'proper' modes of living.

Frederick Turner, the District Officer, is defined as a 'colonial idealist, something of a scholar of poetry, a bit of a rake, perhaps as a man of wit and subtle humour' (Gurnah 2005: 95). As Pujolràs-Noguer observes, he shows a sensitivity channeled through his love for Romantic poetry (Pujolràs-Noguer 2019: 141). Contrary to Burton's argument that Africans need to disappear for Europeans to bring prosperity and order (Gurnah 2005: 84), Turner states that 'if I thought Burton was going to turn out right in his predictions, [...] I'd pack up and go home tomorrow and to hell with the Empire' (Gurnah 2005: 86). In Turner's mind, it is his responsibility to engage with the native population 'to keep an eye on them and guide them slowly into obedience and orderly labour' (Gurnah 2005: 84). Such engagement is not possible, however, since first he does not speak any of the languages local people use: 'I can stir a bit of Hindustani myself, especially if I don't have to understand what the other fellow is saying' (ibid., 92); and, second, because he relies on English Romantic poetry as a basis for his hermeneutical process of understanding the semiospheres of the land he inhabits. As Pujolràs-Noguer puts it:

> Turner tries desperately to understand the strangeness that surrounds him by seeking answers in Romantic poetry. References to Coleridge's 'Kubla Khan,' Shelley's 'Ozymandias,' Swinburne's 'The Forsaken Garden,' and even Rimbaud are called forth as attempts to convert alienation into familiarity, to whiten the space and hence in-habit it, and thus assuage his invincible feeling of loss.
>
> 2019: 141

His discourse could have become a peripheral text that could have transformed the central language of the European semiotic space, but relying on the white hermeneutics in order to understand the world that surrounds him does not allow him to become a valid translator.

In the same way Turner finds in Romantic writers the foundation for his analysis of the semiospheres present in East Africa, Doctor Colin falls back on science and his longed-for *Atlas for Leprosy* (Greene 2001: 20). Compared to Turner's estrangement, Colin initially seems to be a more peripheric element, since he has learnt to accept some defining aspects of the native ontological hermeneutics, such as the fact that Africans can foresee the exact day they will die (Greene 2001: 48).

Yet, in his engagement with the native semiotic space he tries to impose what he considers the certainties of the Western science on his patients. Tellingly, Colin aims to get orthopedic devices for them in an attempt to facilitate the life of the mutilated lepers without questioning himself on whether or not they would like to use them (ibid., 79). As Hill puts it, '[f]or Doctor Colin, the best man can hope to do is improve his little corner of the world or try to provide instruments that will do it for us' (Hill 1999: 77). His true aim in life is to eradicate leprosy (Greene 2001: 22), so he focuses his attention on the symptoms of the illness, and not so much on his patients' suffering. As a result, Colin's effort to engage with his patients is not fruitful since he cannot connect with them at a human level.

While characters such as Burton or Rycker despised the semiosphere(s) with whom they coexist, considering them a no-structure, Turner and Colin do aim to engage with the native population. Nevertheless, they never consider them their equals. In different ways, in both, Turner and Colin's view, Africans need to follow the path of the European civilization and it is their responsibility to act as guides of that process. Their hermeneutic approach towards the different African semiospheres present in the novels is one of well-intentioned paternalism.[7] In this sense, even though Turner and Colin are depicted in a much more favourable light than Burton, Rycker, Father Thomas or Parkinson, the former constitute unsuccessful potential frontier elements within the European semiotic space.

Challenging Bodies in the Experience of Colonization

As Lotman argues, the central languages of a given semiosphere 'lose dynamism and having once exhausted their reserve of indeterminacy they became [sic] inflexible and incapable of further development' (Lotman 1990: 134). Here is where the frontier emerges as 'an area of enhanced meaning generation' (ibid., 2005: 214) and peripheral texts become significant in the semiosphere's transformation process: 'Falling into the category of 'foreigners' within a given system, these texts fulfil the function of a catalyst in the whole mechanism of the semiosphere' (ibid., 214).

According to the Estonian semitiotician, in all semiospheres there are individuals who, due to a particular talent or their occupation, engage with other semiospheres, forming 'a zone of cultural bilingualism, ensuring semiotic contacts between two worlds' (Lotman 2005: 211). As we shall see, in *Desertion* and *A Burnt-Out Case* we find European characters who live in an area of cultural bilingualism and who, as a result, insert 'foreign' texts into their semiotic space that act as catalysts capable of engendering new meanings. As opposed to the hermeneutic approach of imposition and disregard of the normative figures of colonization – Burton in *Desertion* and Rycker as well as Father Thomas in *A Burnt-Out Case* – and to the paternalism shown by Turner and Doctor Colin, these frontier characters challenge the aforementioned hermeneutics with their resistance to colonial embodiment. In this case, I am referring to Martin Pearce in Gurnah's novel and to Father Superior and the other priests in the seminary in Greene's text.

Martin Pearce and Father Superior step down from the hermeneutics of the empire. Following critics such as Richard Dyer and Bill Schwarz, Pujolràs-Noguer contends that the imperial framework established whiteness and monotheism as arbiters of civilization, while savagery was attached to polytheism and the non-white (Pujolràs-Noguer 2018: 597). In that line of thought, colonial hermeneutics marked as 'abnormal' any deviance from the boundaries fixed by empire. In other words, to express it through the lens of Lotman's theory, any frontier element within the European semiosphere was considered 'un-natural' and as a result, dangerous, since it threatened the construction and preservation of colonialism. In an exercise of self-preservation, the European semiosphere regarded the different African semiotic spaces as non-existent, avoiding any encounter (linguistic, cultural and corporeal) with the other that could question the very foundation of the colonial system.

Pearce represents the transgression of the boundaries of the empire at diverse levels. First, language-wise. Whereas Turner is unable to speak any of the languages of the local semiospheres and Burton can only say some words in Swahili, Pearce speaks a little Arabic, which makes possible for him to communicate with the local people. Moreover, as a frontier element, he favours an egalitarian encounter with other semiotic spaces. His presence in Africa, differently than the other two Europeans, is justified by his desire to learn from others, not to civilize them (Pujolràs-Noguer 2019: 144): 'I'm a historian, of a kind. A proper amateur actually. A bit of a linguist, a student linguist' (Gurnah 2005: 51). In the same humble attitude, Pearce declares about his work in Egypt: 'I've been in Egypt the last year and a bit, advising in the department of education. Interfering, rather. [...] I think I learnt a great more deal than the unfortunates who had to listen to my advice' (Gurnah 2005: 92).

Pearce's most significant transgression of the colonial boundaries, however, is his intimate relationship with Rehana, which breaks the rules of the normative sexual desire between white and non-white individuals. In order to avoid being vulnerable, the empire had to limit of such mix-raced encounters to the realm of the private (Pujolràs-Noguer 2018: 597). Having in Turner's phrasing 'a fling with the native girls' (Gurnah 2005: 93), or as Burton puts it, an 'amusing and uncomplicated affair of lust and its gratification' (Gurnah 2005: 119) would not imperil the narrative of the empire. On the contrary, despite his final decision to abandon Rehana and go back to England, Pearce violates what the empire considers appropriate concerning mix-raced relationships making his romance with Rehana blatantly visible. He is a *mzungu*, a European, but even more important, his open and confident encounter with the other makes him an 'aimless wanderer', the literal meaning of the Kiswahili word (Pujolràs-Noguer 2018: 607).

Within the European semiosphere depicted in *Burnt-Out Case* there are characters that constitute frontier elements that are able to engender new meaning, specifically Father Superior. Contrary to Father Thomas, who cannot recognize that his Anglo-Saxon background is as hybrid as any other, the Superior not only recognizes this fact, but he consents to it in a natural way, in line with Edward Said's stance that hybridism is crucial in the foundations of any culture (Dobozy 2002: 443). Tellingly, in his homilies, he mimics syntactically and phonetically the language of the native semiosphere – using 'Klistian' and 'Yezu', and sentences like 'but he a Klistian' (Greene 2001: 80–1) – and borrows words from the Kikongo language, such as 'piccin' (80). He engages with the native semiotic space, challenging the Western view of the world and with this kind of hermeneutical process he triggers reflection, questioning and reinterpretation of the language that gives form to the centre of the European semiosphere, and fostering, at the same time, greater understanding.

Ideologically speaking, the Superior and the rest of the priests in the community – with the exception of Father Thomas – reject, as Martin Pearce does in *Desertion*, the boundaries imposed by the imperial machinery. They are open-minded and willing to accept the ways of living and values of the native population, even in the cases in which those ways are not in accordance with the postulates of the Vatican on moral theology, such as when the priests baptize all children no matter if they have been born out of wedlock (Greene 2001: 120). Actually, moral theology is the least of their worries, and their main duty is not necessarily preaching the Gospel: 'Souls could wait. Souls had eternity' (ibid., 83). It is significant that the Superior and the other priests not only challenge the official teachings of the Vatican on moral theology, but also the empire's dependability on monotheism. First, they work in close proximity with Doctor Colin, a declared atheist (ibid., 82). More importantly, they do not impose the practice of religion as conceived in Europe. Much on the contrary, in their engaging hermeneutical process, they understand the way the natives interpret religion, characterized by syncretism between Jesus and Nzanmbe. As Doctor Colin puts it, 'It's a strange Christianity we have here' (ibid., 58).

As in the case of Martin Pearce in *Desertion*, Father Superior and the other priests acknowledge that the different African semiospheres that inhabit the land in which they also live are linguistically, culturally and religiously as legitimate as the European semiotic space to which they belong. Due to their conscious relinquishing of the hermeneutics of the European colonization, they are depicted in a favourable light in both novels, as '[t]hese characters take Africa as a given, [...] placing service over gain in an attempt to undo or mitigate the harm done in the name of country' (Dobozy 2002: 435).

Conclusion

The analysis of the embodiment of colonization described in Gurnah's *Desertion* and Greene's *A Burnt-Out Case* indicates that the language of the European semiosphere in both novels is far from homogeneous. In an attempt to fortifying the hermeneutics of the European colonization in Africa, we find Burton and Rycker – together with Father Thomas and Parkinson – white characters who are incapable of recognizing their common humanity with African people, giving themselves at the same time a sense of authority and self-importance. Not far from the centre of the European semiotic space and despite their sense of responsibility towards the native population, Turner and Doctor Colin represent unavailing attempts to really engage with the semiospheres of the African people. Their well-intentioned efforts to help are based on their conviction that in order to improve their life conditions, the native population need to, as Achebe would say, grow up with the guidance of Europeans. Finally, within the European semiosphere we find frontier characters – Martin Pearce and Father Superior with the other priests – who recognize the common humanity shared with the natives and, as a result, support a hermeneutics of interaction, respect and understanding with the African semiotic space. In this vein, and in contrast with Pujolràs-Noguer's assertion (2019: 135), not only Gurnah's non-white perspective, but also Greene's white, European depiction of the embodiments of colonization allows us to visualize colonial masculinities as bodies-not-at-home. In this sense, both novels deliver a complementary rebuttal to the imperial narrative.

Pearce and Father Superior's hermeneutic practice is the one favoured by both Gurnah and Greene. On the one hand, as Steiner and Olaussen observe, Gurnah advocates alternative social encounters with 'stories that imagine "Africa" and indeed "Britain" as inter-cultural and inter-linguistic spaces of geopolitical proximity and possible affiliation' (2013: 1–2). In the same line of thought, I conclude with Paula Martín that, following a Lévinassian approach, Greene defends an ethics of the other: 'Greene's work may be said to explore the potential constitution of forms of community based on ethical action, established as alternative – often opposed – to official or institutional communities' (2015: 7). Such frontier characters as Pearce and Father Superior offer more dynamic and complex ways of understanding the world and from that hermeneutic process comes, as Gurnah states, 'a bit of understanding about how we might do things differently' (Iqbal 2019: 39).

Notes

1 As García Ramírez observes, 'Every time Achebe is asked about, he points out that Africa is not the Dark Continent to which most of these writers referred to, but an unknown place unfairly treated' (1999: 38).
2 In this vein, Mazumder points out that *The Heart of the Matter* displays a narrative that is analogous to what Edward Said calls 'Orientalism', that is, 'European ways of creating and seeing the East, where "the idea of European identity as a superior one in comparison with all the non-European peoples and cultures (p. 7) simply prevails"' (2021: 113–14).

3 Tellingly, in her 1997 article, 'Notas sobre la novela colonial de tema africano en Gran Bretaña,' Paula García analyses Greene's books in African soil in the same terms as Aladaylah (2012) and Mazumder (2021). As we can see, this reading of Greene's work has not changed much in over twenty years. In this paper, I hope to contribute an analysis that partly challenges these former readings.

4 Tellingly, Greene scholarship has not only labeled him 'Eurocentric' concerning the image of the African continent in *The Heart of the Matter* or *A Burnt-Out Case*. Talking about his work in general terms, Mudford argues that, '[al]though his novels were set in many different countries, his attitudes and his beliefs were, like those of his contemporaries, Eurocentric' (1996: 12). In fact, critics constantly use 'Greeneland', a term coined by in 1940 by Arthur Calder-Marshall in a review for *Horizon* (McEwan 1988: 17), to refer to the foreign settings in which the British writer set his stories. Greeneland has been interpreted on many occasions as mere mental recreations that have almost nothing to do with the places that inspired those sceneries (Pearson 1982: 214). In the case of *The Power and the Glory*, just to give an example, critics such as Brian Rourke stated that Greene's México is 'a mental entity, a stimulus of the imagination' (1999: 144). In the light of the uncanny similarities between the depiction of the Mexican society in the late 1930s in *The Power and the Glory* and in Juan Rulfo's *Pedro Páramo*, the aforementioned allegations on Greeneland as recreations of Greene's mind become, however, questionable (Valverde 2020: 232).

5 In this line, Gurnah states that one of the central issues to *Desertion* is 'the way European colonialism inserted itself into the lives of people it colonised and the consequences of that intrusion' (Iqbal 2019: 39).

6 Interestingly, in her Doctoral Dissertation *The Image of the European in Nigerian Literature and Culture*, Terri Ochiagha explains that, as Achebe and Irobi observe, in Mbari sculptures, the colonial administrators and estate managers are represented as 'a cultural oddity, an unfathomable alien presence with equally alien characteristics' (Ochiagha 2010: 68). In this sense, 'satire is achieved by exaggerating physical Otherness and by parodying Western culture and political institutions, as well as the cultural and linguistic barriers between colonial administrators and their African aides' (Ochiagha 2010: 69).

7 Significant in this sense is Greene's statement in *In Search of a Character*:

> None the less they [native dancers] were watched by B., the district officer, with smiling proprietorial pride. How often have I seen that smile—like that of a proud schoolmaster watching a school performance of *The Merchant of Venice*, on the faces of British district officers or administrators, in West Africa, or Malaya... at least it is not the stupidity of the *colon*.
>
> Greene 1968: 34, original emphasis

References

Achebe, Chinua. 1988. *Hopes and Impediments: Selected Essays 1965-87*. Oxford: Heinemann.

Aladaylah, Majed Hamed. 2012. 'Postcolonial Reading of a Colonial Text'. *English Language Teaching*, 5 (9): 122–6.

Allen, Jeffrey. 2012. 'Interview with Abdulrazak Gurnah'. *Black Renaissance*, 11 (2/3): 114–222, at 118.

Dobozy, Thomas. 2002. 'Africa and Catholic Crisis: Graham Greene's *The Heart of the Matter* and *A Burnt-Out Case*'. In T. Hill (ed.), *Perceptions of Religious Faith in the Work of Graham Greene*, 427–58. New York: Peter Lang.

García Ramírez, Paula. 1997. 'Notas sobre la novela colonial de tema africano en Gran Bretaña'. *The Grove: Working Papers on English Studies*, 4: 427–44.

García Ramírez, Paula. 1999. 'Chinua Achebe as a Critical Reader of Joyce Cary'. *The Grove: Working Papers on English Studies*, 6: 37–50.

Greene, Graham. 1968. *In Search of a Character: Two African Journals*. London: Penguin Books.

Greene, Graham. 2001. *A Burnt-Out Case*. London: Penguin Books.

Gurnah, Abdulrazak. 2005. *Desertion*. London: Bloomsbury.

Hill, Thomas. 1999. *Graham Greene's Wanderers*. San Francisco, CA: International Scholars Publications.

Iqbal, Razia. 2019. 'Belonging, Colonialism and Arrival'. *Wasafiri*, 34 (4): 34–40. Doi: 10.1080/02690055.2019.1635756.

Lotman, Juri. [1984] 2005. 'On the Semiosphere'. Trans. Wilma Clark. *Sign Systems Studies*, 33 (1): 205–29. Doi: 10.12697/SSS.2005.33.1.09. = Лотман, Юрий М. 1984. О семиосфере. Труды по знаковым системам (Sign Systems Studies) 17: 5–23.

Lotman, Juri. 1990. *Universe of the Mind: A Semiotic Theory of Culture*. Trans. Ann Shukman with an introduction by Umberto Eco. Bloomington, IN: Indiana University Press.

Lotman, Juri. 2005. 'On the Semiosphere'. *Sign System Studies*, 33 (1): 205–29.

Lotman, Juri. 2009. *Culture and Explosion*. Berlin: Mouton de Gruyter.

Martín, Paula. 2015. *The Language of Ethics and Community in Graham Greene's Fiction*. Basingstoke: MacMillan Palgrave.

Mazumder, Tanmoy. 2021. 'Exploring the Eurocentric Heart: A Postcolonial Reading of Graham Greene's *The Heart of the Matter*'. *International Journal of Linguistics, Literature and Translation*, 3 (8): 113–21. Doi: 10.32996/IJLLT.2021.4.8.17.

McEwan, Neil. 1988. *Graham Greene*. Basingstoke: MacMillan.

Mudford, Peter. 1996. *Graham Greene*. Plymouth: Northcote House in association with the British Council.

Ochiagha, Terri. 2010. 'The Image of the European in Nigerian Literature and Culture'. Unpublished PhD diss., Universidad Complutense de Madrid, Madrid.

Pearson, Sheryl. 1982. '"Is There Anybody There?" Graham Greene in Mexico'. *Journal of Modern Literature*, 9 (2): 277–90.

Philips, Caryl. 2003. 'Out of Africa'. *The Guardian*, 22 February. Available online: https://www.theguardian.com/books/2003/feb/22/classics.chinuaachebe (accessed 22 November 2022).

Pujolràs-Noguer, Esther. 2018. 'Desiring/Desired Bodies: Miscegenation and Romance in Abdulrazak Gurnah's *Desertion*'. *Critique: Studies in Contemporary Fiction*, 59 (5): 596–608. Doi: 10.1080/00111619.2018.1459456.

Pujolràs-Noguer, Esther. 2019. 'Imperially White and Male: Colonial Masculinities in M. G. Vassanji's *The Book of Secrets* (1994) and Abdulrazak Gurnah's *Desertion* (2005)'. *Interventions*, 21 (1): 131–49. Doi: 10.1080/1369801X.2018.1487323.

Roos, Henriette. 2009. 'The Sins of the Fathers: The Missionary in Some Modern English Novels about the Congo'. *Tydskrif Vir Letterkunde*, 46 (1): 58–78. Doi: 10.4314/tvl.v46i1.29850.

Rourke, Brian R. 1999. 'Mexicos of the Mind: British Writers of the 1930s in Mexico'. PhD diss., Stanford University, Stanford, CA. Ann Arbor, MI: UMI.

Steiner, Tina and Maria Olaussen. 2013. 'Critical Perspectives on Abdulrazak Gurnah'. *English Studies in Africa*, 56 (1): 1–3. Doi: 10.1080/00138398.2013.780676.

Valverde, Beatriz. 2020. 'Foreign-Space Dramatization in Graham Greene's *The Power and the Glory*: Revisiting Greeneland'. *Roczniki Humanistyczne*, 68 (11): 225–34.

7

The Language of War in the Apocalypse Trope of Meg Elison's *The Book of the Unnamed Midwife*

Almudena Machado-Jiménez

Introduction: Into Elison's World Ending

When Moylan (2000: 111) described dystopias as the 'new maps of hell', his understanding of place was not assumed as a particular geometrical space since 'no dream or trip is taken to get to this place of everyday life' (ibid., 148). Gallardo (2005: 37) adds that 'dystopia is neither a landscape nor a chronoscape', so it cannot be understood as a pre-existent natural 'bad place'. Instead, dystopias are construed regarding the characters' experiences of alienation and distress *living* (in) that cosmos. Dystopia will be comprehended according to the hermeneutical sense of *place* as the site of experience (Olivier 2018; Schlitte 2018). Particularly, Olivier (2018: 14) underpins such notion by remarking that place originates as '*a contextual web of meanings*' after a process of interconnectedness between the individual with the world. Although Olivier's definition of place defies Gallardo's idea of dystopia not as 'a collective state of mind but an individual condition' (Gallardo 2005: 37), dystopia's nightmarish cognitive mapping ultimately emerges after an interchange of meanings has occurred between the narrator and a third entity, usually the reader.

Olivier expounds that this intersubjectivity is based on the platial meaning granted to experience, as it is due to the place that our experiences acquire their full significance: 'experience is not only grounded in but *by* place' (2018: 18). Janz (2018) and Schlitte (2018) agree on the importance of the place to set any narrative: 'Is place textualized as an act of understanding, but could be rendered otherwise, also as an act of understanding?' (Janz 2018: 25). This reciprocity between the place and the text allows the understanding that dystopian narrative is necessarily situated somewhere to interpret the subjects' experience and vice versa – dystopian places *must be narrated* to exist.

The hermeneutic circle can be extrapolated outside the narrative between the texts as products and their situatedness, as 'in order to understand an author's writings, one must understand the language and history of his time, but in order to understand that language and history, one needs to have understood the writings of that time, including the author's' (Schmidt 2014: 15). In science fiction, the creative and cognitive power of the narrative relies on Suvin's notion of estrangement, as this mechanism stimulates 'a reflecting *of* but also *on* reality [...], a creative approach tending towards a dynamic transformation rather than toward a static mirroring of the author's environment' (Suvin 2016: 22). The creative power that comes with the estrangement of cognition enables representing reality as an act of engagement with our bodily experiences, but also enables authors to safely relate their experiences of 'dissatisfaction with [their] political present' (Sargisson 2002: 12) while seeking alternatives that enact social change within/of their environment. Remarkably, feminist science fiction illustrates this dissent, which Sargisson (1996: 68) calls transgressive utopianism, as the genre 'transgresses, negates and creates new conceptual spaces from which to reapproach the world in a non-dualistic way'.

Moreover, unlike other genres that resort to estrangement, e.g. fantasy, Suvin asserts the *novum* introduced is characterized by a scientific logicality (2016: 81) which bridges the realms of fiction and reality. Consequently, dystopias strengthen a hermeneutic loop between the narrator's experiences and the audience's, as the envisioning presented in a particular text represents and makes us realize a plausibly panoramic picture of the future resulting from our contemporary society's wrongdoings. Nevertheless, it is due to the very proximity to the hostile scenarios represented from our reality that feminist dystopias face one of their biggest dilemmas: how to depict female characters beyond the hegemonic patriarchal conceptions denounced while building a feminist narrative toward peace or utopia; how to confront violence without pigeonholing femininity as essentially peaceful. Gursozlu considers this paradigm the main issue of challenging hegemony: 'what needs to be done is to reveal the violent nature of this reality while, at the same time, offering a nonviolent alternative' (2018b: 2).

This study examines that, despite feminist dystopias offering a cognitive critique of patriarchal heteronormativity, they also resort to an essentialist view of the feminine as powerless within conflictual situations, replicating the gendered views on conflict and pre-existent female stereotypes of victims or peacebuilders – the latter role usually restricted and jeopardized by the continuation of violent practices in relationality. To explore this argument, I analyze Meg Elison's *The Book of the Unnamed Midwife* (2014), the first book of her *Road to Nowhere* trilogy. The novel presents an apocalyptic dystopia in which an unknown plague is leading humankind to extinction. Despite the efforts of scientists to understand the causes of this illness and quench it, women around the globe suffer from a deadly fever and neonates are born deceased, killing their mothers at childbirth. And yet, this apocalyptic situation is worsened if one is a female survivor, as her endurance in this androcentric chaos becomes a nightmarish experience, for she will face a worse destiny: sexual exploitation.

Through a series of confessional testimonies collected in her diary, the protagonist – a midwife who recovers from the fever and acts like a heteronormative warlike man to survive – relates her apocalyptic experience in this male-dominated world. Her narrative gathers the shared struggles of female survivors of the plague as if it were a communal hermeneutical approach to the illness. In so doing, this dystopian text/place allegorizes the already hegemonic codes of patriarchal brutality in the pre-apocalyptic civilization, inasmuch as cultural violence tacitly validated the resulting discourses of women's commodification and dislocation during the cataclysm.

Apocalypticality: Unearthing Cultural Violence

Harder (2018: 335) expounds on how art prompts the phenomenological *r*epresentation of our milieu by rethinking the ordinary social constructs under extraordinary uncanny settings. One of the most recurrent hermeneutic devices for representing and understanding our reality in sci-fi narrative has been the trope of the apocalypse. Hongisto's notion of *apocalypticality* approaches the phenomenon both as content and medium, in which the reader becomes an active narratee:

> 'Apocalypticality' results from the feeling of apprehension while one is, through imagistic elements in the Apocalypse, drawn into the possible 'otherness' of the narrative. […] It works towards an understanding of the Apocalypse effected through collective experiential and aesthetic elements that create, by means of reader narrativization and reflection, abstraction and heightened intensity of experience. A description of the engagement with the Apocalypse calls for a term that includes these aspects and transforms the adjective or noun 'apocalyptic', which is content-focused, to an experience-focused word. Similarly,

an addition is needed to the concrete usage of the noun 'apocalypticism', as a type of eschatology and collective behaviour. Apocalypticality embraces the perspective that the reading and performing of the artefact are acts that include the audience, the readers, as narratees.

2010: 115

Remarkably, the prismatic medium to represent the apocalyptical experience in twentieth- and twenty-first-century sci-fi narrative, especially during and after the Cold War, has been conflictual. As Booker explains, the majority of apocalyptic fiction has portrayed human extinction with a 'future war' (2014: 160), e.g. a war between humankind and alien species, a global nuclear war that unleashes a series of environmental disasters or a cyberwar that causes the collapse of modern society. Nevertheless, Elison opts for the motif of the pandemic to represent the epistemic violence that underlies our contemporary society. Despite the impossibility of targetting a tangible enemy in this aversive event, Gomel describes the plague as 'a metaphor for genocide [...], one of the central tropes of biopolitics, shaping much of the twentieth-century discourse of power, domination, and the body' (2000: 406–7). Hence, the 'women's plague' (Elison 2014: 46) ultimately shows the symbolic representation of the female subaltern's experiences within a corrupted system.

The contingency of this form of estrangement confirms Spivak's two-fold notion of representation, considering the strategic deployment of the disease as solely affecting women. In *The Book of the Unnamed Midwife*, the narrative *re*presentation of our contemporary social maladies serves as an exegesis to deconstruct how the hegemonic patriarchal oppressor has historically represented women as the subaltern. The intersubjectivity depicted in the narrative arises from women's shared experiences of dislocation, struggle and illness – characterizing this place (i.e. a representation of patriarchal society) as a 'dysfunctional, disenabling setting' (Olivier 2018: 15). Thus, the apocalypse discloses an interpretive co-relationality between the environment and our embodiment (Aho 2018; Gallagher, Martínez and Gastelum 2018), as only those bodies affected by the plague will suffer the apocalyptic conditions.

Apocalypticality, and notably the women's epidemic, provokes a disruption on the ordinary and, as Aho explains, questions 'our taken-for-granted competencies regarding spatial orientation, intentionality, and motility' (2018: 116), which cannot be extricated from our self-interpretation within the world. The apocalyptic narrative extrapolates the em*bodi*ment of disease to scrutinize the corruption of the dominant political body. In so doing, the estrangement of the body necessarily causes the estrangement of the world, and consequently, it obscures the distinction between illness and war as inward and outward disturbances, respectively. Considering the flesh as the edge where 'the human meets worlds that exceed and entreat it[,] the site of endless transmissions between selves and strangers where 'surplus meaning' comes to remind us that we can never be sufficient to ourselves' (Kearney and Treanor 2015: 11), a carnal hermeneutical understanding of the plague as the conflation of the two modes of struggling enables the audience to interpret Elison's story as an allegory of patriarchal violence.

As the apocalypse anticipates human extinction due to these forms of violence, the anthropocentric misconception of self-sufficiency becomes unstable, disclosing how 'non-human nature has meaning and value independent of any interaction with humans' (Treanor 2015: 62). Indeed, Elison imagines how the apocalypse solely signifies the finitude of human existence while the Earth survives and recovers from the damages of humankind as a species:

> The cities stopped burning. The star filled the skies of places that hadn't seen them since man started burning coal. Herd animals took to the plains. Salmon swelled the rivers. The Earth grew quiet, and everything seemed to teem with life and hold its breath, waiting.
>
> 2014: 282

This delusive arrangement of reality is especially acute when the only ones affected by the disease are women, whom Hernando (2018) characterizes as the relational entities that sustain the patriarchal fantasy of male individuality. In order to secure this hierarchical distinction, the *Anthropos* reinforces gender polarization – a recurrent feature in war, 'the cornerstone of masculinity' (Skjelsbæk 2001: n.p.).

The denouncement of patriarchal violence through the image of the women's plague implies that, whenever humankind faces a conflict, gender performativity becomes highly limited by the masculine/feminine binary opposition, categorizing women as 'victims, but marginal as agents' according to the war codes (Skjelsbæk and Smith 2001). This conjecture can be observed in Goldstein's definition of war as '*lethal intergroup violence*' (2001: 2). As the women's plague accentuates gender inequalities by the impairment of female bodies' health and the rampant rage of male gangs, the apocalypse trope illustrates a conflict in which men and women are the hostile blocs. Hence, sex becomes the only structural power relation regarded, reducing plural multilayered female identities into the monolithic category of *woman* because the downfall of modern society provokes an equalizing effect: '*TOP PRICE PAID FOR FEMALE ANY AGE*' (Elison 2014: 258, original emphasis). Elison interprets how this corporeal deviation is only perceptible after their flesh is treated as bodies-for-others in a violent encounter: women experience the apocalypse only after their bodies have been objectified and incapacitated in/by their interpersonal relationality. Indeed, the apocalypticality of the novel does not rely on the plague itself. Instead, it narrates the apocalypse from the tormenting experiences of female survivors, who are chased and commodified as rare sexual luxuries in a civilization where the ratio of female to male population is one to ten and worsening – considering how sexual brutality aggravates the biological hazards for women in this situation.

Gay explains how violence – which defines the conflictual nature of this apocalypse – cannot emerge from the cosmos itself, as it lacks the volition of executing such brutality:

> To refer to the cosmos as violent characterizes its physical forces like some that are distinctive to creatures with volition and choice. The physical forces of the cosmos or nature are better characterized as indifferent, neutral or, more accurately and to avoid anthropomorphism, as consequences of physically determined causal chains. [...] Violence pertains to creatures with volition and choice—although [...] persons can commit or experience violence in ways where consent is unrecognized or even absent.
>
> 2018: 39

Such a form of non-consensual violence characterizes this disease-war parallelism. Kristeva underscores how the experience of disabled-bodiedness confronts us with mortality due to the intersection between the body scientifically diagnosed as ill and women's phenomenological deviation from the hegemonic constructs of womanhood: 'The nonconformity to the norm, which is the matter at hand in the singularization of disability, is at the crossover with biology (a biological deficit) and with the social response to this deficit: biological and social, nature and culture' (2015: 122).

Nevertheless, the persistence of the female body as diseased, invalidated and on the brink of death is not particularly exclusive to the cataclysm. The unnamed midwife, who worked at a hospital during pre-apocalyptic times, compares the trauma of sexual terrorism perpetrated on female survivors with the cases of rape and gender violence that used to enter the emergency room: 'she'd seen that look before on women who came to the ER, bleeding from one end or the other. Nobody chooses to be a victim, but after a lifetime of practice, it just happens' (Elison 2014: 24). Like in war, Elison's apocalypse through the plague seems solely 'magnification or distortion of "peacetime" violence' (Cohn 2013: 2). Not even at the end of the novel, when the unnamed midwife finds Fort Nowhere as a site of resistance, can female characters find peace. The persistence of violence in the notion of the post-apocalypse – which Gomel describes as a 'backward-looking narrative of trauma' (2000: 408) – is suggested in the final passages about hope, where peace seems arbitrary and security measures for women are reinforced due to their inevitable condition of victims in this apocalypse, as the coming section examines.

Considering the endurance of women's experiences of dislocation before and after the cataclysm, the tensional character of the apocalypse emulates Cockburn's idea of the continuum of violence: 'it is meaningless to make a sharp distinction between peace and war, prewar, and postwar [...] we saw gendered phenomena persisting from one to the next' (2004: 43). And, since the World Health Organization (n.d.) describes health as 'a state of complete physical, mental and social well-being and not *merely the absence of disease* or infirmity', the binary opposition between health and illness is rejected, too. A healthy social condition may not assure the welfare of all its inhabitants – in patriarchy, women – exposing how this well-functioning of our contemporary society conceals and sustains a chronic disease, patriarchal violence.

In this sense, Gadamer's phenomenological approach to health fits Elison's intention to allegorize violence through the apocalypse trope. While health presents the balanced correlation between the subject and the world – 'a condition of being involved, of being-in-the-world, of being together with one's fellow human beings, of active and rewarding engagement in one's everyday tasks' (1996: 113) – Aho remarks that illness is associated to feeling alienated and un-homelike: 'In this state, things that used to be familiar and comforting become unintelligible and strange. The taken-for-granted coherence and intelligibility of my world becomes a disorienting, alienating, even hostile place. Understood this way, *my* world is replaced with *the* world' (2018: 121). With the women's plague, rather than narrating the individual happenings of diseased women, Elison relates their shared misfortunes in a diseased world as a parable about manifold expressions of violence. Nevertheless, the tacit hegemonic agreement on this issue makes us accept violence as part of this peace.

Cockburn explains how gender violence has been a transversal factor in the construction of political bodies: 'the continuum of violence runs through the social, the economic, and the political, with gender relations penetrating all these forms of relations, including economic power' (2004: 43). Nevertheless, the equation of what is understood as violence to only forms of direct and explosive violence leads us to treat many other unacceptable aspects of this social order as peaceful (Gursozlu 2018a). The most straightforward case of direct violence in Elison's apocalypse is rape, which Miller associates with genocide (likewise the plague) and is an integral part of the development of conflict: 'The sexual violence that – on an empirical level – appears to perpetuate a single war, or even war in general, would be the untimely continuation of an "older" war that is more difficult to situate within history' (Miller 2014: 183). As a cautionary tale, Elison portrays the deadly consequences of the legitimization of cultural violence.

Gay (2018: 33) stresses how difficult it is to detect cultural violence due to accepted codes of conduct in our hegemonic society. Similarly to the emergence of the women's plague, this form of violence 'cannot be attributed to an intentional subject' but as Gursozlu demonstrates, '[it] is built into the structure and shows up as unequal power, uneven distribution of resources, and consequently as unequal life chances' (2018a: 84). This unknown illness uncovers the gender differences in women's physical and cultural affordances in society, especially concerning their motility and freedom. Moreover, the plague blurs the division between systemic and personal violence, insofar as rape in these desperate times of human extinction is excused as a sacrifice to uphold the dominant discourse of the survival of the fittest. Although rape is the most radical expression of dominating what now is even more unattainable, the novel presents other indirect forms that contribute to the preservation of this gender violence.

Trying to hide from the dangerous streets during the cataclysm, the unnamed midwife finds shelter in a Mormon community. Their peaceful commitment to save women turns dishonest since the security promised to the female members of this society is given at the expense of their bodily and moral agency under the institution of marriage, which reflects the coercive dogmas of patriarchal fundamentalism:

> I left when the bishop said I would be married in a week to the man of his choosing and that I as being stiff-necked and disobedient and I'd have to learn to submit. He issued like a proclamation that women would be given in marriage by their fathers or by the bishop from now on. Period. We don't get to decide anymore.
>
> Elison 2014: 146

The perpetuation of gender roles is not only on the part of men through conventional matrimony or/and sexual violence. The incorporation of implied constructions on masculinity and femininity is also performed by women in the novel, particularly the protagonist's performance during this conflictual situation.

Apocalypticality helps readers recognize the accepted quotidian violence, as with the women's plague 'one's own body reveals itself as an object of one's attention, an obstacle or barrier that inhibits and disrupts the flow of everydayness' (Aho 2018: 124). Nevertheless, while an excorporating performance of violence helps the midwife survive in this hostile environment, the implicit incorporation and reinforcement of the hegemonic codes of macho man/female victim will ironically perpetuate a conflictual co-relationality in the construction of gender identities, depicting violence as if it were an essential trait of humankind:

> When a discourse of cultural violence becomes hegemonic, that is, when a discourse of cultural violence successfully defines social reality, it does more than legitimizing and making direct or structural violence 'look right—or at least not wrong,' but it naturalizes and normalizes violence by presenting an account of reality that defines violence as reasonable, ordinary, inevitable, and part of everyday life.
>
> Gursozlu 2018a: 89

Hegemonic Embodiments? A Gender(ed) War

Elison's apocalyptic narrative reconsiders the assumed associations between the world and the body, primarily how global hegemony builds gendered experiences. These demarcations can construct social and physical places that reify one's corporeality to suit the other's purposes. Considering Kearney's understanding of the body as 'instrumental' (2015: 30), then female bodies are interpreted as 'the terrain on which patriarchy is erected' (Rich [1976] 1986: 55). Nevertheless, women's corporeality in the novel faces a loss of their productive agency, and also their reproductive agency because the women's plague affects their power of birthing. Women's raped bodies, together with the dying babies and mothers, accommodate and conceive the ill uses of normative hypermasculinity in a hostile environment: 'whatever women are left out there having dead babies are probably dying too, from the fever, from the lack of care and infection. Killed by the men who hold them' (Elison 2014: 56–7). The instrumentality of the body supposes the loss of their freedom and transcendence – a dehumanization that acutely occurs with female survivors. Eventually, as men are the only 'able' bodies in this dystopia, their birthing capacity is ironically limited to, as Scarry (1985) states, the unmaking of the world – destroying patriarchy by the very act of exercising patriarchal power.

The women's plague does not only serve to allegorize gender violence; it displays how gendered violence can be, even within science fiction, by replicating the hegemonic models of the real world. The testimonies of raped women disclose that this is the only form of violence considered before, during and after the plague, illustrating how male integrity perpetuates 'nothing less than an ongoing war of men against women' (Miller 2014: 181). Miller explains how rape usually accompanies war, a characteristic that extends to the women's plague due to its conflictual nature. Nevertheless, rape is an act that exceeds the dimension of war as it is the ultimate expression of epistemic violence:

> rape brings sexual difference into play, it is never simply an isolated crime. It is a historical event that irrevocably transforms bodies, families, and societies. Rape would be the manifestation of an untimely—intersubjective—war that is larger and longer than anything that philosophical and historical discourse would call 'war'; it is a mode of war without war, war beyond war, war before war, and war after war. There is rape in marriage, rape in dating, and rape in war.
>
> Ibid., 181

As 'rape piles vulnerability on vulnerability' (Skjelsbæk and Smith 2001: n.p.), the act of violence aggravates women's already poor health conditions. However, it also reinforces the conventional feminine traits of passivity, fragility and fear – insofar as women assume these conditions of vulnerability, inhibition and abnormality after internalizing the stigmatizing gaze and the forceful touch of a healthy other (Aho 2018: 123). Such alienated self-perception of women's embodiment eventually benefits the old patriarchal arrangement of male supremacy as a restorative measure to control the apocalyptic feminine. Nevertheless, at the same time, it perpetuates Cohn's symbolic gender coding of war (2013: 12) in which men are perpetrators and women victims.

Salla (2001) indicates that gender differences during conflict result from 'socialization rather than biology'. As women have historically been socialized attending to an ethics of care and their identities have been constructed as relational (Hernando 2018; Salla 2001; Skjelsbæk 2001), an active and autonomous role in the military has been usually discouraged, as it would endanger the patriarchal delusive self-perception of male self-sufficiency and power in the universe. And if women participate, the relegated fields have been merely supportive and concerned with peacebuilding processes. Conflict proves to be the most effective tool to build gendered entities, as it limits masculine and feminine life experiences and roles through biological essentialism:

> If we regard motherhood as the central marker of the transition from girlhood to adult womanhood, and war-related activities as markers of the transition from boy to man, [...] femininity is conceptualized as inherently peaceful, it is

the concept of motherhood which is emphasized and cited to legitimize the claim.

Skjelsbæk 2001: n.p.

Skjelsbæk emphasizes how this essentialist understanding of womanhood – in their direct association to motherhood – as inherently antithetical to violence bestows men a justification to execute violent acts as it belongs to their 'true nature'. The configurations of men as naturally violent and women as naturally peaceful and maternal explain the relational dynamics of survivors during the plague. However, the impossibility of women sustaining such an equilibrium of peace and violence because of their disability in bearing progeny exposes the already existing dystopian qualities of society and showcases its latent apocalipticality.

Boesten argues how 'the gender regimes of macho men and available women feed into warfare' (2017: 514), and so it does oppositely since the women's plague 'legitimates' the fallacy of uncontrollable sexual instincts of macho men. Consequently, this assumption brings the slow extinction of women as their bodies are bartered for drugs or weapons between gangs. Indeed, gender reductionism not only presents women as inherently different from men but nullifies any other intersectional factors such as race, class, sexuality, age or disability, which seem inconsequential when women's availability is scarce. Duane Cady observes how this hegemonic violence is the consequence of hegemony itself, as the homogeneization of plural identities eventually legitimizes discourses of violence onto those that do not fit into this particular overdetermination: 'This is why hegemony is violent; it violates, distorts, coerces, dismisses, reduces, diminishes and devalues what it embraces' (qtd in Gursozlu 2018a: 90). Hence, older women, young girls, virgins, infertile, pregnant or wounded; all of them are cast as sperm vessels.

Normative masculinity is gained after violence-related rites of passage; likewise, the continuation of violence against women stems solely from men's belief that 'that is the way to show their masculinity' (Skjelsbæk and Smith 2001) and accordingly, their health, able-bodiedness and dominion in this decaying world. As this gender(ed) violence supposes a reckless endangerment of women's bodies and the oblivion of their identities, the unnamed midwife will perform the hegemonic codes of hypermasculinity intimately linked to violence as a survival and resistance strategy. In so doing, she excorporates the dominant directionality of violence, as she actually uses gender(ed) violence to take care of the female survivors she meets during her journey, collecting their forgotten names and testimonies.

The novel explores Goldstein's approach to gender (2001: 2) as the complex interdependence between biology and culture, considering how the conflict in the novel displays certain limitations in women's gender performativity caused by their bodily experiences of illness and pain. The protagonist remembers the past joys of her sexual freedom and gender equality with her partner before the cataclysm. She did not fit in the female stereotypes of fragility and submission, yet her encounter with the plague and sexual violence leads her to consider her female body 'an object of anxiety' (Aho 2018: 122). She contracted the disease while taking extra turns at the hospital but eventually recovered. Nevertheless, the feeling of unhomelikeness that comes along with the embodiment of the illness persists, making her feel insecure not only living in the world but also living in her body. Her objection towards her female body is overpowering after she suffers an attempt of rape short after she awakes from being unconscious. Rape also illustrates the interdependence between bodies as physical spaces and hermeneutical places, as it

> is a symbolic act of violence committed against a real body; but, worse perhaps, it is a symbolic act of violence committed 'with' a real body, an act of violence that attacks this body as a symbol, exploiting this body as a proxy or effigy in order to destroy something or someone who may be out of reach, unattainable, or untouchable.
>
> Miller 2014: 184

Alone and confused, the unnamed midwife manages to escape from the stranger, but these tragic events leave her body exposed as disabled within this conflictual situation. The possession of female corporeality is automatically diagnosed as an illness, for it 'disrupts the flow of everydayness, [...] not only disabled physically, [but also] as a self-interpreting being, our very identity is threatened' (Aho 2018: 122). Hence, aware of the dangers of being a woman in the apocalypse, she will dress and speak as a man.

Cross-dressing enables her to travel alone without being seen as prey. Despite the possible risks of infection from the women's plague still affecting her health, she rejects the likely determination of her biological sex (re)constructing her identity as a man. In a sense, the power of performance illustrates Aho's concept of a *bodily way of being* rather than being in a body, in as much as the midwife's identity

> [is] a 'self-making' or 'self-constituting' being insofar as [she has] the capacity to *take a stand* on who [she is] by interpreting [her] socio-historical and physiological givenness and engaging in the worldly projects that *matter* to [her] and are made available by the historical context into which [she has] been 'thrown'.
>
> 2018: 119

In a world of violent men, wearing men's clothes is a necessary survival strategy, not only to achieve a camouflaging hypermasculinity but also to regain that compulsory able-bodiedness that is only reserved for men in this gender(ed) conflict. As Heathcote interprets, men's clothes become an exoskeleton that 'render female bodies "closer" to male capabilities in armed conflict situations' (2018: 78). Hence, the representation of her gender identity through clothing is not playful but rather strategic and constrained to the violent and apocalyptic context she finds herself. Indeed, she presents a massive dissonance in her corporeality concerning Butler's dimensions about performativity: anatomical sex, gender identity and gender performance (1990: 137). The protagonist experiences the tensions between her anatomical sex as a woman and her hypermasculine gender performance, and in this intersection, she negotiates the attributes that shape her identity.

The spatial mobility she enjoys by performing as a man enables her to build an independent individuality beyond the chains of those aforementioned conventional feminine traits associated with relational thinking and motherhood. Nevertheless, the midwife does not elude the ethics of care, showcasing a balance between a violent performance and the undercover emotional bonding with other female survivors. In order to help these women, she impersonates the role of the sexual predator and exchanges medicines and weapons with male gangs for some time with the girls they have as prisoners. Though the hypermasculine midwife pretends to have sex in that time, she actually helps these women heal their wounds and provides them with contraceptive methods and other drugs to avoid the risk of infection and deadly pregnancy. Hence, her strategy becomes an act conforming to Sargisson's features of transgressive utopianism (2002: 2), as it is deliberately subversive, resistant to permanence and order and is utopian. Nevertheless, despite subverting women's (potential) victimhood, she also reinforces the gender coding of war when adopting masculinity as armour and equating it to violence.

Apart from cross-dressing, the unnamed midwife's performance as a man relies on the representation of a violent discourse:

Bitch, I am a man. Females. Talk too much. Quit crying. So emotional. Be a man. Man up. Nut up. Jump shot, gunshot, cum shot, money shot. Posing but not to be sexy. Scare me. Lean a little forward. Invade my space. Quit crying. Give you something to cry about.

Elison 2014: 54, original emphasis

Gay considers language to be the most conservative institution in the configuration of our society, and in so doing, it preserves the foundations of epistemic violence, which then naturalizes other forms of social violence: 'Language is inseparable from the distribution of power in society, and these relations are unequal in every society. Language is frequently an instrument of covert institutional violence' (2018: 40–1). The protagonist struggles when presenting a convincing imitation of this violent masculinity, although she has internalzed the idea that the language of violence is gendered, associating it with the conventional qualities of a conflictive hypermasculinity. Thus, even though her performance of a male discourse supposes an excorporation of violence that could allow her to escape from the gender polarization in war personally, the repetition of these social 'masculine' practices legitimizes the public binary gender coding, inasmuch as 'the performance is effected with the strategic aim of maintaining gender within its binary frame – an aim that cannot be attributed to a subject, but, rather, must be understood to *found and consolidate the subject*' (Butler 1990: 140, emphasis added).

Indeed, the foundation of these masculine identities comes with her name change. After the unsuccessful attempt of building a female alter ego at the beginning of the narrative with the name of Karen, the midwife activates her performance as a man. Considering how language is a tool that can enact symbolic violence, Dedaic considers that naming is the most potent mechanism as it is 'a speech act imposed upon us by others' (2003: 3). The midwife is empowered by naming herself as a man, determining this way the rest of her identity. These masculine pseudonyms – Rob, Carl, Alex or Dusty – help consolidate this transformation, changing her character in every new encounter she has. Even though the midwife never reveals her real name, not even in her diary, the woman's name she chooses to have when she arrives at the shelter of Fort Nowhere at the end of the novel allegorizes how structural patriarchal violence is. By calling herself Jane, she represents any woman and all women at once, encapsulating and embodying the experiences of all female survivors during the apocalypse.

In Fort Nowhere, the recovery of a female alias suggests how this place emerges as a utopian community where to perform gender beyond the binary constraints of war codes. This society is described as egalitarian considering that there is no hierarchical distribution of power. Their military services also operate peacekeeping missions outside their fortress to save women from human trafficking and collect anyone who is willing to live there as a feminist ally. Nevertheless, the distribution of these social functions is complementary still, as men – because they are not as affected as women by the disease and not as exposed to the dangers of sex trafficking – can enjoy more free mobility. Women can *accompany* men as long as they carry weapons, too, and drive trucks, like Ava travelling with Dino, the couple that recruited Jane. As she has skills as a nurse and midwife, they invite her to join Fort Nowhere so that she can bring medical knowledge, particularly related to obstetrics, to the people joining the community. The recruiting of women in Fort Nowhere complements and expands the skills of this defensible base, but their inclusion does not actually challenge hegemonic violence and the perpetuation of negative forms of power.

The recovery of Jane's female identity does not pigeonhole the unnamed midwife as ideally feminine, for she does not comply with the attributes of peace and forgiveness. The interiorization of the linguistic codes of war permeates the midwife's relationality with others at the end of the novel, conveying a combination of care and this newly acquired violence. Kearney observes hence that language not only represents but also shapes our experiences: 'The I which speaks words is the I spoken in words. Sensation and language are isomorphic. But they are also transmorphic' (2015: 38). Not long after she settles in Fort Nowhere, a young pregnant girl called Colleen is brought by her rapists looking for guns in exchange. When Colleen comes with her rapists, Jane executes them without hesitation nor remorse: 'I can't fix you. I don't have the time to teach you why you're wrong if you don't already know. So this is it. Stand or kneel?' (Elison 2014: 270). The deaths of the perpetrators are part of a peacebuilding process and security within the community of Fort Nowhere. Nevertheless, the use of forceful tactics perpetuates violence – not only in the physical act but also in the discourse choices – that precisely validates other nodal hegemonic views in the construction of society. The continuation of violence by the midwife fails to comply with Salla's view that women's fundamental participation in the state's decision-making can eliminate violence in the resolution of any conflict. The employment of violence toward other people, even if it is to the criminal, enacts a cyclical motion in which violence prevails, but as Gay concludes, a break from this loop is necessary and must start with the practice of non-violent discourses:

> We can speak and act nonviolently. We can take on the cause to stop the killing— not just at the local level but globally as well. A nonkilling philosophy when focused on efforts to eliminate linguistic violence and to advance the practice of linguistic nonviolence could play a central role in efforts at reducing cultural violence and expanding social justice.
>
> Gay 2018: 59

The justification of sexual violence is also inferred with the messianic birth of a child of rape. The birth of Colleen's daughter, with the assistance of the midwife, marks the promising start of a utopian civilization: 'In the beginning, there was Rhea. Nobody will as why ever again. She is why' (Elison 2014: 288). Rhea comes as a *deus ex machina* that seems to justify all the sacrifice Colleen has suffered and serves ask a simplistic remedy to end the apocalypse without further questioning if that supposes the end of patriarchal violence. As the plague motif serves 'to wipe away existing systems and practices, sometimes clearing the way for better alternatives' (Booker 2014: 184), the Nativity of Rhea is utilized to imagine the end of patriarchy easily. This miracle, together with the survival of the female protagonist, implies that women and their (re)productive power are the only responsible ones in the peacebuilding process. The apocalypse suggests the impossibility of macho men's reformation into equity and sexual education. Instead, it puts hopes on humankind's restoration via conventional procreation forms highly determined by relations of male power and violence rather than seeking mutual pleasure.

After Colleen's labour, a new matriarchal social organization is arranged in Fort Nowhere with the Midwife, Colleen and Rhea as its Holy Trinity. This sacralization of women follows a categorization that depends on women's maternal potentiality, a distinction that sediments in the coming generations to reaffirm the hegemonic understanding of womanhood, mainly if associated with their matrixial potentiality. After establishing the Law of Emily, Fort Nowhere will make a separation between two types of women, those that are fertile and those who are not: 'mothers could not be midwives' (Elison 2014, 289). Women who can beget children will live secluded in the House of Mothers, drastically reducing their mobility beyond this temple. Pregnancy and early childrearing – qualities biologically and conventionally attributed to the feminine biological sex – continue being portrayed as disenabling aspects, hence presenting the female body similarly to the apocalyptic times, as a disabled subject simply because the female sex is the primary affected by the social precariousness and continues being the main victim of epistemic violence, eventually leading women into

> a position of being the 'object of care,' of being 'taken care of,' at best by tenderness, often in neglecting scientific knowledge which succeeds in identifying and in treating specific symptoms, and through a self-indulgence that ends up in infantilization. Indeed, the intrinsic logic of this model slows down the disabled subject: it prevents them from being open to their 'powers,' that is to say to their singular potentialities, and prevents them from turning their solitude, always irrevocable, into its singular creativity, to its initiative which can be shared within its appropriate limits.
>
> Kristeva 2015: 124–125

Even though Fort Nowhere enacts a peacekeeping strategy based on the defence against external violence and the protection of mothers, the radical outcome after the Law of Emily displays an ableist position that perpetuates women as ill and fragile bodies.

And yet, Fort Nowhere is portrayed as the ultimate site of resistance against patriarchal violence, where women can hold a position of power in decision-making and are even deified due to their maternal power. Rhea's Nativity is the ceasefire of apocalyptic cataclysm, but fear and trauma still prevail in the post-apocalypse, for the 'persistence in the continuum of sexual violence against women [...] supersedes the categories of war and peace' (Boesten 2017: 507). The worship of womanhood resides in their capacity of bearing progeny despite their rare affliction. The confinement as if they were an endangered species is thus justified, but it consequently preserves a warlike gender coding that reinscribes the gender binary as determinants for our experiences. This situation enunciates the quandary of whether to use the same patriarchal mechanisms of violence to disintegrate the power structures from within or rather to evade patriarchy using alternative resources. This study has presented how precariousness and conflict become conditioning factors for the configuration and reinforcement of gender polarization, illustrating the multimorphic character of patriarchy and its manifestations of violence. Nevertheless, Elison employs the apocalyptic event to envisage the chances of creation from the scraps of an old system.

Elison's imagery of Fort Nowhere does not contemplate building particular perfectibility as in classic utopias. Rhea's messianic birth portrays the core phenomenon of utopianism, a concept characterized by its non-finitude and social dreaming, an inherent human impulse to aspire for the better (Sargisson 2012: 9). Arendt observes utopianism in the image of natality. Despite Rhea being a child of rape, the newborn denotes the recovery of humanity, boosting the will of change in the inhabitants of Fort Nowhere and many other survivors abroad: 'the new beginning inherent in birth can make itself felt in the world only because the newcomer possesses the capacity of beginning something anew, that is, of acting' (Arendt 1998: 9). Moreover, the glorification of Colleen's raped body emulates Jesus Christ's resurrection because both are elevated even though their bodies have been harmed, as Kristeva notes:

> Does [Jesus] not appear to his apostles, even in his glory, with an 'impaired body,' a damaged body? Here, the wound is not a lack, because it is an integral part of the Glory, itself given and perceived as a singularity.
>
> Kristeva 2015: 126

The contingency of Colleen's success after her experience of trauma is what determines her labour as a miracle. The midwife relates in her diary Rhea's birth as the scene of the Nativity, presenting the newborn as the milestone of a promising era:

> Maybe there was a plan, maybe it's all connected, maybe Rhea will walk on water and raise the dead. Only won by forfeit or default. Not because we really understand or because we deserve it. [...] Don't know why it worked or how we did it. Can't explain method = can't repiclate results. No science [...], just the sound of that baby crying and the whole village coming to see. [...] In the absence of science, we have folk magic. We don't know why it works, but it worked before. Working again. Midwives, working again. Victory?
>
> Elison 2014: 291

Nevertheless, midwives' assistance in labour is acknowledged here, conferring them a power that has been neglected in the history of patriarchy. That Jane, Colleen and Rhea represent the Triple Goddess – Crone, Mother and Maid – and not simply replicate the patriarchal trinitarian divinity leads to new ways of understanding victory. The novel's ambiguous ending does not resolve the issue of apocalyptic violence, but by choosing Rhea's birth as a victory, it breaks with the conventional interpretation of victory as warlike: 'the position or state of having overcome an enemy or adversary in combat, battle, or war; supremacy or superiority achieved as the result of armed conflict' ('victory': n.d.). This victory is non-conflictual, though its interrogation does not guarantee peace. Rhea's birth shows as a non-intentional form of resistance against the apocalypticality of the women's plague, and in so being, it also proves a non-violent victory against patriarchal hegemony, imagining positive forms of showing power and rebuking the previous compulsory warlike codes of sociability.

Elison's final utopia in Fort Nowhere resorts to the initial concept of place, not as a demarcated space on the land, but as a living project that grows and is under construction, in constant need of revisiting and transformation. Even though Rhea's birth supposes a disruption of the violence loop that readers witness between the plague and the sexual violence of this apocalypse, the manifestations of power are still somehow gendered according to a strong hegemony: mainstream masculinity has been portrayed as aggressive; women's power revolves around the event of motherhood. And, as Gursozlu warns, 'what we should be concerned about is not simply the hegemony of a discourse of cultural violence over and within a particular social sphere. We should also pay attention to the possible violence of any form of hegemony' (2018a: 104). The sequels *The*

Book of Etta (2017) and *The Book of Flora* (2019) explore further the development and interpretation of this victory during the post-apocalypse. The answers to this final question '*Victory?*' come in different modes of deconstructing the social conventions within and without Fort Nowhere, attempting to defy hegemony itself and create a place where gender is articulated without constraints.

Conclusion

The Book of the Unnamed Midwife realistically depicts the challenges of feminist sci-fi narratives in their quest to imagine utopias off the shackles of a patriarchal capitalist system. While the world-ending experience enables authors to create a new place by amending the errors of our contemporary dystopian society, the conflictual character of apocalypticality itself hinders a clean detachment towards an alternative sociability. Significantly, violence as a resistance mode supposes an excorporation that defies the uncontested male dominance, but the mere incorporation of violence in the resolution condemning patriarchal brutality maintains hegemonic modes of relationality, which tend to be gendered. This gender polarization is especially acute whenever our biological condition determines our experiences and vice versa, as is the case of the women's plague. The experience of illness has affected women's motility, freedom and comfort not only by the disease itself but by the alienation felt in the world.

Envisaging a matriarchal community after Rhea's birth does not provide the solution to these predicaments, nor does it suppose an end to the apocalypse. Moreover, Elison intentionally precludes the construction of Fort Nowhere as faultless. The fort walls do not evade them from the conflict, people do not live forever, and the disease continues being propagated. Nevertheless, children are also born, and with them, society is reborn. The name of this community shows the oxymoronic essence of Elison's utopia: it is set in a particular place, but it is nowhere; it is enclosed and secured, though it is changing and imprecise, too. The impossibility and refusal to the sedimentation of any cultural and social dogmas despite framing a definite settlement and the recovery of natality as a form of positive power make this novel inherently and successfully utopian.

Science fiction may not bring concrete solutions to the real world's problems – it does not stop conflicts and pandemics. However, its utopian motion invites us to reflect and critical thinking, as these fictional places 'permit us to imagine how our world can be better and that is the first step towards changing it' (Sargisson 2005: 53). In particular, feminist sci-fi narrative faces the challenge of finding a location to freely express women's kaleidoscopic identities – always ever-changing and different, but also mutually reflective and collective. Despite the hurdles in the journey to this particular *nowhere*, the imaginative exercise of conceptualizing a possible place (even if it is only textual or hermeneutical) proves to be the starting point to question the conventions of our dystopian reality:

> We need to imagine a new world in which every woman is the presiding genius of her own body. In such a world women will truly create new life, bringing forth not only children (if and as we choose) but the visions, and thinking, necessary to sustain, console and alter human existence – a new relationship to the universe. [...] This is where we have to begin.
>
> Rich [1976] 1986: 285–6

Elison's novel is about death and violence, but also about life and creation. The women portrayed show the fluctuating nature of these opposites. The midwife has the power to kill as men do and assist the labour of mother Colleen. Colleen, a victim of sexual trafficking, gains ironic agency by deciding to have her baby in a world where pregnancy foretells death. Rhea, a child of rape and death, survives, Fort Nowhere becoming the cradle of a new civilization. In this apocalypse, birth brings death, but it also brings change. Such change takes us to mysterious unmade roads, roads to nowhere, but '*people hope this is the beginning. Beginning. Not the end, the beginning*' (Elison 2014: 288, original emphasis).

References

Aho, Kevin. 2018. 'A Hermeneutics of the Body and Place in Health and Illness'. In Bruce B. Janz (ed.), *Place, Space and Hermeneutics*, 115–127. Berlin: Springer.

Arendt, Hannah. 1998. *The Human Condition.* Chicago, IL: University of Chicago Press.

Boesten, Jelke. 2017. 'Of Exceptions and Continuities: Theory and Methodology in Research on Conflict-Related Sexual Violence'. *International Feminist Journal of Politics*, 19 (4): 506–19.

Booker, M. Keith. 2014. *Historical Dictionary of Science Fiction in Literature.* Lanham, MD: Rowman & Littlefield Publishers.

Butler, Judith. 1990. *Gender Trouble: Feminism and the Subversion of Identity.* London: Routledge.

Cockburn, Cynthia. 2004. 'The Continuum of Violence: A Gender Perspective on War and Peace'. In Wenona Giles and Jennifer Hyndman (eds), *Sites of Violence: Gender and Conflict Zones*, 24–44. Berkeley, CA: University of California Press.

Cohn, Carol. 2013. 'Women and Wars: Towards a Conceptual Framework'. In Carol Cohn (ed.), *Women and Wars*, 1–35. Cambridge: Polity Press.

Dedaic, Mirjana N. 2003. 'Introduction: A Peace of Word'. In Mirjana N. Dedaic and Daniel N. Nelson (eds), *At War with Words*, 1–23. Berlin and New York: Mouton De Gruyter.

Elison, Meg. 2014. *The Book of the Unnamed Midwife*. Seattle, WA: 47North.

Gadamer, Hans-Georg. 1996. *The Enigma of Health: The Art of Healing in a Scientific Age*. Stanford, CA: Stanford University Press.

Gallagher, Shaun, Sergio F. Martínez and Melina Gastelum. 2018. 'Action-Space and Time: Towards an Enactive Hermeneutics'. In Bruce B. Janz (ed.), *Place, Space and Hermeneutics*, 83–96. Berlin: Springer.

Gallardo, Pere. 2005. 'Dystopia is You'. In Fátima Vieira and Marinela Freitas (eds), *Utopia Matters: Theory Politics, Literature and the Arts*, 37–9. Porto: Universidad do Porto.

Gay, William C. 2018. 'The Role of Language in Justifying and Eliminating Cultural Violence'. In Fuat Gursozlu (ed.), *Peace, Culture, and Violence*, 1–63. Boston, MA: Brill.

Goldstein, Joshua S. 2001. *War and Gender*. Cambridge: Cambridge University Press.

Gomel, Elana. 2000. 'The Plague of Utopias: Pestilence and the Apocalyptic Body'. *Twentieth Century Literature*, 46 (4): 406–33.

Gursozlu, Fuat. 2018a. 'Cultural Violence, Hegemony, and Agonistic Interventions'. In Fuat Gursozlu (ed.), *Peace, Culture, and Violence*, 4–105. Boston, MA: Brill.

Gursozlu, Fuat. 2018b. 'Introduction'. In Fuat Gursozlu (ed.), *Peace, Culture, and Violence*, 1–6. Boston, MA: Brill.

Harder, Keith. 2018. 'When the "Here and Now" is Nowhere'. In Bruce B. Janz (ed.), *Place, Space and Hermeneutics*, 333–46. Berlin: Springer.

Heathcote, Gina. 2018. 'War's Perpetuity: Disabled Bodies of War and the Exoskeleton of Equality'. *Australian Feminist Law Journal*, 44 (1): 71–91.

Hernando, Almudena. 2018. *La Fantasía de la Individualidad. Sobre la Construcción Sociohistórica del Sujeto Moderno*. Madrid: Traficantes de Sueños.

Hongisto, Leif. 2010. *Experiencing the Apocalypse at the Limits of Alterity*. Boston, MA: Brill.

Janz, Bruce B. 2018. 'Is Place a Text?' In Bruce B. Janz (ed.), *Place, Space and Hermeneutics*, 23–34. Berlin: Springer.

Kearney, Richard. 2015. 'The Wager of Carnal Hermeneutics'. In Richard Kearney and Brian Treanor (eds), *Carnal Hermeneutics: From Head to Foot*, 15–56. New York: Fordham University Press.

Kearney, Richard and Brian Treanor. 2015. 'Introduction: Carnal Hermeneutics from Head to Foot'. In Richard Kearney and Brian Treanor (eds), *Carnal Hermeneutics: From Head to Foot*, 1–11. New York: Fordham University Press.

Kristeva, Julia. 2015. 'A Tragedy and a Dream: Disability Revisited'. In Richard Kearney and Brian Treanor (eds), *Carnal Hermeneutics: From Head to Foot*, 115–27. New York: Fordham University Press.

Miller, Steven. 2014. *War after Death: On Violence and Its Limits*. New York: University of Virginia Press.

Moylan, Tom. 2000. *Scraps of the Untainted Sky: Science Fiction, Utopia, Dystopia*. Oxford: Westview Press.

Olivier, Abraham. 2018. 'Understanding Place'. In Bruce B. Janz (ed.), *Place, Space and Hermeneutics*, 9–22. Berlin: Springer.

Rich, Adrienne. [1976] 1986. *Of Woman Born:. Motherhood as Experience and Institution*. New York and London: Norton.

Salla, Michael. 2001. 'Women & War, Men & Pacifism'. In Inger Skjelsboek and Dan Smith (eds), *Gender, Peace and Conflict*. London: Sage. Available online: https://ebookcentral.proquest.com/lib/ujaen/detail.action?docID=254759 (accessed 30 March 2022).

Sargisson, Lucy. 1996. *Contemporary Feminist Utopianism*. London: Routledge.

Sargisson, Lucy. 2002. *Utopian Bodies and the Politics of Transgression*. London: Routledge.

Sargisson, Lucy. 2005. 'Why Utopia Matters'. In Fátima Vieira and Marinela Freitas (eds), *Utopia Matters: Theory Politics, Literature and the Arts*, 51–4. Porto: Universidad do Porto.

Sargisson, Lucy. 2012. *Fool's Gold? Utopianism in the Twenty-First Century*. Basingstoke and New York: Palgrave.

Scarry, Elaine. 1985. *The Body in Pain: The Making and Unmaking of the World*. New York: Oxford University Press.

Schlitte, Annika. 2018. 'Narrative and Place'. In Janz B. Bruce (eds), *Place, Space and Hermeneutics*, 35–48. Berlin: Springer.

Schmidt, Lawrence K. 2014. *Understanding Hermeneutics*. Durham: Taylor & Francis.

2001. 'Is Femininity Inherently Peaceful? The Construction of Femininity in the War'. In Inger Skjelsbæk and Dan Smit (eds), *Gender, Peace and Conflict*. London: Sage. Available online: https://ebookcentral.proquest.com/lib/ujaen/detail.action?docID=254759 (accessed 30 March 2022).

Skjelsbæk, Inger and Dan Smith. 2001. 'Introduction'. In Inger Skjelsbæk and Dan Smith (eds), *Gender, Peace and Conflict*. London: Sage. Available online: https://ebookcentral.proquest.com/lib/ujaen/detail.action?docID=254759 (accessed 30 March 2022).

Suvin, Darko. 2016. *Metamorphoses of Science Fiction: On the Poetics and History of a Literary Genre*. Ed. Gerry Canavan. Bern: Peter Lang.

Treanor, Brian. 2015. 'Mind the Gap: The Challenge of Matter'. In Richard Kearney and Brian Treanor (eds), *Carnal Hermeneutics: From Head to Foot*, 57–73. New York: Fordham University Press.

'Victory'. n.d. *Oxford English Dictionary*. Available online: https://www--oed--com.ujaen.debiblio.com/view/Entry/223235?rskey=BsA2lw&result=1&isAdvanced=false#eid (accessed 23 March 2022).

Weber, Samuel. 2015. 'Foreword: One Sun too Many'. In Peter Szendy (ed.), *Apocalypse-Cinema: 2012 and Other Ends of the World*, ix–xx. New York: Fordham University Press.

World Health Organization (WHO). n.d. *Constitution.* Available online: https://www.who.int/about/who-we-are/constitution (accessed 3 April 2022).

8

Prophesizing War in 'The Lament of the Deer' by Christopher Okigbo

Paula García-Ramírez

Introduction

After many years of being unfairly neglected, African poetry is beginning to be recognized as part of the standard literary canon, which has led to greater interest from academic circles. A recent anthology by Christopher Okemwa, sponsored by himself, brings into scenery the poems of more than 150 contemporary poets from the continent with the purpose of demonstrating how 'their poetry is an art that aims at positively effecting and transforming the African society in which they live and in which they write their poetry' (Okemwa 2022: viii). Although the specialized bibliography has grown considerably in recent decades,[1] African poetry remains largely unknown beyond its borders, especially when compared to African narrative, which has made an effective progress in its dissemination to the public, parallel to the consolidation of a critical apparatus around it.

Sub-Saharan African poetry is rooted in indigenous orality, which remains the main unifying element for most of the authors. All of them (mostly men, although there are some notable women) fulfil the prototype of the African artist; that is, they are artists of a broad spectrum and with an indisputable intellectual stamp, who not only cultivate poetry, but also narrative and essay writing, with examples where literature is combined with the visual arts. They also belong to a specific social caste, an elite educated in the best universities on the continent, who have usually completed their training abroad (either in the colonial metropolizes, in the United States, etc.). For this reason, a double tradition coexists in these authors: the word heard and repeated by word of mouth, typical of the culture in which they were born, and the written word, typical of a foreign culture in origin, but of which they have been fully imbued.

Therefore, this dialectic between orality and writing, their far from easy harmonization and the possible conflicts that arise from it, constitute the foundation on which contemporary African poetry is built. To use a neologism that has made a fortune in this field, secular orality and written transmission are combined in an '*orature*' (cf. Chinweizu, Onwuchekwa and Ihechukwu 1983: 2), which reinterprets cultural inheritance through a crosscultural path, whose embodiment may take new or old forms: artistic festivals, plays, proverbs, oral poetry, myths, legends, music and invocations. In the words of Ogundokun (2015: 181): 'form parts of daily life of the African people in which their culture is expressed. All of these depict social realities and help to keep the events of the past and the present for the future generations'.

In close relationship with orality we should focus our attention on the importance of time and the connection with the cycles. Gadamer's theory on time elaborates upon the idea that 'when we are aware of time directly, we are aware of belonging to temporal epochs, of existing within temporal periods either in our life or in history, and not simply of belonging to the continuous flow of time' (qtd by Vessey 2007: 2).

In fact, an essential concept of modernism but also of traditional African poetry is shown in the continuous references to the past and present in African history. Gadamer's concept may apply to our discussion topic. This cyclical idea of history developed among others by Adorno and Yeats might explain the references to the history of some African poets, among them Wole Soyinka (Nigeria), Birago Diop (Senegal) or Toyin Adewale-Gabriel (Nigeria). In the particular case of Christopher Okigbo, African past is used to interpret the events of the present. Throughout Okigbo's poem called 'The Lament of the Deer', which appeared as part of a tale titled *How the Leopard got his Claws* written by Achebe and Iroaganachi in 1972, the reader learns about an indefinite time in which animals had human features.

Attached to the Igbo oral tradition, tale and poem prophesize the war in this land. Strictly speaking, the narration moves into the oral Igbo tradition, though there are elements which resemble the European literary canon. Among the Bolekaja critics (Chinweizu, Onwuchekwa and Ihechukwu 1983), literature may be evaluated on African parameters only. However, I intend to show that a hermeneutic reading of this poem would enrich the understanding of Okigbo's African roots as well as his adopted euromodernist perspectives. Connecting both backgrounds universalizes Okigbo's vision as both a seer and poet.

Encapsulating Meaning: The Intellectual, His Mates and the Biafra War

As an outstanding figure in the context of the first generation of Nigerian writers, Christopher Okigbo has been widely acclaimed by the critics and companions, despite his short life and production. The writer was member of the intellectual elite which was associated to *Government College* at Umuhaia, and he has become one more among the Nigerians who were brought up in a peculiar school essentially devoted to prepare the new rulers of Nigeria at the end of the colonization. Probably, as Terri Ochiagha (2015: 11) clearly pinpoints, the school 'created more spaces of ideological indeterminacy than of willful imperial brainwashing' and the students have found at the school the setting for literary discussions, common readings and an atmosphere which allow them to connect a traditional cultural background recreated at home as well as a British-centred syllabus. Among the students that live together at Government College, Umuahia, we may mention Chinua Achebe, Christopher Okigbo, Wole Soyinka, Chike Momah and Chukwuemeka Ike. All of them had an active role in the decolonization process that was held in Nigeria during the 1960s and most of them had important jobs in the independent Nigerian administration, without mentioning that they are leading intellectual figures of the African continent.

The events that led the country towards independence (1963) and war (1967–70) prevail in the poetry of Christopher Okigbo who will interpret the present using the elements from an undefined time in the past. His influence in a whole generation of African poets has been widely explained but it is worth mentioning how Chinua Achebe, probably the best exponent of his legacy, encompassed the deep influence he had on this future generations as well as the prevalence of the poet-myth:

> The intensity of Christopher's dedication to the Biafran cause was so deep that I remember hearing him get into a raucous debate with his elder brother Pius. Apparently the cause of the flare-up of emotions was a discussion about Biafran sovereignty and its importance for the Easterners, particularly the Igbo, to create a state of their own and secede from the federal Republic of Nigeria.
>
> Achebe 2012: 117

The Nigerian poets who wrote after independence in 1960 share some vital and artistic characteristics. These pioneers shared classrooms in schools in Ibadan and Lagos and, as noted above, completed their education abroad. They have a perfect command of the English language and, on the literary level; they are fully familiar with the Anglo-American tradition. The same influences can be found in their texts as in the verse of Hopkins, Yeats, Eliot, Pound and many others. However, what defines the uniqueness of Nigerian poets in relation to other contemporary authors of the Anglophone domain is that, over and above their contact with the Western tradition, they manifest the need to find an individual voice whose tone is recognizably African.

In this search for the African, two fundamental thematic axes operate. On the one hand, they look to the continent's history in order to disprove the mythical idea, common in the European imagination, that Africa has no history of its own beyond the colonial past. On the other hand, the focus is on the cyclical journey as an essential element in the experience of these authors as poetic subjects. This journey is composed, in accordance with Western patterns, of an exodus, identifiable with academic training abroad and a subsequent return to the roots, which is usually accompanied by a feeling of uprootedness, of feeling rejected and foreign in one's own country.

It is well understood that, from the 1970s onwards, experiences of return are conditioned by the uncertain socio-political evolution of poscolonial countries. Among them, Pol Nnamuzikam Ndu (1940–1976), John Pepper Clark-Bekeredemo (1935–2020) and the Nigerian Nobel Prize Wole Soyinka (1934–) who represent with Christopher Okigbo this first generation of Nigerian poets immersed in the perplexities of the present, while researching on the roots of the past. They share, as I have already examined, a common educational background as well as a temporal space fulfilled with what Gadamer calls a common experience of time:

> In the context of our normal, pragmatic experience of time, we say that we 'have time for something'. The time is at our disposal; it is divisible; it is the time that we have or do not have, or at least think we do not have. In its temporal structure such time is empty and needs to be filled.
>
> Gadamer 1986: 41

This temporal structure coincide with the historical events that affected all these Nigerian poets when the population of Biafra, members of the Igbo ethnical group in its majority, attempted to build an independent state in 1967. This conflict, known as the Nigerian Civil War or the Biafra War, led to one of the most bloody and bitter struggles remembered in the Twentieth century. Christopher Okigbo, the seer-prophet poet, lost his life at the very beginning of the struggle. His death marked the vital path of many of the Nigerian writers of his generation

Christopher Okigbo: Seer-Prophet Poet

Christopher Okigbo (1932–1967), often described as a poet-prophet, has had an enormous influence on many of the poets I have mentioned above and, in general, on the whole African cultural context of the last half century. His poetry is rooted in the Igbo oral tradition, the ethno-linguistic group of southeastern Nigeria from which he hails, and he made his name through books such as *Heavensgate* (1962) and *Limits* (1964). Okigbo participated in many of the cultural enterprises promoted in his country. He was editor of the magazines like *Transition* and *Black Orpheus*.

His great literary projection was cut short by his early death in combat during the early stages of the war in Biafra. In addition to these collections of poems, *Labyrinths* (1971) and *Selected Poems* (1986), which brings together all his work in verse, were published posthumously. *Labyrinths* is probably the most reliable testimony of the author's evolution, since it includes poems from his early youth, clearly subject to an Anglo-American influence, to 'Path of Thunder', written during the war, a few days before his death. Okigbo has a deep knowledge of Igbo oral literary traditions, as well as of Western poetry, both modern and ancient (he studied classical philology). All this is subjected to an elaborate symbolism that allowed him to temper apparently very heterogeneous elements into a unitary whole. Okigbo's extraordinary artistic quality and powerful personality made him the undisputed leader of an entire poetic generation. Moreover, the circumstances of his death have determined his subsequent mythification as a contemporary martyr of the Igbo people, to the extent that he has practically become a legend. This fact also marked the vital path of many of his friends, particularly that of Chinua Achebe, who will rethink his role as an intellectual after that:

> This [the Biafran War] was such a cataclysmic experience that for me it virtually changed the history of Africa and the history of Nigeria. Everything I had known before, all the optimism had to be re-thought.
>
> Searle 1991: 13

A review of Okigbo's life allows us to identify the moment when the poet encountered the literary current of modernism. When he finished his studies, and after doing various jobs in Lagos, he got a job as a Latin teacher at the *Fiditi Grammar School* (1958), near Ibadan. From the beginning he was involved in activities related to the University of Ibadan and contributed to the school's newspaper. He also gave some lectures and, among the young students like John

Pepper Clark-Bekeredemo who spoke of him in the following terms: 'I introduced him to the paper (*The Horn*) as he spouted the Old Classics to me and I the New Greats to him. That's how he met Pound, Eliot, and Yeats ...' (Nwoga 1984: 22). He will complete the journey as a librarian at the University of Nsukka.

The impact, in this case, would come from outside, as Okigbo developed a keen interest in life outside the campus. Rituals, festivals, masked performances and poetry. *Heavensgate* (1962) and *Limits* (1964) were written in Nsukka and published by the Mbari Club, one of the most outstanding cultural events of post-independent Nigeria. Particularly, *Heavensgate* reveals a powerful new voice in Nigerian poetry that compels the reader to recreate into the musicality and hearing of the vernacular tradition through the incorporation of traditional rituals as radically opposed to the more orthodox Christian liturgy:

> The overall meaning of *Heavensgate* emerged when the set of poems to which it belonged was complete and the mythic pattern of Okigbo's development became manifest. What was clear from the beginning was the set of concerns that was featured in the sequence: religion, both Christian and traditional; education and childhood experiences; love and desire; frustration; and, above all, the mentality of a suffering and confused protagonist confronted with these experiences – 'the Orpheus figure at the beginning of his quest'.
>
> Nwonga 1984: 22

Prophesizing War: Interpreting a Tale

When *How the Leopard Got His Claws*[2] was published by Chinua Achebe in 1972, Christopher Okigbo had already died, the Biafra war had ended and many Igbo intellectuals had abandoned Nigeria. The text appeared as a tale for children and has to be understood, basically, as an animal tale.[3] Besides, it is worth mentioning that there are human beings acting (the hunter and the blacksmith), although their role is a secondary one, and there is also a natural force (Thunder) gifted with supernatural character features.

Two animals are the main protagonists of the story. The dog, defined in terms of negative features (individualism, selfishness, lack of empathy) destroys the common good while the leopard justifies his violent and vengeful reaction as a consequence of it: 'I do not blame you' (Achebe with Iroaganachi [1972] 1994) is the sentence repeated as much by the blacksmith as by Thunder when they listen to his story. Nevertheless, his ultimate revenge cannot justify the initial injustice. That is, once the leopard calls for violence, the consequences of his actions seems disproportionate, as he will condemn the community to chaos instead of restoring the pre-established order. Though the dog becomes king, he does not modify the social communal order. At the end, the leopard's revenge will create an authoritarian government.

The story has a strong aetiological value (García-Ramírez 2003), if we bear in mind that it deals with the origins of the leopard's claws but it goes beyond as it also explains the reasons for the violence in the world of animals, the domesticity of dogs and the inherent rage in the animals kingdom. At this point, the conflicts among animals develop into an interpretation of the events that took place in Nigeria after the Independence. Thus, Raisa Simola (1995: 259) remarks that this is the gloomiest of the stories by Chinua Achebe, who wrote it after the end of the war and during Okigbo's mourning. The tragedy outbursts because of an internal conflict in the community. None of the human beings, either the hunter or the blacksmith, intervenes into the events, though they will contribute to the extension of violence.

If we take into account the events described in the story and what we know about Nigerian history, another interpretation is however conceivable. Colonization and the process of Independence hid a deeper conflict that grounded into Nigerian society. Never-ending political, religious and social disputes after the independence will favour the social destruction of the country. In 1967, the Eastern region of Biafra declared the independence from Nigerian Federal territory and an endless Civil War isolated Igboland. The secessionist state suffered incredibly and the consequences of the war devastated the civil population in the area of Eastern Nigeria and three years later, the leader of the Biafran Government, Odumegwu Ojukwu, run away leaving the population defenceless and unprotected.

The Consequences of the War: 'The Lament of the Deer'

Christopher Okigbo composed a poem for the tale *How the Leopard Got His Claws* entitled, 'The Lament of the Deer'. In fact, the word *lament* acquires a deeper meaning if we take into account Okigbo's poetic ideology. Many of his compositions include this word in the title, which allows the poet to connect his poetry with a long tradition. Lament, understood as a 'non-narrative poem expressing deep grief or sorrow over a personal loss', is one of the oldest known poetic modalities. Testimonies are found in Mesopotamia, Egypt, Greece, etc. practically from the origins of written literature.[4] Personally, my belief is that

Okigbo uses this old poetic genre because it constitutes a crossroads where different paths converge: 'SILENCE FACES at crossroads:/Festivity in black [...] (The Passage)' will be the words when he describes his mother's funeral between two cultures. Thus, he delves into the western culture and the oral tradition of his people. The combination of precolonial indigenous and European elements is one of the most salient features of Okigbo's poetry (Richards 2005: 389).

The previously mentioned ideas are set in 'The Lament of the Deer', which follows completely to the canons of the genre. Formally, it has effects such as the presence of refrains. Thematically, it mentions to a collective tragedy, as the dog's violent action will bring about the end of the utopian state in which the animals lived under the leopard's law. Functionally, it is inserted within a narrative context, as an intensifying counterpoint to the climax of the story. However, this narrative context is a fable rather than an epic poem. Actually, it has no consequences at all, for both genres are within the lands of oral literature. In short, Okigbo proves in this brief composition a clear awareness of the *raison d'être* of the lament, a genre that was particularly dear to his heart.[5]

Structurally speaking 'The Lament of the Deer' consists of only fourteen lines, with free meter. A short, synthetic poem inserted into a tale. Moreover, it has only nine different lines as some of them are repeated as refrains. Duplicity and ellipses advocate a rather syncretic structure in which meaning is subjected to the general context of the story. The repetitive formula has a double effect; on one side, it reinforces the drama of the story as the deer has been severely wounded by the dog. Simple sentences develop the causes of a collective tragedy. The repetition of 'the worst has happened to us' (lines 7, 8, 13 and 14) intensifies the force of its content. On the other side, Okigbo supports traditional oral poetry with a mnemonic and musical result, as a way of helping the griot/bard to memorize the content to be sung in front of an audience. In fact, storytelling connects Okigbo with his oral tradition (Anozie 1972: 72) and situates him at the crossroads.

Two clearly separated parts in which the first six lines ask the leopard to return as soon as possible. The second part justifies the urgency for his coming back: the dog has assaulted the communal house and they are defenceless. Consequently, repetitions are not meaningless as they generate a main refrain (the double 'The worst has happened to us') and two secondary refrains: 'Where are you?' in the first part and 'The cruel dog keeps us from it' in the second).

The deer takes special care to show that he only acts as a spokesperson for the whole collective of animals. The systematic use of first person plural forms (our, we, us) demonstrates this. At no point does he allude to his individual suffering from the injuries sustained in the dog attack. He limits himself to lamenting the common tragedy: the destruction of the house, with the awareness that this means the end of an era of happiness that will never be repeated. In short, the poetic voice represented by the deer does not correspond to the individual poetic subject typical of European poetry born out of Petrarchism. It is a voice that returns to the lyrical origins shared by many cultures, and which can be identified with that of the bards/griots of traditional oral poetry. Okigbo thus offers a composition in which European and African poetic sources converge harmoniously.

Conclusion

In the general frame of Okigbo's poetry and significance, 'The Lament of the Deer' is a minor work. However, the poet renounces to his originality to be the voice of other writers; in fact, he uses his voice to the service of the others. Even though the poem is part of a tale for children, he elaborates an intense and emotional composition with a strong syncretic meaning. As I have previously mentioned, a second reading of the poem transfers the reader to the events that took place during the Biafra War.

The aetiological purpose of Iroaganachi and Achebe's story (1972), which is nothing but an enquiry into the causes of evil (cf. García Ramírez 2003: 100–2), is also present in Okigbo's poem. One can only think that, when the deer alludes to the house that the animals built together, the author is referring to the independent Nigeria in which so many young people of his generation had placed their hopes. Hopes that were dashed by political events, to the point of creating an almost unbreathable climate for the Igbo ethnic group. Okigbo was undoubtedly aware that at that time we were witnessing the end of an era of optimism (generated by the decolonization process), which was to give way to a great collective tragedy of incalculable consequences. Probably the poet, as a bard who was a spokesman for his community, was also referring to the Igbo people when he cried out: 'The worst has happened to us,' completing his role as seer and prophet.

Notes

1 Cf., particularly some seminal works by Moore (1963); Hughes (1963); Reed and Wake (1984).

2 *How the Leopard Got His Claws* narrates the story of a group of animals living in the wild forest in an undefined time. Initially, they were very happy under the government of the leopard, however the dog envies the leopard's'good governance. Therefore, the dog has a resentful and hostile attitude towards the rest of the animals. One stormy day, taking advantage of the leopard's absence, the dog enters into the hut violently, hurts the deer and proclaims himself king of the animals. In returning, the leopard fights the dog but he is defeated and the rest of the animals approve the new status quo. Blind with revenge, the leopard visits a blacksmith who builds for him ironed teeth and bronzed claws. Moreover, he asks Thunder for a terrible voice. These new weapons allow him to come back, defeat the dog and extend his vengeance to the rest of the animals of the forest who were unloyal to him. From this moment onwards, animals will live dispersed in the forest and the dog will seek the protection of the hunter. The initial story was created by John Iroaganachi and transformed by Chinua Achebe ([1972] 1994: 8).
3 Chukwuma (1981: 14) claims that, according to the implied characters, most of the traditional African folktales can be grouped in three types: (1) animal tales; (2) tales in which there are human beings and supernatural characters interacting; and (3) tales in which animals and human beings interact.
4 Perhaps the oldest of those preserved is the *Lament for the Destruction of Ur*, while the best known is undoubtedly *the Lamentations* attributed to Jeremiah, which is one of the poetic books of the *Bible*. Also in the origins of English literature, during the Middle Ages, there is a magnificent case of early Anglo-Saxon lament: *Deor's Lament*.
5 Christopher Okigbo had previously used the form of the Lament to write, 'Lament of the Silent Sisters' or 'Lament of the Masks', one of his last poems.

References

Achebe, Chinua with John Iroaganachi. [1972] 1994. *How the Leopard Got His Claws*. Nairobi: East Africa Educational Publishers.

Achebe, Chinua. 2012. *There Was a Country: A Personal History of Biafra*. New York: Penguin.

Anozie, Sunday O. 1972. *Christopher Okigbo: Creative Rhetoric*. New York: Africana.

Chinweizu, Jemie Onwuchekwa and Mabubuike Ihechukwu. 1983. *Toward the Decolonization of African Literature*. London: KPI.

Chukwuma, Helen O. 1981. 'The Oral Tale'. Kiersten Holst Petersen and Anna Rutherford (eds), *Cowries and Kobos: The West African Oral Tale and Short Story*, 12–17. Copenhagen: Dangaroo.

Emenyonu, Ernest N. 1998. '(RE)Inventing for the Past for the Present: Symbolism in Chinua Achebe's How the Leopard Got His Claws'. *Bookbird*, 36 (1): 6–11.

Gadamer, Hans Georg. 1986. *The Relevance of the Beautiful and Other Essays.* Cambridge: Cambridge University Press.
García Ramírez, Paula. 2003. 'Aetiological Values in Achebe's Stories for Children'. *Revista Alicantina de Estudios Ingleses*, 16: 93–109.
Hughes, Langston. 1963. *Poems from Black Africa.* Bloomington, IN: Indiana University Press.
Moore, Gerald. 1963. *Modern Poetry from Africa.* Harmondsworth: Penguin.
Nwoga, Donatus Ibe. 1984. *Critical Perspectives on Christopher Okigbo.* Washington, DC: Three Continents Press.
Ochiaga, Terri. 2015. *Achebe and Friends at Umuahia: The Making of an Elite.* London: James Currey.
Ogundokkun, Sikiru. 2015. 'The Role of Orature in African Sociocultural Space'. *Journal of English Language and Literature*, 6: 179–85.
Okemwa, Christopher. 2022. *The Griots of Ubuntu: An Anthology of Contemporary Poetry from Africa.* Kenya: KTI (Kistrech Theatre International).
Okigbo, Christopher. 1971. *Labyrints with Path of Thunder.* Trenton, NJ: Africa World Press.
Reed, John and Clive Wake. 1984. *A New Book of African Verse.* London: Heinemann.
Richards, David. 2005. 'The Poetry of Christopher Okigbo'. In Richard Danson Brown and Suman Gupta (eds), *Aestheticism & Modernism: Debating Twentieth-Century Literature 1900–1960*, 375–401. London: Routledge.
Searle, Chris. 1991. 'Achebe and the Bruised Heart of Africa'. *Wasafiri*, 14: 12–16.
Simola, Raisa. 1995. *World Views in Chinua Achebe's Works.* Frankfuert am Main: Peter Lang.
Vessey, David. 2007. 'Gadamer's Hermeneutic Contribution to a Theory of Time-Consciousness'. *Indo-Pacific Journal of Phenomenology*, 7: 1–7.

Part Three

Epistemic Spaces in the Geopsychic Universe of Visual and Verbal Communication

9

Local Amazigh Proverbs in Motion

Between Transmission and Interpretation

Fatima Ez-zahra Benkhallouq and Wahiba Moubchir

Introduction

The transmission of knowledge implies social coherence insofar as the dissemination of knowledge constitutes one of the foundations of the social group ensuring cohesion and continuity (Bourdieu [1977] 1995).[1] Being a mirror of continuities and sociocultural transformations, the transmission alone ensures the recognition of a dynamic cultural legacy, thus giving it the legitimacy to be, to evolve and to connect with other visions of the world. It is everywhere in places, in objects and in the dynamism of cultures because there is no isolated culture in the world. Glissant (1996: 27) introduces a key notion in the thought of interbreeding, that of the 'Everyone'. By highlighting the 'histories of peoples' and the 'Relations' between them, he thus goes against the 'absolutes of History'. To think of the world in the transmission is to think of it in diversity and the comings and goings of languages and cultures – this is what Khireddine (2006: 2)[2] calls 'multiple etymology', and Glissant calls 'creolization of the world' (1996: 49).

Omitting the interactions between a way of life (Boukous 2008: 119), a shared knowledge and a sociocultural frame of reference would distort the starting point (Cormier-Salem and Roussel 2005).[3] This is why, from 2002, UNESCO introduced the word 'systems' to account for this dimension that had been excluded until then. Thus, it qualifies this system of natural knowledge as local and indigenous knowledge systems.[4] Everything suggests that in a society where writing is relegated to the background, the only reality that exists is the way of life and the oral literature transmitted by word of mouth and from generation to generation.

Including this article in the framework of transmission presumes that the transhumance of men and cultures is an observation and that cultural and linguistic nomadism does not date from today. Far from manufactured globalization, cultures are by definition composite. In particular, we follow Glissant (1996: 130) in assuming that cultures are of 'rhizome' identity:[5] A rhizome, as a plant with multiple roots, would resemble composite cultures, so entangled that it is difficult to discern a pure origin. In this sense, Glissant criticizes the European tendency to close cultures on themselves:

> 'It is a sublime and mortal conception that the peoples of Europe and Western cultures have conveyed in the world, namely that all identity is an identity with a single root and exclusive of the other. This view of identity (...) is opposed to the real' notion today, in [the] composite cultures, of identity as a factor and as a result of a creolization, that (is to say – to say) of identity as a rhizome, of identity not as a single root but as a root going to meet other roots.
>
> Ibid., 19

In addition, since everything is part of dynamism and a movement, transmission is one of the most complex sending operations in terms of its mechanisms and components. Orchestrated by a power that is both internal and external, conscious and unconscious, it crosses places and people to ensure a permanent passage of culture,[6] ideas, environments and knowledge. This transition, of course, is not always happy, it can be affected by deviations, losses, voluntary or involuntary omissions and it is variable in the circumstances in which it occurs.

The study of the transmission of local knowledge immediately puts us in a multidisciplinary perspective since knowledge appears in the language (the linguistic side), in practice (the social side), in history. We investigate this topic in the example of the intangible heritage of the community of Amazigh-speakers.[7] We focus here on communities living in Morocco. We claim that given the specific pragmatic conditioning of the Amazigh communities, that is, the prevalence of the oral transmission of knowledge and the triglossia (most Imazighen, apart from their native tongue, are fluent in Arabic and French), recovering the thought patterns behind particular proverbs is a specific social hermeneutics (Gadamer), that gives indirect access both to the community dynamics and processes currently affecting those communities.

Formal and Informal Means of Cultural Transmission

The transmission of knowledge highlights the transfer of a way of saying or doing or even of a ritual in its different stages. It is from this point of view necessary to study the forms of transmission, that is to say, the social attitudes, the behavioural conventions, the beliefs which highlight this shared thought or this mode of knowledge instilled to follow up on the past in the present. We can teach or make known formally or informally a way of thinking, doing or acting, a practice, a social code, etc. This is one of the conventional forms of the transmission of knowledge.

The formal mode of transmission is immediately part of a canonical framework governed by formal rules corresponding to a framework and a standard mode of teaching. Indeed, in a society with a written tradition, texts and historical accounts contain the teaching of this kind insofar as they transmit ideas. The relationship between master and a disciple is a relationship of formal transmission, since it is governed by conventional rules, those of the school, the establishment, pedagogy, etc. Another form of formal transmission is conveyed by globalization, by the formalization of a package of knowledge that claims openness and universality. This does not mean that in mountainous areas where the majority is illiterate, this transmission system does not exist. On the contrary, the formal and pedagogical transmission is displayed in Amazigh tales, proverbs, rites and legends. Our first filed survey focuses essentially on the relationship between Amazigh and the natural environment, we have tried to show that this relationship is at the same time existential, substantial and immaterial. The survey was qualitative and touched on the daily life of the Amazighs and their relationship with the animal and natural world in the festivities, the major agricultural events.

Notwithstanding, when we speak of the transmission of local knowledge, of the ancient knowledge of users or peasants, the first mode of transmission that comes to mind is informal, linked essentially to the orality of tradition and the integration of activities into a peasant spatiotemporal framework. Within the family or a restricted group of people belonging to a given linguistic community, the transmission can take the form of the informal in the sense that everything is learning, everything is a transmission. The operation is perceived as a whole, where the only codes that reign are those of the common and sharing.

This form is no longer framed, standardized or formal, but it is open, it crosses the immediate environment: family, friends, the voice of the ancestors via lived and corrected experiences, rites and all the manifestations that go with it. It is therefore essential to consider the knowledge conveyed as a moving process, produced and reproduced through social relations, and not as a set of facts independent of any context and historical evolution which would have remained static in the face of changes in thought patterns.

The incorporation of values through the process of transmission seems important to us to study since the cultural, ritual and even ethical references integrate the body which itself becomes an active actor, consciously or unconsciously, in the transmission of a complex whole: gestures, attitudes, habits and utterances, etc. These ways of doing and acting are embodied, of others to pass on to other individuals who are part of the pastoral community in question. The body thus manifests a multitude of gestures, from the most trivial to the most complex, and therefore becomes the symbolic bearer of the living legacy of deceased ancestors.

We have validated the hypothesis that we have just developed in the previous paragraphs since the beginning of our field survey. Indeed, we felt this omnipresence of bodily teaching, the said and the unsaid, of know-how and know-how to be, shared by all. Moreover, failing to bequeath to the prosperity of works written on classic Amazigh literature which would constitute the collective and immortal memory of those who practice it, the ancestors, have recorded their philosophy and even their trade in forms that measure and musicality doom to eternity.

Since it is a population with an oral tradition, women, men and children repeat proverbs throughout the day. The proverbs, (Amazigh) the *iwaliwən* 'the words' are transmitted from mother to daughter and from father to son. It is obviously an informal but effective learning. Some proverbs are surely lost but others still resonate.

Proverbs and Fixed Expressions as Exponens of Thought Patterns

All languages develop so-called idiomatic, fixed expressions or phraseological units with a global designation that do not necessarily have literal equivalents in other languages. To ignore language forms would be to underestimate a considerable part of language from a linguistic, semantic, stylistic and pragmatic point of view because it is an interesting and frequent phenomenon in languages. For example, there are 40,000 such expressions in French (Salah and Gross 1998) and about 500 fixed Amazigh expressions related to natural elements (Benkhallouq 2016). Fixed expressions are of unknown or uncertain origins, but the transmission ensures their passage from generation to generation thus translating an implicit, even unpredictable meaning.

The adjective 'fixed' which is added to the noun 'expression' or 'phrase' emphasizes two important aspects:

- The impossibility of decomposing the constituent elements of the expression: deletion, addition or even change of order.
- The meaning does not derive from the addition of the semantic features of the constituent elements of the expression. In most cases, the meaning is metaphorical and to be found in the cultural or historical context.

There are two types of fixed expressions:

- *Phrases*: Groups of words, fixed nominal or verbal phrases.
- *Sayings and proverbs*: Phrases that pictorially express general advice or truths. They are fixed by custom or tradition.

It should be noted that in speech, proverbs and fixed phrases play the role of an argument of authority. Bentolila (2004-IRCAM) clearly notes that in a close circle of peers it is sufficient to quote a proverb to catch the attention. Indeed, in the middle of the mountains, among the Amazigh tribes of Morocco, where writing is relegated to the background, the oral language (stories, poems and fixed expressions: proverbs, sayings and phrases) is a key element in maintaining the values and the sharing of a certain number of convictions, both social and religious. It is commonly known that (Amazigh) *Yan wawal ibbi miyya*, 'One word puts an end to a hundred other.'

It must be stressed that the orality in the transmission is fully displayed in the proverbs and locutions coming from a distant period. Collective memory and ancestral wisdom are seen over the years and centuries to acquire argumentative weight in different contexts and situations of daily life. The recognition of this wisdom shared by the entourage which revitalizes these expressions is a conviction in itself of the transmissible continuity of the verbal values transmitted from generation to generation.

Bentolila (1997/1995) returns to a key idea that proverbs are not meant to teach us new things, their success is due to ability to grasp the reality and the gist of individual experience in just a couple of words. Its lapidary form, passed on thought usage, can convey a variety of even complex situations. Crucially, he poses a hermeneutical question of whether it is 'this common fund of human experience that explains why we find similar proverbs in very different cultures?' Recognized by a given linguistic community, proverbs have passed through the ages carrying experiences, truths and wisdom. These coded sentence sequences have been the subject of several linguistic studies, to cite only a few (Greimas 1970; Lundberg 1958).

Indeed, the value of proverbs is, first of all, that of its pre-construction which is grafted around the discourse and forms an integral part of it. What interests us most in this article is the semantic structuring of proverbs and the system of values and beliefs they convey. Let us remember that the competence of the speakers is very desirable insofar as they judge the acceptability of a proverb in a specific context. This clearly shows the difference between a native speaker and a non-native speaker, since non-natives cannot always retrieve a full meaning of a proverb without additional pragmatic explanations.

In a language with an oral tradition such as Amazigh, proverbs and sayings take on a whole new dimension, they translate patterns of thought and construction of mind that traceability does not highlight. By qualifying the proverb as (Amazigh) *awalidderr* 'living word', the Amazigh accentuates the veracity and the force of the words said in the context in question. It is *awal*, 'a word' whose weight is equivalent to an argument from authority. This connotation is enhanced by the qualifying adjective. (Amazigh) *idderr* 'living' to highlight the fact that the proverb lasts and continues to transcend generations. Few words encompass a shared reality and come to illustrate lived situations. In this way, a proverb is a 'folk hermeneutics' of encountered phenomena, through which we have access to the modus of experiencing and valuating the phenomena by their authors.

By changing the language code, we move from one system to another and from one repertoire to another. Among the Amazighs, words symbolize and let out messages more than others. Thus, as a further illustration, (Amazigh) *tasa* 'the liver' as a symbolic organ, translates feelings of love and affection more than (Amazigh) *wul* 'the heart' as it is the case in other cultures.[8] Therefore, a literal translation – just like a literal explanation – will be without fruitful results in this sense.

The literal meaning is now abbreviated as 'LM'. We propose the literal meaning of the proverb as the primary meaning of a sign or signs, to the extent that this meaning is shared by a linguistic community. The sought meaning refers to a cultural or moral value and depends on the context in which this word is used.

In this case, we ask ourselves whether it is necessary to translate, i.e. to carry out the linguistic transfer from a source language to a target language while trying to minimize the cultural differences which result from it, or whether it is sufficient to propose the equivalent of the expression in the target language and to explain the changes which took place while passing from one linguistic system to another. It should be noted that the initial work is done from the Amazigh language to the French language and then to the English language, the language of this article. Comparisons between Amazigh and French proverbs will be made where possible. However, this transition between three languages also points to the difficulty of keeping the gaps small between three culturally different worlds.

Let example (1) be an illustration:

(1) *ku tuyya ṭṭəfaṛ izəġran nəs*
Literal meaning (LM): Every herb follows its roots.
Meaning sought (MS): French proverb: Like father, like son.

This literal meaning is true from the compositional analysis these words offer. The meaning sought or the added informational value is read through the metaphorical value and the context of the communication. We can cite, for example, advice for the choice of a suitable husband or wife, to take into account the origin and the principles of the parents since it is a question of the continuity of transmitted values from parents to children.

Thanks to the concise form of proverbs, we can convey messages relating to both positive and negative human values. Qualities such as 'modesty' are commendable, while faults such as 'pride' and 'pretentiousness' are to be banished.

Given the ensuing example:

(2) *iy tyid afriwn adur tggad lɛdu d wašal*

LM If you manage to have wings, never be the enemy of the earth.

MS The proverb refers to a person whose financial situation has improved but tends to forget their past unfortunates by becoming conceited or arrogant. Here, the statement is presented as a piece of advice for those to whom luck will smile one day. The 'wings' connote a great opportunity that must be seized while being modest. The equivalent proverb in English is, 'Proud and boastful people will be shamed, but wisdom stays with those who are modest and humble.'

The example (3) highlights the true friendship based on virtuous faith far from hypocrisy. To be sustainable, true friendship should be built on sincerity and, above all, on mutual support:

(3) *wənna yran agərrab y smaym iddukkel y lyali*

LM The one who will be in need of the water carrierduring summer (hot) times, must befriend him – in the winter.

MS True friendship perseveres even in times of trouble.

In addition, responsibility towards nature as well as towards animals is openly exhibited through proverbs that reflect a conservation concern. Such a concern being transmitted across generations neither traces back solely to the foundation of NGOs nor the contemporary literary movement.

(4) *iniyi mayd yant lyali iniġaš mayd yant smaym*

    LM   Tell me how winter is, I will tell you what summer will be like.

    MS   The Season of winter already announces the quality of summer.

The proverb in (4) highlights a reality commonly known in several cultures. Generally, when the winter cold is fierce, it can be claimed that the heat of summer will be unbearable. The assumption allows these mountaineers to experience closely climate change, to observe the seasons and to foresee the premises of summer from very specific days in winter (Amazigh) *lyali* 'the forty days that coincide with the longest winter nights (from 20 December to 20 January)'. The degree of cold of the winter nights gives a certain idea of the degree of heat of the hot nights in summer *smaym* 'from 12 July to 20 August'. The proverb in the French version takes up this idea differently, since the cultural and geographical context differs:

(5) (French) *En avril ne te découvre pas d'un fil, en mai fais ce qu'il te plait.*

    LM   In April, do not cover yourself with a thread, in May do what you please.

    MS   October in drizzles, Winter in ruins.

(6) (Amazigh) *ur thasabd xəf iġjden d iširranar d izrey n mars d uhyyan*

    LM   Count your sheep and your children only after Mars and its equinox pass.

English proverb: Cast not a clout until May is out.

To understand the proverb in (6), it is important to dwell on the nature of the draconian conditions that the mountaineers face. Indeed, in the severe context of the fall, the major concern of the Amazigh people is to preserve their economic heritage (Amazigh) *iġjden* 'livestock' and children not to lose them due to the harsh weather of the season. In the French version, the piece of advice is given to a receiver 'you' and concerns the dressing (5).

The relevance of the proverb in this context exceeds by far the value of semantic condensation to offer, in addition to a human experience, a vision of the local world full of multidimensional connotations. A long observation mixed with cumulative wisdom provided this population with skills of acting and saying. Nature, says the peasant, reveals its secrets for those who want to listen and watch.

Table 9.1 juxtaposes main differences in the semantic components of proverbs used by the Amazigh community in Morocco as extracted from the investigated corpus of Amazigh proverbs. The 'weak link' in the Amazigh context is the children and the sheep and it is indeed these two weak elements that find death during the harsh weather of the Atlas Mountains in Morocco.

Another proverb that we take from Bentolila (1997) shows how the peasants, here the Amazighs observed and understood all the natural and animal components that surround them:

(7) *zi kud turiw təġyult urdjin təswi aman zddiynin*

    LM   Since the time the donkey gave birth, she has never drunk clean water. (Her foal's hopping disturbs water.)

He points out in this sense:

> City dwellers' lack of understanding is caused by the fact that we have for the most part never carefully observed the animals and plants. To fully understand the image that 'the donkey never drinks clear water', it is necessary to know that while the donkey is drinking, it has the habit of hitting the ground with its hoofs and thus disturbing its water.
>
> Bentolila 1979: 113, own translation

In a pedagogical dialogue between A and B (Diderot quoted by Bertrand Abraham1989) interprets the nature and traditional society of Tahiti. A society that lives up to the rhythm of nature but within a regulated system. This is what Diderot calls 'the code of nature'. To consider nature here as a 'principle' that regulates the life of men where he observes nature and lives in it. It is a place of teaching and learning.

Table 9.1 Juxtaposition of differences between the Amazigh and French versions of proverbs (our elaboration)

	Amazigh proverb	**French proverb**
1st difference: The target 'Weak link'	• Kids, Lambs & Children • Group	• Receiver You • Person
2nd difference: Risks	Human loss + property loss	Illness 'Flu'
3rd difference: Weather and climates related to geography	In synchrony with the vernal equinox: month of March	Following the vernal equinox of several weeks (in May)

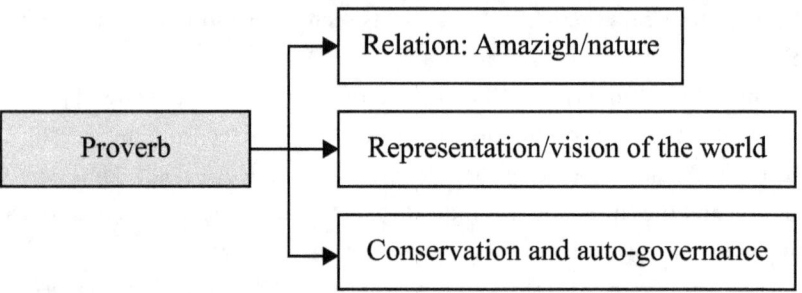

Figure 9.1 Concise form of three levels of analysis (own elaboration).

This shared legislation is obviously important to understand not only the subjective representative world of mountaineers but also the value of respect, accountability and self-governance previously attested.

Second, representations and visions of the world from within, that is, of the local population itself, highlight this harmony between mountain dweller and nature. We have looked at some examples of this. We will detail this in the next section. Finally, the emergence of a common base which is no longer a local and representative one but rather a universal and human one (ecology, self-governance, distinction of animals, etc.) as well as observations that show scientific rigor tinged with culture. This web of interdependencies is shown in the Figure 9.1.

Translate or Interpret the Proverbs?

The translation seems to be one of the most complex and perilous operations. To achieve full performance, translation requires to be operated at both synchronic and diachronic levels, for translating is not only an interaction of linguistic elements, but it is also space for psychological and sociological components to interfere.

Far from any illusion of neutrality, it should be noted that translation changes in content, following the statement by André Markowicz (2018: 16) that: 'by nature, translation is an interpretation'. No objective translation can take place since it is a person who performs the translation. When I say 'by nature' it means that it is neither good nor bad; it is,, rather, a fact of the existing order. So what should we expect from a translation? It is not that it should be faithful, but that it should be consistent, that is, an applied interpretation. A practical reading. There are certainly similar expressions in both languages but limited. They emphasize what is common and universal to all languages.

Translation can also face cultural or ethical obstacles when the source language lends itself to a language that is coded, unfathomable, or deeply rooted in culture, as is the case with proverbs and idioms. There are, indeed, in the examples mentioned above and many others, relevant ties to the cultural background of each language. Interpreting mutually interchanged cultural viewpoints helps to recognize and acknowledge the otherness. Such an assumption transcends the simple understanding of the linguistic dichotomy of the signifier and signified.

The idiomatic expressions below draw on the cultural repository inherent in the Amazigh language (literal translation: LT).

(8) *izwar wullu i lbhaym*

    LT He put the cart in front of the beasts.

    SM Putting the cart before the horse.

(9) *l3aql n ulGem*

    LT Camel's memory.

    SM French proverb: Elephant's memory.

(10) *tghzzat tuSSent*

    LT The she-wolf has bitten him.

    SM To have ants in one's legs, hands, etc. To express the feeling of tingling due to poor blood circulation.

(11) *iSwa am bumhend*

    English idiom: As clever as a monkey.

    TL Cunning or clever as a hedgehog.

    SC To refer to a clever and intelligent person.

Several legitimate questions can be forwarded in this sense: Monkey or hedgehog for cunning? Wolf or ant for tingling? Camel or elephant for memory? The image of unfailing memory is linked in the Amazigh tradition to the camel.

It is an animal that this population has been close to. It is observed that the dromedary has a memory that cannot be mistaken. In the European tradition, this very image sticks to the elephant and its impressive visual memory. As for the Amazighs, they cannot take back such a truth since it is impossible for them to observe elephants at the highest altitudes.

We can thus see here some sort of a hermeneutic universal: interpreting features of human condition through behavioural habits of a creature with which the community is familiar, and thus enriching the linguistic resources with description of that community which has a common knowledge of those habits. Reverting to the example given, for an average member of a community that does not know camel's behaviour, this idiom is completely irretrievable without additional pragmatic support.

Conclusion

It appears that within a fundamentally oral and traditional population, as is the case with Amazigh community, the transmission of values and principles is done through the tribe, this latter representing a moral authority of great magnitude, then the family and the setting, tacitly conveying a common reference. One of its foundations is communal life and sharing since the Amazigh identity takes shape only within the family, the group and the tribe. It is certainly autonomous, but still abiding within the group. It is within the group that an individual manifests one's free and unique existence. This is how the group becomes functional and autonomous. Furthermore, it is within this group that the transmission of the whole of the communicative and cultural system takes place, namely, values, knowledge, practices and perceptions.

In this chapter, we offered a hermeneutic exploration into one of the channels such a transmission takes place, that is, the realm of Amazigh proverbs and idiomatic expressions. The crucial element of the discussion was tracing a clear inner logic that particular proverbs follow and cast them against French proverbs. Most of all, they transmit a system of values, reflcting everyday harships and struggles of the community life, as well as axiological hierarchy. In the first section, we established the basis for the difference between the formal and informal transmission, stressing at the same time their interwining and relating them to the investigated community. The next section looked at proverbs and idiomatic expressions as exponents of thought patterns of a community. We focused on the differences between the French and English correspontents of

Amazigh fixed expfressions, showing how deeply immersed in everyday experience a proverb is.

The final section addressed the issue of translation as interpretation. While translating the proverbs, the translator endeavours to establish a correspondence, a parallel between two visions of the world that sometimes meet and oppose each other. This is why the translation of an idiom requires primarily a good mastery of the meaning and its context before proceeding to work on the equivalent lexicon both from a semantic and pragmatic point of view in the target language. We hoped to show that behind the Atlas Mountains of Morocco lie living knowledge, enduring and shared beliefs, all of which come from nature, applied to this latter and interacting with one another.

Notes

1   All translations in the text are ours.
2   Khireddine (2006: 2) writes in this sense:

> In distant times of prehistory, culture passed from Africa to the North through the Strait of Gibraltar; in antiquity, from the East (Mesopotamia, Asia Minor, Egypt) to Greece, then from there to Europe; in the Middle Ages and the Renaissance, again to North Africa, then to Spain and from there to Europe. In times of war as in times of peace, an uninterrupted exhchange has taken place both by land routes and by sea.

3   Cormier-Salem and Roussel (2005: 521) write:

> the strong return of the local is indisputably linked to the rehabilitation of local naturalist knowledge and know-how, long ignored or even despised by experts in the North, they are now considered by these same specialists, as tools for the conservation of biodiversity and sustainable management of the environment. Local communities, considered the closest to nature, are now presented as the most capable of preserving it (...).

4   Local and Indigenous Knowledge Systems (LINKS), available online: https://en.unesco.org/idil2022-2032.
5   Glissant (1996: 130) explains the notion of 'rhizome' and identity:

> When I approached the question [of identity], I started from the distinction made by Deleuze and Guattari, between the notion of root unique and the notion of rhizome. Deleuze and Guattari, in one of the chapters of Mille Plateaux (which was first published in a small volume under the title Rhizomes), underline this

difference. They establish it from the point of view of the functioning of thought, the thought of the root, and the thought of the rhizome. The single root is the one that kills around it while the rhizome is the root that extends to meet other roots. I applied this image to the principle of identity. And I did it also according to a 'categorization of cultures' that is specific to me, a division of cultures into atavistic cultures and composite cultures.

6   It is generally agreed that culture is a set of codes and norms that allows humans to adapt to their environment while punctuating the different phases of their lives through practices, modes of life, thought, knowledge and institutions. Edward B. Tylor (1873: 72) defines primitive culture as: 'a complex whole which includes knowledge, beliefs, art, morals, laws, customs and all other dispositions and habits acquired by man as a member of a society'. Fruit of experiences and the combination of a past and a present, culture differs according to the geographical environment, social groups and ways of thinking. It follows that an understanding of practices and customs could in no way be made outside the past and historical data.

7   Berber, self-name Amazigh, plural Imazighen, any of the descendants of the pre-Arab inhabitants of North Africa, available online: https://www.britannica.com/topic/Berber (accessed 3 June 2022). We note that the name Berber does refer to the Amazigh community but it was used by the Greco-Romans to designate a civilization foreign to theirs and therefore it remains to be considered as a generic that can refer to all foreign civilizations, to a Roman or Greek origin and the meaning of the word remains as such practically emptied of the connotations and semantic charges that the residue of the *Amazigh* word can convey.

8   It might be noted that the same tendency that is given to the 'liver' as a priority locus can be observed in other languages, e.g. Serbo-Lusatian, where there even occurred a semantic shift, that is, the Old Slavic lexeme for a 'liver' came to mean 'heart', hence, when a Serbolusin speaker says, 'you are liverly welcome', they in fact mean 'you are heartily welcome'. The lexeme, which is Old Slavic, used to mean 'liver', *jatra* (interpolation by the editor, Małgorzata Haładewicz-Grzelak).

References

'Berber'. *Encyclopedia Britannica*. Available online: https://www.britannica.com/topic/Berber (accessed 3 June 2022).

Benkhallouq, Fatima Ez-zahra. 2016. 'Transmission of Local Knowledge in the Middle Atlas -Ait Soukhman Tribe: Anthropological and Linguistic Study'. Unpublished PhD diss., Cadi Ayyad University, Marrakesh.

Bentolila, Fernand. 1993. *Berber Proverbs, Bilingual French-Berber*. Paris: l'Harmattan-Awal.

Bentolila, Fernand. 2004. The Short Forms of Amazigh Literature: Riddles and Proverbs in *Amazigh Literature. Orality and Writing. Specificities and Perspectives*. Proceedings of the International Colloquium, Rabat, IRCAM (Royal Institute of the Amazigh Culture).

Boukous, Ahmed. 2008. 'Le champ langagier, Diversité et stratification'. *Asinag*, 1: 15–37.

Bourdieu, Pierre. 1977. 'Une classe objet'. *Actes de la recherche en sciences sociales*, La paysannerie, une classe objet, 17–18.

Bourdieu, Pierre. [1972]1977/1995. *Outline of a Theory of Practice* (Esquisse d'une théorie de la pratique précédé de Trois études d'ethnologie kabyle, Libraire Droz). Cambridge: Cambridge University Press.

Cormier-Salem, Marie-Christine, Dominique Juhé-Beaulaton, Jean Boutrais and Bernard Roussel (eds). 2005. *Patrimoines naturels au Sud*. Marseilles: IRD Éditions. Available online: http://www.openedition.org/6540 (accessed 4 June 2022).

Diedrot cited by Bertrand Abraham in 'Rousseau, Diderot, Bougainville: Pprotocoles de production et de lecture du récit de voyage au XVIIIème siècle', *Semen*, 4 (1989). Online since 5 June 2008. Available online: http://journals.openedition.org/semen/6973 (accessed 12 September 2022). Doi: 10.4000/semen.6973.

Gadamer, Hans-George. [1960] 1989. *Truth and Method*. London: Sheed and Ward.

Greimas, Algirdas Julien. 1970. 'Les Proverbes et les dictons.' In: *Du Sens. Essais sémiotiques*. Paris 1970, 309–14. Cahiers de lexicologie.

Glissant, Édouard. 1996. 'Il n'y a pas de filiation: L'enfant n'est pas le père de l'homme'. *La revue lacanienne*, 3 (8): 137–53. Doi: 10.3917/lrl.103.0137.

Khireddine, Mourad. 2006. 'Le savoir itinérant et la transhumance du savoir'. Centre Interdisciplinaire de Recherche sur l'Afrique-CIRA-Université Frankfurt Milan.

Local and Indigenous Knowledge Systems (LINKS). Available online: https://en.unesco.org/idil2022 (accessed 3 June 2022).

Lundberg, George A. 1958. 'The Semantics of Proverbs'. *A Review of General Semantics*, 15 (3): 215–17. Available online: https://www.jstor.org/stable/42581747 (accessed 4 June 2022).

Markowicz, André. 2018. 'Translating is Taking into Account the Materiality of Language'. *Le Monde*, p. 30. Available online: https://www.lemonde.fr/culture/article/2018/03/16/andre-markowicz-traduire-c-est-rendre-compte-de-la-materialite-de-la-langue_5271878_3246.

Salah, Mejri and Gaston Gross. 1998. 'Les expressions figées en français. Les noms composés et autres locutions, Ophrys, 1996' (Fixed Expressions in French. Compound Nouns and Other Phrases, Ophrys, 1996). *L'Information Grammaticale*, N. 2, Numero special Tunisie: 57.

Tylor, Edward B. 1873. *Primitive Culture: Researches into the Development of Mythology, Philosophy, Religion, Language, Art, and Custom. In Two Volumes. Vol. II*. 2nd ed. London: Edward Murray.

10

Thirdspace Creation as a Geopsychic Dialogue with Tourists in the Karpacz Holiday Resort, Poland

Joanna Lubos-Kozieł and Małgorzata Haładewicz-Grzelak

Introduction

A Zeppelin 6 majestically crosses the blue sky over the Schneekoppe mountain, while tourists, smiling briskly, lean out of the gondola attached to it, fluttering their hats. On the other side of the mountain, on the rope stretched from the summit, several wicker gondolas can be seen. In the one in the fore, a lady in a violet costume and in a hat with a feather is flying farewell with a scarf. Her companion, in a white shirt, an eyeglass and a tie, grins in a broad farewell smile. The inscription 'Breslau' on the gondola points to the place of destination: a nearby German city. On the adjacent gondola, there is the inscription 'Dresden'. Above the gondolas, there hovers a white airplane. At the foot of the mountain, along a winding, yet comfortable road, other futuristic tourists are taking a perky step to reach the summit of Schneekoppe (Figure 10.1).

This was how authors of a series of postcards from the early twentieth century conveyed their futuristic vision of the spatio-material development of the German tourist complex Krummhübel at the foot of the highest peak of the Riesengebirge (Giant Mountains) - SchneeKoppe. The future would not have brought such spectacular advances as envisaged on the German postcards from the 1900s. Nonetheless, the subsequent history of Krummhübel and its present appearance would certainly be astounding for the authors of these futuristic visions. The locality is currently called Karpacz and lies in the Lower Silesian voivodeship in south-western Poland.

Having been incorporated within the remit of the Polish state after the Second World War boundary shifts, it retained its status as a tourist centre, but now it

Figure 10.1 A futuristic vision of Riesengebirge tourism on a German postcard from the early twentieth century. Postcard from the collections of Joanna Lubos-Kozieł.

attracts mainly Polish tourists for whom Riesengebirge and Scheekoppe – renamed respectively (Polish) Karkonosze and Góra Śnieżka, have become the second most important area of mountain tourism in post-war Poland.[1] Currently, due to the break in its cultural continuity, this tourist resort is something of a heterotopian multilayered palimpsest, shaped and received with a significant amount of mediation (or subject to mediation), some dimensions of which we aim to explore in this contribution.[2] To this aim, we narrate a specific spatial experience of a *flânerie* through the Karpacz holiday resort, which we analytically frame as constructing the experience using the research perspective called 'thirdspace'.

'Thirdspace', introduced by Henri Lefebvre ([1974] 1991) as a specific *dialectique de triplicité*, and further developed by Edward Soja (e.g. [1988] 2000, 1996) into a spatial specificity of urbanism, can be positioned within a larger phenomenological strand of studying culture, known as *spatial turn*. We will trace Lefebvre's 'dialectic of triplicity' through means of experiencing the locality *by* the tourists, intertwined with the means of constructing its urban identity *for* the tourist– and how the perceived, the conceived and the lived space entwines in a fabric of phenomenological dialogue. We propose that Merleau-Ponty's work on the perceived space, entailing the transactional aspects of space, will

Figure 10.2 A venue for the first *flânerie*: transactional tradition in a design of a catering establishment. Left: front view. Right: rear.

contribute to a better understanding of the dynamic aspects of geosocial spatiality. This epistemology naturally entwines with the idea of the hermeneutical dialogue through guided interpretation.

To gather the analytical corpus, we conducted fieldwork in mid-February 2014,[3] during the peak of the winter season, documenting in the form of digital photos and participant observation the publicity related to the tourist industry operating in Karpacz. We compiled a digital documentation of ads placed in the public sphere of the resort for the benefit of a tourist, a sample of which is shown in Figure 10.2.[4] For this report, we will focus on the material collected in the exterior and interior of two catering establishments. We will explore the geopsychical spaces as two phenomenological *lacunae*. One *flânerie* will entail looking at a catering establishment from the outside, the other evolves looking at the interior (from the inside).

The Karpacz Holiday Resort: Historical Vicissitudes

The area of Karpacz ([German] Krummhübel) was already settled by the end of the Middle Ages by lumberjacks and charcoal burners.[5] Its transformation into a German centre of mass tourism began in the second half of the nineteenth century. The most intense development of the village started with the opening in 1895 of the railway line connecting Krummhübel with Jelenia Góra ([German] Hirschberg) and through it with Wrocław (Breslau) and Berlin. The influx of tourists which were able to reach Krummhübel by rail resulted in the construction of numerous guesthouses, hostels, hotels and villas, mostly representing the characteristic forms of wooden and brick architecture typical of German mountain resorts at the turn of the nineteenth and twentieth centuries. In the early twentieth century,

Krummhübel, together with the current Karpacz Górny (then a separate locality called Brückenberg) was not only a summer recreation centre, but also an important modern winter sports hub within the remit of the German state and, the largest tourist venue in the Riesengebirge Mountains.

An important caesura in the history of *Krummhübel* was the year 1945, when, together with the large area of eastern German territories, it was granted to Poland as the aftermath of the Second World War, in compensation for the areas the Republic of Poland lost to the Soviet Union in the east. Within all of the so-called Regained Lands, in parallel to the territories Poland lost in the East, there occurred a population swapping: the autochthon Germans were forced to leave and their lodgings were taken by the influx of Polish settlers. Thus, following the mass population relocations, the locality experienced after 1945 a peculiar break

Figure 10.3 Marking the boundaries of a phenomenological field in a townscape around Bistro *Aurora* (2014).

in tradition and the loss of cultural continuity. In spite of this, soon afterwards, the town resumed its function as a tourist resort and it became one of the most important tourist centres in the Karkonosze Mountains and even in the whole country.

The second caesura in the town's history was the fall of the People's Republic of Poland. One of the outcomes of the 1989 change was deregulation, resulting in economic freedom and fostering new unrestrained business ventures in the region.[6] It brought about the widening and diversifying of Karpacz tourist offerings as well as its peculiar fragmentation, consisting in the proliferation in the market of a multitude of small business ventures and private entrepreneurs running small shops, guesthouses and catering establishments.

In Lubos-Kozieł and Haładewicz-Grzelak (2021: 449ff.), it was established that due to this break in the continuity of tradition in Karpacz [henceforth we will use the current Polish toponym] after 1945, the emerging regionalism acquired a specific character. It mainly consists of attempts to revive regional identity by selectively referring to former German traditions (e.g. the figure of the *Rübezahl* or 'Mountain Spirit') or manufacturing 'regionality'. The other tactics implies relying on the consolidation/incorporation of the Tatra tradition (e.g. availing of elements of the Tatra Mountains, Zakopane, Podhale folklore) and of European traditions in general (e.g. simulations of an Alpine resort).[7] Hence, the geospace of Karpacz is currently definable in relation to the *regionality* and *tradition*, through the combinations of successive layers of visual promotional textuality. The redefinition in terms of a core Polish 'highlanderism' makes it, on the surface at least, distinct from most standard dystopian localities. And, as Gadamer points out (Gadamer 1960 [2013]: xxx) 'appropriating tradition is a hermeneutic task'.

This paper reports the results of two *flâneries* ensuing from our fieldwork in Karpacz, both focusing on sample catering establishments as indexing the process of a transactional thirsdspace construction within what is traditionally called a non-place (Marc Augé), generic space (e.g. Yakhlef 2004) or formalized as Faucauldian 'poly-vocal' heterotopias.

Tourism and the Mediatization of Space

'Space' as a phenomenological concept has long been present in humanities research. For example, Merleau-Ponty observed that just as painting and science, philosophy and, above all, psychology seem to have woken up to the fact that our relationship to space is not that of a pure disembodied subject to a distant object but rather that of a being which dwells in space relating to its natural habitat.

1945: 55

A substantial body of research addresses the topic of the relationship of people to sites which have undergone a considerable amount of mediation (see, e.g., Langerkvist 2009; Jansson 2002; Tomlinson 1999; Miles 2004; Puriton 2023). Media consumption and tourist consumption are regarded as two aspects of spatial appropriation (Jansson 2002) or conflated into one experiential brew (e.g. Campbell 2005: 199). This has been interlined with the larger tendency, called *spatial turn* in cultural studies (e.g. Soja [1988] 2000: 7; Falkheimer and Jansson 2006), focusing on the relationships between mediation and space or on the importance of comprehending the experiential aspect of the changes (e.g. Couldry and McCarthy (2004). Cultural studies scholars thus agree that in order to understand the relationship between communication and space, the concept of *experience* is of paramount importance, which liaises it with a phenomenological approach.

As John Urry ([1990] 2002) emphasized, a pivotal feature of the phenomenon of tourism is the 'gaze' through which the tourist objectifies and interprets the place that he or she visits (see also Lash and Urry 1994). The mediatized gaze entails turning attention to landmarks. The script predating the journey is thus recursively reinforced (Urry [1990] 2002: 151). From this perspective, modern travel turns into a kind of a Mobius strip, a hermeneutic circle where itineraries become scheduled trajectories and the guided gaze follows the predetermined script of representations that had been established long before embarking on the journey (Lagerkvist 2008; Urry [1990] 2002; Duncan and Gregory 1999). In this contribution, we tried to formalize that gaze through a perceptional dialogue which identifies three levels of interaction with the site during our *flânerie* through the locality of Karpacz.

Quite often studies on consuming and producing the materiality of the urbanscape involve some forms of spatial trialectics, with the concomitant mediatization of tourism experience. To name a few examples: Jody Baker in a study of Algonkin National Park traces the way two Canadian cultural archetypes are negotiated through the geopsychical entity of Algonkin Park: one of the industrial nation and that of wilderness. She points out that 'wilderness spaces are imbricated in various histories of economic activity, ecological exploitation and systems of representation. People make geographies and ecologies as they make history. Analysis can compel those geographies and ecologies to speak their histories' (Baker 2002: 199).

Yakhlef (2004), using some aspects of Lefebvre's tripartite conceptualization of space, analyses brands as generic spaces, which are lived and embodied experientially, in the case study of Best Western hotels. Amanda Lagerkvist (2008: 355) shows how the USA after the Second World War, has, by means of mediation, become a geopsychical space across the globe – 'completely familiar and yet unfathomable'. Focusing attention on a specific spatial experience and mediatized sense of space, she showed how Swedes both consumed and produced the materiality of the American continent.

There is also a vein of seminal studies focusing on particular venues as indexing larger geopsychical and geo-historical issues. For example, Tzanelli (2012) offers an ethnography of a café in Thessalonica as embodying a particular cosmogony. Her analysis, being on the one hand, a study about the politics of social interaction, shows how the 'café owners narrate their business custom in audio-visual and olfactory ways through the "absent presence" of Thessalonica's Ottoman Turkish past'. She identifies a peculiar diforia: 'a self-presentational technique which bifurcates according to the audience to which it is addressed' (ibid., 28).

Mediation, as Lash and Friedman (1992: 20) observe, perform a dyadic teleology, whereby communication entails *circulation* on two levels: (1) the exchange of symbolic messages and (2) the material means and media forms physically present in the constructed environment of lived world [Lebenswelt]. It is important to be aware of the degree of mediation involving the visual language. When attending to spaces interspersed with technology-produced visuality artefacts, 'we keep adjusting the present and developing new languages, as well as the routines, postures, and even gestures of communication' (Chmielewska 2005: 351).

An urbanscape thus does not only involve clearly distinguishable traditional dystopias in the Foucauldian sense, as, e.g., of the type of an airport, but on a meta-level, a locality with all its phenomenological space can become generic.[8]

Spatial Trialectics and the Phenomenology of Perception

Henri Lefebvre claimed that if we agree that space is a product, accordingly 'our knowledge of it must be expected to reproduce and expound the process of production' (Lefevre [1974] 1991: 36). The domains that he identified in searching for a unified theory of spatiality are: (1) of the physical, (2) the mental, including logic and abstractions and (3), the social, each of which is to be seen at the same time as real and imagined, concrete and metaphysical. Analytically, they translate into: (1) spatial practice, (2) representations of space and (3) spaces of representation.

The spatial practice of a society, which can be analytically uncovered by the study of the society's space, in Lefebvre's definition, 'secretes that society's space, it propounds and presupposes it, in a dialectal interaction. It produces it slowly and surely, as it masters and appropriates it' (Lefebvre [1974] 1991: 38). Representations of space are defined as 'conceptualized space, the space of planners, urbanists, technocratic subdividers and social engineers, as of a certain type of artist with a scientific bent, all of whom identity what is lived and what is perceived with what it is conceived' (ibid., 38). This is, according to Lefebvre, the predominate mode in any society tending towards the verbal sign type (ibid., 49).

The category of representational spaces entails looking at space as directly *lived* through the images and symbols ascribed to it. Hence, it is on the one hand the space of 'inhabitants' and 'users' and on the other, of artists and scholars who describe it. It constitutes 'the dominated - and hence passively experienced space - which the imagination seeks to change and appropriate. It overlays the physical space, making symbolic use of its objects' (ibid., 39).

In our analysis, we will rely on Soja's extension of Lefebvre's work. Edward Soja, expanding on Lefebvre's theory through 'critical spatial imagination' (Soja [1988] 2000: xiv), proposes to highlight the intrinsic spatiality. Firstspace epistemologies (ibid., 1996: 74) - Lefevre's the *perceived* space of materialized Spatial Practice - focus attention on the analytical deciphering, 'material and materialized 'physical' spatiality that is directly comprehended in empirically measurable *configurations*: in the absolute and relative location of things and activities, sites and situations' (Soja 1996: 74).

From the firstspace perspective, the city space can be studied as a set of materialized spatial practices, ranging from an idiosyncratic personal space to the spatial grid of social practices (ibid., 74–5). The cityscape is here perceived as a conjoint of mappable and measurable patterns of our lifeworlds, combinations, cause and effect structures (ibid., 75). From a secondspace perspective, the city can be studied as a sort of ideational or mental mapping, grounded in imagery and symbolic modality. This conceived *space of imagination*, Soja proposes to call 'urban imaginary' (ibid., [1988] 2000: 11), as an example being given on the one hand, an inner, mental map of a city each of us is able to elaborate upon, and on the other, 'the envisioning of an urban utopia, an imagined reality which can also affect our urban experience and behavior' (ibid.). Secondspace, as an ideational quality, 'is made up of projections into the empirical word from conceived or imagined geographies' (ibid., 1996: 79).

A clear opposition thus arises, between objective, quantitative, engineering schemas of conceiving the city (perceived space) and qualitative, artistic, subjective perspectives concentred with 'thoughts about the space' (conceived space) (Soja [1988] 2000: 11; ibid., 1996: 78). However, limiting the investigative space to these two perspectives, according to Soja mutes the inherently dynamic aspect of space. The solution he proposes is epistemological trialectics, giving rise to a Thirdspace. The emerging quality is thus grounded in a fundamentally open perspective, which Soja calls 'thirding as othering' and which is to transcend epistemological binarisms (Soja 1996: 5).

As the scholar upholds (ibid., [1988] 2000: 11), the pivotal argument in coining 'thirdspace' was to posit the existence of another means to conceptualize the social generation of human spatiality, which would incorporate both first and secondspace perspectives and concomitantly, would open up the room for spatial (geographical) imagination. Within such a perspective, 'the spatial specificity of urbanism is investigated as a fully lived space, a simultaneously real-and-imagined, actual-and-virtual, locus of structured individual and collective experience and agency' (ibid., 11).

The starting-point for this strategy, as Soja emphasizes, is shifting the focus from epistemology to ontology, in particular, to the trialectic of Spatiality-Historicity-Sociality. Such an ontological repositioning is aimed at recentring 'knowledge formation first around the long-submerged and subordinated spatiality of existential being and becoming, and then in the spatialization of historicity and sociality in theory-formation, empirical analysis, critical inquiry and spatial practice' (ibid., 1996: 81–2). This trialectic ontological premise is usually cast against Pierre Bourdieu's' habitus. In this contribution, we however propose to enhance the analytical perspective with phenomenological insights by Maurice Merleau-Ponty, focusing on his theory of perception. The concept of thirdspace has strong implications and potential for phenomenological research, due to the possibility of postulating various levels of spatial analysis. Additional underpinnings from Merleau-Ponty's work (in particular, those elaborated in this book *Phenomenology of Perception*) will expose the issue of constructing new experiential identities through the use of media in a case study of a selected holiday resort.

The phenomenology of Merleau-Ponty is particularly suitable for thirdspace studies since for that scholar, phenomenology combines both its focus on essences (following Husserl) and it is also the philosophy that

> puts the essences back in existence and does not think that we can understand man and the world only from their 'facticity'. It is a transcendental philosophy which suspends the affirmations of the natural attitude in order to understand them, but it is also a philosophy for which the world is always 'already there' before reflection (...). It is the ambition of a philosophy which is an 'exact science' but it is also an account of space, time, the lived world.
>
> Merleau-Ponty 1945: i

In Merleau-Ponty's work, the space is oriented, and this directionality is elaborated 'with a series of beautifully conducted critical analyses of the distinction between concrete and abstract actions' (Macann 1993: 173–4). Such a directionality will be explored as a transactional aspect of the social space.

We propose to cast the thus elaborated methodological support against Gadamerian 'critical moment' of consciousness (1967: 158). As the philosopher maintains, we are always faced with the necessity of gaining a new awareness of the impact that is being exerted on us, such that everything from the past that we have just experienced compels us to take it as a burden and thus, to somehow assume it as truth (ibid., 158). Basically, it implies that for Gadamer, 'understanding is not a state but an event – a happening in history that stirs us to wonder – where the world is brought to life by being "made present"' (Turnbull 2004: 173). Hence, in hermeneutic terms, it transpires that 'it is not "we" who speak language, but the historically constituted world that in some sense "speaks to us" in ways that are mediated and assimilated by the linguistic element' (ibid., 172–3).

Flâneuries through *Fusions of Horizons*: Hermeneutics of Catering in Karpacz Resort

Flânerie One: Juggling Regionality and Tradition in a Spatial Fusion

Gadamer claims that effective history influences the understanding of tradition. Contingent on that is a certain legitimate ambiguity in the concept of historically affected consciousness (*wirkungsgeschichtliches Bewusstsein*) (...). This ambiguity is that it is used to mean at once the consciousness effected in the course of history and determined by history and the very consciousness of being thus affected and determined.

Gadamer [1960] 2013: xxx

Our first *flânerie* precisely relates to the node of hermeneutic consciousness and 'the naïve appropriation of tradition' as 'retelling' (Gadamer [1960] 2013: xxxi).

Figure 10.2 shows the target of our first *flânerie*: an example of a catering establishment evoking the traditional wooden architecture from the Tatra Mountains. The restaurant *Zagroda góralska* (Highlander's Inn), is designed in a quasi-Zakopane style, with a multiayered fusion of Tatra traditional elements and components referring to *Rübezahl* (legendary Karkonosze Mountain Spirit) and to the Karkonosze Mountains. It inscribes into a larger tendency within the Karpacz endemic space of using the motifs of the Tatra mountains for tourism purposes, that is why we chose to analyse it as a token of that strategy.[9]

Looking at the entrance and the rear part of the catering establishment in question, the most basic phenomenological level is that of the immediate materiality of real physical contact, utility and patterns connected with the restaurant, implying encounters with the physical world. We can touch its décor accessories, we can order a 'traditional' meal, recognizing the somatic feeling of being hungry, or drink a 'traditional' beer. This layer entails looking at those visual texts from a purely teleological and utilitarian perspective in a generic sense. The restaurant we see here, on the level of immediate experience, is a place enticing tourists to get a nourishing 'traditional' meal.

On the secondspace level, it is a venue for interaction – both subjective and intersubjective. The type of interaction we mean here could be for example, evaluation – do I like the decoration, do I like the people that go there or also intersubjective interactions, did I have a good time eating there or having a drink? Will it be a convenient place for a successful and pleasant communicative interaction? But there is also a constructivist force driving the choice of visual and verbal textuality enveloping the venue and encroaching upon subjectivity.

First, the establishment, as mentioned before, has the conspicuous architectural features of a traditional Zakopane (Podhale) mountain hut, reinforced by the verbal text with the name 'Zagroda góralska' (Highlanders' Inn). In the previous study on Karpacz (Lubos Kozieł and Haładewicz-Grzelak 2021), we established that the references to this type of highlander culture are the most frequent in Karpacz and they usually carry the most prestige. It is as if the Podhale region was 'by default', or even by antonomasia the determinant of Polish '*highlander culture*' and all the positive connotations that go with it. Yet, if in a locality references to Zakopane occur alongside references to Mont Blanc, Holland, the seaside (which is actually geographically at the other, opposite part of Poland), and all that is bound and labelled as 'regional'/'traditional', this means the social space of that locality is transactional and negotiated through the lens of the reference to a geopsychical space.

Let us briefly revert to the Gadamerian question about the 'universality of the province of hermeneutics'. The philosopher, defying the metaphysical conclusion of 'everything' being only 'language and linguistic event' posits that:

> the infinity of the dialogue in which the understanding is achieved makes any reference to the ineffable itself relative. But is understanding the sole and sufficient access to the reality of the history? Obviously, there is a danger that the actual reality of the event, especially its absurdity and relativity will be weakened and misperceived by being seen in terms of the experience of meaning.
>
> Gadamer 2013: xxxiii

Clearly what happens with retelling the tradition here is beyond the reality of the encounter and beyond the experience of what is meant by being in a traditional highlander inn in a place, where has never been a (Polish) highlander culture. There was, of course, a culture of German settlers, coalminers, with their proper dialect of German, their proper costumes and food, which, as their entire heritage, was lost after their relocation.

Let us enumerate parts of that secondspace script in the outside of the catering establishment in question as a phenomenological transaction of the geospace. Flanking the door, there are two wooden sculptures of young brigands ([Polish] '*harnasie*') from the Tatra mountains. On the door itself, there is a carving of a young waitress with long braids, traditionally worn by highlander women in Podhale.

However, the sculpture shows the woman/waitress dressed in a miniskirt – attire that a highlander woman would never wear. Hence, we can see a double transaction here: (1) a reference to the region that has the most prestige when it comes to mountain tourism (Podhale), but also generally the most salient in Poland, by incorporating as part of the decoration a carving of a highlander waitress, grafting it as a default highlander attribute of Karpacz (which, let us recall, lies in the Karkonosze mountain chain); and (2) the second transaction occurring in the created geospace is the choosing of the miniskirt as part of the canonical regional dress of highlanders. This is one of the exponents of a simulated dialogue with a tourist. Nonetheless, this dialogue already is effectuated in the thirdspace – an imaginary and at the same time, material space.

Over the entrance, there is also the inscription, *Witojcie Dudki łostowiojcie* ('Welcome and do leave [here] your dosh'). This inscription is also a part of an imaginary dialogue in the thirdspace because it is transcribed in a simulation of the Podhale highlanders' dialect, having certain formulaic phonetic features connoted with this variety.[10] In this context, the rendition of a simulation of a dialect actually softens the strong message and even makes it sound hilarious. Hence, the message, phenomenologically, is already 'there' embedded in space, before the experience, before the gaze but it anticipates and guides the direction of that gaze. These are thus examples of a transaction: between the anticipated gaze, shared cultural assumptions in the form of stereotypes and potential first space transactions in the form of the purchasing of particular dishes.

On the roof, we can see a wooden figure of Rübezahl – the spirit of the Karkonosze Mountains, which – in line with the iconographic tradition developed in the nineteenth century – was depicted as an old man with long hair and a beard. Another reference to Rübezahl and the Karkonosze traditions is the carving of a wooden throne with the inscription *Siedzisko Ducha Gór Karkonoszy Liczyrzepy* ('The Seat of the Spirit of the Karkonosze Rübezahl').[11]

Near the door there is an inscription *łotwarte* ('opened'), again in a simulation of the Tatra highlanders' dialect. A recurring decorative motif, visible, among others, in the restaurant sign and the eaves of the roof, are stylized representations of edelweiss flowers (Leontopodium alpinum) – a traditional plant that grows in Poland only in the Tatra Mountains. These are but sample aspects of grafting the 'highlander' attributes present in the exterior décor.

The catering establishment in question inscribes into the townscape of the locality, blending onto an amalgam of nineteenth- or early-twentieth-century German buildings, interspaced with contemporary detached house architecture. A tourist thus at the same time feels the thrill of novelty, being away from their dwelling, but also at the same time, realigns with a broader tone of familiar visual culture, blended with stereotypes of a highland mountain locality, a patina of bygone times with an anticipated comfort of accommodation. We can thus see here an intersubjective world at work, spanned by a phenomenological interplay involved in the production of a territory.

Our first *flânerie* shows how a secondspace script in Karpacz balances 'the known and the expected' in references to a culturally prestigious high mountain region in Poland, thus how the asymmetrical dialogic indexes a thirdspace. The social space thus has a certain phenomenological directionality: preferably pointing to the highest cultural prestige as a stake in dialectal transaction. Phenomenologically, that aspect was captured by Merleau-Ponty, who claimed that being-in-the-world must not be comprehended in a concentrical way, that is, as a relation between a central entity and the milieu around it, but rather it needs to be comprehended via pending actions or tasks to be done, through

> a free space which outlines in advance the possibilities available to the body at any time. In turn these possibilities have to be understood not as the possibilities of a perceptual presentation or conceptual representation of the world but as the possibilities of action in a world.
>
> Macann 1993: 173

What is at stake here thus, can be defined as a potential for action on the part of a tourist, invitation to interaction of pre-connived space, which in Gadamerian sense, is effected as understanding in *aprioristic* prejudices (Heideggerian *pre-conceptions*).

Flânerie Two: Juggling History and Ideology in a Temporal Fusion

Let us recall that in general hermeneutics is not limited to a canonical structural analysis of texts (cf. Introduction), but is primarily concerned with the universe emerging between authors, readers and texts themselves (cf. Kearney 1988: 6). For Gadamer, architecture (cf. Gadamer 2006) as a dialogue between pragmatic needs and art carries certain weight and is bestowed with space-creating function, alike all of the enactment processes of art. Nonetheless, the philosopher does not consider architecture a mere construction of a product with a purpose (a concert hall, a theater, an art gallery, etc.) Rather, 'architecture is true to what it is designed to be in a double respect' (Gadamer [1992] 2006: 79).

The Karpacz townscape matches however rather what Gadamer calls a problematic concept of the decorative.[12] Due to the lack of any official restrictions on placing advertisements, the venue propagates a loud visual cacophony reflecting the fierce competition in the resort's townscape. Most frequently, one business advertises its offerings using many publicity elements, e.g., Bar Baca (*baca* is a 'chief shepherd'), where we counted as much as 7 different banners around the establishment with its name. But a reverse strategy can also occur, that is, one company can also have several names or multiple versions of a name.

One of the examples of such nominal proliferation is Bistro 'Aurora' (henceforth, *Bistro*, Figures 10.3 and 10.4) which at the same time bears the name *Mini Muzeum Socrealizmu* (Mini Museum of Socialist Realism) and *Rosyjska restauracja rekomendowana przez National Geographic* (Russian restaurant recommended by National Geographic).[13] To that, there is a communist 'logo' of a sickle, hammer and a star, as well as a profile image of Lenin on the restaurant's red banner. That Bistro was the second spot where we, in the guise of the two *flaneuses*, plunged into the endemic phenomenological space.

The photo in Figure 10.3 (level of urban planning – *secondspace*), shows how the Bistro's publicity is embedded within the heterotopian townscape, operating with the staple symbolism associated with the period of Leninism. The verbal and visual congestion of several banners advertising the spot intertwine with the spatial congestion: the entrance to the Bistro is through a show alley, in the vicinity of other, crouched one next to another, buildings of the public space. As typical of any tourist Polish resort, around it there is a proliferation of stands selling all type of merchandise, mostly recalling the various handicrafts from the Tatra mountains. As we enter, we are suddenly enveloped in an alternative idiosyncratic reality, of which a glimpse can be seen in the two sample photos in Figure 10.4. The immediate materiality of the contiguous urban spatiality disappears into a carefully scripted internal décor, marketed as 'museum' and as an immersion into the socialist experience.

First of all, the 'exhibits' profusely collated on the walls form a cacophony which would never be possible in a true museal institution.[14] In fact, it is an absolute refutation of all that a museum's mission statement is. In a (state) museum, there is a script for each exhibition, but such an exhibition script sometimes is being prepared for years, taking careful consideration not to slant the general picture of the issue being presented, and to be objective in its presentation. The museum exhibition script has the goal to preserve and illustrate a particular issue from the past. It does not rely on what a potential visitor expects, it usually can run counter to the expectation, presenting unknowns and unexpected facets. The selection of artefacts featured in the Bistro are not exhibits in fact, but a skeuomorphic reflection of exhibits: both on the level of form and of content, and that is why we claim that they are another example of creating a transactional thirdspace.

On the level of content, there is thus a priming of the issues related to the socialist period in a hypothetical dialogue of the owners with the clients, negotiating a stereotype of socialist esthetics. Hence, the resulting lived space, relating to Merleau-Ponty's perspective, is oriented through the scripted and guided motility of the guests. The result is a no-place (the bistro) embedded

Figure 10.4 Photos of the interior of the Bistro Aurora. Left: Portraits of Lenin and Brezhnev. Right: interior wall of the bistro, incorporating newspaper clippings and a poster by Valery Barykin.

within a larger no-place, the Foucauldian heterotopia (Karpacz), a scripted and imagined place at the same time.

Both Gadamer and Ricoeur emphasize that understanding is a process, evolving in a dialectic way. This is particularly true of relating to art (cf. Gadamer [1996] 2006). In the case of dystopias, the Lotmanian game of art is however scripted. In our flaneuries the skeuomorphic play is obtained through immediate contact with the 'exhibits' such as a gun (replica?) in an exhibition case, painted portraits of Vladimir Ilyich Ulyanov (Lenin) and Leonid Ilyich Brezhnev. The thirdspace teleology, the lived experience, is to feel cozy and safe here and now (*Dasein*), with the simultaneous thrill of being under a prison (interrogation) lamp and of having a drink with a gun behind your back. The thirdspace message is constructed forwarding the claim of socialism and communism in Russia being a friendly, good old bygone and exotic time.

Another prominent decoration type which inscribes itself into the dialectics of the interior are copies of posters (authored by Valery Barykin) – an artist, who artistically reworks canonical motifs known from socrealist art into a humorous reflection 'à rebours' with an erotic tint. It is indeed telling that instead of tokens or reproductions of paintings produced actually as socrealist art in 1949–53, the interior features only artistic dialogues which in fact defy all the ideological underpinnings of socrealism, while presenting a very general formal reference to that art.

The second *flânerie* illustrates the issue of constructing experiential identities and objectivation through the use of script as media: (1) immediate perception;

(2) representation of a skeuomorphic aspect; and (3) priming the experience: leading to the perception of communism as a jolly period. Accordingly, the social space appears as a tool for shaping the imagination. The thirdspace emerges as a dialogically constructed intersubjectivity, concatenating in a phenomenological field. What is directly apprehended in such a transaction are objectified qualia, grafted onto the no-place of the larger phenomenological field of Karpacz.

Conclusion

In this chapter, we adopted an approach elaborated by Edward Soja of the 'third space' creation, coupling it with Gadamerian hermeneutics and Maurice Merleau-Ponty's phenomenology to investigate transactional nature of spatio-temporal endemic universe of the Karpacz holiday resort, Poland. Edward Soja, in defining thirdspace, points out its volatile character by specifying that it is a heuristic and purposefully flexible notion, aiming to grasp 'what is actually a constantly shifting and changing milieu of ideas, events, appearances and meanings' (Soja 1996: 2). This formulation, in accordance with Lefebvre's stance, brings to the fore the interconnectivity of temporality, historicity and spatiality. In this contribution, we focused on such interconnectivity in domain of the hermeneutics of tourism in the case study of two catering establishments in a Karpacz holiday resort.

For our methodical framework, we also proposed to enrich Soja's theory with a transactional aspect of social space, in line with Merleau-Ponty's phenomenology, and with emergent hermeneutic dialogue. Hermeneutics as a meta-perspective was particularly useful, since as Misgeld (1979) points out, it can liaise between phenomenology and canonical language analysis because rather than focusing on rule-driven processes or conventional teleology of speech, it can delve into intentions to apprehend what is at work at that discourse stretch (ibid., 223).

We pursued the investigation into that 'hermeneutical moment', focusing on how the Karpacz space phenomenologically interacts with tourists as subjects who transform it, and how the subjects turn into objects, receiving the transformation from the predetermined script and reinforcing the script. The resulting geospace avails of scripts of regionality (references to a prestigious mountain culture in Poland) and historicity (the Aurora bistro). The study thus uncovered the dialogical relationships in the site: with tourists active as the subject (driving the transformation) and as the object (receiving the transformation and being affected by the perceived materiality).

Enriching the trichotomy of space with an additional phenomenological look brought to the fore dialogisms implicated in actually negotiating the space for the tourist. At the first stage, the 'imagery' is negotiated by the authors of the script: in the first *flânerie*, we saw how the particular choice of reference for a 'prestigious' region and not any other is grafted onto the already heterotopian space. In the second, the phenomenological dialogue occurs between the script of primed communist canons and the guests. The space is thus transactionally marketed as being submerged into actuations of a particular region and history.

The carving of a waitress wearing a miniskirt (from the Podhale region, not the Karkonosze Mountains), the omnipresence of the German Mountain spirit on the same building as the Podhale Edelweiss motif, and a subjectivize vision of socialist realism aesthetics in a restaurant that self-identifies as 'a museum' are just a few examples of the material exponents of those phenomenological translations. In particular, the choice of the artistic vision of socrealism, being in fact socrealist art *a rebours*. Seeing the phenomenological directionality of the space, in the perspective by Merleau-Ponty, prompts the relation of the Dasein to the world 'not to be understood in terms of objective distances but in terms of a sort of primordial coincidence or coexistence of the body with that towards which it enacts itself, mobilizes itself, projects itself' (Macann 1993: 176). The mobilization of the phenomenological body occurs through skeuomorphic references to real places: the posited reality of a quality of being 'regional' or 'historic' and not heterotopian.

This transactional interaction can be compared to the traditional ideas of the Gadamerian hermeneutic circle: before visiting the Karpacz resort, a visitor has an idea of what to expect there based on a patchwork of prototypical details like, for example, a seaside inn, a Silesian inn, an Alpine inn, a highlander inn, regional Czech beer, regional pizza, or regional hamburgers. (cf. Lubos-Kozieł and Haładewicz-Grzelak 2021). These specifics generate an emergent unity, which comforts the tourist, is understandable and makes the tourist feel safe, immersed in a sense 'that concerns him' (Turnbull 2004: 173):

> In this way, the sense sought by the ontological demand that we understand 'what happens to us', is brought to light by a concern for what the always and already historically constituted world delivers over to us by dint of our inevitable participation with it and in it. (...) Understanding is not a state but an event – a

happening in history that stirs us to wonder – where the world is brought to life by being 'made present' (and with this, one's awareness of one's own historical subjectivity is brought into play).

Ibid.

The results thus pointed to the indivisible connection of the mediatization with tourism and to creating a thirdspace (a real-and-imagined place) for the benefit of tourism. Working at the intersection of tourism, hermeneutics and phenomenology, brings additional insights into mediation and the world of life as such, resulting in the mapping of a type of sociophysical geography. Thus, a geopsychic space is constructed, actualizing the idea of a non-place, fostering a guided apprehension. The tourist experience is scripted though a complex interaction with skeuomorphic references to regionality and history in a fused, metaphysical horizon.

Notes

1. The unquestionable lead in terms of mountain tourism in Poland is taken by the Tatra Mountains – the highest mountain range in Poland, with its landmark resort, Zakopane, which is considered to be the most prestigious tourist venue.
2. This article forms part of our larger project on Karpacz resort. In the previous strand of the research (cf. Lubos-Kozieł and Haładewicz-Grzelak 2021), apart from providing more in-depth historical insights, we also addressed the topic of constructing the 'regional tradition' in Karpacz for the benefit of the tourist and we presented in more detail the corpus of all the types of visual texts we studied. The results of the present research were presented to the academic audience during the 36th International Human Science Research Conference, *Between Necessity and Choice: Existential Dilemmas in the Human Life-World*, Jelenia Góra, Poland, 11–14 July 2017. To the best of knowledge, there have not been any studies of the townscape of Karpacz apart from our work. All the translations and all the photos in the text, unless otherwise indicated, are our authorship.
3. A follow-up research study conducted in 2021 did not show any substantial variegation with our previously completed database. There were changes in the decor of some catering establishments, some disappeared, but also new ones came into being with a similar rotor of simulacrum. The changes after the pandemic would require a separate longitudinal study of its own, hence we decided to focus on a uniform material collected at the major field study.

4   Our study concerned only Karpacz Dolny, that is, only the former Krummhübel, without the Brückenberg locality, which was later added to it, and which is now called Karpacz Górny.
5   The historical dimension of the town and the region is provided in, e.g., Mateusz J. Hartwich (2012), Alicja Hirsch-Tabis and Ewa K.Tabis (2005). See also the official webpage of the town: https://www.karpacz.pl/historia.
6   It should be noted that the fall of communism in addition to changing the economic situation, also brought about ideological changes, which among other things, spurred interest in the previously neglected and left unsaid, former German past of the village and of the region.
7   Karpacz regionalism was studied by us in the context of advertising and as a component of advertising. A key analytical finding in that paper was establishing a semiotic rotor for glocalization: in the dystopian locality of that type everything was posited to be *regional*. We arrived at the heuristic value [+regional] as the default one, which translates into the ease of adopting multifarious and disjointed elements that can be sold to tourists as *regional*.
8   For example, pointing to the importance of the lived experience in understanding spaces, Yakhlef observes that:

> [g]eneric spaces are deterritorialized, disembodied, and lifted out from their context. Once cut loose from the joints of time and space, they take on features that are associated with the logic of flows (such as money, airports, hotels, information, etc.), which turns them into a direction rather than a reference that anchors them into a specific organizational culture or a specific nation.
>
> Yakhlef 2004: 239

9   See Lubos-Kozieł and Haładewicz-Grzelak (2021) for more details.
10 The message in the standard (colloquial) Polish would be: *Witajcie i zostawcie [tu] swoja kasę*. It should be remembered here that in this particular region historically there has never been any indigenous Slavonic dialect spoken, the Tatra highlanders' dialect least of all.
11 Including the two names (Mountain Spirit and *Liczyrzepa*) are due to the fact that Rübezahl counting turnips – has never had a unified Polish name, but several competing names, since the figure was grafted onto the Polish cultural milieu only after 1945, from German and Czech traditions.
12 'What we call 'decorative' is already thought of in relation to the concept of art, and if we find a painting to be decorative, this is almost a criticism of it. Nothing mysteriously comes forth from it, or perhaps there is nothing in the painting to come forward' (Gadamer [1992] 2006: 80).
13 The design as of year 2014. The name 'Aurora', possibly unretrievable semantically anymore to the average contemporary visitor of the catering establishment in

question, refers to the name of an armoured Russian cruiser. Supposedly a blank shot on 24 October 1917 (Old Style), fired from one of her guns was to signal the assault on the Winter Palace. That shot is canonically assumed to be the inception of the October Revolution.

14 See a sample web page showing the specifics of exhibitions at the Museum of Opole Silesia, Opole, Poland, available online: https://muzeum.opole.pl/en/ (accessed 29 July 2023).

References

Baker, Jody. 2002. 'Productions and Consumption of Wilderness in Algonkin Park'. *Space and Culture*, 5 (3): 198–210.

Campbell, Neil. 2005. 'Producing America: Redefining Post-Tourism in the Global Media Age'. In David Crouch, Rhona Jackson and Felix Thompson (eds), *The Media and the Tourist Imagination: Converging Cultures*, 198–214. London: Routledge.

Chmielewska, Ella. 2005. 'A Close Reading of the Iconoshpere of Warsaw'. *Space and Culture*, 8 (4): 349–80.

Chmielewska, Ella. 2007. 'Framing [Con]text: Graffiti and Place'. *Space and Culture*, 10 (2): 145–69.

Couldry, Nick and Anna McCarthy. 2004. 'Introduction. Orientations: Mapping Media Space'. In Nick Couldry and Anna McCarthy (eds), *Mediaspace: Place, Scale and Culture in a Media Age*, 1–18. London: Routledge.

Duncan, James and Derek Gregory. 1999. 'Introduction'. In J. Duncan and D. Gregory (eds), *Writes of Passage: Reading Travel Writing*, 1–13. London: Routledge.

Falkheimer, Jasper and André Jansson (eds). 2006. *Geographies of Communication: The Spatial Turn in Media Studies*. Gothenburg: Nordicom.

Gadamer, Hans-Georg. [1960] 2013. *Truth and Method* (Wahrheit und Methode. Tuebingen). Translation revised by Joel Weinsheimer and Dolan G. Marshall. Bloomsbury Revelations. London and New York: Bloomsbury Academic.

Gadamer, Hans-Georg. 1967. *Kleine Schriften I. Philosophie, Hermeneutik*. Frankfurt am Main: Tübingen.

Gadamer, Hans-Georg. [1992] 2006. 'Artworks in Word and Image "So True, So Full of Being!" (Goethe)'. *Theory, Culture & Society*, 23 (1): 57–83.

Gadamer, Hans-Georg. 2013. Foreword to the second edition. In Gadamer (1960/2013), xxv–xxxvi.

Hartwich, Mateusz J. 2012. *Das schlesische Riesengebirge. Die Polonisierung einer Landschaft nach 1945*. Wien: Böhlau Verlag.

Hirsch-Tabis, Alicja and Ewa K. Tabis. 2005. *Karpacz – Krummhübel, dzieje miasta pod Śnieżką* (Karpacz – Krummhübel. The History of the Town under the Śnieżka Mountain). Mysłakowice: Związek Gmin Karkonoskich.

Jansson, André. 2002. 'Spatial Phantasmagoria: The Mediatization of Tourism Experience'. *European Journal of Communication*, 17 (4): 429–43.

Jansson, André. 2006. 'A Sense of Tourism: New Media and the Dialectic of Encapsulation /Decapsulation'. *Tourist Studies*, 7 (1): 5–24.

Karpacz. n.d. 'Historia', by Ryszard Rzepczyński. Available online: http://www.karpacz.pl/historia (accessed 26 August 2022).

Kearney, Richard. 1988. 'Paul Ricoeur and the Hermeneutic Imagination'. In T. P. Kemp and D. Rasmussen (eds), *The Narrative Path: The Later Works of Paul Ricoeur*, 1–31. Cambridge, MA: MIT Press.

Lagerkvist, Amanda. 2008. 'Travels in Thirdspace: Experiential Suspense in Mediaspace: The Case of America (Un)known'. *European Journal of Communication*, 23: 343–63.

Lash, Scott and Jonathan Friedman. 1992. 'Introduction: Subjectivity and Modernity's Other'. In Scott Lash and Jonathan Friedman (eds), *Modernity and Identity*, 1–30. Oxford: Blackwell.

Lash, Scott and Jonathan Friedman (eds). 1992. *Modernity and Identity*. Oxford: Blackwell.

Lash, Scott and John Urry. 1994. *Economies of Signs and Space*. London: Sage.

Lefebvre, Henri. [1974] 1991. *The Production of Space*. Oxford: Blackwell.

Lubos-Kozieł, Joanna and Małgorzata Haładewicz-Grzelak. 2021. 'Defaulting [+traditional] in the Karpacz HolidayRresort (Poland)'. In A. Pawelec and G. Szpila (eds), *Text – Image – Music: Crossing the Borders. Intermedial Conversations on the Poetics of Verbal, Visual and Musical Texts*, 445–70. Frankfurt a/M: Peter Lang.

Macann, Christopher. 1993. *Four Phenomenological Philosophers: Husserl, Heidegger, Sartre, Merleau-Ponty*. London: Routledge.

Merleau-Ponty, Maurice. 1945. *Phénoménologie de la perception*. Paris: Gallimard.

Miles, Malcolm. 2004. *Consuming Cities*. London: Bloomsbury Academic.

Misgeld, Dieter. 1979. 'On Gadamer's Hermeneutics'. *Philosophy of the Social Sciences*, 9: 221–39.

Muzeum Sportu i Turystyki w Karpaczu. n.d. Available online: http://www.muzeumsportu.org/index.php?option=com_content&view=article&id=5&Itemid=4&lang=pl (accessed 26 August 2022).

Pierce, Joseph. 2019. 'How Can We Share Space? Ontologies of Spatial Pluralism in Lefebvre, Butler, and Massey'. *Space and Culture*, 25 (1): 1–13.

Polska. n.d. Available online: https://polska-org.pl (accessed 26 August 2022).

Purinton, Malcolm F. 2023. *Globalization in a Glass: The Rise of Pilsner Beer through Technology, Taste and Empire*. London: Bloomsbury Academic.

Soja, Edward. [1988] 2000. *Postmetropolis*. Oxford: Blackwell.

Soja, Edward. 1996. *Thirdspace: Journeys to Los Angeles and Other Real-and-Imagined Places*. Oxford: Blackwell.

Turnbull, Neil. 2004. 'Making "It" Happen: Philosophy, Hermeneutics and the Truth of Art. [A review of] *The Philosophy of Gadamer* by Jean Grondin, translated by Kathryn Plant London: Acumen, 2003, 180 pp.'. *Theory, Culture & Society*, 21 (6): 171–8.

Tzanelli, Rodanthi. 2012. 'Domesticating the Tourist Gaze in Thessaloniki's Prigipos'. *Ethnography*, 13 (3): 278–305.
Urry, John. [1990] 2002. *The Tourist Gaze*. 2nd ed. London: Sage.
Urry, John. 1995. *Consuming Places*. London: Routledge.
Yakhlef, Ali. 2004. 'Global Brands as Embodied "Generic Spaces": The Example of Branded Chain Hotels'. *Space and Culture*, 7 (2): 237–48.

Creating Common Epistemic Spaces through Multimodal Stance-Taking Practices

Valentyna Ushchyna

Introduction

Lately, stance-taking as a multifaceted and multilayered discursive activity has gained an unprecedented attention of the researchers from all over the world (cf. Biber and Finegan 1989; Du Bois 2007; Jaffe 2009; Kiesling et al. 2018).[1] In the last few decades, stance has been studied from different angles and perspectives – as a way of expressing the speaker's / writer's opinion on a certain problem, as a means the users of language use to position themselves in conversation in terms of certainty or emotion, as a linguistic expression of the speaker's / writer's attitude towards the object of communication, the person's likes or dislikes and knowledge of the discussed topic. But most importantly, stance has become a focal notion of the studies concerned with the discursive construction of social meanings in language and by means of language.

Many researchers noted that 'stance' is inseparably connected with 'persona' (Eckert 2012), 'style' (Johnstone 2009), or 'identity' (Bucholtz and Hall 2004) of the speakers. Manifold of stances reflect the consistent patterns of individuals' speech behaviour, or their linguistic selves. Moreover, stance is not only agentive discursive-semiotic practice, it is also inherently intersubjective. To find their existential places in society, to grasp their social space and 'social orientation' (Langlotz 2015: 1), people often rely on their mental representations about the world, theirs and their interlocutors', basing their knowledge on their stances, interactively constructed in various situations of life.

Stance cannot be studied without referring to the notion of 'stance-taking'. Some researchers treat them as close equivalents but I believe stance can be seen as a result (though never finite) of stance-taking – a continuous intersubjective process of stance construction and stance negotiation in discursive interaction. According to Scott Kiesling, the most important difference between stance and stance-taking is that 'stancetaking moves the focus of the term from static noun to a dynamic verb' (2021: 410). Stance and stance-taking, as explained by Kiesling, are 'related concepts that help to explain patterning of language and the motivations for the use of lexical items, constructions, and discourse markers' (ibid., 409). These linguistic means of marking stances are indicating the relationships of the speaker to other participants of conversation, as well as the content of the interaction. Therefore, stance-taking is always indexical. In Michael Silverstein's terms, it indicates 'momentary relational attitudes and affects' (Silverstein 2021: 13), and, thus, it's situationally and contextually bound.

Stance-taking activities are traditionally viewed as a unity of knowledge of speakers about the objects of stance-taking (epistemic stance) and their feelings and emotions concerning it (affective stance). Stances are formed and later formulated on the basis of epistemic and affective evaluations of various discursive dimensions (including sociocultural, conversational and sociolinguistic variables) that the stance-takers have in their disposal. In this chapter, I will mainly concentrate my attention on the epistemic dimension of stance-taking in an attempt to explain how the level of knowledge (or a lack of it) influences the ways people express their attitudes towards the problem they discuss.

Consequently, I will demonstrate that individual epistemic stances do not only reflect the epistemic spaces they represent but they also shape these spaces. Due to their active circulation in virtual (Internet) discourse, individual stances mold certain ideological planes, recognizable by the in- and out-group members. They often serve as indexical signs of certain socio-cultural communities, united by similar views, values and beliefs – the so-called 'ideological bubbles', existing in such social networks as Facebook, Twitter, or Instagram. In such bubbles, people have their own order of 'semiotic dialectic' (Silverstein 2021: 13), reflecting certain epistemic spaces.

According to David Chalmers, epistemic space consists of imaginative space of possible scenarios:

> If a subject did not know anything, all scenarios would be epistemically possible for the subject. When a subject knows something, some scenarios are excluded. Every piece of substantive knowledge corresponds to a division in epistemic space: some scenarios are excluded out as epistemically impossible for the subject, while others are left open. More specifically, it is natural to hold that for

a given *p*, there may be scenarios in which *p* is the case, and scenarios in which p is not the case. Then when a subject knows that *p*, scenarios in which *p* is not the case are excluded, while others are left open. The scenarios that are epistemically possible for a subject are those that are not excluded by any knowledge of the subject.

Chalmers 2011: 61

Hence, people build their stances based on the scenarios that are epistemically possible for them, on the scenarios that are not eliminated due to their knowledge of the subject matter. Following Chalmers who writes, 'there are many ways things might be.... [I]t might be there is life on Jupiter, and it might be that there is not' (ibid., 61), we may presume that it might be that Covid-19 vaccines will kill you or it might be that they will not. Or even better: it might be that Covid-19 vaccines will poison you, or implant the chips into your bodies or it might be that they will not. So, to make this picture complete, we might suppose that epistemic spaces are not only 'the spaces of ways things might be' (ibid., 63), but also the ways things might have been (Jago 2009: 327). Or in other words, they include counterfactual spaces with epistemic possibilities of possible (sometimes unreal) worlds. Epistemic possibilities as well as truth conditions and (un-)certainty in the expressed propositions comprise epistemic stances and can be accessed via words, word combinations and/or sentences that served the basis for our further analysis.

Data and Methods

The data for this study were gathered from the blogs of popular Ukrainian bloggers Karl Volokh (Карл Волох) and Garik Korogodski (Гарік Корогодський), published on Facebook during the period of three months: from December 2021 till February 2022. Both of these bloggers are well known in Ukraine and can be considered Ukrainian opinion-makers. The average number of their followers is around 100000 people (as of August 2022, Karl Volokh had 90,597 subscribers, while Garik Korogodski had 153,000 followers). Karl Volokh leads his blog in Ukrainian, while Garik Korogodski usually wrote in Russian before Russia launched its war on Ukraine, lately he often resorts to the Ukrainian language in his blog. They have different political views, support different political parties and political actors, though both of them take very patriotic pro-Ukrainian positions.

As is well known, before 24 February 2022 – the date of the Russian invasion that drastically changed the lives of all Ukrainian people – the most topical issue that had been actively communicated around the globe with a fare level of intensity was Covid-19 pandemic. So, the main object of stance-taking in the texts that have been analysed in this study, is Covid-19 and vaccination against it, which was profusely discussed at the period of data gathering not only on Facebook and other social media, but also in public discourse and mass media.

General methodological framework for this study was offered by objective hermeneutics – an approach that allows reconstruction of the hidden structures of discourse. Theoretical development of objective hermeneutics as the method of textual analysis is connected with the need of giving explanations to the processes of social semiosis in postmodern, heavily computerized and highly virtualized world. Representatives of objective hermeneutics support the idea that meaning is a social category (Ley 2010; Oevermann 2002; Wagner 2001).

Because objective hermeneutics assumes that speech behaviour of individuals depends on interactively shared rules and, therefore, meanings are rather intersubjective than subjective, it can serve a good instrument for the reconstruction of the discourse stances, built in online communication. Moreover, in contrast to other qualitative methods of discourse analysis (e.g. critical discourse analysis or narrative studies), objective hermeneutics is not about reproducing a meaning intended by the author, but rather about determining the latent (i.e. unconscious) meanings of the text.

Objective hermeneutics offers a peculiar view of the relationships between a person and a society, which is based upon the balancing between the subjectivity of individual positioning and objectivity of social interaction. Within the framework of objective hermeneutics, analysis of stance-taking presupposes taking into account personal attitudes of a stance-taker (including the person's knowledge of the stance object and emotions concerning it), along with the domineering social structures framing the person's discursive actions and interactions with others.

As it was already mentioned earlier, the focus of this study is on the epistemic component of stance, because knowledge (or a lack of it) plays an exclusively prominent role in Covid-19 discourse. Moreover, knowledge concerning Covid-19 is a priori insufficient, due to novelty of the disease and, therefore, limited amount of checked and scientifically proven data that would be a reliable source of information about it. Such insufficiency creates epistemic spaces with numerous epistemic possibilities of possible (sometimes unreal) worlds, for instance attempts to explain the essence of Covid-19 by various conspiracy theories or mysterious intentions of secret elites. Besides, everything that has been discussed in this thematic realm is associated with lots of uncertainty and necessity of decision-making: be it the decision to wear a mask or the decision to be vaccinated. In addition, as it happens, uncertainty usually motivates engaged and opinionated discussions where epistemic stances are formed, expressed and negotiated.

Linguistic Expression of Eepistemic Stance

Whether during face-to-face encounter or in online conversations, discourse subjects represent their knowledge of the situation in which they find themselves, while constructing their epistemic status in discursive interaction. Consequently, they inform their interlocutors of: (1) the ways information had been obtained; (2) their certainty in the truthfulness of the utterance; and (3) their commitment to the validity of the proposition. Besides, they evaluate epistemic status(-es) of their interlocutor(s) and formulate their utterances accordingly.

Thus, while stance in general embraces such categories as emotions and feelings (affective stance), as well as attitudes and evaluations (attitudional stance), its epistemic part relates to the speaker's knowledge and the person's commitment to the propositional content of the utterance (Hyland 1999: 101). The researchers' attention to the ways knowledge or a lack of it is expressed by means of language is as old as linguistics itself, but particular interest to epistemic stance (Biber and Finegan 1989; Biber 2004) was ignited by the attempts to grasp the interrelation between the speakers' pragmatic attitude (i.e. their own motivations in the process of knowledge processing and the evaluation of their interlocutors' knowledge and motivations) with propositional attitude (i.e. internal structure of information conceptualization and verbalizing by means of language).

Epistemic component of stance is marked in discourse by means of linguistic tools that indicate the speaker's commitment to the truthfulness of the offered proposition, the source of information, and the level of the person's certainty in the validity of their own judgement (Chafe 1986: 264). Therefore, epistemic stance comprises information about the source from which the knowledge was obtained (evidentiality) and the stance-taker's subjective reflections based upon the parameters of current situational context (modality). In the subsequent sections I will illustrate the use of these language tools deployed by the stance-takers in online discussions, extracted from my corpus.

Modality

The concept of modality (from Latin *modus* – mode, measure) has been studied within the framework of formal logic (Kripke 1963; Garson 2021), philosophy (Marcus 1993; Wright 1989) and linguistics (Alexander 1988; Fintel 2007; Lyons 1977; Palmer 1979, 1986). Modality reflects subjective aspects of human thinking. While cognizing the world around them, people make their own judgments about it and express their personal attitudes towards it, which is later objectivized in language as a category of modality. The relationship between modality and stance is determined by their correlation with the ways the speaker presents himself and his attitude to the referential situation in communicative interaction. As M. A. K. Halliday (1994: 88) stated, modality is the intermediate point between the positive or the negative poles. He further mentioned that it refers to the area of meaning that lies between 'yes' and 'no' – the intermediate ground between positive and negative attitude (ibid., 356). Similarly, linguistic expression of modality marks positive and negative stances built in discursive interaction.

Usually, modal expressions are considered to have two types of meaning: epistemic and deontic. Epistemic is 'concerned with matters of knowledge or beliefs on which basis speakers express their judgements about state of affairs, events or actions' (Hoye 1997: 42), while deontic refers to the 'necessity of acts in terms of which the speaker gives permission or lays and obligation for the performance of actions at some time in the future' (ibid., 43). In this chapter, I will mainly focus on epistemic modality as a part of epistemic positioning in discourse.

Epistemic modality relates to propositional attitude of the speakers and, thus, serves a basis for their stances. It appertains their commitment to the truthfulness of the expressed propositions (Kärkkäinen 2003:150). Reflecting the degree of completeness of the speaker's knowledge of the event, epistemic modality is associated with the assessment by the speaker of his capabilities and the identification of the degree of confidence in his own assumptions (Thornborrow 2005: 18).

Being a key feature of epistemic modality, subjectivity underlies the design of stance-taking in discourse. It is associated with the very definition of epistemic modality as the expression of the speaker's attitude to the person's own utterance (Palmer 1979: 3). Subjectivity is the background for stances that a discourse subject occupies in relation to: (1) the person's knowledge of the discussed matter, (2) the reliability of the information offered by to the person and (3) the person's certainty/uncertainty in the truthfulness of the proposition. Such positions are treated as epistemic stances. They usually reflect the subjective inferencing of the speaker rather than an objective reality. E.g.: '*I mean*, *I don't think* the lions had much to chat about with the lambs' (Segal 1988: 41, emphasis added).

In the above sentence, the speaker does not affirm the fact that the lions did not have '*much to chat about with the lambs*', but he metaphorically expresses his disbelief in the communicative ability of people of different psycho-types and with different social statuses to find their common ground in conversation. Subjective attitude of the speaker is marked by the personal pronoun *I* and the verb *mean*, which is later intensified by the stance phrase '*I think*,' used in a negative grammatical form.

In any utterance, there is always a subjective variable, even if the proposition contains an objective information, independent from the communicative situation or from the participants of this situation. For instance, in the statement by Karl Volokh published in his post on Omicron in early December 2021, 'Дозволю собі висловити кілька припущень (дилетантських, але базованих на стеженні за ситуацією)' (I will let myself make some presumptions (dilettante, but based on the situation watch)) one may see that the speaker tries to mitigate categoricalness of his judgment by emphasizing the inherent subjectivity of his reasoning and acknowledging his own incompetence in self-evaluative commentary (*dilettante, but based on the situation watch*). Further, he continues by explicitly expressing his insufficient knowledge and uncertainty in formulation of his arguments:

> Якщо я помиляюся і справа лише в тому, що в нас Омікрон з'явився й поширюватися почав значно пізніше, ніж там, то Україну чекають дуже важкі часи [if I'm mistaken and the reason is only in the fact that omicron appeared and was spread in our country much later that there [in Europe], then Ukraine is going on face very difficult times].

As we may see in the given example, Karl Volokh formulates modality of uncertainty by presupposing that his arguments could be faulty (*if I'm mistaken*). At the same time, the use of such communicative strategy produces an opposite pragmatic effect on his followers. Instead of weakening his position, it enhances the validity of the proposition, and in such a way, strengthens the trustworthiness of the blogger's stances.

The described subjectivity variables concern the evaluation of the information validity by the speaker, the person's beliefs, attitudes and intentions, and, thus, they serve the basis for epistemic stance-taking. It is an evaluation of a possibility that a certain hypothetical state of affairs is untrue or probably true (as well as true or definitely true). In the above-mentioned examples, the speaker uses epistemic stance-markers of uncertainty, '*I will let myself make some presumptions*', '*if I'm mistaken*', which can be interpreted as his doubtfulness in the truthfulness of the expressed proposition. Such stance-forming expressions are seen as a modality of unsure knowledge, which is characteristic for constructing epistemic stance of uncertainty.

Hence, any verbalized statement is not only a speech materialization of speakers' mental representations but also the person's actualization of discursive and, consequently, social activity. An inseparable part of such activities consists in subjects' construing their discursive positions concerning their certainty or uncertainty in the validity of the utterance contents, or epistemic stances, which are expressed through epistemic modality. English, as it were, has a quite ramified system of language means for expressing epistemic modality that can be ranged in the scale from '*I know*' via '*I suppose*' to '*I don't know*'. Modal expressions include lexical (e.g. modal words, evaluative adjectives, interjections), syntactic (specific syntactic structures, e.g. cleft sentences or ellipsis), pragmatic (e.g. different discourse markers) and phonetic (intonation, volume, prosody, etc.) means. Modal expressions create a range of modal meanings – certain modal metatext, by means of which the stances of discursive subject (speaker or writer) are explicated. Fairly often, linguistically objectivized modality enables the listeners' perception of the speaking subject's mental representations.

Modality as a part of the stance-taking activities is characterized by linguistic variability and depends on social and psychological factors. The semantics ranges along the continuums of 'possibility' – 'impossibility', 'possibility' – 'coercion', 'possibility' – 'logical necessity'. By linguistic means of expressing epistemic modality, speakers index their epistemic stances, as well as mark the amount of their knowledge about the stance objects. They range from confidence and certainty to doubt and uncertainty, which can be depicted on the geometric axis on which we place these positions, as shown in Figure 11.1.

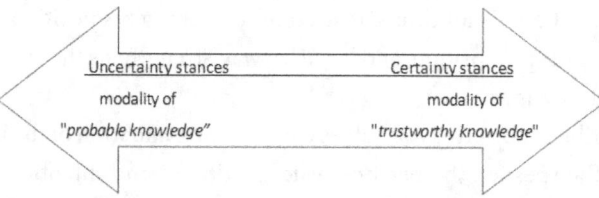

Figure 11.1 Modality on the axe of epistemic stance-taking (own elaboration).

Therefore, the speaker's assessment of the degree of truthfullness is included in the modal part of the statement and expresses attitude of the speaker to reality in terms of reliability / unreliability, confidence / doubt, certainty / uncertainty, as well as associates modality with evidentiality that together make up the epistemic stance of the subject. In other words, speech behaviour of the discourse subjects during their stance-taking activities is determined by their knowledge about the situation and their assuredness in the validity of this knowledge (modality), as well as by the source of this knowledge (evidentiality).

Evidentiality

Many world languages have specific linguistic tools for indication an information source, or *evidentiality*. In some languages, evidentiality is grammaticalized via particular grammatical elements (affixes, clitics, or particles), in other languages (including English) evidentiality is expressed through various lexical means that usually are optional. In linguistics, evidentiality has been recognized since Boas (1938), but only recently it has come to attention of a larger number of linguists (Narrog 2005). The best known monograph on linguistics of evidentiality was written by Alexandra Aikhenvald, who defines this concept as 'a grammatical category that has source of information as its primary meaning' (Aikhenvald 2006: 320). Following Aikhenvald, we will treat evidentiality as a set of grammatical or lexical means that serve to index the source of information the speaker / writer mentions in their utterances.

Researchers studying evidentiality (Aikhenvald 2006, 2015; Bybee 1995; Chafe 1986; Chung and Timberlake 1985; Willet 1988), categorize it in different ways, but almost all of them agree that evidential meanings can be classified based on the ways speakers accessed information – directly or indirectly. Direct evidentiality presupposes that the speaker bases his statements on his own experience. Either he / she has seen the situation with the person's own eyes (visual evidence), has heard what happened (auditory evidence), or attested to the events in any other way (e.g. somatic bodily reactions).

In the fragment of the Facebook post by Garik Korogodski, the author describes his being sick with Covid-19 as a ground for his stance on vaccination boosters (the original text is in Russian):

[2]

    Второй ковид намного легче первого. Но – внимание – это не простуда, хуже. Перенес легко, посмотрим, как пойдет восстановление. Неделю отсидел в изоляции. Две вакцины, третью не успел. ['Second Covid is much easier than the first one. But – attention – this is not a flu, it's much worse. I endured it easily. Let's see how recovery will go. I was in isolation for a week. Two vaccines, the third was not got yet']

As we may see, the author bases his judgements on his own experience: he himself was twice sick with Covid and compares the severity of his encounters with the disease (*Second COVID is much easier than the first one*), evaluates the severity of the illness with the reference to a regular flu (*But – attention – this is not a flu, it's much worse*) and, finally, comes to a conclusion that he '*endured it easily*' due to two vaccines he received earlier.

Indirect evidentiality or indirect evidence means that the speaker was not an immediate participant of a situation but obtained his information about it in a different way – by reported evidence or hearsay. This means that the person's judgements are based on somebody else's evidence or on inferences (based on background knowledge, available proofs or intuition). In the following example [3], we can find the reference to information which is commonly available in the media. Garik Korogodski offers a reported evidence about successful results of vaccination experience in Great Britain:

[3]
Пример Англии, которая достигла уровня вакцинации 85% с двумя дозами и 66 с тремя и сняла все ограничения, включая маски, перед глазами ['In front of your eyes there is an example of England that could lift all the restrictions because it reached 85% of vaccination by two doses, and 66% by three doses']

Further, he explicitly criticizes evidential 'hearsay':

[4]
Да, и рассказы, что от вакцины на лбу может вырасти нечто. к сожалению, так и остались рассказами [So, the stories about the possibility of the vaccines to grow horns on one's forehead, unfortunately, remain just the stories]

Thus, in the given fragment, the blogger uses all known types of evidentiality – starting from his perceptual experience (direct evidentiality) through the reported evidence up to hearsay (indirect), see Figure 11.2.

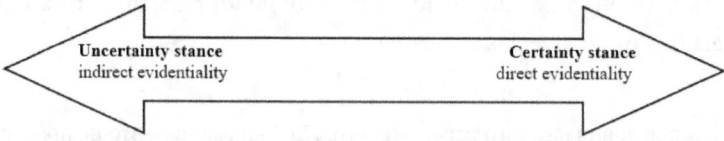

Figure 11.2 Evidentiality on the axe of epistemic stance-taking (own elaboration).

Placed on the geometrical axe of epistemic stance-taking, direct evidentiality tends to be part of certainty stances, while indirect evidentiality, contrarily, is characteristic for stances of uncertainty. In the next section, I will show how modality and evidentiality are used in common epistemic spaces creation.

Sequential Dynamics of Epistemic Stance-Taking and Creating Common Epistemic Spaces in Online interaction

The stance-taking process requires from the stance-takers cognitive conceptualization of the situation in which they find themselves. Such conceptualization includes not only framing of the situation by its subjects and further construing its prototypical script or scenario, but also imagining their possible actions in the situational conditions, 'trying on' different alternative results of these actions. It is obvious that such 'trying on' greatly depends upon the level of knowledge stance-takers possess about the situation in general and about the object of their stance-taking in particular. They cognitively build possible futures that serve as a foundation for their stances. In communicative situations where vaccination against Covid-19 is the object of stance-taking, the discussion has a prognostic character where epistemic stances constitute the problematic nature of proclaimed judgments. In other words, stances are verbalized in statements, based on assumptions rather than on reliable knowledge. Hypothetical and epistemically unjustified character of judgments is actualized through uncertain modality and indirect evidentiality. It is determined not by epistemic but by ontic possibility of some events' future realization (Heidegger's 'ontic possibility').

Therefore, an individual's ability to imagine the consequences of different ways events might develop in the future, underlies the person's stances taken in certain situational conditions. Depending on what they know about the situation they are in, on the level of their confidence in their knowledge and on the reliability of the information available to them, the participants construct possible scenarios of their behaviour in this situation, contemplating their possible actions and their consequences, which eventually cannot be fully foreseeable or clear. According to John Heritage,

> the states of knowledge can range from circumstances in which speaker A may have absolute knowledge of some item, while speaker B has none, to those in which both speakers may have exactly equal information, as well as every point in between.
>
> Heritage 2012: 4

Consequently, the level of knowledge can be assessed via 'the informative sequences' or manifested stances. These are the sequences in which the interlocutors show different degrees of knowledge concerning some item and drive their talk in order to rebalance the initial epistemic imbalance (ibid., 2012: 4). Usually, their knowledge determines their epistemic stances and/or their attitudes.

Let me illustrate the dynamics of epistemic stance-taking on the example of reaction to the Facebook post by Karl Volokh concerning 'Omicron' and Covid-19 vaccines. The fragment given below in [5] is a chain of comments made by six different people, marked as Subject$_{1,2...n}$. All comments were made either in Ukrainian or in Russian.

[5]

>   **Subject 1:** <u>The bad thing about this omicron is</u> that it spreads very, very quickly. You can 'pick it up' with lightning speed, even if someone sneezed on the other side of the road. <u>According to my personal experience</u>, people do not do tests, do not go to the doctors, if the course of the disease is within the limits of 'can be sustained'. <u>My son brought omicron from a trip after the New Year.</u> His wife's test showed nothing, but their symptoms were the same. by frivolity, all the relatives around him, of course, fell ill. none of us went to the doctors. based on our family statistics, the incidence rate can be safely multiplied by 5. <u>And we are all vaccinated with 2 doses</u> [паршиве в цьому омікроні те що він дуже-дуже швидко поширюється. 'підхопити' його можна блискавично, навіть якщо хтось чихнув з іншої сторони дороги. По особистому досвіду – люди не роблять тестів, не йдуть до лікарів, якщо перебіг хвороби в межах 'можна витримати'. Мій син привіз омікрон з мандрівки після Нового року. у дружини його тест нічого не показав, але симптоми у них були однакові. по легковажності всі родичі кругом нього звісно захворіли. ніхто з нас до лікарів не ходив. виходячи з нашої сімейної статистики показник захворюваності можна сміливо множити на 5. І ми всі вакциновані 2-ма дозам.]
>
>   **Subject 2:** If you continue to call a spade a spade, then vaccination is not needed for those who are already sick, but is needed for the risk group. [Якщо продовжити називати речі своїми іменами, то вакцинація не потрібна тим, хто вже хворів, але потрібна для групи ризику.]
>
>   **Subject 1: (Addresses Subject 2 by name)**: I've been fully vaccinated, and I've been sick FOUR times but mildly! It's complete nonsense that those

who had been sick don't need to be vaccinated!! That is a suicidal position. [Я вакцинована повністю, перехворіла ЧОТИРИ рази, в легкій формі! Повна ДУРНЯ, що перехворівшим не потрібна вакцинація!! то є позиція самобивці.]

Subject 3: (Addresses Subject 1 by name): Just another proof that this vaccine is like a Band-Aid. [Лишнее доказательство того, что эта вакцинация – как мёртвому припарка.]

Subject 1: (Addresses Subject 3 by name): Then don't use it! And you'll be a handsome band-less dead. [Не припарюйтесь, будете красивим мертвим.]

Subject 4: Similarly – three times. [аналогічно – тричі.]

Subject 5: They kind of predict an omicron peak at the end of February in our country, at least that's what Mr. Liashko said. [Наче прогнозують у нас пік 'омікрона' у кінці лютого, принаймні так сказав пан Ляшко.]

Subject 6: Vaccination is not a panacea, it is only a training for the body, it teaches you to fight. This is what I say to all anti-vaxxers. [Вакцинація не панацея, вона є лише тренінгом для організму, вона вчить боротися. Таке я кажу всім антиваксам].

Reading the above excerpt, taken from the thread of commentaries reacting to Karl Volokh's post on Facebook published in early February 2022, it is easy to recognize Covid-19 as the situational context for the given act of stance-taking. The stance object is explicitly outlined in the very first line. It is 'Omicron' – the then-new variety of Covid-19 virus, as well as vaccination against it. Following the 'stance triangle' methodology by John Du Bois (Du Bois 2007: 163), we can identify three main vectors in the stance-taking activities: evaluation, stance choice and stance alignment. The act of evaluation is inseparably connected to epistemic stance and, thus, is often expressed through the linguistic means of modality and evidentiality.

For instance, Subject$_1$ uses explicitly evaluative statement *the bad thing* in their comment: '*The bad thing about this omicron is that it spreads very, very quickly*'. She intensifies her stance by hyperbolizing the virus's ability to spread through the use of: (1) consecutively repeated lexeme *very*, (2) metaphoric epithet *lightning* ('*with lightning speed*') and (3) unreal conditional '*if someone sneezed on the other side of the road*', emphasized by *even*. To justify the validity of their own judgement, the commenter refers to direct evidentiality in their next statement '*According to my personal experience*'. Pursuing the same pragmatic aim, she later resorts to reported evidentiality and describes the experience of her son and her daughter-in-law in the next sentences. And, finally, she mentions that all the members of her family including herself were vaccinated twice: '*And we are all vaccinated with 2 doses*.' There is a possibility of two different interpretations of this statement: (1) vaccination is important because it helps to tolerate the disease in a mild form; and (2) vaccination is not important as it does not protect from infection. And further we can see this discrepancy of meaning-making in the process of sequential online stance alignment and stance adjustment.

In the above thread, alignment is realized through mentioning the names of Subject-addressee, as well as through using reference to previously formulated stances or mentioned judgments. For example, Subject$_2$ refers to the part of previous comment where Subject$_1$ mentioned her vaccination. And his comment is based on the interpretation where vaccination is not helpful in protecting against omicron: '*If you continue to call a spade a spade, then vaccination is not needed for those who are already sick, but is needed for the risk group*.' However, in the following reply where Subject$_1$ explicitly addresses Subject$_2$, we find a contradictory statement by which she disagrees with her interlocutor. She not only offers an explanation to her otherwise unclear and therefore misinterpreted stance towards vaccination (*I've been fully vaccinated, and I've been sick FOUR times but mildly!*), but she also negatively evaluates Subject$_2$'s statement, calling it a 'nonsense' (*It's complete nonsense that those who had been sick don't need to be vaccinated!!*) and explicitly labels his stance as dangerous for himself (*That is a suicidal position*).

The discussion is developed in the next comment where Subject$_3$ joins the conversation addressing Subject$_1$ but supporting the stance of Subject$_2$. They proclaim futility of vaccination in a categorical statement with deployment of the rhetorical device of simile: *Just another proof that this vaccine is like a Band-aid*. The beginning of this sentence '*Just another proof*' implies that there supposedly exist more facts proving the ineffectiveness of the vaccine. Besides, the commenter explicitly expresses his view of vaccination as ineffective comparing it to '*a Band-aid*'. So, the given utterance allows to decode the speaker's stance towards vaccination as negative – anti-vaccine.

However, it's interesting to trace how stance alignment is dynamically unfolding in the direction of pro-vaccination attitude. Subject$_1$ immediately reacts to a new comment by an imperative construction (*Then don't use it!*) and offers a doom prognosis for her vis-a-vis' reckless actions (*And you'll be a handsome band-less dead*). In the following comment, the object of stance-taking is not clear – it may be either a vaccination or a disease itself. Subject$_4$ only mentions the quantity of 'something unspecified', without direct naming what they mean ('*Similarly – three times*').

Further, Subject$_5$ resorts to an authoritative evidentiality, starting with nameless '*They*' and finishing with mentioning the name of Ukrainian Minister of Health (*They kind of predict an omicron peak at the end of February in our country, at least that's what Mr. Liashko said*). It is worth noting that collocation '*kind of*' expresses modality 'I suppose' or epistemic stance of UNCERTAINTY, which is characteristic for the given context. Finally, Subject$_6$ winds up this discussion by giving an unbiased evaluation of vaccine efficiency (*Vaccination is not a panacea, it is only a training for the body, it teaches you to fight*) and outlining their own stance as different from 'anti-vaxxers' (*This is what I say to all anti-vaxxers*).

As the stance-taking activity associated with the stance-choosing and stance-alignment is characterized by interactivity and intersubjectivity, its implementation depends on multiple cognitive representations and pragmatic expectations of all the communication participants. Fairly often stances do not coincide as they are based on different or even opposite epistemic and emotional assessments of the stance object. Aligning their stances, participants of online interaction create common discursive interactional environment, where its epistemic part is decisively important.

Conclusion

Common epistemic spaces are discursively constructed through epistemic stance-taking, linguistically objectivized as epistemic modality and evidentiality. Epistemic modality expresses the relation of the content of the statement to reality, established by the speaker in terms of its reliability. Because of this, along with the term 'epistemic modality', the term 'modality of truthfullness' (Peacocke 1978) is also used, which indicates the evaluative nature of this category, and reflects the semantic basis of the assessment – the degree of awareness and the nature of the subject's knowledge about reality. Evidentiality is the way sources of information are comunicated, which range from direct (experiential) to indirect (hearsay).

The study illustrates how common epistemic space is created in online interaction through discursive activity of stance-taking on Covid-19, as exemplified by analysis of pandemic discussions in social networks. I have shown that different stances are constructed, adjusted and reconstructed in interaction that takes place in the discursive environment of an internet blog. On the one hand, followers of a certain blogger construct common epistemic spaces, having similar views and values, exchanging knowledge concerning certain problems, supporting or disagreeing with each other's stances. On the other hand, their stances reflect their identities, their belonging to certain social groups, having certain worldviews and following certain ideologies.

In the above described case, the collective stance of the discussion group towards Covid-19 as the object of stance-taking, underlying their discussion, can be formulated as follows: 'Covid-19 is a dangerous disease; 'Omicron' is a specific variety of Covid-19 virus and it is very infectious; vaccination does not solve all the Covid-19 problems but plays an important role in fighting this disease.' Speaking of its epistemic component, it is rather a stance of CAUTIOUS CERTAINTY, expressed through modality I SUPPOSE and direct (experiential) and indirect (reported and authoritative) evidentiality.

If we place both evidentiality and modality onto the axis of epistemic spaces (Figure 11.3), built in discursive interaction, then direct (experiential) evidentiality which is based on the stance subject's personal perceptual and cognitive experience, will be located closer to the 'I KNOW' modality and therefore, can be treated as the representation of epistemic stance of CERTAINTY. At the same time, indirect (reported or hearsay) evidentiality must be placed closer to 'I DON'T KNOW' modality, which is characteristic for building epistemic stances of UNCERTAINTY.

Thus, building common epistemic spaces online is based on the ability of the stance subjects to cognitively structure the virtual world around them, similar to the possibility of their sensory orientation in real (physical) time and space. Accordingly, their epistemic statuses are co-constructed and co-determined in discursive interaction of all discursive activity participants. By building their own status in discourse, people simultaneously build statuses of those with whom they communicate, marking them through their stance-taking. Therefore, on the one hand, the design of epistemic spaces built in discursive interaction depends on the knowledge possessed by all of its participants. On the other

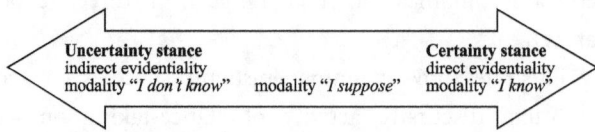

Figure 11.3 Axe of epistemic stance-taking (modality+evidentiality) (own elaboration).

hand, epistemic spaces influence their epistemic statuses, molding and changing them. So, building common epistemic spaces in online discourse interaction is sociosemiotic process of constructing meanings that reflect the surrounding social reality.

Notes

1 All the translations from Ukrainian and Russian in the chapter are mine.

References

Aikhenwald, Alexandra Y. 2006. 'Evidentiality in Grammar'. In Keith Brown (ed.), *Encyclopedia of Languages and Linguistics*, 320–5. Oxford: Elsevier.

Aikhenvald, Alexandra Y. 2015. *The Art of Grammar: A Practical Guide*. Oxford: Oxford University Press.

Alexander, Louis G. 1988. *Longman English Grammar*. London: Longman.

Biber, Douglas. 2004. 'Historical Patterns for the Grammatical Marking of Stance: A Cross-Register Comparison'. *Journal of Historical Pragmatics*, 5 (1): 107–36.

Biber, Douglas and Edward Finegan. 1989. 'Styles of Stance in English: Lexical and Grammatical Marking of Evidentiality and Affect'. *Text*, 9 (1): 93–124.

Boas, Franz. 1938. *Language*. In F. Boas (ed.), *General Anthropology*, 124–45. Boston, MA, and New York: D. C. Heath.

Bucholtz, Mary and Kira Hall. 2004. 'Language and Identity'. In A. Duranti (ed.), *A Companion to Linguistic Anthropology*, 369–94. Malden, MA: Blackwell.

Bybee, Joan. 1995. 'An Introductory Eessay'. In J. Bybee and S. Fleischman (eds), *Modality in Grammar and Discourse*, 1–14. Amsterdam: Benjamins.

Chafe, Wallace. 1986. 'Evidentiality in English Conversation and Academic Witing'. In W. Chafe and J. Nichols (eds), *Evidentiality: The Linguistic Coding of Epistemology*, 261–72. Norwood, NJ: Ablex.

Chalmers, David J. 2011. 'The Nature of Epistemic Space'. In Andy Egan and Brian Weatherson (eds), *Epistemic Modality*, 60–107. Oxford: Oxford University Press.

Chung, Sandra and Alan Timberlake. 1985. 'Tense, Aspect and Mood'. In Timothy Shopen (ed.), *Language Typology and Syntactic Description, Vol. III: Grammatical Categories and the Lexicon*, 202–7. Cambridge: Cambridge University Press.

Du Bois, John. 2007. 'The Stance Triangle'. In R. Englebretson (ed.), *Stancetaking in Discourse: Subjectivity, Evaluation, Interaction*, 139–82. Amsterdam: John Benjamins.

Eckert, Penelope. 2012. 'Three Waves of Variation Study: The Emergence of Meaning in the Study of Variation'. *Annual Review of Anthropology*, 41: 87–100.

Fintel, Kai von and Anthony S. Gillies. 2007. 'An Opinionated Guide to Epistemic Modality'. In *Oxford Studies in Epistemology*, 32–62. Oxford: Oxford University Press.

Garson, James. 2021. 'Modal Logic'. *The Stanford Encyclopedia of Philosophy*. Summer 2021 Edition, Edward N. Zalta (ed.). Available online: https://plato.stanford.edu/archives/sum2021/entries/logic-modal/ (accessed 31 March 2022).

Halliday, M. A. K. 1994. *An Introduction to Functional Grammar.* London: Edward Arnold.

Heritage, John. 2012. 'Epistemics in Action: Action, Formation and Territories of Knowledge'. *Research on Language and Social Interaction*, 45 (1): 1–29.

Hoye, Leo. 1997. *Adverbs and Modality in English*. Harlow: Longman.

Hyland, Ken. 1999. 'Disciplinary Discourses: Writer Stance in Research Articles'. In H. Candlin and K. Hyland (eds), *Writing: Texts, Processes and Practices*, 99–121. London: Longman.

Jaffe, Alexandra (ed.). 2009. *Stance: Sociolinguistic Perspectives*. Oxford: Oxford University Press.

Jago, Mark. 2009. 'Logical Information and Epistemic Space'. *Synthese*, 167 (2): 327–41.

Johnstone, Barbara. 2009. 'Stance, Style, and the Linguistic Individual'. In A. Jaffe (ed.), *Stance: Sociolinguistic Perspectives*, 29–52. Oxford: Oxford University Press.

Kärkkäinen, Elise. 2003. *Epistemic Stance in English Conversation: A Description of Its Interactional Functions, with a Focus on I Think*. Amsterdam: John Benjamins.

Kiesling, Scott F., Umashanthi Pavalanathan, Jim Fitzpatrick, Xiaochuang Han and Jacob Eisenstein. 2018. 'Interactional Stancetaking in Online Forums'. *Computational Linguistics*, 44 (4): 689–718. Availale online: https://www.academia.edu/38162880/Interactional_stancetaking_in_online_forums (accessed 1 August 2023).

Kiesling, Scott F. 2021. 'Stance and Stancetaking'. *Annual Review of Linguistics*, 8: 409–26. Doi: pdf/10.1146/annurev-linguistics-031120-121256.

Kripke, Saul A. 1963. 'Semantic Considerations on Modal Logic'. *Acta Philosophica Fennica*, 16: 83–94.

Langlotz, Andreas. 2015. *Creating Social Orientation through Language: A Socio-Cognitive Theory of Situate Social Maning*. Amsterdam and Philadelphia, PA: John Benjamins.

Ley, Thomas. 2010. *Introduction to the Method of Objective-Hermeneutic Sequence Analysis*. Frankfurt am Main: Publishing House for Police Science.

Lyons, John. 1977. *Semantics*. Cambridge: Cambridge University Press.

Marcus, Ruth Barcan. 1993. *Modalities: Philosophical Essays*. New York: Oxford University Press, 1993.

Narrog, Heiko. 2005. 'Aikhenvald, Alexandra (2004), "Evidentiality (Oxford Linguistics). Oxford: Oxford University Press. Pp. xxvii, 452. Book Review". *SKY Journal of Linguistics*, 18: 379–88. Available online: https://www.academia.edu/79302171/Aikhenvald_Alexandra_2004_Evidentiality_Oxford_Linguistics_ (accessed 1 August 2023).

Oevermann, Ulrich. 2002. *Clinical Sociology Based on the Methodology of Objective Hermeneutics – Manifesto of Objective Hermeneutic Social Research* (Klinische Soziologie auf der Basis der Methodologie der objektiven Hermeneutik – Manifest der objektiv hermeneutischen Sozialforschung). Frankfurt am Main: Instituts für hermeneutische Sozial- und Kulturforschung e.V. Mode of Access: https://www.ihsk.de/publikationen/Ulrich_Oevermann-Manifest_der_objektiv_hermeneutischen_Sozialforschung.pdf (accessed 25 May 2022).

Palmer, Frank Robert. 1979. *Modality and the English Modals.* London; New York: Longman.

Palmer, Frank Robert. 1986. *Mood and Modality.* Cambridge: Cambridge University Press.

Peacocke, Christopher. 1978. 'Necessity and Truth Theories'. *Journal of Philosophical Logic,* 7: 473–500.

Segal, Erik. 1988. *The Class.* New York: Bantam Books.

Silverstein, Michael. 2021. 'The Dialectics of Indexical Semiosis: Scaling Up and Out from the "Actual" to the "Virtual"'. *International Journal of the Sociology of Language,* Special Issue, *Language Ideologies and Social Positioning: Structures, Scales, and Practices,* 272: 13–45.

Thornborrow, Johanna. 2005. 'The Sociolinguistics of Narrative: Identity, Performance, Culture'. In J. Thornborrow and J. Coates (eds), *Sociolinguistics of Narrative,* 1–16. Amsterdam: John Benjamins.

Wagner, Hans-Josef. 2001. *Objective Hermeneutics and Formation of the Subject.* Weilerswist: Velbrück Science.

Wierzbicka, Anna. 1972. *Semantic Primitives.* Frankfurt/M.: Athenaum.

Willet, Thomas L. 1988. 'A Cross-Linguistic Survey of the Grammaticalization of evidentiality'. *Studies in Language,* 12 (1): 51–97.

Wright, Crispin. 1989. 'Necessity, Caution, and Scepticism'. *Proceedings of the Aristotelian Society Supplement,* 63: 203–38.

Elaborating a Heuristic Tool to Determine Fluency Spectrum for Deaf Pupils in Poland

Marta Wrześniewska-Pietrzak

Introduction: Diversification of Linguistic Communication in the Deaf Community and the Language of School Education

Sign languages, as noted by most researchers (including Kotowicz 2018; Tomaszewski and Piekot 2015; Wrześniewska-Pietrzak 2017 and others) are a natural means of communication for deaf people[1] who are unable to acquire phonic language. In the case of this diverse social group (Tomaszewski and Piekot 2015), first language acquisition may proceed in various ways, depending on many pragmatic factors. For example, the degree of acquiring sign language fluency by a child can be determined by the language their parents communicate in, the milieu where they live, and it is also related to the chosen educational path, e.g. integration classes in mainstream schools, or instruction in special schools for deaf children and young people (see Woźnicka 2017; Świdziński 2014).[2]

However, this choice for the hearing impaired children is not unequivocally related to matching the path between the education in Polish and their bilingual education (that is, signed / written bilingualism). Moreover, language competences of hearing impaired pupils are not comparable (see, e.g., Tomaszewski, Niedźwiecka and Majewska 2018) and, as a result, the language of education imparted is not always a choice adequate to the deaf pupil's communication abilities and competences. The direction of matching rather tends to be the opposite – it is the child who is to adjust to the educational situation they are being thrown in.

A hearing-impaired child can either be mainstreamed into a public school (either to the provided *integrative programme* or to with an ordinary comprehensive programme) or be offered education in special schools. The educational reality in Poland shows that even special schools for hearing impaired pupils do not always have the staff sufficiently prepared to conduct classes tailored to the communication needs of a deaf pupil, especially the one who communicates using the natural sign language (henceforth the acronym of the Polish name will be used – *Polski Język Migowy*, PJM).[3] This is due to the fact that courses and studies that help to improve the knowledge of sign language are still not sufficiently popular in Poland. As a result, specialists working in a special school as part of the required studies in the field of surdopedagogy do not learn sign language to the extent to be able to communicate fluently with a student for whom PJM is the first language, the language of his parents and family environment.

At this point, it should also be emphasized that language education in a special school for the deaf does not have a systemic teaching curriculum that takes into account a bilingual, Polish-sign language education path (cf. Tomaszewski 2014). Bilingual education (as opposed to the oralist approach) for deaf children and adolescents provided in special institutions which are supposedly established for this group of pupils is not guaranteed, as it is specified by appropriate regulations and educational documents.[4] This means that the form of language education that would reduce communication barriers for the hearing impaired depends largely on the awareness of diagnosticians (psychologists, educators and surdopedagogues working in counseling centres), as well as on the possibilities of the school itself, which should in this case be understood as being prepared for teaching Polish as a *foreign* language and teaching Polish Sign Language in such a way that it can become the educational language of a pupil.

As a result, an overall evaluation of a deaf child cognitive capabilities is made solely in written/spoken Polish and the child can be unjustly diagnosed as cognitively inferior to their hearing peers. As shown by psychologists (Wiśniewska-Jankowska 2016, 2019), it is difficult to fully diagnose this situation due to the lack of diagnostic tools that would allow the assessment of language competences of deaf schoolchildren, respectively in written and in sign languages. What is more, the existence of that type of diagnostic tools would not solve all problems, because diagnosticians working with deaf pupils hardly ever communicate fluently in PJM.

It is worth noting here that the language competences of deaf pupils are not comparable (see Tomaszewski, Niedźwiecka and Majewska 2018). The characteristics of this community in terms of the knowledge of Polish and sign language communication means are usually described as a linguistic continuum, extending from communicating in (standard verbal) Polish, that is, learned speech and speech reading (PL), communication in Signed Polish and/or in PJM.[5] This diversity makes the definition of the native language, often called the first language, difficult in the case of the Deaf, as it requires an attempt to characterize the idiolect of each pupil taking into account the varying degrees of fluency both in PL, and in the PJM. Most often, even deaf people born in deaf families who communicate in sign language on a daily basis function in an educational reality dominated by written Polish, which becomes the educational language, and often also functionally, the first one of a deaf pupil. This is because teaching materials, as well as the educational system in Poland related to passing through the subsequent educational stages, are mainly related to communication in written language. The exams after the second and thirrd stage of education (the so-called *eighth-grade exam* and *matura exam*) are also mostly written exams.

The statistical data clearly confirm that the definition of both the first language (the so-called mother tongue) and communication competences is, for the vast majority of the hearing impaired (pupils), a task to be faced by a diagnostician. Only in a small group (about 10% of children born in deaf families; Tomaszewski 2000: 23) it can be expected that the language acquired, developing correctly and allowing for free communication in various communication situations, is the sign language considered as the first language (Tomaszewski 2014: 17). Thus, the figures show that the vast majority, as many as 90 per cent of hearing impaired children are born in hearing families, which are communicating in a phonic language, unavailable to a deaf child through natural acquisition (cf. Wiśniewska 2019: 159). Therefore, this group of children does not have the conditions for the acquisition of the phonic Polish language – the language of parents and the family environment. Furthermore, there is no possibility of immersion in the sign language (parents, as hearing persons, do not know the sign language) which means that the communicative competence in both Polish and the sign language is lower than that of their signing peers (raised in signing) families which results in educational underperformance.

The presented situation of communication heterogeneity in the group of deaf people means that phonic Polish as the language of school education is not always a choice adequate to the pupil's communication abilities and competences. Despite this, as it was mentioned earlier, the direction of matching adopted in the Polish education system is the opposite – it is the child who is to adjust to the educational situation. The system only allows to implement activities supporting this imposed direction of matching (by means of speech therapy, revalidation classes, etc.). In an educational space constructed in this way, a deaf child born in a hearing and non-signing family often functions as a person who does not communicate effectively in written and / or sign language (PJM).

At this point, communication efficiency should be understood as language proficiency insufficient to start instruction at school. As a result, an overall evaluation of a deaf child cognitive capabilities is made solely in phonic (written or verbal) Polish and the child can be unjustly diagnosed as underperforming and cognitively inferior to their hearing peers.[6] As shown by psychologists (Wiśniewska-Jankowska 2016, 2019), it is difficult to fully reckon with this situation due to the lack of diagnostic tools that would allow the assessment of the overall language competence of a deaf pupil in written and in sign language PJM). What is more, the existence of such tools would not solve all problems, because diagnosticians working with deaf children do not always communicate fluently in PJM. Therefore, the awareness of diagnosticians regarding the communication heterogeneity in the deaf community is far from satisfactory. Knowledge alone, without the possibility of verifying the child's full communication potential, is insufficient to make a decision, issue an opinion on the basis of which education and the revalidation system are organized.

To remedy to some extent these basic imbalances, which result in ambiguities surrounding a deaf child in the context of education in Poland, as well to reckon with the diagnosticians' situation,[7] an attempt was undertaken under my leadership as a cooperation between the Adam Mickiewicz University (Poznan, Poland) and Poradnia Psychologiczno-Pedagogiczna No. 2 in Poznań (the Psychological and Pedagogical Clinic No. 2 in Poznań) to develop an innovative tool (an online app).[8] The team involved in devising the tool is composed of linguists, glottodidacticians, sign linguists, a surdopsychologist and a native PJM user.[9] The testing tool was designed to allow to define the preferred language of a bilingual deaf primary school pupil (their written Polish skills versus their fluency in PJM limited to the receptive ability in lexis).

It is worth emphasizing that this tool does not consist of two parallel ranking/placement tests that make it possible to determine the level of language proficiency in Polish and in PJM. The proposed tool is innovative because it makes it possible to compare the passive knowledge of vocabulary resources of a child both Polish and sign language vocabulary within one the same evaluation attempt. Then at the normalization stage, the results a child obtained are compared to two peer groups: one of hearing and the other, of deaf pupils in a primary school. Finally, it should be pointed out that administering the test, as well interpreting the test result does not require the diagnostician to be fluent in PJM, but only to be aware of various forms of communication in the d/Deaf community.

The subject of this contribution will therefore be to present both the test functionality that influenced the formula of the test application, and the methodological assumptions for testing proficiency in both the Polish language and in PJM. The solutions developed in the multidisciplinary team will be shown against the background of existing tests assessing the language and communication skills of a d/Deaf child. The developed TEST LEKSYKA PJM-PL will also be presented in terms of how to build a tool that compares fluency in languages with two different modalities (the phonic and visual-spatial one). In addition, the assumptions made in the test will be compared with the results of research on the acquisition of sign language as a second language (cf. a collaborative project between University College London (UCL) and Stockholm University on how adults learn sign languages, 2022). In this way, the tool will be seen as a dialectal matching in the nested web of relations between various communication modalities, between the needs of deaf children and their diagnosticians as well as an advance in language testing as such.

TEST LEKSYKA PJM-PL – Concept, Structure and Functionality of the Tool in the Light of the Perceived Diagnostic Needs

Taking into account both the linguistic needs of a hearing impaired pupil[10] and the situation of the diagnostician as presented above, as well as noticing the lack of tools allowing to diagnose communication competences of a deaf child, both in sign language (PJM) and in Polish, translated into an attempt to develop an innovative tool that would allow to define the preferred language of an elementary school pupil. Preferred language is understood to be one which is communicatively easier (cf. Dunaj 2015: 179, 198–200) to use in communication (both in transmitting and receiving information). The proposed tool does not determine a 'stronger' language based on the determination of the proficiency levels of each of the tested languages. Its functionality was designed to support the process of diagnosing the broadly understood communication competence of a pupil.

When starting to construct a tool that was a response to the problem indicated above, the authors of the solution were guided by the following criteria: (1) the tool should be easily accessible to diagnosticians working with deaf pupils; (2) the test should enable diagnosis for both languages differing in modality (both phonic and visual-spatial); (3) due to the assumed addressee of the test – a hearing impaired child, the test checking the passive knowledge of the Polish language has been limited to the written version of Polish, which is in line with the concept of signed-written bilingualism in this social group (cf. Kotowicz 2018);[11] (4) the structure of the test should not be based on the fact that the test in one language version will be translated into a test in a language with a different modality (this assumption allowed to avoid a learning effect that could affect the pupil's score); (5) the result of the test in both languages should enable conclusions to be drawn both for each language separately and for comparative purposes; (6) the pupil's result in each of the languages should make it possible to see the obtained result against the background of the comparison group of hearing and deaf pupils/ peers; (7) conducting the test and reading the result obtained by a pupil cannot depend on the language competences in PJM of the diagnostician.

In addition to these criteria, there were temporal and financial limitations assumed in the grant project under which TEST LEKSYKA PJM-PL was developed. The described tool was prepared under the grant project Incubator of Social Innovation Accessibility Generator, which is financed under the Operational Program Knowledge Education Development 2014–2020 from the European Social Fund. This grant involves a three-month process of developing a prototype, and then a maximum six-month long stage of testing the prepared solution. In the case of the proposed solution, this meant the development of a fully functional test prototype within three months. Due to this short time span allotted, the scope of the tested areas of linguistic competence had to be significantly constrained, which in practice implied limiting the test to checking passive knowledge of lexis.

The selection of lexis in turn was conditioned both by glottodidactic criteria[12] and by educational criteria. In the process of creating the test, concepts were used that indicated the relationship between understanding /comprehending number of the text and the years of education of a an individual. Therefore, in the selection of tested units, the designers of the tool used lexicographic studies allowing to indicate the basic vocabulary for the Polish language (Zgółkowa 2013), while for the sign language, the selection of the lexis was associated with availing of the vocabulary present in the Corpus Dictionary of Polish Sign

Language (Łacheta, Linde-Usiekniewicz and Rutkowski 2016) ([Pol.] *Korpusowy słownik polskiego języka migowego*) as well as *Słownik polskiego języka migowego* (The Dictionary of the Polish Sign Language, available on the platform migaj.eu, which is a dictionary of Polish sign language developed by Olgierd Kosiba).

The selection of lexical units for each of the languages allowing the comparison of passive knowledge of lexis implied the determination of similar or tantamount semantic fields, while the selection of the appropriate lexeme resulted from the level of difficulty, which was determined on the basis of both the glottodidactic and educational criterion. The introduction of the educational criterion to the tool was associated with the use of the plain language standard present in linguistic research and related research showing the relationship between language comprehensibility and the educational stage of the examined person. Therefore, determining the degree of difficulty of selected lexical units was related to taking into account both the age and the propaedeutic content of instruction at the first and second stages of education (currently at the primary school stage).

It is also necessary to emphasize the difficulty of building a test for diagnosing the knowledge of lexis in PJM. When developing this part of the test, the authors used the experience of Anna Wiśniewska-Jankowska, who in her previous research prepared the Test for Assessing the Knowledge of Lexis in Polish Sign Language ([Pol.] *Test do Oceny Znajomości Leksyki w Polskim Języku Migowym* (TOZL PJM) TOZL PJM) (Wiśniewska 2016). Conclusions from the development of that tool contributed to the elaboration of the following assumptions: (1) TEST LEKSYKA PJM-PL should, in the part concerning sign language, provide the possibility of viewing the sign being performed, and not just seeking its drawing visualization; and (2) the form of the proposed tasks should check the knowledge of lexis and ignore logical operations related to the categorization of concepts according to the semantic hyperonymous, hyponymous or antonymic relation.

The elaboration of these criteria prompted the decision that the test should be available as a computer application that would allow the respondent to see the sign in a form as close to natural as possible. This meant that each sign is to be presented in the application as a video file in which a native Polish Sign language user flashes the target sign in isolation. Moreover, due to the fact that, as indicated earlier, the sign language test was not to contain any associated elements from the phonic Polish (written) language, the test questions (instructions) about the selection of the appropriate lexical unit were constructed on the following basis:[13]

1. multiple choice: selecting one out of the four lexemes according to the meaning of the object;
2. selecting for a given lexical unit one of out the four illustrations that best reflects its meaning;
3. selecting a synonym for a lexical unit in a given language from among four lexical units in a given language.

These criteria are illustrated in the Figure 12.1, which juxtaposes the didactic strategies adopted, respectively, for Standard Polish (PL version, left-hand side) and PJM (Polish Sign Language version), right hand side.[14]

An important role in the compilation of the list of test lexemes for each language was the participation of a native Polish language user and a PJM user at this stage of the tool development. According to the elaborated structure of the test, the lexis was divided into four groups related to the categorization by part of speech in each of the languages. Therefore, tasks were distinguished to check the knowledge respectively, of nouns, verbs, features (adjectives and

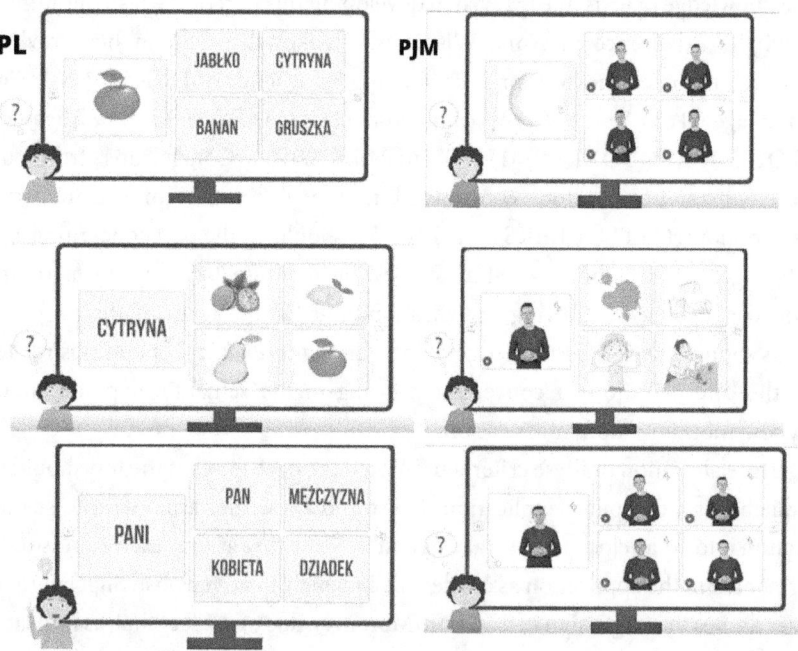

Figure 12.1 Sample tasks from the application displayed to the respondent in the animated instruction prior to starting the test. Standard Polish and Polish Sign Language. The illustrations and videos in the application are colorful.

adverbs) and numerals. Within each group there were words assigned by the authors to three levels of difficulty (easy, medium, difficult). This difficulty grading was determined with the help of expert analysis (a sign language linguist, a Polish language glottodidactician, as well as a native PJM user with philological education).

Already at this heuristic stage, it is worth emphasizing that the development of a solution responding to the perceived lack of a diagnostic tool allowing for the comparison of the knowledge of Polish and sign language (for example in the field of passive knowledge of lexis) requires a wide range of competences of specialists from several scientific disciplines, the most important of which are: sign linguists, Polish philologists, surdoglottodidacticians, Polish language glottodidacticians as well as native users of sign language and Polish. The competences of these people allowed for the development of the test form and selection of test tasks.

Yet, the expertise of a team thus constructed would still be insufficient to develop one of the most important functionalities of the tool from the perspective of a diagnostician. The innovative nature of the proposed application is related not only to the fact that it allows you to compare the passive knowledge of the vocabulary in Polish and the sign language, but, which is the most important from a diagnostic perspective, it also allows you to relate the result obtained by a given student to the peer cohort of hearing and deaf students. Such solutions do not occur when constructing tools to assess the knowledge of lexis from a given language (native or foreign / second). The reason is that for a glottodidactician or Polish philologist, the reference point are the standards and guidelines contained in curricula or documents indicating the requirements related to a specific level of language proficiency. The introduction of this functionality was implemented from psychological tests, in which the result obtained by the respondent is most often shown against the background of the so-called standardization group. This method of research is most often used in psychometry, it allows to show the correlation between the result obtained on the basis of a given test and the distribution of results characterizing a specific population. In this case, due to the study on sign-phonic bilingualism, the obtained results had to be related to the results of two standardization groups – hearing and deaf students of the second stage of education (grades 4–8 of primary school).

Pursuant to this, the student's result obtained in the PJM test and in Polish can be seen against the background of the community of deaf students and it can be stated whether this result is average for a given group, or whether it can be characterized as below / above the norm. Due to the differences in the communication skills of a deaf student described in the first part of the text and the need to function in an educational language (Polish as an educational language), an important element was the presentation of the result achieved by a deaf student against the background of the normalization group of hearing students, the results of which were also divided according to three-point scale: lower than typical score/ typical score/ higher than typical score.

Relating the result of a deaf student obtained in the Polish language test to the characteristics of the standardization group will allow the diagnostician to see whether this result allows to build an educational path based on the written Polish language, or whether it is worth considering linguistic adaptations that will allow the student to further their education in the way which will be communicatively propitious. The introduction of this functionality, as well as the ability to automatically check the answers in the application mean that carrying out and reading the test result does not require the diagnostician to be fluent in PJM, but only to be aware of various forms of communication in the Deaf community.

What are the Perspectives/Prospects of Using the LEKSYKA PJM-PL TEST?

The tool developed in our multidisciplinary team that allows to compare the passive knowledge of the lexis of Polish and sign language in relation to a representative group of hearing and deaf pupils is, of course, a response to the creation of instrumentarium that can be used by a diagnostician who is faced with the task of assessing communication skills of a deaf student. However, it seems that the obtained result may also help a diagnostician in developing further indications concerning special educational needs, subsuming communication needs, of a young person.

The complex analysis of communication skills is paramount to determining the possibility of assessing the pupil's potential as an individual. It would also help delineating further educational activities which would allow to build language proficiency enabling communication independence both in everyday communication and on the educational path. In other words, a comprehensive diagnosis allows, first of all, to support the student's preferred language, make it the educational language and to use this language to build a second- / foreign-language fluency. As a result, two main ways of language education would be possible: with the leading PJM and Polish taught concomitantly with glottodidactic methods or with the leading Polish language and with PJM taught as a second/foreign language. The second of these paths, in the case of language skills in Polish, which does not adversely affect communication and education, could provide a chance to learn the sign language, which is a natural key to the Deaf community.

Due to the fact that the standardization group examined with the test was not large – it comprised 42 pupils – the designers of the tool are aware that this tool has the potential to prepare a standardization test that will allow to show the result of the examined student against the background of 3 groups: (1) hearing students; (2) deaf students born in families of the hearing impaired; and (3) deaf students born in hearing families. This would allow to show the differences with regard to the ways of learning and acquiring Polish as a second / foreign language, as well as research conducted in this area on the acquisition of sign language as a foreign / second language.[15] In the present situation, the number of deaf students in Poland studying at the second stage of education who meet the criteria for selection into the standardization group was so small that such a division was impossible. At this stage we have to appreciate that the developed test formula and the selection of tasks differentiate the normalization groups of both hearing and deaf students. Therefore, the standardization study has become an additional, third stage of verifying the reliability and validity of the tool's operation.

This means that further work on the improvement of diagnostic tools could use the solutions elaborated so far and foster constructing a test that checks other language subsystems based on the criteria adopted in the prepared application, taking into account also the result related to the determination of the language proficiency level in PJM and in Polish. Such prospects for the development of the tool are potentially possible, especially since the effects of work on the development of Polish CEFR for sign languages can be noticed in the last two years.[16] Research is also undertaken on the development of tests for productive skills in PJM, which gives ground to foresee that soon it will be possible to fully assess language proficiency in PJM, taking into account both passive, receptive and productive skills.

Conclusions

This chapter aimed to attend to several research goals. The first and foremost was to relate to the question: Is TEST LEKSYKA PJM-PL ('The PJM-PL vocabulary test') – a tool comparing lexical competences of students in languages with different modalities (Polish Sign Language and written Polish) a response to the needs of the d/Deaf pupils and their diagnosticians? To answer that question, first I sketched the background of the educational functioning of the community of the d/Deaf in contemporary Polish society. This community communicates in several unrelated languages systems in different modalities, with PL as a superstrata and PJM being the underestimated substratum variety. There is no knowledge of the actual bilingual composition in the linguistic resources of individuals.

The exposition meant to show that the education paths of hearing-impaired children in Poland are far from satisfactorily prepared or regulated. What is more, the final evaluation of propaedeutic process is done solely in written Polish, disregarding the fact that for a large percentage of the hearing impaired this is a second language which might be acquired at later educational stage. This usually leads to the educational underperformance. Furthermore, no guidance as far as the task of the diagnosticians is concerned who are supposed to assess the cognitive abilities of a hearing impaired pupil and hardly ever they are able to converse in PJM. Finally, there is lots of work to be done to integrate the PJM into the CEFR framework which would help introducing bilingualism approach in schools.

The tool that was presented can thus be seen as a small step towards that integration and as a result, towards remedying some of the quandaries besetting the educational path of d/Deaf pupils. I showed the problems encountered during the elaboration of that tool as well as constraints on its scope and functionality. For illustrative purposes, samples of potential tasks were provided. Finally, the discussion brought to the fore the limitations (a necessary small sample size) as well as the potential for expanding the scope implicit in the design. The tool allows a simultaneous appraisal of the knowledge of two languages (PJM and PL), allows their mutual ranking but it also allows to place the result of the tested person against the results obtained by the peer cohort, also with reference to both languages.

As far as hermeneutical implications are concerned, several observations are in place. The first area concerns the traditional hermeneutic (Ricoeurian) assumption of the paramount importance of the (written) text. If we admit that the general idea behind the hermeneutic approach is extracting the inner logic of a piece of text and through engaging with that textuality, reaching beyond its immediate givenness towards the implicit core of 'humanness', then the hermeneutic horizon of the sign language in Poland as a viable means and resource for communication faces severe social ostracism. As a result, the situation of the Deaf community as a diaspora amongst the sonic milieu in Poland seems to be a kind of refutation of a dialogic interaction.

A hearing-impaired child, which is in predominant majority born into a hearing family, faces a wall of isolation from the very start, even in their own families which are forcing the child to bend to their preferred communication need. The situation only gets worse at later educational stages, regardless if the child is raised in dormitories of OSW (school and educational centres; [Pol.] *ośrodki szkolno-wychowawcze*) since the instructors there are not always required to converse in PJM. Hence there are pronounced communicative misbalances: between the members of the Deaf community and the sonic world, between the d/Deaf themselves, since as was mentioned before, in practice each of them might communicate in a different modality and with varying degrees of proficiency in any of those modalities, and between the educational system and requirements as compared with the educational offer to cater for their needs.

Between the phonic Polish, which deaf citizens are somehow implicitly assumed to know as any other citizen should, and PJM, which is the denied the status of the full-fledged language even today. With these perspective, the tool TEST LEKSYKA PJM-PL can be seen as a hermeneutic praxis to offer a due assessment (interpretation) and from there, by establishing a comparative platform, to reach towards a dialogue: across modalities and across sonic and gestural worlds.

Notes

1   In the context of Polish research on hearing impaired, there is an issue of capitalizing the lexeme 'deaf'. If it is used in an adjectival function, we leave it, as canonically accepted in scholarly environment, without capitalization, however, when it is used in a nominal function, relating to the members of a particular community, it is spelt in a capital letter.

2   It is assumed that about 90 per cent of Polish deaf children are born into hearing families (cf. Tomaszewski 2000: 23; Bartnikowska 2010: 86). Accordingly, those children in the vast majority have contact only with the phonic language. Parents in such cases prefer to choose the oralist approach to the education of their hearing impaired children following the predominant directives of surdopedagogists. The oralist approach puts emphasis on learning the verbal (phonic) speech, on the visual perception of speech, and on speech-reading. Of great importance are medical

activities, aiming to make use of residual or remaining hearing. The aim of this strategy is, as Tomaszewski (2000: 23) points out, to help a deaf child integrate into the sonic world. Concomitantly, all forms of para-verbal gestures (the use of sign language are strongly discouraged in that approach since it is argued that gestural input impedes the process of learning the spoken language (ibid., 23)).

3 The text evolves around two varieties across different modalities: Polish Sign Language and phonic Polish (both in its written and spoken form). For clarity of exposition, I will refer to the Polish Sign Language as PJM (the acronym of the name in Polish) and to the phonic Polish as PL. It also should be observed here that apart from the PJM, two other signematic systems also function in Poland: Signed Polish SP (Polish, *system językowo-migowy* (henceforth, SJM) and Polish Pidgin Sign language (Polish, *polski migowy typu pidgin PMP*). SJM constitutes an arbitrary visualization of spoken Polish, carefully preserving its grammatical structure and desinences, combining that with some ideography borrowed from the PJM (Tomaszewski and Rosiak 2003: 156ff.), signs of the SJM function as a sort of illustration to an enunciation in the national language. The existence of that variety, although of course in specific areas indispensable for communication unfortunately backgrounds the status of the PJM. Crucially, it is an arbitrarily created system, in which authors of particular dictionaries (which not always feature the stipulation that they are dictionaries of SJM rather than of the PJM not infrequently invent new signs themselves or avail of those proposed for *Gestuno*; cf. Grzesiak 2006).

4 For example, an educational project on bilingual education of the deaf, prepared and developed by Magdalena Dunaj, despite positive opinions and recommendations, has not been adapted as a systemic solution (as of September 2022).

5 Some insights into the conundrums of that continuum are provided in Włodarczak et al. (2019: 84ff.). A crucial feature of that situation is that the coexisting communicative means lack any interconnectedness. As a result, deaf children even living in the same area might not be able to communicate with each other. Additionally sign language is used with success to communicate with, e.g., an autistic, although hearing child (augmentative and alternative communication (AAC). Finally, there is a situation of a hearing children born of deaf parents, who acquired PJM as the first language from their parents. Often the Deaf themselves cannot distinguish between the usage of PJM and SJM, not to mention official courses, where SJM can be taught as PJM. As a safe rule of the thumb though, it might be posited that a person who cannot converse in PJM cannot be considered to belong to Deaf culture (Włodarczak, Ruta-Korytowska and Wiśniewska-Jankowska 2019: 84ff.).

6 For example, the research by Schlesinger and Meadon ([1972]) as cited in Tomaszewski (2000: 23) done in deaf and hearing children in the kindergarten age

who followed the oralist programme shows that 75 per cent of deaf children at the age of 4 possess the lexical repertoire of the corresponding child of the age of 2.
7   The diagnostic difficulties and problems encountered by employees of psychological and pedagogical counseling centres related to the process of diagnosing deaf students were known to us directly, due to the fact that one of the co-authors and originators of the tool – Anna Wiśniewska-Jankowska works as a diagnostician for deaf children and adolescents on a daily basis. Having described the tools used in the diagnostic process (Wiśniewska-Jankowska 2019) basing on those experiences, she showed the functioning of tools or assessing the knowledge of sign language in children (Wiśniewska-Jankowska 2016; Kip 2009).
8   Available after verification at: TL PJM-PL (test-leksyka.pl) (accessed 22 September 2022).
9   It is a social grant, within the framework of *Generator Dostępności – Inkubator Innowacji Społecznych* (Accessibility Generator – Social Innovation Incubator). It is an example of creating solutions for people affected by exclusion. Link to the grant information page at: https://innowacje.spoldzielnie.org/aplikuj/ (accessed 22 September 2022).
10 At this point, it is worth pointing to an interesting concept by Katarzyna Karpińska-Szaj, who, writing about individualization related to language education, suggests using the term of 'special linguistic or communication needs' (Karpińska-Szaj 2022: 21).
11 At this point a caveat is in order: the result of the lexical comprehension test would not prove the (lack) of knowledge of the meaning of a given of a given lexical unit, but it could be the result of many other variables, including listening comprehension skills.
12 The degree of difficulty of the selected lexemes was determined on the basis of semantic fields indicated at individual levels of language proficiency in the European System for the Description of Education.
13 The illustrative material of the test tasks for this chapter is taken from the test instructions. It is not possible to publish the test content questions. Open access to individual questions and their formulas would mean that the test could no longer be used by diagnosticians as a reliable assessment of passive knowledge of the lexis.
14 A caveat: the photos forming part of the Figure 12.1 are publicly available on the test website: TL PJM-PL (test-leksyka.pl) (click: *dowiedz się więcej* 'Learn more'). The test itself, as indicated in the introduction, was created under EU funds, so the developed solutions are widely available. It should also be emphasized that the particular task sheets under consideration, are sample illustrations of proper question formats and are not part of the test. The illustrative material of the test tasks for this chapter is taken from the test instructions. It is not possible to publish the test content questions. Open access to individual questions and their formulas would

mean that the test could no longer be used by diagnosticians as a reliable assessment of passive knowledge of the lexis. So it is not that we are revealing one of the questions in each category in this way. Proper test questions are available only when doing the proper test available only for professionals (psychologists or teachers at schools for deaf pupils).

15 Currently, within a framework of a project developed by University College London and Stockholm University research is being conducted on how adults learn sign languages, available online: https://mediacentral.ucl.ac.uk/Play/80732 (accessed 22 September 2022).

16 Such integration has been done many years ago for the French Sign language and subsequently, for the Spanish sign language as an adapted translation from the French one. See also URL to the starting page of the Library of signs '*Biblioteca de signos*', which form part of the Virtual Library, *La Biblioteca Virtual* 'Miguel de Cervantes', available online: http://www.cervantesvirtual.com/seccion/signos/.

References

Bartnikowska, Urszula. 2010. *Sytuacja społeczna i rodzinna słyszących dzieci niesłyszących rodziców*. Toruń: AKAPIT.

Dunaj, Magdalena. 2015. *GŁUCHY-ŚWIAT. Głuchota w perspektywie antropologii zaangażowanej*. Łódź. Available online: https://core.ac.uk/download/pdf/71973611.pdf (accessed 22 September 2022).

Grzesiak, Iwona. 2006. 'Słowniki języków wizualno-przestrzennych jako teksty kultury'. In J. Mazur and M. Rzeszutko-Iwan (eds), *Teksty kultury, oblicza komunikacji XXI wieku*. Lublin: Wydawnictwo UCMS.

Karpińska-Szaj, Katarzyna. 2022. *Niezwykłe dzieci, nieobce języki. O indywidualizacji w kształceniu językowym*. Kraków: Wydawnictwo Impuls.

Kip, Paulien. 2009. *The Comparability of Language Assessment Instruments for Sign Language of the Netherlands, the NGT-OP and the T-NGT – Master Thesis Linguistics*. Amsterdam: University of Amsterdam.

Kotowicz, Justyna. 2018. *Dwujęzyczność migowo-pisana dzieci głuchych. Komunikacja i procesy poznawcze* (Signed-Written Bilingualism of Deaf Cchildren: Communication and Cognitive Processes). Kraków: Wydawnictwo Naukowe Uniwersytetu Pedagogicznego.

Kotowicz, Justyna. 2020. 'Pamięć werbalna w języku migowym u osób G/głuchych'. *Niepełnosprawność. Dyskursy Pedagogiki Specjalnej*, 4: 44–56.

Łacheta, Joanna and Czajkowska-Kisil, Małgorzata and Linde-Usiekniewicz, Jadwiga and Rutkowski, Paweł (eds). 2016. *Korpusowy słownik polskiego języka migowego*. Warszawa: Wydział Polonistyki Uniwersytetu Warszawskiego. Availale online: https://www.slownikpjm.uw.edu.pl/ (accessed 22 September 2022).

Piekot, Tomasz Zarzeczny, Grzegorz and Ewelina Moroń. 2019. 'Standard Plain Language w polskiej sferze publicznej'. In M. Zaśko-Zielińska and K. Kredens (eds), *Lingwistyka kryminalistyczna. Teoria i praktyka*, 197–214. Wrocław: Quaestio.

Rutkowski, Paweł (ed.). 2017. *Ikoniczność w gramatyce i leksyce polskiego języka migowego (PJM)*. Warszawa: Wydział Polonistyki Uniwersytetu Warszawskiego.

Świdziński, Marek (ed.). 2014. *Sytuacja głuchych w Polsce. Raport zespołu ds. g/Głuchych przy Rzeczniku Praw Obywatelskich*. Warszawa: Biuro Rzecznika Praw Obywatelskich.

Tomaszewski, Piotr. 2010. *Fonologia wizualna*. Warszawa: MATRIX.

Tomaszewski, Piotr. 2014. 'Funkcjonowanie poznawcze i językowe u dzieci głuchych'. In M. Sak (ed.), *Edukacja głuchych*, 17–34. Warszawa: Wydawnictwo Biuro Rzecznika Praw Obywatelskich.

Tomaszewski, Piotr. 2000. 'Rozwój językowy dziecka głuchego: wnioski dla edukacji szkolnej' (Linguistic Development of Deaf Child: Conclusions for School Education)'. *Audiofonologia*, 16: 21–57.

Tomaszewski, Piotr and Tomasz Piekot. 2015. 'Język migowy w perspektywie socjolingwistycznej'. *Socjolingwistyka*, 29: 63–87.

Tomaszewski, Piotr and Paweł Rosik. 2002. 'Czy polski język migowy jest prawdziwym językiem?' In Grażyna Jastrzębowska and Zbigniew Tarkowski (eds), *Człowiek wobec ograniczeń. Niepełnosprawność. Komunikacja. Terapia*, 133–165. Lublin: Fundacja ORATOR.

Tomaszewski, Piotr and Mariusz Sak. 2014. 'Is it Possilble to Educate Deaf Children Bilingually in Poland?' In M. Olpińska-Szkiełko and L. Bertelle (eds), *Zweisprachigkeit und bilingualer unterricht*, 129–49. Peter Lang Press.

Tomaszewski, Piotr, Alicja Niedźwiecka and Marta Majewska. 2018. 'Kompetencje dzieci głuchych w posługiwaniu się językiem migowym – metody oceny i jej kliniczne znaczenie'. *Edukacja*, 4 (147): 136–48.

Wiśniewska, Dominika. 2019. 'Dziecko słyszące rodziców niesłyszących. Kontekst rozwojowy, możliwości wspierania'. *Edukacja*, 4 (151): 157–65.

Wiśniewska-Jankowska, Anna. 2016. 'Test do Oceny Znajomości Leksyki w Polskim Języku Migowym (TOZL PJM) – Konstrukcja i charakterystyka psychometryczna'. *Studia Psychologiczne*, 54: 17–29.

Wiśniewska-Jankowska, Anna. 2019. 'Narzędzia do oceny znajomości języka migowego u dzieci – przegląd'. *Nowa Audiofonologia*, 8 (1): 72–9.

Włodarczak, Aleksandra, Agnieszka Kossowska and Małgorzata Haładewicz-Grzelak. 2019. 'Understanding Loans from Standard Polish into the Polish Sign Language by the Deaf: A Perception Study'. In Marta Bogusławska-Tafelska and Małgorzata Haładewicz-Grzelak (eds), *Communication as a Life Process: Volume 2: The Holistic Paradigm in Language Sciences*, 73–104. Newcastle upon Tyne: Cambridge Scholars Publishing.

Woźnicka, Elżbieta (ed.). 2017. *Edukacja niesłyszących – wczoraj, dziś i jutro*. Łódź: Wydawnictwo AHE.

Wrześniewska-Pietrzak, Marta. 2017. *Aksjologiczne wyznaczniki tożsamości w wypowiedziach g/Głuchych i czasopiśmie środowiskowym 'Świat Ciszy'*. Poznań: Rys.

Wrześniewska-Pietrzak, Marta, Ruta-Korytowska, Karolina and Wiśniewska-Jankowska, Anna. 2020. 'Słowniki polskiego języka migowego dostępne on-line. Krytyczna analiza leksykograficzna'. In M. Bańko, W. Decyk-Zięba and E. Rudnicka (eds), *Leksykografia w różnych kontekstach. Tom 2*, 227–44. Warszawa: Wydawnictwa Uniwersytetu Warszawskiego.

Zgółkowa, Hanna. 2013. *Słownik minimum języka polskiego*. Kraków: UNIVERSITAS.

13

The Concept of *Wenming* (文明) ('Civility') as an Edusemiotic Strategy

Katarzyna Mazur-Włodarczyk, Małgorzata Haładewicz-Grzelak, Elżbieta Karaś, Joanna Kolańska-Płuska and Przemysław Misiurski

Introduction

The Chinese lexeme *wenming* (文明) ('civility') may be translated into English in several semantic dimensions, that is e.g. as: (1) 'nature', 'natural phenomenon'; (2) 'culture' (association with the character [文] constituting the word *wenming*); (3) 'something new', 'modern', or even 'western' (used in this context during the Quing dynasty and the early Republic of China); (4) 'civilization', that is, achieving a certain level of social advancement and the sum of material and non-material wealth achieved by the given society; (5) 'civilizational advancement', achieving a higher level of culture, 'becoming civilized' – acquiring good manners; (6) 'good manners', 'politeness'; and (7) 'civility', 'good upbringing', displaying good manners or creating and spreading culture.[1] This plethora of potential translatory target domains is usually referred to as 'a functional imbalance' (Dranseika, Berniūnas and Silius 2018). Moreover, one of the meanings the word *wenming* refers to, that is, 'civilization' indicates a connection with a very broadly defined concept.[2]

Etymologically, 文 (wén) in its earlier form (Figure 13.1a) showed a man with a piece of text on his chest (Gu 2008: 981). This character is associated with the script as such, with written language in general and with Chinese characters, i.e. the main civilization factors (Działoszyński 2018: 12–13; Erbaugh 2008: 639). By extension, it denotes also the entire concept of culture or cultivation through which civilization manifests itself (Sickman and Soper [1956] 1984: 485). The second constituent character (明) (míng), on the other hand, refers to the quality of being bright, well-lit, sparkling and clear, like the sun (日) and the moon (月), or the light coming through a window (囧) or an eye (目) (Gu 2008: 37), as shown in Figure 13.1b. Therefore, in general terms, the word *wenming* indicates

Figure 13.1 The characters 文 and 明 are written in the calligraphic style *jiaguwen* and *jinwen*. Drawing by Katarzyna Mazur-Włodarczyk. Based on: *Chinese Language Dictionary* (a) and (b). *Chinese Language Dictionary* (a) (in Chinese: 汉典), *Ming* (in Chinese: 明), n.d., available online: https://www.zdic.net/hans/%E6%98%8E (accessed 4 February 2020); and *Chinese Language Dictionary* (b) (in Chinese: 汉典), *Wén* (in Chinese: 文), n.d., available online: https://www.zdic.net/hans/%E6%96%87 (accessed 4 February 2020).

that a person experiences the world around him, tries to remember it and write it down, to substantiate it. The purpose of that consolidation is to obtain knowledge on the basis of which one can influence others, so that they can move in the right direction, become possessors of certain virtues and, thus, be enlightened and civilized (Deng, et al. 2014). *Being civilized* thus indicates being transformed, in particular, transformed by writing (Thao Thi Phuong Nguyen 2012: 61).

In addition to the wide span of translational target domains for *wenming*, there is also a question of a certain blending between *wenming* concept and *wenhua*, (文化) the latter usually being translated as 'civilization'. Erbaugh (2008: 639) points out that since *wenhua* 'civilized' has also assumed the meaning of 'literate', both terms ultimately 'pay homage to the scholar-official'. Furthermore, both *wenming* (in Erbaugh's translation – 'civil' or 'enlightened') and *wenhua*, rather than relating to citizenship, a royal court, or city life, connote literacy and education (Erbaugh 2008: 639).[3]

Deng, Zhang and Wen (2014), providing a detailed diachronic study of the sematic development of the *wenming* constituent characters conclude that in ancient Chinese, there is a non-symmetry in word derivation between 'civilization' and '*wenming*', since the lexeme 'civilization', coming from 'civil', patterns the derivation on 'civis', or 'civilitas' in Latin, 'civil' implying the relation to citizens (inhabitants of a town/city). Nonetheless, the radical factors of the meaning of the word 'civilization' are 'make' and 'development'. They focused on the 'town' and 'city', namely, the process of cumulating wealth and remolding the nature through human being intervening in nature actively. But the source of 'wenming' stress to experience the nature, to cultivate the inner world. With the help of this process, one can have enlightenments and knowledge, so one can improve ordinary people, and make them far away from the savage condition.

Deng, Zhang and Wen 2014: 413

In the chapter, we will consider the *wenming* concept as a social engineering strategy to 'ecologize' Chinese society in accordance with the Ricoeurian hermeneutics of explaining and understanding. We will also apply the edusemiotic approach, relying on the concept of *Bildung* as a dialectic between the subject and the world, or between actantial subjects. The paper is part of a trailblazing project (Mazur-Włodarczyk et al., submitted), the implementation of which would enable the analysis of *wenming* as one of the components of Chinese culture, from the point of view of elements having a significant impact on the environment in which economic processes take place.

The chapter is informed by a corpus of digital documentation of tokens of visual and verbal texts related to propagating this concept (with the embedded visual or verbal reference to *wenming*), collected by Katarzyna Mazur-Włodarczyk (17 tokens) and Natalia Brede (70 tokens) in the years 2010–21. The documented data was produced in the form of banners, posters and announcements placed in public space (lawns, banners on walls, billboards, lawns, subway, etc.). The photos were documented as tokens, which are certain types of emerging schema of wider spectrum of items. Therefore, there were many more combinations of visual textuality with variants occurring as ubiquitous constituents of urbanscape, but, within the accessible scope, there were no new verbal textuality variants.

The documentation we are analysing was mainly collected in the municipalities of Beijing and Shanghai, and the cities of Kunming in Yunnan Province and Fuzhou in Fujian Province. It should here be pointed out that the city of Kunming is subject to the Wenming Kunming (文明昆明) project, to transform it into a fully civilized city to achieve a full set of socialist values and to create the ecological civilization (Chang et al. 2019; De Jong 2019). This analysis is of an exploratory nature, aiming to establish a general research plateau from which further strands can be subsequently pursued, such as, e.g., visual and written references to Chinese culture appearing in these advertisements, as well as an analysis in terms of visual grammar or more specific relations with the hermeneutical approach. The current stage of research has been dedicated to classifying the collected types of texts and determining their main semiotic intertextual relations.

Wenming in the Pragmatic Background

Multidimensional categories, such as exemplified by the term *wenming*, are important for numerous reasons, e.g. in terms of Chinese cultural heritage (which includes art, literature, philosophical and religious trends), the need for coexistence between man and nature, its topicality apparent e.g. in contemporary speeches of Chinese politicians. No preliminary research has been carried out so far devoted strictly to *wenming*, nevertheless, research on *harmony – hexie* (和谐) – a category that also influences the shaping of Chinese economic culture – conducted by Mazur-Włodarczyk (e.g. 2021) in recent years, points to the fact that:

1. multifaceted categories influencing the shaping of Chinese economic culture result from the exceptional diversity of the Chinese society (e.g. the existence of diverse ethnic groups, the level of socio-economic development, generational affiliation), but also from the living spaces they relate to.
2. multifaceted categories are important from the point of view of:
   - Chinese cultural heritage (including art, literature, philosophical and religious trends),
   - the need for human coexistence with nature,
   - in speeches by contemporary Chinese politicians, but also associated with only declarative attitudes and not very spontaneous official speeches containing the required keywords in their content (including *hexie* and *wenming*),
3. multifaceted categories also have implications in relation to economic activity, subsuming policies on the international markets, as well as in connection with business activity – in the management space. They also belong to the group of factors that educate and motivate the Chinese to adopt a pro-entrepreneurial attitude.[4]

Wenming, as an example of such a multidimensional category, should also pragmatically be viewed in the context of political discourse in China, referring to building a socialist society (a socialist civilization) in which ideological culture is described as the soul of the country and nation (Li 2016: 18). *Wenming* is thus also a political concept utilized to establish a classification system based on rather abstract categories for a good citizen (Figure 13.2). In such a perspective, 'civilization' is also defined as a system of moral, hygienic and pragmatic values closely intertwined with Confucian doctrine (Romero 2018).[5]

Contemporary spiritual civilization with Chinese specificity refers to specific behavioural habits of an individual. For example, Li (2016) observes that 'if someone manages interpersonal relationships and participates in social interactions in a polite and reasonable manner in everyday life, his behavior can then be perceived as correct in terms of behavioral habits' (Li 2016: 7.) On that take, the benchmark of civilization is the awareness of the need to act according to socially established norms, manifested, inter alia, in waiting in lines, obeying road traffic regulations and not entering the personal zone of another person (ibid., 12). This propaedeutic stipulation also entails the stigma related to behavioural failures.

With the view of the above, 'undesired' habits of PRC citizens 'under radar' include:

(1) not queuing (e.g. when entering public transport); (2) not giving way to people with special needs – the elderly, the sick, with disabilities, pregnant women and those caring for children (e.g. in public transport); (3) crossing streets in forbidden places, not obeying traffic regulations (especially ignoring red light); (4) spitting, swearing, shopping in pajamas (Strittmatter 2010: 134, 139); (5) excessively loud behaviour in public places; and (6) littering; and (7) smoking in places marked with a no-smoking sign.

In order to counteract and rectify such behaviours, in the 1980s a number of remedial actions were initiated by the Chinese Communist party, related to the education of PRC citizens, subsuming for example the development and distribution of educational guides for correct behaviour. According to Mary S. Erbaugh (2008), China has overtaken Europe in publishing courtesy guides that are not aimed at individuals but at the collective level. They relate to practically each of the above-mentioned manners.

Another wide spanning project initiated in the 1980s by the Chinese Communist Party aimed at promoting verbal hygiene, that is, the use of civilized and polite language, including the use of five main politeness phrases: good morning (你好, nǐ hǎo), please (请, qǐng), sorry (对不起, duìbùqǐ), thank you (谢谢, xièxiè) and goodbye (再见, zàijiàn), mapping thus a deep realignment of social relations (Erbaugh 2008: 622).

This policy also took the form of social propaedeutics. For example, during the Expo 2010 World Fair in Shanghai hand paper fans in the form of a water

Figure 13.2 A canonical urban decoration showing 12 features of a socialist society, into which *wenming* is embedded: prosperity and power (of the country) (富强), (socialist) democracy (民主), civilization (civilization development) (文明), harmony (和谐), freedom (自由), equality (平等), justice (公正), the rule of law (法治), patriotism (爱国), dedication to work (respect for work) (敬业), honesty (诚信), friendliness (友善). Author: Natalia Brede.

droplet – the symbol of EXPO 2010 – were distributed (a token shown in Figure 13.5). It was at that international event when *wenming* policy can be said to have been officially triggered. The fans contained educational slogans, encouraging the participants to act like civilized visitors (文明观博), which we will also subsequently see in other material bearers within urbanscape. To wit, according to the stipulations contained on the fan, the visitor (to the fair), among other things, was supposed: not to cut lines but wait patiently for his turn (耐心等候不插队); to take care of the exhibits (not to touch them) (爱护展品不乱碰); to selectively dispose of garbage and not to litter (垃圾分类不乱); not to smoke in prohibited zones (控烟区域不吸烟); to accept gifts (freebies) without a fight for them[6] (领取赠品不争抢); not to make noise and to use civilized (polite).[7]

As a contemporary extension, a new category of 'civility' has also emerged which is directly related to the Internet. It is dubbed as the civilized use of the

Figure 13.3 [遵守公共道德争当文明市民] This photo says: Observe public morality and strive to be a civilized citizen. Author: Katarzyna Mazur-Włodarczyk.

global network (文明上网, *wénmíng shàngwǎng*), as well as the attitude of a civilized Internet user (文明网民; *wénmíng wǎngmín*) (De Seta 2018). This extension, of base category implies not only references to opposing vulgarity, respecting others and other behaviours shown in the international netiquette, but also the issue of not publishing information that could threaten, inter alia, national security, undermining social stability and social morality (Civilized Internet Access, Building Harmony Proposal 2021).[8]

Methodological Foundation: Edusemiotics as Social Hermeneutics

The term 'edusemiotics' was coined by Marcel Danesi in 2010, as an amalgam of several epistemologies: *semiotics* being a science of signs, *theory of learning* (i.e. theory of how signs are learned) and *education*, which he describes as 'philosophy coupled with the practical art/science of teaching individuals of how to interpret and understand signs' (Danesi 2010: vii). The motivation for such a move was that semiotics, as a science of signs, is an intrinsically suitable tool to investigate how signs are learned (ibid., vii).[9]

As that scholar further observes, learning, since the earliest childhood behaviours, is a semiotic process (Danesi 2010: ix). After the exploratory phase of sensory cognizing, the emerging units of knowledge enable the child 'to recognize' the same entity so as not to have to re-examine it sensorily. With time, engaging in semiotic behaviour increases, transcending that primary sensory cognition. Subsequently, the child develops a 'psychosocial connection' between their corporality and conscious thinking related to the surrounding world. Here Danesi observes the paramount importance of signs, which, constituting a sort of 'representational glue', interconnect in a holistic manner the mind with the body, and with the world around. The posted inbuilt learning system, as the scholar further upholds, is shaped by culture and context as well as experience, serving for the developing human being as a 'filter that allows him/her to reorganize the raw, yet functional, information: to process it into meaningful wholes' (Danesi 2010: ix–x).

A concise motivation for edusemiotics was also put forth by Winfred Nöth, singling out two main aspects of the mutual feedback: (1) teaching and learning as processes of semiosis have semiotic effects; (2) the learning and teaching process can also provide insights into the ontological aspects of signs, that is the study of the sign ontogeny. The areas where there is most overlap between the two disciples include for example, methodological and practical aspects of education, theoretical foundations (epistemological perspective), as well as communicative competence (Nöth 2010: 1).[10]

Throughout the years, edusemiotics thus has solidified as a platform and point of contact for the scholars developing theories of education with those engaged in semiotic practices.[11] That is, the bourgeoning framework has intended to host both the research evolving round the question of what semiotics tells us about education, and its reverse, that is, investigating what education can tell us about semiotics (Semetsky, Stables and Pesce 2016: 2–3). Although *edusemiotics* currently implies multifarious theoretical frameworks and developments – pragmatism included – the edusemiotic model is in broad terms characterized by anti-dualistic and holistic approach, the focus on the existential dimension and interpretation, embodied cognition and the focus on a process, rather than a product (ibid., 2).

The processual aspect of pedagogy endorses, among else, the synergy of arts and sciences of communication to enhance the 'pragmatic awareness of the systems of thought and habits of learning' (Peterson 2016: 24). Such a perspective entails a wider stance on the ontology of education.[12] For example, Stables singles out education as a process which emphases 'the becomingness of all personal and social being, whether or not it is consciously goal-directed' (Stables 2016: 56).

Here we arrive at the key notion for our edusemiotic analysis of *wenming*, that is, the concept of (German) *Bildung*[13] as elaborated by Gadamer. Having emphasized its importance for the human science, the philosopher endorses a basic definition given by Herder as 'rising up to humanity through culture' (Gadamer 2013: 9). Crucially, the German philosopher notes that there has occurred a shift of focus: from the attention and primacy given to *Bildung* as a natural form, in gist referring to external appearance or shapes created by nature, *Bildung* has come to be associated with the concept of culture.

Through that, Gadamer proposes to see *Bildung* a task for man, which entails renouncing from the particular for the sake of the universal. Nonetheless, 'sacrificing particularity means the restraint of desire and hence freedom from the object of desire and freedom for its objectivity' (Gadamer 2013: 12). Pursuing that thread, he follows in the footsteps of Hegel, in elaborating a free self-consciousness 'in-and-for-itself'. In restraining desire, working consciousness presents itself as independent consciousness. Selflessly concerned with the universal, the working consciousness can thus raise itself beyond the mundane aspect – the immediacy of its mere existence, to reach the universal: 'by forming the thing it forms itself' (Gadamer 2013: 12).

For Hegel thus 'the self-awareness of working consciousness contains all the elements that make up practical *Bildung*: the distancing from the immediacy of desire, of personal need and private interest and the exacting demand of the universal' (Gadamer 2013: 13). From this elaboration of the practical *Bildung* by Hegel, Gadamer extracts one basic idea: 'To recognize oneself in the alien, to become at home in it, is the basic movement of spirit, whose being consists only in returning to oneself from what is other.' What follows, any formal, *Bildung* such as e.g. foreign language instruction, constitutes the continuation of that 'underlying' *Bildung* (Gadamer 2013: 13).

Kukkola and Pikkarainen (2016) provide a concise retrospective of that Kantian concept, observing, first of all, that there is no unanimous, common definition of its content. That is why there is no uniform translation of that German lexeme in English. Among the possible translations the authors enumerate 'culture', 'growth,' or 'formation'. Furthermore, the authors stipulate three key aspects that relate to the concept in question: (1) *Bildung* is conceived of as a developmental process, implying the changes of the subject in the form of its growth and self-formation; (2) it implies the relationship between the subject and the umwelt, or relationships holding with other subjects; and (3) it implies the dynamism of activity of the subject, who, rather being a passive object of environmental forces, engage in active and creatively self-formation, in this way, *Bildung* liaises with the pragmatist understating of *experience* (Kukkola and Pikkarainen 2016: 200).

Existential-Hermeneutic pedagogy as developed, e.g., by Otto-Friedrich Bollnow shifts the focus from the subjectivity included in the concept to the mundane power that can exert influence on us (Kukkola and Pikkarainen 2016: 205). ([German] *Geisteswissenschaftliche Pädagogik*, as those scholars further observe, constitutes the basis for Bollnow's understanding of education as based on a hermeneutic tradition of educational theory. In particular, the investigative object is 'educational reality' ([German] *Erziehungswirklichkeit*), which can be understood as 'a part of human reality, a specific area of human existence, and therefore as a part of the totality of historical-cultural conditions' (Kukkola and Pikkarainen (2016: 205).

The concept of *Bildung* is the point of departure for the *geisteswissenschaftliche* tradition, serving as a basis for deriving subsequent key notions, e.g. *Bildsamkeit*, 'educability'. Here lies the gist of what Kukkola and Pikkarainen (2016) refer to as 'Kant's pedagogical paradox':

> the process of *Bildung*, also understood as the formation of an individual, does not occur by itself, spurred only by the abilities of this individual; but the individual is in need of pedagogical intervention so, 'how is it possible that we become autonomous and rational persons, when this result relies on coercive educational action? (...) Educational coercion is thus seen as the very opposite of what the development of human being's skills and capacities ought to amount to. This coercion has been mandated by the abovementioned notion of Bildsamkeit, the fundamental human ability to learn skills and competence.'
>
> Kukkola and Pikkarainen 2016: 205

Bollnow's work on pedagogy was called as, stipulated above, Existential-Hermeneutic Pedagogy. But we can derive linkages between edusemiotics and hermeneutics on a much more general level. Let us recall some general aspects of hermeneutical thought as established by Ricoeur (cf. Peface, this volume). In brief (assuming that all the terminological aspects in any theory is fluid and subject to constant change), Ricoeur adopts a working defining of hermeneutics as the theory of the operations of understanding with reference to the text interpretation. This liaises with the French philosopher's firm refutation of the

Diltheyan opposition of explication and understanding, as well as searching for the complementarities concerning the two terms, rather than dichotomizing them (Ricoeur [1981] 1989: 191).

In Dilthey's philosophy, to recall, the issue of understanding was related to the modes of understanding the Other that appears to us through their message. Heidegger shifted that focus of the ontological problem, through his Dasein entity (*Dasein* – as being-here, as *we* being here) from the question of another human being to the mundane question (Ricoeur [1981] 1989: 208ff.). Gadamer turned the analytical attention in turn to the issue of *Zugehörigkeit*, (pertaining) and its opposite – the creation of the distance. 'Belonging' thus was conceptualized in terms of the historicity, that is, being part of a historical process and belonging to a linguistic community (German) *wirkungsgeschichtliches Bewusstsein* ('awareness of the historicity of the outcomes (Ricoeur [1981] 1989: 218).[14] It means that individual's participation in tradition or in traditions is achieved by interpreting the signs of works and texts in which the heritage of the past is inscribed and given to us to decipher (Ricoeur [1981] 1989: 222). In the subsequent analysis we will see how the concept of *wenming* binds the two paths: the education, in particular with the emphasis on *Bildung*, and on meaningful experience through action with the hermeneutic grounding.

Analysis: Visual Propaedeutics of *Wenming* as *Bildung*

We will now move on to the analysis of collected tokens from the database described above. To recall, the documentation as tokens means that there are many more combinations of visual textuality with variants of verbal textuality, but they do not bring any new content: the same texts are repeated with different visual textualities. The general categorization of *wenming* pragmatic extensions proposed by the Chinese themselves, was documented on one of the banners: (1) creating a civilized city and (2) creating civilized and ethical citizens (centre headings) through eight groups of rituals/ ceremonies:

1. 仪式之礼 – ritual ceremony (honouring, admiring, celebration, respecting etiquette);
2. 行走之礼 – traffic (including compliance with regulations) showing kindness, helping the elderly and the weaker, giving way during commuting);

3. 餐饭之礼 – eating (including paying attention to hygiene, nurturing food, not wasting food and eating elegantly);
4. 旅游之礼 – traveling (e.g. being kind to the landscape, cultivating cultural monuments, respecting folk customs and observing public morality);
5. 诗人之礼 – erudition (including respect for teachers, relatives, tolerance, kindness and honesty);
6. 言谈之礼 – language (e.g. civilized language, calmness, patient listening, honesty and friendliness);
7. 观赏之礼 – sightseeing (e.g. proper behaviour, respecting the natural environment, admiring and appreciating);
8. 仪表之礼 – personal appearance (e.g. well-kept image, natural appearance, good manners).

We have re-grouped that categorizing key of the eight groups of rituals into more general domains. Due to the richness of the collected material, as well as the multiplicity of analytical threads implicated in the database which cannot be covered within one canonical academic paper, in this analysis we focus on 'ecology' framed in the database as caring for nature. This will be related to searching for the predominant contexts and references to nature in the corpus (hermeneutical dimension). We decided to start from that thematic vein since verbal and visual textuality related to the concept of *nature* are the most numerous sections of the collected corpus. What is important, the preponderance of the refences to well-kept natural habitat occurs with the concomitant absolute lack of refences to *techne* (technological aspects of civilization). That thread, as we will see, is closely linked to the phenomenon of caring for the *other* as an example of rituals related to being a good citizen (edusemiotics dimension). Recalling once more a general Gadamerian context of Bildung, that concept is not to be envisaged solely as the process of historically elevating the mind to the universal; but 'it is at the same time the element with which the educated man (*Gebildete*) moves' (Gadamer (1960 [2013]: 16).[15]

'Wengming publicity' documented as our corpus that contains some form of reference to natural habitat are in the form of: flowers (also painted in traditional, Chinese graphic style, green areas and landscapes. The reference to 'nature' is effectuated also through placing hoardings /boards directly in a green area (e.g. in parks). Moreover, the shape of those boards is significant, since they are usually in the shape of a heart or a creature, e.g. a frog. The verbal textuality accompanying the character wengming in that case does not have to relate to nature. In this way, the context is given priority in retrieving the final message.

Figure 13.4 Example of textuality relating *wenming* to propadeutic dimension ecological and natural aspects. (Beautiful scenery for people to enjoy Virtue makes people admire them. Photo: Natalia Brede.

Sample visual textuality is juxtaposed in Figures 13.4 and 13.5, featuring the main types of both visual and verbal exponents of ecology.

Other phrases related to nature and propadeutics from the database and not adduced as a visual support here include:

(a) 温馨提示 – tips; 创建文明城市 – creating a civilized city; 提倡文明礼仪 – promote civilized etiquette; 弘扬社会公德 – promote social morality; (b) 创建全国文明城市，打造世界春城花都 – creating a civilized city throughout the country, building the world, spring flower capital; 社会注意价值观 – values of socialism; (c) 创建文明城市 – creating a civilized city; 文明是最美的风景 – civilization-civility is the most beautiful scenery; 旅游美时美刻，文明随时随地 – beautiful moments while traveling, civility anytime, anywhere; 社会注意价值观 – values of socialism; (d) 文明一个人温暖一座城 – civilizing one man warms the city; 文明贵在一言一行，环保重在一点一滴 – civilization is

Figure 13.5 A paper fan as a tourist brochure handed out at EXPO 2010. Photo: Katarzyna Mazur-Włodarczyk.

valuable in words and deeds, environmental protection is important piece by piece; 社会注意价值观 – values of socialism; (f) 文明昆明 – civilized Kunming; 关丽春城诗如画，文明旅游同行同心 – picturesque city of spring (this is another name for Kunming), civilized tourism directed towards the centre; 社会注意价值观 – values of socialism; (g) 文明昆明 – civilized Kunming; 绿水青山，就是金山银山 – green waters, blue mountains (as green nature) are mountains of gold and silver; 社会注意价值观 – values of socialism; (h) 关爱青少年，守护为明天 – caring for young people, caring for tomorrow. 和谐文明 – harmonized civilization (or harmony, civilization), Civilized Kunming, (middle) 我的城市我的家，文明城市靠大家 – my city my home, a civilized city depends on everyone; 文明昆明 – civilized Kunming) 用行动呵护美景，用文明装点心灵 – take care of beauty through action, decorate the mind with civilization; 文明昆明 – civilized Kunming, (top middle) 创建全国文明市 – creating a civilized city throughout the country, 关爱未成年人成长，托起明天的太阳 – caring for the development of minors, keeping tomorr'w's sun; 色环保，垃圾分类 – green environmental protection, garbage segregation, 文明昆明 – civilized Kunming, (middle) 关爱老人，关爱自己的未来 – caring for seniors, caring for the future.

We can see here several threads that are prominent in trying to capture the hermeneutic 'density' of the *wenming* concept with respect to references to nature, which as we recall, was also in the past connected with the concept of Bildung. Apart from the connection with the cultivation of natural habitat as the most salient feature, the corpus allows to specify the following aspects:

1. *Wenming* as a reflection of the natural habitat – as Lebenswelt – and of citizen's inner spirituality, natural habitat outside and inside [civility is the most beautiful scenery, it is something that you can decorate the mind with; something to possess as an individual, green waters, blue mountains (as green nature) are mountains of gold and silver], external image of civilization;
2. *Wenming* as a ceremony to be practiced step by step: [civility is valuable in words and deeds, environmental protection is important piece by piece, civility anytime];
3. It implies the fortitive process [civilizing one man warms the city, guarding the morrow, enhancing honesty and quality; gradational process and taking place on a micro-scale (piece by piece, one man's civility).
4. It requires action on the part of the subject [take care of beauty through action], it can be précised as a community behaviour and as micro-scale (individual's responsibility, creating a civilized city throughout the country).
5. It has a centripetal dynamics [civilized tourism directed towards the centre] and that dynamics it translates here as fostering the aspect of belonging: *my city my home, a civilized city depends on everyone*, caring for youth, guarding tomorrow, strengthening honesty and quality tourism directed towards the centre, my city, civilized city, civilized health, caring for seniors, caring for their future;
6. it involves a certain awareness of historicity (Gadamerian historic progress) and awareness of belonging linked in this case to the context involving ecology of the habitat [caring for young people, caring for tomorrow, harmonized civilization (or harmony, civilization), caring for

the development of minors, keep tomorr'w's sun, caring for seniors, caring for the future;
7. embedding to into a general horizon of socialist values [to recall, from Figure 13.2, posited as: prosperity and power (of the country) [富强], (socialist) democracy [民主], civilization (civilization development) [文明], harmony [和谐], freedom [自由], equality [平等], justice [公正], the rule of law [法治], patriotism [爱国], dedication to work (respect for work) [敬业], honesty [诚信], friendliness [友善].

These heuristic domains involve a lot of overlap and blending. Most of all, we can directly connect the aspect of practicing community behaviour with caring for one's elders (predecessors and the future generations (posterity) and the centripetal (bonding) dynamics. Hence an individual is immersed into a historical process of becoming, which is a classical hermeneutic Gadamerian tenet (cf. Rÿoeurur 1989: 220 and above). Furthermore, Gadamer also proposes the dialectics of participation and alienation, framed as (German) *Horizontverschmelzung* (the fusion of horizons) which basically implies that where a specific situation occurs, there also comes into being a dynamic horizon. The crisscross of that horizon warrants the communication between two divergently situated subjectivities (Ricoeur 1989: 222).

Moreover, if we juxtapose the translatory domains for the concept of *Bilding* with that for *wenming*, there seem to emerge several parallels, beyond the semantic layer. Let us recall that the lexeme *wenming*, which is usually translated into English as 'civility' or 'civilization', can also be understood as 'formation', 'growth', 'culture', 'cultivation'. The collected tokens, as evident from the preceding exposition preclude any connection with the '*techne*' aspect of civilizational advancement, while at the same time, there is a strong connection with the environment and nature. Hence, the cultivation is understood ecologically, as the cultivation of the Lebenswelt.

Conclusion

In this chapter, we undertook several research goals. First, the subject of the study, i.e. the concept of *wenming* itself, has been briefly presented, both in semantic aspect as well as against the pragmatic and ideological background. Then, we presented the assumptions of the research perspective and the possibility of further exploration in relation to the concept *of Bildung*. At the end, a preliminary typology of the collected research data was presented, according to the category of eight social rituals and environmental ecology. The current stage of research was to establish the main semiotic intertextual relationships, considering the multifaceted nature of the *wenming* category as an educational category as regards references to nature and habitat. In particular, we focused on the parallels between the concept of Bildung and wengming. At the same time, we did not analyse the aspect of the ideological (political) embedding of the concept.

The features we singled out that define the semiotic prominence of the concept were: references to nature, with concomitant total absence of references to *techne*, processual character, centripetal, cohesive dynamics (towards the centre, which is of course also related to the fact that China is referred to as *a country of the centre*) with the absence of centripetal dynamics; being an attribute to be possessed. It involves fortitive aspect, fusion of horizons, *wenming* wax thus isolated as a paramount edusemiotics marker, of hermeneutical nature, pivotal in creating an ecosystem of cultural significance.

Relations with the *Bildung* concept based on the analysed domains would imply: (1) Processual character: *wenming* as a process of improving oneself and society, as a process of caring for society through education – corrective actions; (2) References to growth (self-)formation, cultivation; and (3) Education as formation in semiosis.

Within the last category, we can trace the convergent nexus of all the three perspectival axes exposed so far: education, semiotics and hermeneutics. The *Wenming* concept entails references to semiotics as interpretation relating to the fact that it also can *denote* writing – as has been exposed in the introductory section, 'script' semantically, features as one of the possible translations of that character (as a direct denotation). As a result the characters [文明] convey semiosis on two levels: as a character being written, that is, as a linguistic sign, paradigmatically replaceable by any other item of script, and on the semantic plane, denoting 'script'.

Let us point out here that in Ricoeurian hermeneutics, the phenomenon of *script* has a pivotal status, relating to the wider dialectal construction of the concept of meaning. In brief, solidifying discourse by means of writing implies the autonomy of the psychological meaning from the textual meaning. Writing thus leads to the liberation of the text from the conditioning established by a conversation. That liberation is effectuated through the act of reading (Ricoeur 1989: 237). A hermeneutic repercussion of that process, is that, as the French philosopher upholds, the effect of the distance is no longer seen as a being 'parasitic' and affixed, but it becomes constitutive of the phenomenon of text as writing After having been transferred from the epistemological sphere (methodological) into the ontological sphere it becomes a prerequisite for interpretation (Ricoeur 1989: 238).

Wenming this is a specific hermeneutic plateau, showing interpretative potential by the blend of denotation and connotation. Moreover, the analysis traced coextensive-ness with both hermeneutics and education: the action of signs does not only occur at the graphic level but also on the visual textuality level and on the meaningful embedding within wider pragmatic horizon.

Acknowledgements

The article received funding under the internal university grant 'Delta' (Opole University of Technology). We would like to thank Natalia Brede for letting us include photos of her authorship in this paper.

Notes

1 All translations from Chinese in the paper are mine, Katarzyna Mazur-Włodarczyk. All remaining translations are ours, Katarzyna Mazur-Włodarczyk and Małgorzata Haładewicz-Grzelak.
2 Adamski (2003: 548–51); see also Deng, Zhang and Wen (2014).
3 She further indicates that it was Meiji Japanese scholars who in the in the late nineteenth century coined the modern two-syllable lexeme for 'civilization' (*wenhua*) after having translated European works of sociology (Marx included). It was done by combining the Chinese characters (*wén*) as 'script' and (*hua*) ('transformation'). Subsequently 'civilized' *wenhua* has merged its semantic field with 'literate', which tightened the link between the concept of 'education' and that of 'civilization'. On a related note Erbaugh also observes that in fact a considerable number of modern Chinese words, subsuming also lexemes such as 'factory', 'car', 'republic', 'citizen', or 'constitution', were ideated by Japanese modernizers (Erbaugh 2008: 639).
4 The above information is the starting point for the planned research on the category of civilization (cf. Mazur-Włodarczyk et al., forthcoming), addressing research questions such as, e.g.: What influences the shaping of the Chinese category of *wengming*? Is the feature of *civilization / civility* really still important in the life of modern Chinese? Or is it merely an attractive rhetoric used by the rulers? Is the

drive to civilization evident in China in connection with economic activity? According to the definition of economic culture, does the category of civilization constitute the background of economic processes as an unconscious stimulus for making decisions on an economic basis?

5   More detailed relations with Confucianism cannot be covered within the scope of this paper and are left for a follow-up research.
6   Which is to say that visitors should not push and fight over freebies given away at the fair.
7   This aspect will not be analysed in the scope of this paper.
8   '文明上网从我做起，争做文明上网使者), (2021) Civilized Internet Access Starts from Me, Striving to Be a Civilized Internet Messenger!' (in a Chinese URL, no longer active).
9   Semiotics is ultimately a form of inquiry into how humans shape raw sensory information into knowledge-based categories through sign-interpretation and sign-creation, that is, through the use of forms that stand for the categories. Signs that penetrate the flux of information are intelligent selections which are taken in by our senses or our intuitions, allowing us to encode what we perceive as meaningful in it and, thus, to learn and remember it.

    Danesi 2010: ix

10 The same reference for a detailed overview of the retrospective of interrelations between semiotics and education. For example, the scholar observes that: 'The pedagogical insight that knowledge is 'a process, not a static structure to be learned and remembered' (Cunningham 1987b: 214) has its semiotic foundation in Peirce's theory of semiosis as an infinite progress of becoming by which signs and meanings are connected by the human mind' (Nöth 2010: 3).
11 In particular, see here works such as, e.g., Stables (2005); Stables and Semetsky (2015).
12 Along these lines, Fornasa as cited in Peters 'Ex-ducere (to bring out) and ad-prendere (to grasp in the chaos by giving form and sense to the event) are processes epistemologically and relationally opposite the customary instructional modalities of in-ducere (to insert something within insofar as it is lacking) and insegnare (to impress a form from outside) – as every schoolchild knows...' (Fornasa 1998: 204), as cited in Peterson (2016: 22).
13 Translated in Gadamer (2013: 9) as 'culture'. The following is a synopsis of Gadamer (2013: 9–16).
14 The ontological moment, as Ricoeur ([1981] 1989: 212) emphasizes elaborating on Heidegger's *Sein und Zeit*, appears only with the emergence of the third segment of the triad: situation – understanding – interpretation. Prior to the text exegesis there is thus the exegesis of the world and of life. What follows, interpretation for Heidegger is most for of all, explication as an expansion of understanding and the enunciation does not reveal its subject per se, the enunciation only articulates its

subject. That, for Ricoeur (1989: 214), implies that in the oeuvre *Sein und Zeit*, (German) *reden* 'to say' has a priority over (German) *sprechen* 'to speak' (Ricoeur [1981] 1989: 214).

15 In particular,

> every single individual who rises himself out of his natural being to the spiritual, find in the language, customs and institutions of his people a pre-given body of material, which as in learning to speak, he has to make his own. This every individual is always engaging in the process of Bildung and in getting beyond his naturalness, inasmuch as the world into which he is growing is the one that is humanly constituted through language and customs.
>
> Gadamer [1960] 2013: 14

References

文明上网从我做起，争做文明上网使者. 2021. 'Civilized Internet Access Starts from Me, Striving to Be a Cvilized Internet Mmessenger!' In Chinese. URL no longer accessible.

Adamski, Franciszek. 2003. 'Cywilizacja'. In *Encyklopedia pedagogiczna*, XXI w.), vol. I, 548–51. Warszawa: Wydawnictwo Akademickie 'Żak'.

Bollnow, Otto F. 1966. *Krise und neuer Anfang: Beiträge zur pädagogischen Anthropologie*. Heidelberg: Quelle & Meyer.

Chang I-Shin, Wang Wenqi and Wu Jing. 2019. 'To Strengthen the Practice of Ecological Civilization in China'. *Sustainability*, 11: 4661. Doi: 10.3390/su11174661.

Chinese Language Dictionary. n.d. (a) (In Chinese: 汉典), *Ming* (in Chinese: 明). Available online: https://www.zdic.net/hans/%E6%98%8E (accessed 4 February 2020).

Chinese Language Dictionary. n.d. (b) (In Chinese: 汉典), *Wen* (in Chinese: 文). Available online: https://www.zdic.net/hans/%E6%96%87 (accessed: 4 February 2020).

Cunningham, Donald J. 1987. 'Outline of an Education Semiotics'. *American Journal of Semiotics*, 5: 201–16.

Danesi, Marcel. 2010. 'Foreword'. In Inna Semetsky (ed.), *Semiotics Education Eperience (Educational Futures: Rethinking Theory and Practice*, vol. 43, vii–xi. Rotterdam: Sense.

De Jong, Martin. 2019. 'From Eco-Civilization to City Branding: A Neo-Marxist Perspective of Sustainable Urbanization in China'. *Sustainability*, 11: 5608. Doi: 10.3390/su11205608.

De Seta, G. 2018. 'Wenming Bu Wenming: The Socialization of Incivility in Postdigital China'. *International Journal of Communication*, 12: 2010–30. Doi: 1932-8036/20180005.

Deng, Fei, Li Zhang and Xu Wen. 2014. 'Exploring the Non-Symmetry of Word Derivation in Chinese-English Translation—"Wenming" for "Civilization"'. *Open Journal of Modern Linguistics*, 4: 407–14.

Dewey, John. [1934] 1980. *Art as Experience*. New York: Perigee.

Dranseika V., R. Berniūnas and V. Silius. 2018. 'Immorality and Bu Daode, Unculturedness and Bu Wenming'. *Journal of Cultural Cognitive Science*, 2: 71–84. Doi: 10.1007/S41809-018-0013-Y.

Działoszyński, Bartosz. 2018. *Cywilizacja. Szkice z dziejów pojęcia w XVIII i XIX wieku* (Civilization: Sketches from the History of the Concept in the 18th and 19th Centuries). Warszawa: Wydawnictwo Uniwersytetu Warszawskiego.

Erbaugh, Mary S. 2008. 'China Expands Its Courtesy: Saying "Hello" to Strangers'. *Journal of Asian Studies*, 67 (2): 621–52.

Fornasa, Walter. 1998. 'Maestro perché le cose finiscono in disordine? Epistemologia ecológica e processi educativi'. In Sergio Manghi (ed.), *Attraverso Bateson. Ecologia della mente e relazioni sociali*, 201–12. Milan: Raffaello Cortina.

Gadamer, Hans-Georg. [1960] 2013. *Truth and Method* (Wahrheit und Methode. Tuebingen). Bloomsbury Revelations. Trans. and revised by Joel Weinsheimer and Dolan G. Marshall. London and New York: Bloomsbury Academic.

Gadamer, Hans-Georg. 2013. 'Foreword to the Second Edition'. In Gadamer ([1960] 2013), xxv–xxxvi.

Gu Jianping (ed.). 2008. *Chinese Character Graphic Dictionary* (in Chinese: 顾建平，汉字图解字典，中国出版社集团). Shanghai: China Press Group.

Kukkola, Jani and Eetu Pikkarainen. 2016. 'Edusemiotics of Meaningful Learning Experience: Revisiting Kant's Pedagogical Paradox and Greimas' Semiotic Square'. *Semiotica*, 212: 199–217.

Li Xiaodong. 2016. *Cywilizacja* (Civilization). Trans. Dorota Arendt-Mendoza. Toruń: Adam Marszałek.

Ma Ying, Zhao Yandong and Liao Miao. 2015. 'The Values Demonstrated in the Constitution of the People's Republic Of China'. In Ladikas Miltos, Chaturvedi Sachin, Zhao Yandong and Stemerding Dirk (eds), *Science and Technology Governance and Ethics*, 73–81. Dordrecht: Springer Open. Doi: 10.1007/978-3-319-14693-5.

Mazur-Włodarczyk, K., P. Misiurski, M. Haładewicz-Grzelak, E. Karaś and J. Kolańska-Płuska. Submitted. 'China's Energy – Sytainable Strategies'.

Nöth, Winfried. 2010. 'The Semiotics of Teaching and the Teaching of Semiotics'. In Inna Semetsky (ed.), *Semiotics, Education Experience (Educational Futures: Rethinking Theory and Practice 43)*, 1–19. Rotterdam: Sense.

Peterson, Thomas E. 2016. 'Contemporary Approaches to a Pedagogy of Process'. *Semiotica*, 212: 7–26.

Ricoeur, Paul. 1989. *Język tekst, interpretacja. Wybór pism*. (Language, Text, Interpretation: Selected Writings, trans. Katarzyna Rosner and Piotr Graff). Warszawa: PIW.

Romero, Aran Moreno. 2018. 'From Process of Civilization to Policy of Civilizaton: A Holistic Review of the Chinese Concept of Wenming'. *Revista D'Antropologia I Investigacio Social*, 8: 1–14.

Schönfeld, Martin and Chen Xia. 2019. 'Daoism and the Project of an Ecological Civilization or Shengtai Wenming 生态文明'. *Religions*, 10 (11): 630. Doi: 10.3390/rel10110630.

Semetsky, Inna, Andrew Stables and Sébastien Pesce. 2016. 'Editorial'. *Semiotica*, 212: 1–5.

Sickman, Laurence and Aleksander Soper. [1956] 1984. *Sztuka i architektura w Chinach* (The Art and Architecture of China, trans. Mieczysław J. Künstler). Warszawa: Państwowe Wydawnictwo Naukowe.

Stables, Andrew. 2005. *Living and Learning as Semiotic Engagement: A New Theory of Education*. Lewiston, NY: Edwin Mellen Press.

Stables, Andrew. 2016. 'Edusemiotics as Process Semiotics: Towards a New Model of Semiosis for Teaching and Larning'. *Semiotica*, 212: 45–57.

Stables, Andrew and Inna Semetsky (eds). 2015. *Edusemiotics: Semiotic Philosophy as an Educational Foundation*. London: Routledge.

Strittmatter, Kai. 2010. *Chiny. Instrukcja obsługi* (Gebrauchsanweisung für China, no indication of a translator). Kraków: Wydawnictwo Astraia.

Suggestions of the Central Committee of the Communist Party of China on Formulating the Fourteenth Five-Year Plan for National Economic and Social Development and the Vision for 2035, Xinhuanet (in Chinese: 中共中央关于制定国民经济和社会发展第十四个五年规划和二〇三五年远景目标的建议, 新华网). Available online: http://www.xinhuanet.com/politics/zywj/2020-11/03/c_1126693293.htm?mc_cid=afeb03209b&mc_eid=53701013ad (accessed 8 January 2022).

Thao Thi Phuong Nguyen. 2012. 'The Discourse of Wenming ("Civilization"): Moral Authority and Social Change in Contemporary Shanghai'. Unpublihsed PhD diss., University of Western Australia, Perth.

Wulf, Christoph. 2003. *Educational Science: Hermeneutics, Empirical Research, Critical Theory*. Münster: Waxmann. Available online: http://www.pedocs.de/volltexte/2010/1564/pdf/Educational_Science_final_D.pdf (accessed 8 January 2022).

Wetzel, Alexandra. 2008. *Chiny. Leksykon cywilizacji* (China: Lexicon of Civilizations). Trans. Maria and Ksenia Zawanowskie, no indication of the original title. Warszawa: Arkady.

Thematic Index

apocalypse xxxii, 28, 41, 125, 127–32, 136, 138, 140, 142–5, 147
   apocalyptic dystopia 127
   apocalyptic fiction 128
   apocalyptic narrative 129, 133
   apocalyptic violence 142
   apocalyptically 135
   post-apocalypse 141
   trope xxxii, 125, 127, 128, 129, 131
art xvii, xviii, xix, xxiii, xxv, xxvi, xxvii, xxviii, xxix, xxx, xxxi, xxxii, xxxv, xxxvi, 3–19, 23–4, 28–31, 33–7, 39–44, 59, 61, 63–4, 66, 75, 77, 87, 95, 99, 100, 127, 149, 192, 194, 196, 244, 247
   abstract xxii, 12, 29, 30, 33–4, 40, 42, 71, 75, 76, 188, 245
   history xxi, 5, 24, 26, 30, 37, 39, 41, 90, 96, 101, 103, 104, 126, 132, 142, 150, 152, 153, 155, 163, 164, 179, 182, 183, 185, 188, 189, 190, 192, 196, 197
   icon 23, 24, 26, 35, 36, 37, 40, 41, 95, 100
   Silver Age art 24
   symbolism 153, 193

Baroque xxxi, 31, 56, 58, 59, 61, 62, 64, 66
   iconography xxxi, 55, 61, 66
   Silesia (region) xxxi, 55
beat 76, 81
biopolitics 128
body 7, 22, 31, 33, 45, 48, 57, 83, 90, 91, 99, 128, 130, 133, 136, 140, 141, 144–6, 166, 184, 192, 196, 215, 217, 248, 260
   able-bodiedness 135, 137
   disabled-bodiedness 130
   female 130, 136, 140

character 8, 11, 20, 75–80, 89, 104, 105, 109–12, 115, 117–23, 125, 126, 131, 138, 141, 143, 154, 158, 183, 195, 213, 241, 242, 252, 257, 258, 261

civilization xxxi, 19, 30, 38, 46, 110, 114, 117, 118, 127, 130, 140, 144, 176, 241–5, 252–6, 258–62
   citizenship 242
   habits 166, 174, 176, 245, 246, 248
clause 81
colonization xxix, xxxii, 27, 99, 100, 109, 111–21, 123, 151, 155
   British iv, 80, 99, 107, 109–11, 114, 122–4, 151
   European Community 110
   experience xi, xviii, xix, xxv, xxvii, xxix, xxxi, xxxiii, xxxiv, xxxv, xxxvi, 3–8, 10, 12, 13, 15–19, 22, 28, 35, 36, 42, 45–8, 60, 61, 66, 71, 73, 75–7, 81, 87, 88, 90–2, 95, 102, 111–13, 115, 116, 118, 125–8, 130, 131, 133, 134, 136–9, 141–3, 146, 152–4, 165, 167, 170, 174, 175, 176, 180, 184–91, 193–5, 197, 198, 200, 211, 212, 214, 215, 218, 229, 237, 242, 243, 248, 250, 251, 261
   non-Europeans 110, 111
   paternalism 117, 118
   performance 73, 80, 82, 83, 104, 111, 115, 122, 132, 133, 136–8, 154, 172, 208, 221
   stereotypes 109, 126, 136, 191, 193
communication xvii, xviii xix, xxiii-xxxvii, 9, 12, 16, 23, 24, 28, 42, 43, 53, 87, 95–7, 105, 111, 114, 115, 161, 184, 185, 199, 200, 203, 206, 217, 223–7, 232, 233, 235–9, 248, 256, 260
   acquisition 100, 223, 225, 227, 233
   deaf people 223, 225
   education xix, xxxv, 100, 119, 140, 151, 154, 223–6, 228, 229, 231–7, 239, 242, 246–51, 257–62
   ideograms 96, 103
   sign language xxix, xxxiv, xxxv, 223–34, 236–9

composer 71, 78–80
concert 71, 73, 192
    cello concerto xxxi, xxxii, 71, 72, 75, 77, 80–4
conductor 76, 82
conflict xxix, xxxiii, 38, 126, 129, 132, 134, 136, 137, 139, 141–4, 146, 150, 152, 155
    armed 137, 142
    death 26, 38, 44, 52, 59, 130, 139, 144, 146, 152, 153, 171
    gender 92, 94, 107, 129–38, 141, 143–6
    gendered 126, 131, 133, 134, 138, 142, 143
    violence 135, 140, 144, 145
Covid-19 xxxiv, 205, 206, 211–18
culture xviii, xix, xxi, xxiii, xxiv, xxxiii, xxxiv, xxxvi, 19, 25–8, 31, 36–54, 88, 100–8, 119–23, 130, 136, 145, 149, 150, 156, 163, 164, 172, 173, 175–7, 180, 189–91, 195, 198–201, 221, 236, 241, 243, 244, 248, 249, 256, 259
    Adinkra symbols xxx, xxxii, 87, 88, 90, 91, 92, 95–7, 100, 101, 105, 106
    Akan xxxii, 87, 94–7, 105–8
    Amazigh xxx, xxxiii, xxxiv, 163–73
    aso ebi 87, 92–8, 101–3, 107
    message xxxii, 12, 17, 23, 35, 42, 44, 45, 78–80, 87, 94, 97, 98, 100–2, 168, 169, 185, 191, 194, 198, 251, 252
    proverbs xxx, xxxiii, xxxiv, 3, 96–8, 101, 107, 108, 150, 163–77
    rituals 154, 251, 252, 257
    transmission xxxiii, 47, 48, 129, 150, 163–7, 169, 171, 173, 174–6

discourse xvii, xx, xxii, xxvii, xxix, xxx, xxxi, xxxii, xxxiv, xxxvi, xxxvii, 1, 32, 66, 71, 73, 75–83, 89, 90, 94, 99, 102, 103, 105, 108, 114, 117, 127, 128, 132, 133–5, 137–9, 142, 168, 195, 204, 206–8, 210, 211, 218–20, 244, 257, 262
    dominant 6, 40, 81, 128, 132, 135
    male 89, 92, 96, 99, 104, 105, 108, 111, 115, 124, 127, 129, 130, 134, 137, 138, 140, 143
    meaning xxi, xxii, xxx, xxxiii, xxxiv, xxxvii, 5, 8, 18, 23, 29, 31, 39, 42, 43, 45, 46, 58, 75, 88, 89, 91, 94, 98, 103, 112, 118, 119, 125, 129, 151, 154–7, 159, 166–9, 175, 176, 190, 206, 208, 211, 216, 219, 230, 237, 242, 243, 257
    non-violent 139, 142
    social knowledge 89
    subject xxi, xxii, xxiv, xxviii, xxxi, 11, 12, 23, 28, 30, 31, 60, 79, 89, 106, 131, 132, 138, 140, 153, 157, 167, 180, 184, 196, 204, 205, 208, 210, 211, 214–17, 221, 227, 243, 249, 250, 255, 256, 260
    violent 126, 127, 130, 135, 137–9, 142, 154, 156
disease 128–31, 136, 138, 143, 206, 212, 214, 216, 218
    chronic 131
    embodiment of 45, 111, 116, 120, 128, 136
    female body as 130
dystopia xxix, 125–7, 133, 135, 145, 146, 185, 194
    apocalyptic 127
    contemporary 143
    dystopian narrative 125
    dystopian society xxxiii, 143
    feminist 126

ecology xxxiv, xxxvii, 50, 172, 252, 255, 257
education xix, xxxv, 100, 119, 140, 151, 154, 223–51, 257–62
    efficiency 217, 226
    Polish educational system 225
    PJM (*Polski Język Migowy*) xxxiv, 224–39
    TEST LEKSYKA PJM-PL 227–9, 233, 235, 237
environment 92, 95, 126, 128, 133, 165, 175, 176, 185, 217, 218, 224, 225, 235, 243, 252, 256
    environmental disaster 128
    estrangement 4, 117, 126, 128
    hostile 133
epistemology 181, 186, 187, 219, 220, 247
    epistemic modality 208, 210, 217–20
    epistemic space xxx, xxxiii, xxxiv, 161, 203–6, 213, 217–20
    epistemic status 207, 218, 219

Thematic Index

evidentiality 207, 211–21
experience xviii, xix, xxv, xxvii, xxix, xxxi,
    xxxiii, xxxv, xxxvi, 3–22, 35, 36,
    42–8, 60–1, 66, 71–7, 87–95, 102,
    111–18, 125–46, 152–4, 167, 170,
    175, 176, 180–200, 211–18, 229, 237,
    242, 243, 248, 250, 251, 261
  apocalyptical 128
  mediatized gaze 184
  shared 128
  socialist experience 193

female 130, 136, 140
  body 130, 136, 140
  corporeality 133, 136, 137
  identity 129, 139
  stereotypes 126, 136
  survivors 127, 130–8
  victims 133
fiction xxxii, 75–84, 90, 94, 99, 103–10,
    123–8, 133, 143, 144, 146
  narrative fiction xxxii, 75–90

gender 92, 94, 107, 129–38, 141–6
  coding of war 134, 137
  conflict xxxiii, 129, 132–7, 141–6
  female 130, 136, 140
  health 129–36
  identity 133, 137
  pandemic xiii
  performance 137
  phenomenological approach to 131
  polarization 129, 138, 141, 143
  reductionism 135
  violence 130–3

hegemony 26, 46, 126, 133, 135, 142–5
  hegemonic codes 127, 133, 135
  hegemonic constructs 130
  hegemonic embodiments 133
  patriarchal 142
hermeneutics xvii–xxii, xxv–xxxviii 3,
    7–29, 42, 43, 50, 61, 66, 85, 87, 88,
    92, 94, 105, 111–21, 126, 127, 144–6,
    150, 159, 164, 168, 174, 183, 184,
    188–98, 200, 206, 220, 221, 234, 235,
    243, 247, 250, 251, 255–8, 262
  Existential-Hermeneutic Pedagogy 250
  hermeneutic consciousness 189

hermeneutic encounter xvii
hermeneutic plateau 258
hermeneutical moment 195
  methodological xxi
  ontological xxi 117
  objective xxxiv, 206, 220, 221
  place 136
  understanding 129
human xvii, xviii, xx, xxiii–xxxviii, 3, 7, 9,
    18–21, 24, 25, 28, 34, 35, 39–43, 53,
    57, 59–64, 66, 107, 114, 117, 128,
    129, 131, 132, 138, 141, 144, 150,
    154, 155, 158, 167, 169–72, 174, 187,
    197, 208, 243, 244, 248–51, 259
  extinction 128, 129, 132
  female corporeality 136
  heteronormative 127
  hypermasculinity 133, 135, 137, 138
  language xvii, xxiv, xxix, xxxii, xxxiv,
    xxxv, 12, 23, 26, 33, 40, 44, 49, 50, 53,
    56, 62, 71, 73, 75, 77, 88, 89, 96, 101,
    102, 104, 106, 108, 112–14, 117–23,
    125, 126, 137–9, 145, 151, 159, 164,
    166, 167, 168, 173, 175, 177, 185,
    188, 190, 195, 203–10, 219–21,
    223–42, 246, 249, 252, 260, 261
  man xix, xx, 23, 26, 28, 29, 32, 33, 36, 44,
    59–61, 66, 92, 108, 114, 116, 117,
    127, 129, 132–8, 176, 188, 191, 241,
    244, 249, 252, 253, 255
  trafficking 138
  warlike 127, 141, 142

illness 117, 127–32, 136, 143, 144, 171, 212
interaction xviii, xix, xxxi, xxxiv, 14, 17, 23,
    42, 63, 79–82, 103, 121, 129, 172,
    184–6, 189, 192, 196, 197, 204,
    206–8, 213, 217–20, 235
interpretation xviii, xx, xxi, xxii, xxv, xxix,
    xxx, xxxii, xxxv, xxxvi, 3–26, 41, 42,
    56, 59, 110, 128, 142, 143, 155, 163,
    172–5, 181, 216, 235, 248, 250, 257,
    258, 259, 261
  phenomenological vii, xi, xxxiv, 3, 5, 6,
    10, 13, 20–3, 28, 88, 127–31,
    180–200

key xx, xxi, 5, 34, 73, 76, 79, 80, 83, 90, 163,
    167, 198, 208, 233, 249, 250

locations 44, 104, 106, 144, 186
  heterotopias 183
  Karpacz (Krummhübel) xxxiii, xxxiv, 179–84, 188–200
  tourist resort 180, 183

masculinity 111, 129, 132, 135, 137, 138, 142
  mainstream 24, 142, 223
  normative xiii, 113, 118, 119, 133, 135
  violent 126, 127, 130, 135, 137–9, 142, 154, 156
midwife xxxii, xxxiii, 28, 125, 127, 128, 130–3, 135–40, 142–5
motherhood 90, 92, 93, 98, 106, 107, 134, 135, 137, 142, 146
move xviii, 15, 76, 81, 168, 242, 247, 251
music xvii, xxviii, xxix, xxx, xxxi, xxxii, 14, 34, 35, 71, 73, 75–84, 150, 200
  absolute music 73
  piece 71, 75, 77, 82
  vocal music 73
mystical xxxi, xxxii, 25, 28, 33, 34, 37, 38, 40, 41, 45, 46, 52, 53, 56–62, 64–6
  confraternity 56, 57, 65
  exponents 56
  fraternal 57, 58
  prayers 40, 43, 57, 59, 62, 115

narrativity xvii, xxxi, xxxii, 71, 73, 75–7, 80–2, 84
narrator 75–82, 111, 114, 125, 126
  opening move 81
novum 126

obstetrics 139
orality 149, 150, 165, 167, 177
  orature 106, 159
  storytelling 93, 156

pandemic xxxiv, 128, 143, 197, 206, 217
patriarchal 126–34, 138, 140–3
  fundamentalism 132
  hegemony 26, 46, 126, 133, 135, 142, 143, 145
  heteronormativity 126
  violence 129, 131, 138, 140, 141
peace 37, 39, 41, 44, 49, 126, 131, 135, 139, 141, 142, 144, 145, 146, 175

peacebuilding process 134, 139, 140
peacekeeping missions 138
peacetime violence 131
performance 73, 80, 82, 83, 111, 115, 122, 132, 133, 136–8, 172, 208, 221
phenomenology xxxiv, xxxvii, 6, 7, 11, 14, 19–23, 53, 88, 108, 159, 185, 187, 188, 195, 197
  Dasein xxii, 194, 196, 251
  flânerie xxxiv, 180, 181, 183, 184, 188–92, 194, 196
  phenomenological body 196
  phenomenological field 182, 193, 195
pictorial xxxii, 47, 61
  illustrations 61, 62, 65, 77, 95, 230, 237
  scene 5, 14, 15, 20, 55, 56, 58, 59, 61–4, 109, 142
  spirituality 35, 46, 65, 255
  strategies xxxii, 61
place xxii, xxvi, xxxiv, 23–7, 33, 38, 40, 42, 59–65, 91, 98, 104, 114, 121, 122, 125–38, 142–6, 155, 157, 163, 164, 168, 171, 172, 174, 175, 179, 183, 184, 189, 190–201, 203, 210, 213, 218, 226, 234, 243, 246, 255
  hermeneutical 136
  physical 133
plague 127–36, 140, 142, 143, 145
  women's 128–36, 142, 143
poetry xxix, xxxiii, 84, 106, 116, 117, 149–51, 153–7, 159
  African 149, 150
  lament v, xxxii, 149, 150, 155–8
  modernism 150, 153, 159
  Nigerian 154
power xxxiv, 8, 23, 26, 36, 42, 65, 73, 89, 96, 99, 122, 124, 126, 128, 129, 131–4, 136, 138–44, 164, 245, 250, 256
  distribution of 132, 138
  maternal 141
  patriarchal 133
  reproductive 133
  structural 129

relationality 127, 128, 130, 133, 139, 143
  co-relationality 128, 133
  hegemonic 113, 126–8, 130–5, 139, 140, 143
  interpersonal 9, 12, 130, 245

religion xxxvii, 22, 26, 29, 36, 39, 47, 48, 50, 52, 104, 113, 120, 154, 262
  iconosphere 55
  mysticism 36, 37, 56, 57, 59, 62, 65–7
repetition 31, 43, 76, 81, 93, 138, 156
reporting clause 81
representation 34, 36, 42, 43, 47, 55–66, 71, 73, 77, 79, 87–91, 95, 98, 99, 103, 105, 107, 109–11, 127, 128, 137, 172, 184, 186, 191, 192, 195, 203, 210, 217, 218, 248
  of kisses 59
rhythm 35, 44, 71, 73, 171

science fiction 126, 133, 143, 144, 146
score xxxii, 71, 72, 75–7, 80, 82, 228
semiotics xx, xxxii, 88, 110, 112, 247, 248, 250, 257, 259–62
  cultural 110, 112, 113
  frontier 110, 112, 113, 116–19, 121
  intercultural xxxiv, 111
  semiosphere 112–23
  signs xxvi, 31, 42, 43, 71, 95, 168, 200, 204, 236, 238, 247, 248, 251, 258, 259
  space 110, 112, 113, 116–21
  symbolical ii, 34, 36, 43, 48, 58, 61, 62, 66, 87, 105, 112, 113, 128, 134, 136, 138, 166, 168, 185, 186
sexual 119, 127, 130, 132, 134–7, 139–42, 144
  exploitation 127
  freedom 136
  terrorism 130
  trafficking 144
  violence 132, 136, 139, 141, 142, 144
signature 31, 73, 76, 83
soloist 82
space xvii, xix, xxviii, xxx, xxxiii, xxxiv, 3, 13, 15, 17, 18, 27, 31–3, 35, 36, 41, 44, 45, 48, 91, 103, 110, 112, 113, 116–21, 124–6, 136, 137, 142, 144–6, 151, 152, 159, 161, 172, 179–81, 183–201, 203–6, 213, 217–20, 226, 243, 246
  mediatization 18, 184, 197, 200
  representations of space 186
  social space 188, 190, 191, 195, 203
  spatial appropriation 184
  spatial practice 186, 187

spatial trialectics 184, 185
spatial turn 180, 184, 199
spirituality 35, 46, 65, 255
  ascension 26, 29, 36, 43, 61
  henosis 27, 28, 42, 43
  hermeticism 26, 29, 38, 45, 50
  hieratic xxxi, 23, 42, 43
  neoplatonism 29, 43, 46, 47
  Russian Christian Orthodoxy 37
  symbol xviii, xxii, xxx, xxxii, 23, 24, 26, 28, 31, 33–51, 58, 61–6, 87–107, 113, 136, 138, 186, 246
  theosophy 29, 43, 47, 50
  theurgy 42, 43, 45, 47, 48, 50, 54
stance xviii, xviii, xxii, xxxiii, xxxiv, xxxv, xxxvi, 71, 79, 119, 195, 203–20, 249
  affective stance 204, 207
  epistemic stance xxxiii, xxxiv, 204, 205, 207, 209–20
  stance alignment 215, 216
  stance triangle 215, 219
  stance-taker xxxiv, 204, 206, 207, 213
  stancetaking xxxiii, xxxiv, 203–18
story xxxii, xxxiii, 44, 52, 73, 75–82, 92, 114, 129, 154–8
stylistics 73, 76
  discourse stylistics 73, 76
survivors 127, 130, 133, 135, 137, 138, 141

text xvii-xxv, xxviii-xxxv, xxxvii, 5, 7, 8, 12, 15, 23, 43, 57, 61, 62, 65, 67, 71, 73, 77, 82, 88, 89–93, 96–8, 101–3, 105, 111, 113, 115, 117, 118, 123, 125, 126, 127, 145, 152, 154, 165, 189, 192, 199, 200, 206, 211, 219, 220, 228, 232, 234, 241, 243, 244, 250, 251, 257–9, 261
  music text 73, 75, 82
  narrative text xxxvii, 71
tonic 81, 83
tourism 180, 181, 183, 184, 189, 190, 195, 197, 199, 200, 254, 255
tradition xix, xxv, xxix, xxxiii, xxxvi, xxxvii, 39, 41, 44, 49, 54, 92–4, 97, 101, 104, 105, 107, 149, 150, 152–6, 165–8, 17, 181–3, 188, 190, 191, 197, 250
  break 182, 183
  scripts of regionality 195
translation xxxiv, 15, 22, 50, 77, 84, 94, 123, 168, 171, 172, 173, 175, 196, 197,

199, 219, 238, 242, 249, 257, 258, 261
trauma 102, 130, 131, 141, 142
trope xxxii, 92, 96, 125, 127–9, 131
  apocalypse xxxii, 28, 41, 125, 127–32, 136, 138, 140, 142–5, 147

unio mystica xxxi, 55, 59–66
  human xvii, xviii, xx, xxiii, xxiv, xxv, xxvi, xxix, xxxi, xxxii, xxxiii, xxxiv, xxxv, xxxviii, 3, 7, 9, 18–21, 24, 25, 28, 34, 35, 39, 40, 42, 43, 53, 57, 59–64, 66, 107, 114 ,117, 128, 129, 131, 132, 138, 141, 144, 150, 154, 155, 158, 167, 169–72, 174, 187, 197, 208, 243, 244, 248–51, 259
  marriage 12, 56, 57, 64, 65, 132, 134
  path xvii, xx, xxix, xxx, xxxvi, 29, 30, 32, 51, 59, 60, 61, 80, 117, 150, 152–6, 159, 200, 223, 224, 232–4, 251
  spiritual xvii, xxxii, 25–53, 57–65, 87, 97, 103, 105, 109, 245, 260
  Trinity 56–9, 62, 65, 140
urbanscape xxix, xxxv, 184, 185, 243, 246
  catering establishment xxxiv, 181, 183, 189–91, 195, 197, 198
  dystopias xxix 185
  landmarks 184
utopianism 54, 126, 137, 141, 146
  transgressive 126, 137

values xxiv, xxv, xxxiii, 9, 120, 135, 159, 166–9, 174, 204, 218, 243, 245, 253, 254, 256, 261

aetiological xxxiii, 155, 157, 159
re-presentation 88, 89, 97–105
representation
violence xxix, xxxiii, 48, 126–46, 154, 155
  continuum of 131, 141, 144
  cultural 127, 132, 133, 139, 142, 145
  epistemic 128, 134, 138, 140
  excorporation of 138
  hegemonic 135, 139
  patriarchal 129, 131, 138, 140, 141
  peacetime 131
  sexual 132, 136, 139, 141, 142, 144
  structural 133

war xxviii, xxxii, xxxiii, 9, 38, 44, 99, 102, 125, 128–34, 137–47, 149–59, 175, 179, 180, 182, 185, 205
  Second World War 179, 182, 185
  Biafra 151–8
  Civil 152, 155
  Nigeria 151, 152, 154
  prophesizing xxxii, 149, 154
  violence xxix, xxxiii, 48, 126–46, 154, 155
wenming xxxiii, xxxv, 241–62
  civility xxxiii, xxxv, 241, 246, 253–8
women xxxii, xxxiii, 44, 87–9, 92–4, 97–100, 105–8, 127–40, 144–9, 190, 246
  African xxxii, 87–94, 97–107
  motherhood 90–3, 98, 106, 107, 134, 135, 137, 142, 146
  mothering 92
  womanist 92
  writers 87–94, 97–100, 105

www.ingramcontent.com/pod-product-compliance
Lightning Source LLC
Chambersburg PA
CBHW071804300426
44116CB00009B/1203